Irshad Manji

The Queer Muslim Activist Defying Tradition – Unfiltered

Amir Garba

ISBN: 9781779696885
Imprint: Telephasic Workshop
Copyright © 2024 Amir Garba.
All Rights Reserved.

Contents

Unveiling a Warrior

Discovering Identity

Early Years in Uganda

In this subsection, we delve into the early years of Irshad Manji's life in Uganda. The fascinating journey of this LGBTQ activist began in East Africa, where she first encountered the complexities of identity and the challenges of living in a traditional Muslim society.

Born in 1968 in Kampala, Uganda, Irshad Manji grew up in a multicultural and diverse community. Uganda, at the time, was a country filled with natural beauty, but it was also deeply entrenched in conservative religious values and social norms. Irshad's family belonged to the Ismaili sect of Islam, which followed a progressive interpretation of the religion.

Growing up, Irshad witnessed the intersections of religion and culture. While her family emphasized the importance of education, they also embraced traditional values and customs. This mix of influences shaped her perspective and compelled her to question societal norms.

Despite her relatively privileged upbringing, Irshad faced challenges with her identity from an early age. She was aware of her queer orientation, which clashed with the heteronormative expectations of her community. Uganda's society, like many others at the time, viewed homosexuality as taboo and sinful.

Irshad's experience in Uganda exposed her to the complexities of being queer in a traditional Muslim setting. She witnessed the struggles of LGBTQ individuals who lived in fear of discrimination, persecution, and exclusion. These experiences ignited a fire within her to challenge the status quo and fight for equality and acceptance.

The turmoil of the Idi Amin regime and the subsequent expulsion of South Asians from Uganda in the early 1970s deeply affected the Manji family. This experience of displacement had a profound impact on Irshad's understanding of cultural identity and resilience.

In 1972, as a result of the expulsion, the Manji family immigrated to Canada, seeking a safe and welcoming environment. The move allowed Irshad to attend school in a Western context, where she encountered a different cultural landscape. Canada provided her with opportunities to explore her individuality and express herself freely.

However, the challenges she faced in Uganda did not disappear overnight. Adjusting to a new country, culture, and educational system came with its own set of difficulties. Irshad's dual identity as a queer individual and a Muslim migrant added complexity to her journey of self-discovery and acceptance.

Throughout her early years in Uganda and Canada, Irshad grappled with questions of faith, identity, and belonging. She began to critically examine her religious beliefs, searching for a way to reconcile her queer identity with her Islamic upbringing. This exploration marked the beginning of her lifelong dedication to activism, interfaith dialogue, and reformation within the Muslim community.

Irshad Manji's early years in Uganda laid the foundation for her journey as a fearless LGBTQ activist. The challenges she faced as a queer Muslim woman in a conservative society fueled her determination to challenge societal norms, fight for LGBTQ rights within Islam, and bridge divides between communities. In the following sections, we will explore her deepening commitment to activism, faith, and the impact she had on LGBTQ Muslims worldwide.

Relocating to Canada

Relocating to a new country can be a daunting and life-changing experience. In this subsection, we explore Irshad Manji's journey of relocating to Canada and the impact it had on her life as a queer Muslim activist.

A Leap of Faith

Leaving behind her homeland in Uganda, Irshad Manji took a leap of faith and embarked on a new chapter in Canada. It was a bittersweet departure, leaving behind familiar faces and places, but with an indomitable spirit and determination to create a better future for herself and others.

Adapting to a New Culture

Canada provided Irshad Manji with a fresh start and an opportunity to embrace her identity fully. Adjusting to a new culture, language, and way of life presented its own set of challenges. From navigating the Canadian education system to building new friendships, Irshad had to learn to not only adapt but also educate others about her unique experiences as a queer Muslim.

Finding a Supportive Community

As Irshad settled into her new life, she discovered a vibrant LGBTQ+ community in Canada. Joining support networks and engaging with local advocacy groups enabled her to connect with like-minded individuals, share stories, and contribute to the ongoing fight for LGBTQ+ rights. Through these connections, Irshad found solace, encouragement, and inspiration to continue her activism.

Redefined Freedom and Independence

Canada offered Irshad Manji a sense of freedom and independence that she had longed for. The country's commitment to human rights and inclusivity allowed her to explore her identity without fear of persecution or discrimination. This newfound freedom became a catalyst for Irshad's journey of self-discovery and paved the way for her to make a significant impact in the LGBTQ+ movement.

Navigating Cultural Differences

Despite the embrace of her new home, Irshad faced challenges in reconciling her diverse identities with Canadian culture. Navigating the intersections of her Muslim and LGBTQ+ identities was an ongoing process, as she confronted societal stereotypes, biases, and misconceptions. However, through open dialogue, education, and community engagement, Irshad was able to bridge the gap between diverse cultures and foster understanding and acceptance.

Building Bridges Across Communities

Relocating to Canada not only provided Irshad Manji with a safe haven but also presented an opportunity to bridge the divide between the LGBTQ+ and Muslim communities. By engaging in conversations and fostering dialogue, she aimed to dispel misconceptions and challenge the prevailing narrative of conflict between these communities. Irshad believed in the power of unity and collaboration, recognizing that the fight for equality was interconnected and required collective effort.

A New Beginning

Relocating to Canada marked a new beginning in Irshad Manji's journey as a queer Muslim activist. It offered her a platform to amplify her voice and advocate for change. This section of her life demonstrated her resilience, adaptability, and unwavering commitment to challenging societal norms and creating a more inclusive world for all.

Note to the Reader:

Relocating to a new country can be both exciting and challenging. It presents an opportunity for personal growth, cultural exchange, and the exploration of new identities. For individuals like Irshad Manji, who live at the intersection of multiple identities, moving to a diverse and inclusive country can provide a platform for their activism and an environment where they can freely express their true selves. In the following section, we will explore the struggles and triumphs Irshad faced as she grappled with personal identity and embarked on her journey of activism.

Struggles with Identity

The journey of self-discovery is often fraught with challenges and obstacles, and for Irshad Manji, this was especially true. Growing up in Uganda, Manji found herself in an environment where discussions about sexual orientation and gender identity were largely taboo. As she navigated her own path of self-acceptance and understanding, she encountered numerous struggles with identity that shaped her into the fearless activist she is today.

Intertwined Cultures and Conflicting Messages

Manji's upbringing in Uganda exposed her to a cultural landscape that often clashed with her own experiences and understanding of her sexuality. Although Uganda is a country known for its strong religious and traditional beliefs, she also witnessed a vibrant LGBTQ community that struggled to find acceptance. Balancing these conflicting messages and understanding her own identity within such a complex cultural context became a source of immense struggle for her.

Self-Doubt and Internalized Homophobia

Like many individuals who come to terms with their sexual orientation, Manji battled with self-doubt and internalized homophobia. Society's negative portrayal of LGBTQ individuals and the lack of positive representation led her to question her own worth and identity. The internalized stigma created a mental and emotional barrier that hindered her self-acceptance and ability to embrace her authentic self.

Fear of Rejection and Isolation

In conservative societies like Uganda, being queer often means facing potential rejection and isolation from family, friends, and even the wider community. Manji experienced the fear of losing important relationships and being cast out from the support network she had come to rely on. This fear created a profound sense of isolation and made it challenging for her to find the strength to embrace her identity fully.

Navigating Cultural Expectations

Cultural expectations and societal norms can significantly impact an individual's journey of self-discovery. Manji grappled with the pressures of living up to these expectations, including conforming to traditional gender roles and fulfilling the expectations placed on her as a woman. Overcoming these expectations and finding her own authentic path became a crucial aspect of her struggle with identity.

Secrecy and Fear of Judgment

In a society where being queer was stigmatized, Manji felt compelled to keep her true identity a secret. The fear of judgment and potential harm prevented her from embracing her sexuality openly. Living in the shadow of secrecy added an extra layer of complexity to her struggle with identity, compelling her to constantly negotiate between her true self and the expectations imposed on her.

Finding Strength in Community and Activism

Despite the challenges she faced, Manji was fortunate to find allies and support within the LGBTQ community. Connecting with others who shared similar experiences allowed her to build a network of support and encouragement. This support system became a vital source of strength as she embarked on her journey of self-discovery and activism.

Embracing Intersectionality

Manji's struggle with identity was not solely confined to her sexuality. As a queer Muslim, she faced the additional challenge of navigating the intersectionality of her multiple identities. Balancing her religious beliefs with her queer identity required a deep exploration and understanding of both aspects of her identity. This journey of self-interrogation and exploration ultimately led her to embrace her unique intersectional identity with pride.

Breaking the Chains of Internalized Oppression

Internalized oppression is a deeply ingrained system that perpetuates self-hatred and reinforces societal biases. Manji recognized the need to break free from these chains and challenge the oppressive norms that had shaped her understanding of her own identity. Through self-reflection and actively questioning the narratives imposed upon her, she was able to dismantle the internalized oppression that hindered her growth and acceptance.

Embracing Vulnerability and Authenticity

One of Manji's biggest breakthroughs in her struggle with identity came when she embraced vulnerability and authenticity. Rather than hiding or denying her true self, she learned to openly share her story and experiences. By owning her truth, Manji not only empowered herself but also inspired countless others to embrace their authentic selves.

Cultivating Empathy and Compassion

Manji's personal struggles with identity have deeply informed her approach to activism. Through her own journey, she developed a profound sense of empathy and compassion for individuals grappling with their own identities. This understanding fuels her commitment to creating inclusive spaces where all individuals, regardless of their sexual orientation or gender identity, feel seen, heard, and accepted.

Unconventional Example: The Power of Memoirs

Memoirs have the unique ability to capture the nuanced struggles of individuals and serve as powerful tools for generating empathy and understanding. Manji's own memoir, "The Trouble with Islam Today," not only provided a platform for her to share her personal struggles with identity but also sparked much-needed conversations about the intersections of faith, sexuality, and culture. By sharing her story in an authentic and vulnerable way, Manji expanded the boundaries of what it means to be a queer Muslim activist and encouraged others to embrace their true identities.

In the next section, we will delve deeper into Manji's journey of reconciling her faith and sexuality as she navigates the complexities of her Islamic upbringing. Stay tuned to explore the intersections of faith, activism, and LGBTQ rights in Islam.

A Queer Awakening

In this subsection, we delve into the enlightening journey of Irshad Manji as she undergoes a profound, transformative experience of self-discovery and acceptance. Her queer awakening not only involves embracing her sexual orientation, but also finding strength, purpose, and a profound sense of activism in her identity.

Embracing Authenticity

Growing up in Uganda, Irshad Manji was no stranger to the struggles of living in a society that rigidly adhered to traditional values and norms. She felt suffocated by societal expectations and the pressure to conform. This battle for authenticity intensified when she relocated to Canada, where she encountered different cultural norms and experienced a sense of liberation.

Through self-reflection and introspection, Manji began to fully acknowledge her true identity, recognizing her attraction to individuals of the same gender. This realization marked a significant turning point in her life and became the catalyst for her journey toward embracing her queerness.

Confronting Internalized Homophobia

Like many individuals who come to terms with their sexual orientation, Manji grappled with internalized homophobia. She had absorbed society's negative messages about LGBTQ+ individuals, and this self-hatred hindered her from fully embracing her queerness.

To overcome this, Manji embarked on a process of self-education and connecting with LGBTQ+ communities. She sought out resources, engaged in open conversations, and exposed herself to diverse perspectives. Gradually, she began to challenge and dismantle the internalized homophobia that had plagued her for years.

Gaining Confidence through Community

Finding a supportive network of friends and allies played a pivotal role in Manji's queer awakening. She discovered the power of community and the transformative effects of connecting with individuals who shared similar experiences and faced similar challenges.

By actively participating in LGBTQ+ events, joining support groups, and engaging in online communities, Manji found solace and encouragement. These connections not only bolstered her self-confidence but also exposed her to the experiences, stories, and resilience of other queer individuals, which further fueled her determination to advocate for LGBTQ+ rights.

Discovering Activism as Identity

As Manji delved deeper into her queer awakening, she realized that activism was an inherent part of her identity. She recognized the necessity of using her unique experiences and platform to advocate for the rights and visibility of LGBTQ+ individuals, especially within Muslim communities.

This realization marked a turning point for Manji, as she began to merge her queerness, her Muslim background, and her passion for social justice. She understood that her activism was not only about her personal journey but also about challenging societal norms and creating a more inclusive society for all.

Empowering Others through Visibility

Manji recognizes the profound impact of visibility in empowering others to embrace their sexual orientation and gender identity. Inspired by the trailblazers who had paved the way before her, she understood the importance of being unapologetically authentic and sharing her story with others.

By speaking openly about her queer identity, Manji challenged societal taboos and stigmas, paving the way for others to do the same. Her visibility not only offered hope and inspiration but also fostered a sense of community and belonging for queer individuals who struggled with their identities.

Making Strides in the Queer Muslim Community

As Manji embraced her queer awakening, she recognized the unique challenges faced by LGBTQ+ individuals within Muslim communities. Determined to effect change, she turned her attention to advocating for LGBTQ+ rights within a religious context.

Manji passionately engaged in dialogue with religious scholars, challenging conservative interpretations of Islamic teachings that perpetuated prejudice and discrimination against queer individuals. She worked diligently to foster understanding, promote inclusion, and create safe spaces for LGBTQ+ Muslims, ultimately striving for a more progressive and accepting Muslim community.

Embracing the Complexities

Throughout her queer awakening, Manji understood that the intersectionality of her identities as a queer Muslim woman was both a source of strength and a complex challenge. She learned to navigate the intricacies of faith, sexuality, and cultural expectations, embracing the richness and diversity of her experiences.

By embracing the complexities of her identity, Manji became a beacon of hope for individuals grappling with similar intersections. She showed that it was possible to reconcile faith with queerness, challenging long-standing dogmas and contributing to a more inclusive understanding of spirituality.

In conclusion, this subsection explores Irshad Manji's profound journey of self-discovery and acceptance as she embraces her queer identity. Through confronting internalized homophobia, gaining confidence through community support, and recognizing activism as an innate part of her identity, Manji's queer awakening shapes her path as a trailblazing advocate for LGBTQ+ rights within Muslim communities. Her story showcases the power of visibility and the transformative effects of embracing authenticity.

Embracing Activism

In this section, we delve into Irshad Manji's journey of embracing activism and the impact it has had on her life and the LGBTQ community. Activism is the driving force behind Manji's mission to challenge societal norms and promote equality, acceptance, and understanding.

Discovering the Power of Activism

Growing up, Manji faced numerous challenges as she navigated her identity as a queer Muslim. These experiences sparked a fire within her to make a difference and create change. Manji recognized that embracing activism would allow her to challenge the status quo and advocate for LGBTQ rights within the Muslim community and beyond.

Finding Her Voice

Finding her voice was a transformative moment for Manji. It empowered her to express her thoughts, beliefs, and experiences openly. Through activism, she realized that her voice had the power to inspire and influence others, especially those who were struggling with their own identities.

Starting Small, Making an Impact

Manji began her activism journey by engaging in meaningful conversations within her community and initiating dialogue about LGBTQ rights and acceptance. She understood that change starts at the grassroots level and that every small step towards progress counts.

To make an impact, Manji encouraged open discussions, organized workshops, and created safe spaces for LGBTQ individuals to share their stories and experiences. By providing a platform for marginalized voices, she aimed to challenge preconceived notions and foster empathy and understanding.

Collaborating with Allies

Recognizing the importance of allyship, Manji actively sought and collaborated with individuals and organizations that shared her vision of inclusivity and equality. Allies played a crucial role in amplifying the LGBTQ rights movement and challenging societal stigmas.

By working together, Manji and her allies promoted awareness, educated communities, and challenged discriminatory practices and attitudes. This collaboration helped create a supportive network that uplifted voices from different backgrounds and mobilized for change.

Mobilizing for Change

Activism requires action, and Manji consistently mobilized her efforts to effect tangible change. She organized rallies, demonstrations, and campaigns to raise awareness about LGBTQ issues and call for equal rights and treatment under the law.

To amplify her impact, Manji harnessed the power of social media and utilized strategic communication techniques to reach a wider audience. Sharing personal stories, experiences, and resources, she aimed to educate and inspire others to join the fight for LGBTQ equality.

Expanding the Movement

Manji recognized the importance of expanding the LGBTQ rights movement by engaging with diverse communities and creating alliances. She understood that inclusive activism meant actively seeking to address the intersectionality of identities and amplifying marginalized voices.

By building bridges and fostering understanding between different communities, Manji aimed to challenge stereotypes, combat discrimination, and promote acceptance. Through her efforts, she highlighted the shared struggles faced by individuals of different faiths, cultures, and sexual orientations.

Leading by Example

As an activist, Manji understood the power of leading by example. She encouraged others to embrace their identities and be unapologetically themselves. By embodying authenticity and resilience, she inspired fellow LGBTQ individuals to find their voices and fight for their rights.

Manji's steadfast commitment to activism, paired with her unwavering authenticity, has served as a beacon for those seeking to challenge societal norms and promote equality. Her personal journey and dedication have motivated countless individuals to embrace activism and make a difference in their own communities.

In the next section, we explore how Manji navigated the intersectionality of faith and sexuality, and the role that religion played in her journey of self-discovery and activism.

Coming Out to Family and Friends

Coming out to family and friends can be both a liberating and challenging experience for queer individuals. It is a deeply personal journey that involves revealing one's true self and facing the reactions and acceptance of loved ones. In this subsection, we will explore the various aspects and dynamics of coming out within the context of Irshad Manji's life as a queer Muslim activist.

Navigating a Complex Web of Emotions

Coming out is an emotional rollercoaster for both the individual and their loved ones. Irshad Manji's experience was no exception. With her traditional Muslim background and upbringing, Irshad knew that revealing her true identity as a queer woman would likely be met with mixed reactions from her family and friends.

Fear, anxiety, and uncertainty can be overwhelming during this process. It is essential to recognize that individuals may have different coping mechanisms and reactions. Some may experience shock, denial, or even anger, while others may be immediately accepting and supportive.

Manji's journey of self-acceptance and self-love served as a pillar of strength during this challenging time. It is crucial for individuals coming out to prioritize their mental well-being and avoid internalizing negative responses.

Honest and Open Communication

Communication is key when coming out to family and friends. Manji advocated for open and honest conversations, providing her loved ones with an opportunity to understand her journey and perspectives.

Having meaningful discussions about sexual orientation, religious beliefs, and cultural norms can help bridge the gap between personal experiences and societal expectations. It allows for a deeper understanding of the complexities involved in being both queer and Muslim.

During these conversations, it is essential to approach the topic with sensitivity and empathy. Offering educational resources, such as books, documentaries, or online materials, can help facilitate discussions and provide a broader context for exploration.

The Role of Allies and Support Networks

Manji's experience highlighted the importance of allies and support networks when coming out. Allies, whether family members, friends, or members of the LGBTQ+ community, play a crucial role in providing emotional support and validation.

Support networks, such as LGBTQ+ organizations, can connect individuals with resources, counseling services, and peer support groups. Sharing experiences with others who have gone through similar journeys can foster a sense of belonging and empowerment.

For Manji, finding allies within her family and community helped empower her voice and create a space for open dialogue. Allies can challenge stereotypes, break down societal barriers, and advocate for acceptance and equality within their own circles of influence.

The Power of Empathy and Education

Empathy and education are powerful tools when coming out to family and friends. It is essential to acknowledge that loved ones may come from different cultural, religious, and generational backgrounds, which can impact their understanding and acceptance.

Providing educational resources, such as books, articles, or documentaries, can help dispel myths and misconceptions surrounding homosexuality and Islam. This encourages empathy and fosters a more informed dialogue.

Manji's personal journey of reconciling her faith and sexuality serves as an example of how education and self-reflection can lead to personal growth and acceptance. By sharing her story and engaging in respectful conversations, she helped challenge preconceived notions and fostered understanding within her community.

Resilience and Setting Boundaries

Coming out is not always met with immediate acceptance, and it is essential to acknowledge and prepare for various reactions. Sometimes, loved ones may need time to process and understand the information before fully accepting and supporting an individual's sexual orientation.

Manji's journey of resilience reminds us of the importance of self-care and establishing healthy boundaries. It is crucial to prioritize one's own well-being and emotional health throughout the coming-out process.

Setting boundaries may involve limiting exposure to hurtful or disrespectful reactions, seeking professional support, or pursuing activities that bring joy and healing. Fostering resilience is vital to navigate the complexities and challenges that may arise during this period.

Living Authentically and Embracing Queer Muslim Identity

Coming out is a transformative experience that allows individuals to live authentically. For Manji, embracing her queer Muslim identity meant navigating the intersection of her sexual orientation and religious beliefs.

Living authentically does not always require compromising or rejecting one's faith. Manji's journey demonstrates the importance of finding personal interpretations of religious texts and engaging in ongoing dialogue regarding LGBTQ+ inclusion within religious spaces.

By embracing her queer Muslim identity, Manji has become a beacon of hope and inspiration for individuals around the world who face similar challenges. She has shown that it is possible to reconcile faith, sexuality, and cultural expectations while advocating for equality, acceptance, and love.

Personal Reflections and Transformation

Manji's coming-out journey serves as a testament to personal growth, resilience, and the power of authenticity. Coming out to family and friends is a deeply personal and courageous act that allows individuals to live true to themselves.

However, it is important to remember that every individual's coming-out journey is unique and may have different outcomes. While some may experience immediate acceptance and support, others may face rejection or adversity. It is crucial to seek out supportive networks and resources to navigate these challenges.

By sharing her story and advocating for LGBTQ+ rights within Islamic communities, Manji has become a pioneer in the movement for acceptance and equality. Her transformation and continued activism inspire others to celebrate their identities proudly and work towards a more inclusive world.

Exercises

Exercise 1: Reflection and Self-Acceptance

Take a moment to reflect on your own journey of self-acceptance. Consider the following questions:

1. What steps have you taken to embrace your authentic self? 2. How have your experiences shaped your understanding of your sexual orientation or gender identity? 3. What challenges have you faced along the way, and how have you overcome them? 4. How do you prioritize your mental well-being during times of self-discovery and coming out? 5. In what ways can you advocate for yourself and others within your own circles?

Write a short reflection on your personal growth and the lessons you have learned throughout your own journey of self-acceptance. Consider the ways in which your experiences can inspire and empower others.

Exercise 2: Developing Empathy

Empathy is a crucial component of building understanding and acceptance. Engage in an empathetic exercise by following these steps:

1. Choose a close friend or family member who may have difficulty understanding your sexual orientation or gender identity. 2. Put yourself in their shoes and consider their perspective. What cultural, religious, or societal factors may influence their understanding and acceptance? 3. Write a letter or have an open conversation with them, explaining your experiences, thoughts, and feelings. Use empathy and understanding to foster a compassionate and open dialogue. 4. Reflect on the conversation or letter exchange. What did you learn about their perspective, and what did they learn about yours? How can you continue to build empathy and understanding in your relationship?

Remember, conversations about sexual orientation and gender identity can be challenging, but cultivating empathy and understanding is essential for creating a supportive and inclusive environment.

Exercise 3: Building Support Networks

Support networks are crucial during the coming-out process. Consider the following exercise to help build your personal support network:

1. Research LGBTQ+ organizations, support groups, or online communities that align with your religious or cultural background. 2. Attend local events or connect virtually with individuals who share similar experiences. 3. Engage in

thoughtful conversations and share your story. Listen to others and provide support and validation. 4. Stay connected with your support network through regular check-ins, meetings, or online forums. 5. Consider involving allies, such as family members or friends, who are supportive of your journey.

Building a strong support network can provide a sense of belonging and empowerment, especially when faced with challenges or moments of self-doubt.

Additional Resources

+ **Book:** "Faith Beyond Belief: Stories of Good People Who Left Their Church Behind" by Margaret Placentra Johnston.

+ **Documentary:** "Trembling Before G-d" directed by Sandi Simcha DuBowski.

+ **Online Resource:** LGBTQ+ Muslims: Resources for LGBTQ+ Muslims and Their Allies - www.lgbtqmuslims.com.

+ **Support Group:** The Muslim Alliance for Sexual and Gender Diversity - www.muslimalliance.org.

Note: These resources are provided as a starting point for further exploration and support. It is important to research and find resources that are relevant to your specific needs and location.

Finding Acceptance in Society

Finding acceptance in society as a queer individual can be a challenging and sometimes daunting task. Irshad Manji, a queer Muslim activist, has faced these challenges head-on and has paved the way for others to find acceptance and fight for their rights. In this section, we will explore the journey of finding acceptance in society, highlighting the struggles faced by LGBTQ individuals, the importance of community support, and the role of allies in creating an inclusive society.

Challenges Faced by LGBTQ Individuals

For many LGBTQ individuals, finding acceptance in society can be an uphill battle. Homophobia, transphobia, and discrimination are still prevalent in many parts of the world. These attitudes can lead to exclusion, bullying, and even violence against queer individuals. Moreover, societal expectations and traditional values often perpetuate stereotypes and stigmatize those who deviate from the norm.

Creating Supportive Communities

One of the crucial steps in finding acceptance in society is creating and fostering supportive communities. LGBTQ individuals often find solace and understanding within these communities, which provide a safe space for self-expression and personal growth. These communities offer a sense of belonging and support, where individuals can connect with others who have similar experiences and challenges.

Irshad Manji recognized the importance of community support and played a pivotal role in creating safe spaces for LGBTQ Muslims. Through her activism, she initiated conversations and facilitated dialogue among individuals who were facing similar struggles, providing them with a supportive network and access to resources.

The Role of Allies

Allies, individuals who support and advocate for LGBTQ rights, play a significant role in fostering acceptance in society. They use their privileged positions to challenge discrimination and promote inclusivity. Allies can be vital in breaking down stereotypes and educating others about LGBTQ experiences and issues.

Irshad Manji acknowledges the importance of allies in her journey towards acceptance. She actively engages with individuals from different backgrounds, encouraging them to learn, empathize, and stand in solidarity with LGBTQ individuals. By building bridges and forming alliances, she has helped create a more inclusive society.

Social Media and Visibility

In the digital age, social media platforms have played a pivotal role in finding acceptance in society. LGBTQ individuals have leveraged social media to share their stories, connect with others, and form virtual support networks. Visibility through platforms such as Instagram, Twitter, and YouTube has helped challenge stereotypes and humanize the LGBTQ experience.

Irshad Manji, through her extensive social media presence, has amplified the voices of queer Muslims and provided them with a platform to share their stories. This visibility has helped challenge misconceptions and create spaces for dialogue, paving the way for increased acceptance in society.

Shifting Societal Norms

Acceptance in society is not a static concept. It evolves as societal norms and values change over time. Through tireless advocacy and raising awareness, individuals like

Irshad Manji have contributed to the shifting of societal norms and the acceptance of LGBTQ individuals.

By challenging preconceived notions and engaging in conversations with diverse audiences, Manji has encouraged critical thinking and reflection. Her efforts have contributed to more inclusive conversations surrounding gender, sexuality, and religion, ultimately leading to greater acceptance in society.

Embracing Diversity and Intersectionality

Finding acceptance in society requires recognizing and embracing the diverse identities and experiences within the LGBTQ community. Intersectionality, the recognition of how different forms of oppression intersect and compound, is crucial in understanding and addressing the unique challenges faced by individuals who hold multiple marginalized identities.

Irshad Manji emphasizes the importance of intersectionality in her activism. She strives to create inclusive spaces that recognize and embrace the diverse backgrounds and experiences of LGBTQ individuals. By highlighting the intersections of faith, sexuality, and culture, Manji encourages dialogue and understanding, fostering greater acceptance in society.

Case Study: "Queer and Muslim" Support Group

To illustrate the power of finding acceptance in society, let's explore a case study of a "Queer and Muslim" support group. This support group provides a safe space for queer individuals who identify as Muslim to connect, share experiences, and discuss their unique challenges.

The group not only offers emotional support but also provides educational resources on LGBTQ rights, Islamic teachings, and how to reconcile faith with queerness. Through guest speakers, workshops, and community events, the group aims to foster acceptance within Muslim communities and society in general.

The support group acts as a catalyst for change, inspiring its members to become activists and advocates for LGBTQ rights within their own communities. This domino effect helps create a ripple of acceptance, leading to societal change and a more inclusive future.

Conclusion

Finding acceptance in society as a queer individual is a journey that requires resilience, community support, and allyship. Through the efforts of individuals like Irshad Manji, the barriers to acceptance are slowly being dismantled. By fostering inclusive communities, shifting societal norms, leveraging social media, and embracing diversity, we can work towards a future where acceptance is the norm, regardless of one's sexual orientation or gender identity. The path to acceptance may be challenging, but it is through collective action and unwavering determination that we can create a more inclusive and accepting society for all.

Allies and Support Networks

In the journey towards acceptance and equality, allies and support networks play a crucial role in the lives of LGBTQ individuals. They are the backbone of the LGBTQ rights movement and provide valuable resources, advocacy, and emotional support. This subsection will explore the importance of allies and support networks in the queer Muslim community and their contribution to creating a more inclusive society.

Understanding the Role of Allies

Allies are individuals who actively support and advocate for the rights and well-being of the LGBTQ community, despite not identifying as LGBTQ themselves. They recognize the injustices and discrimination faced by queer Muslims and use their privilege and influence to challenge social norms and misconceptions surrounding sexual orientation and gender identity.

The Power of Allyship

Allyship has the potential to reshape conversations, challenge prejudices, and dismantle systemic discrimination. Allies can amplify the voices of LGBTQ individuals and help create safe spaces where Queer Muslims can thrive. By supporting and uplifting their queer Muslim friends and acquaintances, allies send a powerful message of acceptance and empathy that can have a profound impact on an individual's well-being.

Support Networks for Queer Muslims

Support networks are vital for the well-being and empowerment of queer Muslims. These networks provide a safe and understanding environment where individuals can share their experiences, seek guidance, and develop connections with like-minded individuals. Whether they are in-person communities or online support groups, these networks offer a sense of belonging and solidarity.

Building Bridges Between Communities

Allies and support networks can play a crucial role in bridging the gap between the LGBTQ and Muslim communities. By acting as intermediaries, they initiate conversations and facilitate understanding about gender and sexual diversity within religious contexts. Through dialogue and education, they help dispel stereotypes and misconceptions and promote inclusivity and acceptance.

Advocacy and Activism

Allies and support networks have the power to create tangible change within society. They can engage in advocacy efforts, raise awareness about LGBTQ rights, and challenge discriminatory policies and practices. Their commitment to justice and equality strengthens the LGBTQ movement and paves the way for a more inclusive future.

Proactive Listening and Learning

Effective allyship requires proactive listening and continued learning. Allies should actively seek to educate themselves about LGBTQ experiences, terminology, and issues. By staying informed and engaged, they can better support and advocate for queer Muslims, fostering a more inclusive and understanding environment.

Intersectionality and Allyship

Recognizing the intersectionality of LGBTQ and Muslim identities is essential for effective allyship. Allies should understand that individuals may face multiple forms of discrimination and privilege based on their race, ethnicity, and socioeconomic status. By acknowledging and addressing these intersecting identities, allies can work towards a more equitable society for all.

Taking Action

Allyship is not a passive state but an ongoing commitment to action. Allies can actively participate in LGBTQ events, attend workshops and seminars, and support LGBTQ organizations financially and through volunteering. By using their platforms and networks, allies can amplify the voices of queer Muslims and contribute to tangible change.

The Importance of Self-Care for Allies

It is crucial for allies to prioritize self-care and well-being while supporting LGBTQ individuals. The emotional labor and potential backlash associated with advocating for LGBTQ rights can take a toll on allies. Engaging in self-care activities, seeking support from other allies, and setting boundaries are essential for sustaining long-term allyship.

An Unconventional Approach: The Power of Storytelling

An unconventional yet impactful method for allyship is the power of storytelling. Listening to and sharing personal stories can foster empathy, understanding, and connection. Allies can create platforms for queer Muslims to share their experiences, breaking down barriers and humanizing the struggle for LGBTQ acceptance within the Muslim community.

Conclusion

Allies and support networks play a vital role in the fight for LGBTQ acceptance and equality, particularly within the queer Muslim community. Through their support, advocacy, and commitment to learning, allies bridge the gap between communities and create a more inclusive society. Their actions contribute to the well-being and empowerment of queer Muslims and pave the way for a more accepting future.

The Power of Visibility

Visibility has always been a potent tool in the fight for LGBTQ rights and acceptance. Irshad Manji understood this power early on in her journey as a queer Muslim activist. In this section, we will explore how visibility can create positive change, dismantle stereotypes, and pave the way for a more inclusive society.

The Impact of Representation

Representation matters. When marginalized communities are visible in society, it challenges prevailing narratives and helps to break down stereotypes. For too long, LGBTQ individuals and Muslim communities have been erased or portrayed negatively in mainstream media. However, through her activism and unapologetic visibility, Irshad Manji has shown that there is not just one narrative, but a diversity of experiences within these communities.

By sharing her story and amplifying the voices of other queer Muslims, Manji has helped to redefine what it means to be both LGBTQ and Muslim. Through her work, she has inspired countless individuals to embrace their authentic selves and reject the limiting constraints of societal expectations.

Creating Safe Spaces

Visibility not only challenges societal norms but also creates safe spaces for LGBTQ individuals. When queer Muslims see others like them being visible and proud of their identities, it instills a sense of belonging and acceptance. It sends the message that they are not alone and that there is a community that supports and understands them.

Irshad Manji's advocacy for LGBTQ inclusion in religious spaces has been instrumental in creating safe spaces for queer Muslims. By engaging with religious leaders and challenging conservative interpretations, she has opened doors for LGBTQ individuals to practice their faith without fear of discrimination or exclusion. Through her work, she has inspired the establishment of LGBTQ-friendly mosques and other faith-based organizations that provide support and acceptance.

Challenging Stereotypes

Visibility is a powerful weapon in dismantling stereotypes. By being visible as a queer Muslim, Irshad Manji has shattered the misperception that one cannot be both LGBTQ and religious. She has shown that faith and queerness are not mutually exclusive, and the two can be reconciled.

Through her public speaking engagements, workshops, and books, Manji has been able to challenge stereotypes and misconceptions surrounding Islam and LGBTQ identities. By sharing her insights and personal experiences, she demonstrates that the intersection of faith and queerness is not something to be feared or hidden but celebrated.

Inspiring Change

The power of visibility lies in its ability to inspire change. When LGBTQ individuals see others like them who have overcome adversity and achieved success, it instills hope and motivates them to advocate for their rights and fight for equality. Irshad Manji's visibility as a queer Muslim activist has inspired countless individuals to take action and create positive change in their communities.

Through her writing, public speaking, and advocacy work, Manji has empowered others to speak out and challenge discriminatory practices and laws. Her courage and resilience have shown that one person can make a difference, and that change is possible even in the face of adversity.

The Path Forward

The power of visibility cannot be underestimated. As we look to the future, it is crucial that we continue to support and uplift LGBTQ individuals and Muslim communities in their efforts to be visible and proud of their identities.

Creating safe spaces, challenging stereotypes, and inspiring change through visibility are just a few of the ways we can work towards a more inclusive society. It is up to each of us to celebrate and support the visibility of marginalized communities, amplifying their voices and creating a world where everyone can live authentically and without fear.

Let us remember the powerful impact visibility can have, and let us continue to fight for a future where all LGBTQ individuals, including queer Muslims, can live their lives openly, proudly, and without discrimination. Our collective activism and commitment to visibility will shape a more inclusive and accepting world for generations to come.

Key Takeaways:

+ Visibility challenges stereotypes and breaks down societal barriers.

+ Representation is crucial in redefining narratives and fostering acceptance.

+ Creating safe spaces for LGBTQ individuals is essential for their well-being and sense of belonging.

+ Challenging stereotypes through visibility helps to dismantle discriminatory beliefs.

+ Visibility inspires change and motivates individuals to advocate for their rights.

Self-Reflection Questions:

+ How can I contribute to the visibility of marginalized communities?

+ In what ways can I challenge stereotypes and misconceptions?

+ How can I create safe spaces for LGBTQ individuals in my own community?

+ What steps can I take to inspire change and promote inclusivity?

Embracing Queer Muslim Identity

Background and Introduction

Embracing one's identity as a queer Muslim can be a complex and transformative journey. This subsection focuses on the challenges, triumphs, and strategies involved in accepting and celebrating this intersectional identity. It explores the experiences of queer Muslims, highlights their contributions to activism, and provides support and resources for individuals navigating this unique path.

The Intersection of Queerness and Muslim Identity

Being both queer and Muslim can often feel like navigating between two worlds. Muslims who identify as LGBTQ+ may face social and religious pressures that can cause confusion, isolation, and internal conflict. However, it is important to recognize that being queer and Muslim is not inherently contradictory; rather, it is a beautiful expression of diversity within the Muslim community.

The Importance of Community and Support

For queer Muslims, finding like-minded individuals and support networks is crucial. These communities can provide understanding, empathy, and a safe space to explore the complexities of their identity. Building connections with others who share similar experiences can validate their feelings and help to counteract the isolation often associated with this dual identity.

Navigating Religious Spaces

One of the significant challenges faced by queer Muslims is finding acceptance within religious spaces. Many traditional interpretations of Islamic teachings may view homosexuality as incompatible with religious beliefs. However, it is essential to recognize that Islam is a diverse religion, and there are interpretations that promote inclusion and acceptance. Engaging in respectful dialogue, challenging harmful interpretations, and advocating for change can foster more inclusive spaces for queer Muslims.

Reconciling Faith and Sexuality

Reconciling faith and sexuality is a deeply personal and individual journey. Queer Muslims often grapple with questions of religious legitimacy and self-acceptance. They may seek guidance from progressive religious scholars who advocate for a reevaluation of traditional religious teachings through a lens of inclusivity. The process of reconciling faith and sexuality requires self-reflection, critical thinking, and a deep exploration of personal values and beliefs.

Advocacy and Visibility

Embracing queer Muslim identity also involves advocating for the rights and visibility of this often marginalized community. Through activism, queer Muslims can challenge societal norms, combat homophobia within Muslim communities, and promote understanding and acceptance within wider society. Visibility through sharing personal stories, engaging in public speaking, and participating in LGBTQ+ and Muslim organizations can create a transformative impact and inspire others.

Resources and Support Networks

Access to resources and support networks is vital for queer Muslims to navigate their identity confidently. LGBTQ+-inclusive mosques, organizations, counseling services, and online platforms can provide a sense of belonging and provide essential guidance. Education resources that tackle intersectional challenges, mental health support, and advocacy toolkits can empower queer Muslim individuals and build resilience within the community.

Contemporary Challenges and Opportunities

The journey of embracing queer Muslim identity continues to face contemporary challenges, but it also presents opportunities for growth and change. As queer Muslims continue to speak out, engage in dialogue, and advocate for their rights, they create space for future generations to embrace their identities freely. It is essential to recognize and address the unique challenges faced by queer Muslims and collaborate with other activist movements to foster social change.

Conclusion

Embracing queer Muslim identity is a courageous and transformative journey that requires self-reflection, resilience, and support from the community. By navigating the complexities of their dual identity, queer Muslims can challenge harmful narratives, promote inclusion, and create a more accepting and compassionate world. It is through their activism and visibility that they inspire future generations of queer Muslims to embrace their identity unapologetically.

Key Takeaways and Exercises

1. Reflect on your own understanding of queer Muslim identity. How can you challenge your own biases and prejudices to promote inclusivity within your community? 2. Research and explore the stories of queer Muslim activists who have made significant contributions to LGBTQ+ and Muslim rights movements. How have their experiences informed their activism? 3. Engage in respectful dialogue with individuals from different backgrounds and intersections of identity, fostering understanding and empathy. 4. Connect with online LGBTQ+ Muslim communities and organizations that provide resources and support for individuals navigating the complexities of their dual identity. 5. Use social media platforms to amplify the voices of queer Muslims, promote inclusive narratives, and challenge harmful stereotypes. 6. Educate yourself on the progressive interpretations of Islam that advocate for LGBTQ+ inclusion. How can you be an ally to queer Muslims within your local religious community?

Remember, embracing queer Muslim identity is a deeply personal journey, and everyone's experience is unique. The most important aspect is to approach it with empathy, respect, and a commitment to creating a more inclusive and accepting world.

Navigating Faith and Sexuality

Traditional Islamic Upbringing

Growing up in a traditional Islamic household, Irshad Manji's journey was deeply influenced by the conservative values and beliefs that shaped her early years. Islam, as a religion, plays a significant role in the lives of millions of people around the world, and understanding its teachings and practices is crucial to comprehending the complexities of Manji's story.

1. The Pillars of Islam: The foundation of Islamic faith lies in the Five Pillars of Islam, which are the five core principles that every Muslim is expected to follow. These pillars are: - Shahada: The declaration of faith in one God, Allah, and the acceptance of Muhammad as God's final messenger. - Salah: The obligation of offering five daily prayers towards Mecca. - Zakat: The act of giving alms or charitable donations to those in need. - Sawm: Fasting during the holy month of Ramadan, from dawn until sunset. - Hajj: The pilgrimage to the holy city of Mecca, which every Muslim should strive to undertake at least once in their lifetime, if physically and financially able.

2. Gender Roles and Expectations: Traditional Islamic upbringing often assigns specific roles and responsibilities to individuals based on their gender. Men are expected to lead the family, be the breadwinners, and exert authority, while women are typically responsible for household chores, child-rearing, and maintaining modesty in their appearance. These expectations can vary widely depending on cultural practices and interpretations of Islamic teachings.

3. Importance of Family and Community: Family plays a central role in traditional Islamic upbringing, and strong family ties are highly valued. The concept of community is also significant, with Muslims encouraged to support and care for one another. Islamic scholars and religious leaders, such as imams, hold positions of authority and provide spiritual guidance to the community.

4. Religious Education: From an early age, Muslim children are exposed to Islamic teachings and practices through religious education. This education emphasizes the study of the Quran, the holy book of Islam, as well as the Hadith, which are the sayings and actions of the Prophet Muhammad. Learning about

Islamic history, jurisprudence, and principles of ethics and morality are also important aspects of religious education.

5. Modesty and Hijab: Modesty is a core value in Islam, and many Muslim women choose to observe hijab, which refers to the modest dress and behavior that aligns with Islamic teachings. The hijab is a symbol of piety and adherence to Islamic values and varies in style and interpretation across different cultures and regions.

6. Respect for Authority: Respect for authority, particularly religious leaders and scholars, is ingrained in traditional Islamic upbringing. Religious teachings are often accepted as the ultimate source of guidance and knowledge, and questioning or challenging these teachings may be discouraged or even considered taboo.

7. Balanced Approach to Life: While traditional Islamic upbringing emphasizes religious devotion and adherence to religious obligations, it also encourages a balanced approach to life. Islam promotes ethical behavior, kindness, compassion, and social responsibility. It encourages Muslims to excel in both worldly pursuits and spiritual endeavors, aiming for a harmonious integration of faith, family, and society.

However, it is essential to note that interpretations of Islamic teachings can vary, and individuals may have different perspectives on how to reconcile these teachings with contemporary issues such as LGBTQ rights and gender equality. Manji faced her own challenges in navigating her traditional Islamic upbringing while embracing her queer identity and advocating for inclusion and acceptance within Muslim communities.

Understanding the traditional Islamic upbringing provides a context for the struggles and conflicts that Irshad Manji experienced as she embarked on a journey of self-discovery, challenging traditional norms, and seeking to reconcile her faith with her queer identity. In the following subsections, we will delve deeper into Manji's quest for LGBTQ rights within Islam, her engagement with religious scholars, and her efforts to create spaces of inclusion and acceptance for LGBTQ Muslims.

Questioning Religious Beliefs

In this section, we delve into Irshad Manji's journey of questioning her religious beliefs and the impact it had on her identity and activism. This exploration represents an essential aspect of her path towards embracing her queer Muslim identity and challenging traditional Islamic interpretations.

The Turmoil of Doubt

Irshad Manji's traditional Islamic upbringing initially provided her with a solid foundation of faith and belief. However, as she navigated her journey of self-discovery, she began to question the ways in which her religion addressed issues of gender and sexuality. This questioning process led her to confront an internal turmoil of doubt, as she grappled with reconciling her faith with her personal experiences and understanding of the world.

Exploring Alternative Interpretations

To address her doubts and seek clarity, Irshad Manji delved into the world of Islamic scholarship and alternative interpretations of the Quran and Hadiths. She engaged with diverse voices within the Muslim community and studied the works of progressive Muslim scholars. Through this exploration, she discovered that Islam is a dynamic and multifaceted religion, capable of accommodating a range of perspectives.

Confronting Homophobia in Religious Texts

One of the major challenges Irshad Manji faced was reconciling the presence of homophobic verses in religious texts with her belief in equality and justice. She examined the historical and cultural context in which these verses were revealed, recognizing the need to reinterpret them in a way that aligns with contemporary understandings of human rights and LGBTQ inclusion.

Redefining Religious Authority

Irshad Manji began to question the traditional sources of authority within Islam and the monopoly of interpretations held by religious scholars. She argued that the voice and lived experiences of marginalized individuals, including LGBTQ Muslims, should be included in shaping the understanding of Islamic teachings. This redefinition of religious authority contributed significantly to her activism, challenging the prevailing orthodoxy and advocating for a more inclusive and compassionate Islam.

The Evolution of Belief

Through her exploration and questioning, Irshad Manji's beliefs regarding LGBTQ rights and religious inclusivity evolved. She came to understand that her faith and sexuality could coexist, and that her identity as a queer Muslim did not contradict her devotion to Islam. This evolution encouraged her to challenge the status quo and advocate for change within Muslim communities, highlighting the necessity of ongoing dialogue and the acceptance of diverse perspectives.

Engaging in Critical Analysis

A crucial aspect of Irshad Manji's questioning involved engaging in critical analysis of religious texts and teachings. She encouraged individuals, regardless of their religious background, to critically examine the ethical and moral implications of traditional interpretations. This analytical approach allowed her to push boundaries and challenge discriminatory norms, opening up avenues for an inclusive understanding of faith.

Acknowledging Complexities and Controversies

While questioning religious beliefs, Irshad Manji also recognized the complexities and controversies surrounding these discussions. She acknowledged the diversity of viewpoints within the Muslim community and encouraged respectful and constructive dialogue on these sensitive topics. It is important to approach these discussions with empathy, understanding, and a commitment to fostering unity and acceptance.

Reconciling Personal Faith and Advocacy

Irshad Manji's journey of questioning religious beliefs ultimately led her to reconcile her personal faith with her activism. She recognized that advocating for LGBTQ rights and challenging oppressive norms within her faith did not diminish her devotion to Islam but rather enhanced it. This reconciliation became a driving force behind her work, inspiring others to question and challenge entrenched beliefs.

Unconventional Exercise: Rewrite a Homophobic Verse

As an unconventional exercise, individuals can be encouraged to rewrite a homophobic verse from a religious text in a more inclusive and compassionate manner. This exercise fosters critical thinking, creativity, and empathy, urging individuals to examine the impact of language and explore alternative interpretations that prioritize equality and justice.

Additional Resources

1. "Progressive Muslims: On Justice, Gender, and Pluralism" by Omid Safi 2. "Sexuality and Eroticism Among Males in Muslim Societies" by Arno Schmitt and Jehoeda Sofer 3. "Queer Jihad: LGBTQ Muslims on Coming Out, Activism, and the Faith" edited by Afdhere Jama and Parvez Sharma

Exploring LGBTQ Rights in Islam

In this section, we delve into the complex and often controversial topic of LGBTQ rights within the context of Islam. By exploring the teachings, interpretations, and historical perspectives of Islam, we aim to shed light on the diverse range of opinions and debates surrounding queer identities in this religion.

Islam, like any other major religion, is not immune to differing viewpoints on LGBTQ individuals and their rights. While some scholars argue for a more progressive and inclusive interpretation of Islamic principles, others hold more conservative beliefs that view same-sex relationships as sinful and immoral. It is essential to recognize this diversity of opinions within the Muslim community when discussing LGBTQ rights and Islam.

Islamic Teachings and Perspectives

The Quran, the central religious text of Islam, does not explicitly mention homosexuality. However, certain verses and stories have been interpreted by scholars in different ways regarding same-sex relationships. Some scholars argue that the Quran condemns homosexual acts based on the story of Lot, while others suggest alternative interpretations that emphasize the importance of love, compassion, and avoiding harm in all relationships.

Hadiths, the sayings and actions of the Prophet Muhammad, are also significant in shaping Islamic beliefs. However, determining the authenticity and relevance of specific hadiths regarding homosexuality remains a topic of ongoing debate among scholars. It is important to approach these texts with a critical mindset and consider the cultural and historical contexts in which they were formed.

Progressive Interpretations and Advocacy

In recent years, there has been a growing movement within Islam to advocate for LGBTQ rights and inclusion. Progressive scholars argue that Islam's core principles of justice, compassion, and equality should extend to all individuals, regardless of their sexual orientation or gender identity. They emphasize the importance of contextualizing Quranic verses and hadiths to accommodate modern understandings of human sexuality and relationships.

Progressive scholars also highlight historical evidence of same-sex relationships being accepted in some Muslim societies, such as the existence of same-sex marriages in pre-modern Islamic empires. They argue that Islam's rich diversity allows for different understandings of gender and sexuality and that contemporary Muslim societies should be open to embracing LGBTQ individuals.

Challenges and Controversies

While there is a progressive movement within Islam, it is essential to acknowledge the ongoing challenges and controversies surrounding LGBTQ rights. Conservative interpretations, societal stigma, cultural norms, and fear of backlash hinder the progress of LGBTQ inclusion within Muslim communities. LGBTQ individuals may face social isolation, discrimination, and even violence in some contexts.

Engaging in open and respectful dialogue within Muslim communities is crucial in addressing these challenges. It requires creating safe spaces for discussions, challenging harmful stereotypes and assumptions, and highlighting the lived experiences of LGBTQ Muslims. Allies within the Muslim community can play a pivotal role in facilitating these dialogues and promoting understanding and acceptance.

Resources and Support

Numerous organizations and activists are dedicated to supporting LGBTQ Muslims and promoting LGBTQ rights within Islam. These organizations provide resources, education, and support for individuals navigating their sexual orientation or gender identity within the context of their faith.

Some organizations and online platforms offer inclusive interpretations of Islamic teachings and provide resources for LGBTQ individuals seeking religious guidance and community. Additionally, counseling services, support groups, and helplines specifically catering to LGBTQ Muslims are available to tackle the unique challenges they face.

The Importance of Inclusivity

Exploring LGBTQ rights in Islam is not solely an intellectual exercise but one that has real-world impact on the lives of individuals struggling with their sexual orientation or gender identity within a Muslim context. It is crucial for Muslim communities to foster inclusivity, empathy, and support for LGBTQ individuals, while also recognizing the rich diversity of opinions and interpretations within the religion.

Engaging in a compassionate and respectful dialogue helps create an environment where LGBTQ Muslims can reconcile their faith with their identity, navigate societal challenges, and promote progressive change within their communities. By striving for inclusion and understanding, we can work towards a world where LGBTQ individuals can fully embrace their identity without fear of discrimination or rejection.

Allies and Allieship

In the journey towards acceptance and equality, allies play a crucial role in supporting and advocating for the LGBTQ community. An ally is someone who may not identify as LGBTQ themselves but supports and stands up for the rights and well-being of LGBTQ individuals. Allies can be a powerful force for change, helping to shift societal attitudes, challenge discrimination, and create safer and more inclusive spaces for everyone.

Understanding the Importance of Allies

Allies are instrumental in promoting LGBTQ rights because they possess certain privileges and social capital that can be leveraged to challenge and dismantle systems of oppression. They can use their voice, privilege, and influence to amplify LGBTQ voices and advocate for change within their own circles of family, friends, and workplaces.

Educating and Raising Awareness

One way allies can make a meaningful difference is by educating themselves and others about LGBTQ experiences and issues. By understanding the challenges faced by the community, allies can dispel stereotypes, challenge misconceptions, and foster empathy and understanding. This can be achieved through reading books and articles, attending workshops and seminars, and engaging in open and respectful discussions with LGBTQ individuals.

Creating Safe Spaces

Allies play a vital role in creating safe spaces where LGBTQ individuals can freely express themselves without fear of discrimination or judgment. This can be accomplished by actively supporting LGBTQ-inclusive policies and practices in schools, workplaces, and other community settings. Allies can also help establish LGBTQ support groups or organizations, organizing events, and providing resources to foster a sense of belonging and acceptance.

Using Privilege to Advocate

Allies have the advantage of being heard and respected in spaces where LGBTQ voices might be silenced or marginalized. They can use their privilege to speak out against discrimination and advocate for equal rights and opportunities, both individually and within institutions. This may involve challenging homophobic or transphobic comments, supporting LGBTQ-inclusive legislation, or partnering with LGBTQ organizations to advance LGBTQ rights.

Active Listening and Validation

Being an ally involves actively listening to LGBTQ individuals, validating their experiences, and offering support. This means taking the time to understand the unique challenges faced by different members of the LGBTQ community, such as the intersectionality of identities, and acknowledging that everyone's experiences can be different. By providing a safe and non-judgmental space for LGBTQ individuals to share their stories, allies can contribute to a greater sense of acceptance and understanding.

Advocacy and Empowerment

Allies can also play a vital role in advocating for policies and legislation that promote LGBTQ equality. This may involve working with LGBTQ organizations, attending rallies and protests, and engaging in conversations with policymakers. Allies can also empower LGBTQ individuals by amplifying their voices and sharing their stories, whether through social media, writing op-eds, or organizing public speaking events.

Responsive and Respectful Relationships

Creating meaningful relationships with LGBTQ individuals is an essential aspect of being an ally. Allies should strive to build connections based on understanding, mutual respect, and support. This means actively seeking feedback, acknowledging and learning from mistakes, and continuously working to improve allyship skills.

Challenging Homophobia and Transphobia

Allies have a responsibility to challenge homophobia, transphobia, and other forms of discrimination wherever they occur. This can be done by calling out offensive language, supporting LGBTQ-inclusive policies, and engaging in conversations that address harmful stereotypes. Allies can also participate in anti-bullying initiatives and promote LGBTQ-inclusive education to combat prejudice and promote acceptance.

Showing up in Times of Need

Supporting the LGBTQ community means being there for them during challenging times, such as when they face discrimination or violence. Allies can provide emotional support, offer resources and information, and connect them with appropriate organizations or services. It is crucial for allies to stand up against hate and ensure that LGBTQ individuals feel supported and protected.

Continual Learning and Growth

Allyship is an ongoing journey that requires continuous learning and growth. Allies must commit to understanding and challenging their own biases, acknowledging the intersections of privilege and oppression, and actively seeking opportunities to support and uplift the LGBTQ community. This may involve attending workshops, engaging in self-reflection, and remaining open to feedback and new perspectives.

Unconventional Example: Using Comedy for Education

An innovative approach to allyship involves using comedy as a tool for education and advocacy. Comedians can use their platform to challenge stereotypes, shed light on LGBTQ experiences, and provoke thoughtful discussions. By combining humor with social commentary, they can engage audiences who might otherwise not be receptive to serious conversations about LGBTQ issues. Comedy has the power to break down barriers, challenge prejudices, and provide a unique way of fostering understanding and acceptance.

In conclusion, allies are pivotal in the fight for LGBTQ equality. Through education, advocacy, creating safe spaces, using their privilege responsibly, and continually learning, allies can contribute to a more inclusive and accepting world. By standing alongside LGBTQ individuals, allies can play a vital role in dismantling systems of oppression and creating an environment where everyone can thrive and live authentically.

Building Bridges, Breaking Barriers

Building bridges and breaking barriers are essential for creating a more inclusive and accepting society for LGBTQ individuals, especially within religious communities. In this section, we will explore the strategies and approaches that Irshad Manji has employed to foster dialogue and understanding between different groups, ultimately paving the way for greater acceptance and equality.

The Need for Dialogue and Understanding

One of the key principles underlying Manji's work is the belief that true progress can only be achieved through open and honest dialogue. Building bridges between different communities requires a willingness to engage with diverse perspectives, even those that may initially seem at odds with one's own beliefs.

Manji recognizes that breaking down barriers is not a one-way process. It requires individuals from all sides of an issue to come together and find common ground. By facilitating conversations and creating spaces for dialogue, Manji encourages both LGBTQ individuals and religious communities to listen and learn from one another.

The Role of Education and Awareness

Education and awareness play a crucial role in breaking down barriers and challenging discriminatory beliefs. To foster understanding, Manji is committed to providing accessible resources and engaging in educational initiatives.

Through her workshops and training sessions, Manji equips both LGBTQ individuals and religious leaders with the knowledge and tools they need to navigate the intersection of faith and sexuality. These sessions enable participants to engage in informed conversations and challenge misconceptions about LGBTQ rights within religious contexts.

Additionally, Manji collaborates with LGBTQ organizations to develop resources and toolkits that promote inclusivity and support within religious spaces. These resources provide guidance and practical steps for fostering acceptance and breaking down barriers.

Empathy and Compassion as Catalysts for Change

Empathy and compassion are powerful tools for bridging the gap between different communities. Manji emphasizes the importance of cultivating empathy and understanding towards those with different perspectives and lived experiences.

By fostering conversations that focus on personal stories and lived realities, Manji helps individuals develop empathy for the challenges faced by LGBTQ individuals within religious communities. This approach not only breaks down barriers but also humanizes the struggles and triumphs of LGBTQ individuals, making it harder to dismiss their experiences.

Collaboration and Solidarity

Collaboration and solidarity between LGBTQ individuals and religious communities are vital for creating lasting change. Manji encourages LGBTQ individuals to seek allies within religious communities and engage in grassroots activism together.

By working together, LGBTQ individuals and religious allies can challenge homophobic beliefs and practices within their own communities. This collaboration sends a powerful message that being LGBTQ and religious are not mutually exclusive identities.

Furthermore, Manji advocates for LGBTQ activists to engage in cross-movement collaboration. By connecting LGBTQ rights with other social justice causes, activists can amplify their impact and create a more inclusive society for all marginalized communities.

Unconventional Approach: Creative Storytelling

An unconventional but highly effective approach that Manji employs is the use of creative storytelling. Stories have the power to transcend boundaries and evoke emotions, making them a powerful tool for breaking down barriers.

Manji leverages the art of storytelling to bring to light the experiences of LGBTQ individuals within religious communities. By sharing personal narratives, either her own or those of others, she challenges preconceived notions and encourages empathy and understanding.

Through books, speeches, and social media, Manji's storytelling approach humanizes LGBTQ individuals, allowing for a deeper emotional connection that can break through the walls of prejudice and discrimination.

Examples and Case Studies

To illustrate the impact of building bridges and breaking barriers, let's explore a couple of examples:

Example 1: LGBTQ-Inclusive Mosques   Manji advocates for the creation of LGBTQ-inclusive mosques, where LGBTQ individuals can feel accepted and affirmed in their religious practices. She has collaborated with religious leaders to develop guidelines and resources for establishing welcoming spaces.

One such example is the Unity Mosque in Toronto, Canada, which welcomes individuals of diverse sexual orientations and gender identities. Through dialogue, education, and support, this mosque provides a safe and inclusive environment for LGBTQ Muslims to practice their faith.

Example 2: Engaging Religious Scholars   Manji recognizes the importance of engaging with religious scholars to challenge conservative interpretations of religious texts. By initiating conversations and providing resources, she encourages religious scholars to reexamine their teachings and consider more inclusive interpretations.

One successful case study is Manji's collaboration with renowned Islamic scholars to reinterpret Quranic verses traditionally perceived as condemning homosexuality. By delving into historical context and linguistic nuances, they provide alternative interpretations that emphasize inclusivity and love.

Resources and Further Reading

For readers interested in learning more about building bridges and breaking barriers, the following resources are recommended:

+ "Allah, Liberty and Love: The Courage to Reconcile Faith and Freedom" by Irshad Manji

+ "The Trouble with Islam Today: A Muslim's Call for Reform in Her Faith" by Irshad Manji

+ "Queer Jihad: LGBT Muslims on Coming Out, Activism, and the Faith" edited by Afdhere Jama et al.

+ "Progressive Muslims: On Justice, Gender, and Pluralism" edited by Omid Safi

By embracing dialogue, education, empathy, and collaboration, Irshad Manji has made great strides in building bridges and breaking barriers between LGBTQ individuals and religious communities. Through her innovative and compassionate approach, she lays the foundation for a more inclusive and accepting world.

Reconciling Faith and Sexuality

In this subsection, we delve into the complex and personal journey of reconciling faith and sexuality. Irshad Manji's experience as a queer Muslim provides valuable insights and lessons on navigating the intersections of these two fundamental aspects of identity.

Challenges in Reconciling Faith and Sexuality

The intersection of faith and sexuality can often present challenges for individuals, particularly those who belong to religious communities that have historically held conservative views on LGBTQ issues. For many LGBTQ Muslims, the teachings and doctrines of their faith may seem at odds with their sexual orientation or gender identity. This conflict can bring about feelings of guilt, shame, and confusion.

Irshad Manji recognizes the difficulties faced when trying to reconcile these seemingly contradictory aspects of identity. She understands the pain that can arise from feeling rejected by religious institutions and grappling with the fear of losing one's faith entirely.

A Shift Towards Progressive Interpretations

One of the key aspects of Manji's work is her advocacy for progressive interpretations of religious texts and teachings. She encourages a critical examination of traditional interpretations that may perpetuate discrimination and prejudice against LGBTQ individuals.

By engaging with religious scholars and encouraging dialogue within religious communities, Manji promotes a more inclusive understanding of faith. This entails challenging the rigid and often outdated interpretations of sacred texts and promoting an environment that embraces diversity.

The Importance of Inclusivity in Islam

Manji emphasizes the importance of inclusivity within Islam and highlights the need to create safe and welcoming spaces for LGBTQ Muslims. She believes that faith communities should be at the forefront of promoting love, acceptance, and support for all individuals, regardless of their sexual orientation or gender identity.

Through her work, Manji encourages Muslim leaders and communities to actively challenge homophobia and transphobia within Islamic spaces. This involves reevaluating traditional teachings and working towards a more compassionate, understanding, and inclusive interpretation of Islam.

Promoting Dialogue and Education

Another crucial aspect of reconciling faith and sexuality is through dialogue and education. Manji advocates for open conversations and the sharing of personal stories and experiences, creating opportunities for understanding and empathy.

By speaking at universities, conferences, and mosques, Manji aims to raise awareness and foster dialogue around LGBTQ rights and acceptance in Muslim communities. These platforms provide valuable opportunities for individuals to engage with the topic, ask questions, and challenge preconceived notions.

Balancing Personal Faith and Queerness

Manji's own journey of reconciling faith and sexuality reminds us that it is a deeply personal endeavor. She encourages individuals to find their unique path in navigating their faith and queerness, acknowledging that everyone's journey is different.

Finding a balance between personal convictions and LGBTQ identities may involve seeking guidance from queer-friendly religious leaders, engaging with support networks, and engaging in personal introspection. It is essential to recognize that the path to reconciling faith and sexuality is not linear and may involve self-discovery and continuous growth.

Empowering LGBTQ Muslims

In her work, Manji strives to empower LGBTQ Muslims by creating resources, toolkits, and safe spaces for them to flourish. By amplifying the voices and experiences of LGBTQ Muslims, she seeks to inspire others who may be grappling with their faith and sexuality.

Manji actively mentors LGBTQ youth and encourages them to embrace their whole selves, affirming that being queer and Muslim is not mutually exclusive. Her efforts extend beyond personal empowerment, as she advocates for policy changes and legal reforms that protect the rights of LGBTQ individuals within Muslim communities.

The Path to Reconciliation

Reconciling faith and sexuality is an ongoing process, one that requires self-reflection, education, and open-mindedness. The journey to finding harmony between these two aspects of identity is unique for each individual.

As Irshad Manji has demonstrated, it is possible to reconcile faith and sexuality by challenging traditional interpretations, fostering inclusive communities, engaging in dialogue, and empowering LGBTQ individuals within religious spaces. By embracing compassion, understanding, and love, we can pave the way for a more accepting and inclusive world that fully honors the diversity within both faith and sexuality.

Cultural Contexts

It is important to note that the experiences of LGBTQ Muslims may differ based on cultural contexts and geographic locations. The challenges faced by LGBTQ individuals within Muslim-majority countries may be distinct from those in Western societies. It is crucial to have an awareness and understanding of these diverse experiences when advocating for greater acceptance and inclusivity within religious communities.

Further Resources

For those interested in exploring the topic of reconciling faith and sexuality further, the following resources may be helpful:

- "Queer Jihad: LGBT Muslims on Coming Out, Activism, and the Faith" edited by Afdhere Jama

- "Progressive Muslims: On Justice, Gender, and Pluralism" edited by Omid Safi

- "Living Out Islam: Voices of Gay, Lesbian, and Transgender Muslims" by Scott Siraj al-Haqq Kugle

- The Queer Muslim Project (queermuslimproject.org) – an online platform for LGBTQ Muslim voices and resources

These resources provide valuable insights, personal stories, and practical guidance for individuals navigating the intersection of faith and sexuality.

Exercise

Consider your own faith and how it relates to LGBTQ rights and inclusion. Reflect on any conflicts or challenges you may have faced reconciling these aspects of identity. Engage in open-minded self-reflection and consider ways in which you can promote greater acceptance and inclusivity within your faith community.

Challenging Homophobia within Muslim Communities

Homophobia is a deeply entrenched issue within many religious communities, including Islam. While it is important to recognize and respect religious beliefs and traditions, it is equally important to challenge homophobic attitudes and create safe spaces for LGBTQ individuals within these communities.

Understanding Homophobia

Homophobia is the fear, hatred, or intolerance towards individuals who identify as LGBTQ. It often stems from a lack of understanding, ignorance, and societal stereotypes. It manifests in various ways, such as discriminatory laws, exclusionary language, and acts of violence targeting LGBTQ individuals.

In Muslim communities, homophobia can sometimes be influenced by conservative interpretations of religious texts that condemn same-sex relationships. It is crucial to recognize that these interpretations are not the only valid ones and that alternative, inclusive interpretations are possible.

Promoting Dialogue and Education

One of the most effective ways to challenge homophobia within Muslim communities is through open and respectful dialogue. By engaging in conversations about LGBTQ issues, individuals can gain a better understanding of homosexuality and overcome their prejudices.

Educational initiatives are also essential in combating homophobia. Mosques and Islamic organizations can organize seminars, workshops, and panel discussions on LGBTQ rights in Islam. These initiatives can provide a safe space for questions, discussions, and the dissemination of accurate and inclusive information.

Highlighting LGBTQ Muslim Voices

LGBTQ Muslims face unique challenges and often feel isolated within their communities. By amplifying their voices and sharing their stories, we can challenge the stereotypes and misconceptions surrounding homosexuality in Islam.

Supporting LGBTQ Muslim individuals to publicly come out and share their experiences can be a transformative force in breaking down barriers and fostering understanding within Muslim communities. Their stories can humanize the struggle for acceptance and help dispel the notion that being LGBTQ is incompatible with being Muslim.

Creating Inclusive Spaces

It is essential to create welcoming and inclusive spaces within Muslim communities where LGBTQ individuals can feel accepted and supported. Mosques can play a vital role in this by actively working towards inclusivity and challenging homophobia.

This can be achieved through implementing LGBTQ-inclusive policies, providing resources and support for LGBTQ individuals, and establishing LGBTQ support groups within mosques. By actively working to challenge homophobia, mosques can become beacons of acceptance and love for all members of the community.

Addressing Homophobic Attitudes and Beliefs

Challenging homophobia within Muslim communities requires addressing and dismantling homophobic attitudes and beliefs. This task can be accomplished through engaging with religious scholars, challenging conservative interpretations of religious texts, and promoting critical thinking.

Engaging with religious scholars who advocate for LGBTQ rights can provide a more nuanced understanding of Islam's stance on homosexuality. By supporting progressive Muslim scholars and encouraging the exploration of alternative interpretations of religious texts, we can foster a culture of inclusivity and acceptance within Muslim communities.

Advocacy and Activism

To challenge homophobia effectively, it is crucial to engage in advocacy and activism on both individual and collective levels. This can involve participating in Pride events, joining LGBTQ Muslim organizations, and showing support for LGBTQ rights.

Activism can also take the form of advocating for policy changes within Muslim communities and working towards the inclusion of LGBTQ individuals in mosque leadership positions. By actively promoting LGBTQ rights and challenging homophobia, we can push for lasting change within Muslim societies.

Confronting Intersectionality

It is important to recognize and address the intersectionality of identities within Muslim LGBTQ individuals. Many LGBTQ Muslims face discrimination not only based on their sexual orientation or gender identity but also on their race, ethnicity, and religious beliefs.

Efforts to challenge homophobia within Muslim communities must also address the racism, xenophobia, and Islamophobia that intersect with LGBTQ discrimination. By fostering solidarity and understanding between diverse communities, we can create a more inclusive and accepting society for all.

In conclusion, challenging homophobia within Muslim communities requires open dialogue, education, amplifying LGBTQ Muslim voices, creating inclusive spaces, addressing beliefs and attitudes, and engaging in advocacy and activism. By working towards acceptance and understanding, we can create a future where all LGBTQ individuals, regardless of their religious beliefs, can live authentically and with dignity.

Intersections of Faith and Activism

Faith and activism are two powerful forces that, when brought together, can create significant change and transform societies. In this subsection, we will explore the intricate relationship between faith and activism, understanding how they intersect and complement each other in the context of LGBTQ rights and the fight for equality.

Faith as a Motivator for Activism

For many individuals, faith serves as the foundation for their values, ethics, and guiding principles in life. It provides them with a sense of purpose and a moral compass from which they navigate the world. Within various religious traditions, there are teachings and beliefs that emphasize love, compassion, justice, and equity, which align with the core principles of activism.

When individuals with a deep-rooted faith embrace activism, they channel their spiritual beliefs into tangible actions that seek to address social injustices, confront discrimination, and advocate for equality. They draw strength and inspiration from their religious teachings, seeing their commitment to activism as an embodiment of their faith.

Example: A Muslim activist, driven by their faith, might strive to challenge homophobic practices within their community and advocate for LGBTQ rights by quoting passages from the Quran that emphasize compassion, respect, and the importance of social justice.

Activism's Influence on Faith

While faith can motivate activism, the act of engaging in activism also has the power to shape and transform an individual's faith. Through their involvement in advocating for LGBTQ rights, individuals may question and reevaluate certain interpretations, traditions, or practices within their religious community that perpetuate discrimination or exclusion.

Activism serves as a catalyst for critical thinking and dialogue within religious communities. It prompts individuals to challenge deeply ingrained beliefs and structures that may have been used to justify discrimination or marginalization. This process can lead to a more inclusive and progressive understanding of faith, where traditional religious teachings are revisited and reinterpreted in light of the principles of equality and social justice.

Example: The experience of advocating for LGBTQ rights may prompt an individual to question their religious institution's stance on same-sex relationships. Through conversations, activism, and engagement with religious scholars, they may seek alternative interpretations of religious texts that embrace and affirm queer identities.

Building Interfaith Alliances

Interfaith alliances play a crucial role in creating a more inclusive society. By fostering understanding, respect, and collaboration between different religious traditions, these alliances can be powerful agents of change in promoting LGBTQ rights and challenging discriminatory practices.

Interfaith activism recognizes that diverse religious communities share common ground when it comes to principles of justice, compassion, and equality. By working together, individuals from various faith traditions can leverage their collective influence to challenge discriminatory policies, advocate for LGBTQ-inclusive legislation, and support marginalized individuals within their respective communities.

Example: LGBTQ activists and religious leaders from different faiths might come together to hold interfaith dialogues, where they explore the intersections between faith and LGBTQ rights. These conversations can help break down barriers, foster empathy, and build bridges between communities.

The Importance of Faith-Inclusive Spaces

To create a truly inclusive society, it is essential to ensure that faith communities are safe spaces for LGBTQ individuals. Intersectional activism recognizes that individuals can simultaneously hold multiple identities, including their faith and their queerness. Activists advocating for LGBTQ rights in religious spaces work towards dismantling homophobia, transphobia, and discrimination and fostering acceptance and inclusion.

Faith-inclusive activism involves challenging discriminatory practices within religious institutions and engaging in dialogue to educate congregations about LGBTQ issues. It also involves creating resources, toolkits, and support networks within religious communities to assist LGBTQ individuals, their families, and allies.

Example: An activist working within a religious institution might initiate workshops or educational programs to promote LGBTQ inclusion. Through these initiatives, they aim to challenge negative perceptions, share personal stories, and encourage empathy and understanding among community members.

Navigating Challenges and Resistance

Intersections of faith and activism are not without their challenges. Progress towards LGBTQ inclusion often faces resistance from within religious communities, as some traditional interpretations may condemn homosexuality or gender diversity. Activists working in faith spaces must navigate these challenges with patience, persistence, and strategic advocacy.

They utilize their knowledge of religious texts, engage with religious scholars, and leverage the power of personal narratives to dismantle harmful beliefs and promote alternative interpretations that affirm LGBTQ identities. Activists also draw strength from the history of successful social justice movements to inspire and mobilize their communities for change.

Example: LGBTQ activists advocating for religious inclusivity might face backlash and resistance from members of their faith communities. To overcome this, they might organize conferences or panels where LGBTQ individuals and allies share their stories, demonstrating the importance of accepting and embracing diverse identities.

The Power of Personal Faith Journeys

In the intersection of faith and activism, personal faith journeys play a vital role. LGBTQ individuals who navigate the complexities of reconciling their queer identities with their faith can inspire others by sharing their experiences and leading by example.

These personal faith journeys offer guidance, solace, and hope to individuals who are struggling to reconcile their religious beliefs with their sexual orientation or gender identity. By telling their stories of self-acceptance and religious growth, individuals can provide a sense of community and foster understanding among LGBTQ individuals who may be grappling with similar challenges.

Example: A queer Christian activist who went through a transformative faith journey might write a memoir or blog about their experience. Through their storytelling, they can articulate the complexities they navigated, the moments of doubt and eventual self-acceptance, and how their faith and activism intertwine to promote equality and inclusion.

In conclusion, the intersections of faith and activism in the fight for LGBTQ rights demonstrate the transformative power of bringing together deeply held religious beliefs with social justice efforts. Faith can serve as a driving force for activism, while activism can reshape faith traditions, challenge discriminatory practices, and create inclusive spaces within religious communities. By recognizing these intersections, individuals and communities can work towards a more equitable and inclusive world where faith and LGBTQ identities are celebrated, not in conflict, but in harmony.

Promoting Inclusion in Religious Spaces

Promoting inclusion in religious spaces is a crucial aspect of Irshad Manji's activism. She recognizes the fundamental need for LGBTQ individuals to feel safe and accepted within their religious communities. In this subsection, we will explore the challenges and strategies involved in promoting inclusion, as well as the importance of creating welcoming spaces for LGBTQ individuals within religious contexts.

Understanding the Challenge:

Religious spaces often uphold traditional beliefs and teachings that may conflict with or exclude LGBTQ individuals. This poses a significant challenge in promoting inclusion and acceptance. Many religious communities view homosexuality as a sin or consider it incompatible with their faith. Consequently, promoting inclusion requires navigating deeply rooted cultural and religious norms.

Strategies for Promoting Inclusion:

1. **Education and Awareness:** The first step in promoting inclusion is creating awareness and educating religious communities about LGBTQ+ identities and

experiences. This can involve organizing workshops, seminars, or panel discussions to initiate honest and respectful dialogue. It is important to approach these conversations with empathy and understanding, encouraging people to question their preconceived notions and engage in critical thinking.

2. **Engaging Religious Leaders:** Religious leaders hold a significant influence over their communities. Engaging them in discussions about LGBTQ+ inclusion can help shift attitudes and promote change from within. Building relationships and fostering open dialogue with religious leaders can lead to their increased understanding and acceptance of LGBTQ+ individuals. This can be facilitated through interfaith dialogues and collaboration.

3. **Advocacy from Within:** LGBTQ+ individuals and their allies within religious communities can play a vital role in promoting inclusion. By sharing personal stories and experiences, they challenge stereotypes and break down barriers. Forming support groups or LGBTQ+ affinity groups within religious institutions provides a safe space for individuals to connect, share experiences, and advocate for change.

4. **Inclusive Policies and Practices:** Religious institutions should actively work towards adopting inclusive policies and practices. This can include creating safe spaces, revisiting teachings and interpretations, and updating codes of conduct to explicitly include protections for LGBTQ+ individuals. By openly welcoming diversity and affirming LGBTQ+ identities, religious communities can foster an inclusive environment.

5. **Interfaith Collaboration:** Collaborating with other faith-based organizations and religious communities is essential in promoting inclusion. Engaging in interfaith dialogues and joint initiatives can help break down barriers, share resources and best practices, and work collectively towards creating more inclusive religious spaces.

The Importance of Inclusive Religious Spaces:

Creating inclusive religious spaces has several benefits:

1. **Support and Acceptance:** Inclusive religious spaces provide LGBTQ+ individuals with the support and acceptance they need to navigate their identities within their faith. It offers them a sense of belonging and community, reducing feelings of isolation and rejection.

2. **Faith and Identity Reconciliation:** LGBTQ+ individuals often face challenges reconciling their faith with their sexual orientation or gender identity. Inclusive religious spaces offer a platform for individuals to navigate this reconciliation process, promoting a harmonious relationship between their faith and identity.

3. **Positive Role Models:** Inclusive religious spaces provide LGBTQ+ individuals with positive role models within their faith communities. Seeing LGBTQ+ individuals who are leading fulfilling lives while maintaining their faith challenges stereotypes and empowers others to embrace their identities.

4. **Social Change:** Promoting inclusion in religious spaces can have a broader impact on society. Religious communities often hold significant influence within their larger communities, and their acceptance of LGBTQ+ individuals can contribute to wider social acceptance and equality.

Challenges and Caveats:

Promoting inclusion in religious spaces is not without challenges and potential pitfalls. Religious beliefs and traditions vary widely, and progress towards inclusivity can be slow. Resistance to change, fear of backlash, and deep-rooted cultural norms can hinder progress. Additionally, some individuals within religious communities may reject the idea of LGBTQ+ inclusion, resulting in tensions and divisions.

It is crucial to approach these challenges with empathy and patience. Change takes time, and it requires ongoing dialogue, education, and advocacy. It is important to remember that promoting inclusion is a collective effort, involving the broader LGBTQ+ community, allies, religious leaders, and the community at large.

Conclusion:

Promoting inclusion in religious spaces is essential for LGBTQ+ individuals to fully embrace their identities within the framework of their faith. It involves education, dialogue, advocacy, and the creation of supportive and affirming spaces. By promoting a culture of inclusivity, religious communities can play a significant role in fostering acceptance, understanding, and equality for all. The journey towards inclusion may be challenging, but it is a vital step towards creating a more inclusive and equitable society as a whole.

The Importance of Religious Freedom

Religious freedom is a fundamental human right that is essential for creating a more inclusive and diverse society. In the context of LGBTQ activism, the importance of religious freedom cannot be overstated. It is a crucial aspect of fostering understanding, acceptance, and equality for queer individuals within religious communities.

1. The Challenge of Balancing Faith and Identity

Many LGBTQ individuals face the challenge of reconciling their sexual orientation or gender identity with their religious beliefs. This can be particularly difficult in religious traditions that hold conservative views on homosexuality or transgender issues. The struggle to find acceptance within their faith community often leads to feelings of isolation and the internalization of shame.

2. Embracing Pluralism and Accommodation

The importance of religious freedom lies in the ability of religious communities to adapt their doctrines and practices to accommodate the diversity of their members, including LGBTQ individuals. This requires a shift from exclusivity and judgment to a more inclusive approach that embraces pluralism.

3. Nurturing Safe and Inclusive Religious Spaces

Religious freedom should be seen as an opportunity to create safe and inclusive spaces within religious communities. These spaces can foster dialogue, understanding, and compassion, allowing LGBTQ individuals to fully participate in the life of the community without fear of discrimination or marginalization. It is essential to challenge homophobia, transphobia, and other forms of discrimination within these spaces.

4. Collaboration between LGBTQ Activists and Religious Leaders

To promote religious freedom and LGBTQ inclusion, it is crucial to foster collaboration between LGBTQ activists and religious leaders. This collaboration can help bridge the gap between faith communities and queer individuals, allowing for open and honest conversations.

5. Promoting Legal Protections

Religious freedom also extends to legal protections. It is important to advocate for laws that protect LGBTQ individuals from discrimination based on their sexual orientation or gender identity within religious contexts. These protections can ensure that religious organizations, such as schools, hospitals, and social services, do not discriminate against LGBTQ individuals.

6. Providing Education and Resources

Promoting religious freedom requires providing education and resources to both LGBTQ individuals and religious communities. LGBTQ individuals need support and guidance to navigate the intersections of their faith and identity. Religious communities need resources to foster inclusive practices and challenge harmful interpretations of religious texts.

7. Emphasizing the Principle of Love and Acceptance

An important aspect of religious freedom is the emphasis on the principle of love and acceptance. This principle cuts across religious traditions and forms the basis for nurturing understanding and respect for LGBTQ individuals. It is crucial to highlight the divine love that transcends religious boundaries and includes all individuals, regardless of their sexual orientation or gender identity.

8. Engaging in Interfaith Dialogue

Interfaith dialogue plays a critical role in promoting religious freedom and LGBTQ inclusion.   By engaging with individuals from diverse religious backgrounds, we can challenge prejudices and stereotypes, foster empathy, and collectively work towards creating a more inclusive society.

9. Acknowledging the Impact of Religion on LGBTQ Activism

Religion has played a significant role in the lives of many LGBTQ activists throughout history. It has provided them with inspiration, a sense of purpose, and a framework for advocating for equality. Recognizing and honoring the role of religion in LGBTQ activism helps to bridge the gap between religious and secular LGBTQ movements.

10. Creating Space for Intersectionality

When discussing the importance of religious freedom, it is essential to recognize intersectionality, which refers to the interconnectedness of various social identities and systems of oppression. LGBTQ individuals from marginalized communities often face additional challenges due to their race, ethnicity, socioeconomic status, or disability. Promoting religious freedom must include an understanding of these intersecting identities and work towards dismantling multiple forms of discrimination.

In conclusion, religious freedom is a vital aspect of LGBTQ activism. It requires creating safe and inclusive spaces within religious communities, challenging harmful interpretations of religious texts, and fostering collaboration between LGBTQ activists and religious leaders. By promoting religious freedom, we can create a more compassionate and inclusive society that embraces the diversity of LGBTQ individuals and their faith.

Facing Adversity and Courageously Speaking Out

Confronting Homophobia

Homophobia is a deeply ingrained issue in society, and it poses significant challenges to LGBTQ individuals. In this subsection, we will explore the various ways in which Irshad Manji confronted homophobia, both within her own community and on a larger scale. By shedding light on this deeply rooted problem and providing strategies for combating it, Manji has become a beacon of hope for those facing adversity.

Understanding Homophobia

Homophobia refers to the irrational fear, hatred, or prejudice against individuals who identify as LGBTQ. It manifests in various forms, from discriminatory laws and policies to acts of violence and bullying. Homophobia can be deeply rooted in cultural, religious, or societal norms, making it a complex issue to address.

To confront homophobia effectively, it is crucial to understand its origins and the harmful effects it has on individuals. Manji delves into the historical context of homophobia and its impact on LGBTQ individuals. By exploring the experiences of those affected by homophobia, Manji humanizes the issue, allowing readers to empathize with the struggles faced by LGBTQ individuals.

Challenging Stereotypes and Misconceptions

One way Manji confronts homophobia is by challenging stereotypes and misconceptions about LGBTQ individuals. She recognizes that homophobia often stems from ignorance and a lack of understanding. By providing education and promoting awareness, Manji challenges the preconceived notions that fuel homophobia.

Manji takes an innovative approach to combatting homophobia by incorporating personal stories and real-life examples. She highlights the diversity within the LGBTQ community, breaking down stereotypes and showcasing the wide range of experiences. This approach helps dismantle biases and fosters a more inclusive and accepting society.

Promoting LGBTQ Rights and Inclusion

Addressing homophobia requires advocating for LGBTQ rights and promoting inclusion. Manji identifies the importance of legislation that protects LGBTQ individuals from discrimination and violence. She encourages readers to engage in advocacy efforts, such as supporting LGBTQ organizations and contacting policymakers to push for inclusive policies.

In addition to legal protections, Manji emphasizes the significance of creating inclusive spaces for LGBTQ individuals. She highlights the role of schools, workplaces, and religious institutions in fostering acceptance and removing barriers. Manji provides strategies to challenge homophobia within these spaces and encourages dialogue and understanding.

Empowering the LGBTQ Community

Confronting homophobia also involves empowering the LGBTQ community to stand up against discrimination. Manji recognizes the importance of self-advocacy and encourages individuals to assert their rights. She provides resources, such as support networks and organizations, where LGBTQ individuals can find empowerment and strength.

Manji's approach to empowering the LGBTQ community involves promoting self-acceptance and building resilience. She encourages individuals to embrace their authentic selves and find pride in their identities. By sharing personal stories of triumph over homophobia, Manji instills hope and inspires others to take action.

Embracing Allieship

Allieship is another crucial aspect of confronting homophobia. Manji emphasizes the need for allies within the LGBTQ community and beyond. She explores ways in which individuals can become allies by educating themselves, challenging their biases, and speaking out against homophobia.

By supporting the LGBTQ community, allies can play a significant role in confronting homophobia. Manji highlights the impact of allies in creating safer spaces and driving societal change. She provides practical strategies for allies to actively engage in combating homophobia and fostering inclusivity.

Overall, Manji's approach to confronting homophobia combines education, advocacy, empowerment, and allieship. By shedding light on the harmful effects of homophobia and providing actionable strategies, Manji inspires individuals to take a stand against discrimination and work towards a more inclusive and accepting society.

Challenging Patriarchy

In this subsection, we delve into Irshad Manji's efforts in challenging patriarchy within LGBTQ communities and society at large. Manji understands that the fight for equality extends beyond sexual orientation and religious identity, as gender inequality and rigid patriarchal structures often undermine the progress made by marginalized communities. By highlighting the intersections of patriarchy, Islam, and LGBTQ rights, Manji aims to dismantle systemic discrimination and create spaces that are truly inclusive and empowering for all.

Understanding Patriarchy

Before we can challenge patriarchy, it is important to understand its underlying principles and mechanisms. Patriarchy refers to a social system in which men hold primary power and dominate in roles of political leadership, moral authority, social privilege, and control of property. This system perpetuates the belief that male values, perspectives, and experiences are superior, while devaluing and subordinating those of women and non-binary individuals.

Patriarchy manifests in various ways, including gender-based violence, wage gaps, limited reproductive rights, and rigid gender expectations. It reinforces harmful stereotypes, restricts opportunities, and perpetuates discrimination against women, LGBTQ individuals, and minority groups. Challenging patriarchy is essential in building a more equitable and just society.

Unveiling Gender Stereotypes

One of the key aspects of challenging patriarchy is debunking and dismantling gender stereotypes that confine individuals to narrow roles and expectations. Irshad Manji emphasizes the importance of breaking free from societal expectations and encouraging individuals to embrace their authentic selves, regardless of gender norms.

By challenging gender stereotypes, we can create spaces where everyone feels empowered to express themselves freely. This involves understanding that femininity does not equate to weakness and masculinity does not equate to strength. Manji confronts the patriarchal notion that femininity and associated traits are inferior, while highlighting the diversity and value of all gender expressions.

Promoting Intersectional Feminism

Manji recognizes the significance of intersectionality in dismantling patriarchy. Intersectional feminism acknowledges the interconnected nature of various systems of oppression, including those related to race, sexuality, gender identity, religion, disability, and social class. It recognizes that different individuals experience patriarchy in unique ways and advocates for inclusive and nuanced approaches to challenge these structures.

By promoting intersectional feminism, Manji aims to bridge gaps between diverse communities and foster solidarity. This involves actively amplifying the voices and experiences of marginalized individuals, particularly those who are often overlooked or silenced. Manji encourages conversations and collaborations that challenge the hierarchical power dynamics perpetuated by patriarchy.

Building Allies and Support Networks

Challenging patriarchy requires a collective effort, and allies play a crucial role in dismantling patriarchal structures. Irshad Manji emphasizes the importance of building strong support networks and fostering allyship between marginalized groups and individuals.

Allies are individuals who support and advocate for equality, even if they do not personally identify with the marginalized group. Manji encourages open dialogue and education to foster understanding and empathy among allies. By promoting allyship and collaboration, we can create inclusive spaces that challenge patriarchal norms and promote equity.

Addressing Toxic Masculinity

Toxic masculinity is a subset of patriarchal norms that glorify traits such as aggression, dominance, and emotional repression, while stigmatizing vulnerability, empathy, and emotional expression in men. It perpetuates harmful behavior and limits the personal growth and emotional well-being of individuals.

Irshad Manji emphasizes the need to address toxic masculinity within LGBTQ communities and beyond. By challenging the societal expectations that restrict emotional expression and enforce harmful gender norms, we can create environments where individuals of all genders can thrive. This involves promoting healthy relationships, emotional intelligence, and open communication.

Educating and Empowering

Education and awareness are vital tools in challenging patriarchy. Manji advocates for comprehensive sex education and gender studies that dismantle harmful stereotypes and promote discussions on consent, equality, and healthy relationships. By empowering individuals with knowledge and critical thinking skills, we can challenge the patriarchal narratives that perpetuate inequality.

Additionally, Manji emphasizes the importance of creating safe spaces for individuals to share their experiences, concerns, and aspirations. This can be achieved through support groups, workshops, and community initiatives that uplift and empower marginalized voices. By providing access to resources and mentorship, we can nurture future leaders who will continue the fight against patriarchy.

An Unconventional Approach: Leveraging Pop Culture

In her unique and unconventional approach, Irshad Manji utilizes pop culture to challenge patriarchal norms. By engaging with popular music, movies, literature, and social media, Manji encourages critical thinking and fosters discussions on gender representation and stereotypes.

Through the lens of pop culture, Manji seeks to expose harmful narratives, highlight the diversity of experiences, and promote inclusive storytelling. This approach allows for a broader audience reach and creates opportunities for transformative conversations.

Example: Challenging Gender Expectations in the Workplace

One example of challenging patriarchy and its impact on LGBTQ individuals is addressing gender expectations in the workplace. Patriarchal norms often influence workplace dynamics, leading to gender-based discrimination, wage disparities, and limited opportunities for advancement.

An intervention strategy to combat this issue could involve promoting inclusive hiring practices, equal pay policies, and offering mentorship programs that support individuals who do not conform to traditional gender norms. By challenging patriarchal structures within organizations, we can create environments where LGBTQ individuals feel valued, heard, and supported.

Summary

In this subsection, we explored Irshad Manji's efforts to challenge patriarchy within LGBTQ communities and society. Understanding the underlying principles of patriarchy, addressing gender stereotypes, promoting intersectional feminism, building allies, addressing toxic masculinity, educating and empowering individuals, and leveraging pop culture are all crucial aspects of overcoming patriarchal norms. By embracing an intersectional lens and actively engaging individuals and communities, we can foster spaces that are inclusive, equal, and empowering for all.

Battling Islamophobia

Islamophobia, the fear and prejudice against Islam and Muslims, continues to be a pressing issue in many societies. Addressing and combating Islamophobia is a crucial aspect of Irshad Manji's activism, as she understands the detrimental effects it has on Muslim individuals and communities. In this subsection, we will explore the strategies and approaches that Manji employs to challenge and overcome Islamophobia.

Understanding the Root Causes of Islamophobia

To effectively battle Islamophobia, it is vital to understand its underlying causes. Islamophobia can often stem from ignorance, stereotypes, misinformation, and a lack of exposure to diverse Muslim perspectives. Manji believes that by addressing these root causes, we can begin to dismantle Islamophobic attitudes and promote greater understanding and acceptance.

Education and Awareness Campaigns

Education plays a pivotal role in combating Islamophobia. Manji advocates for comprehensive initiatives aimed at dispelling misconceptions about Islam and Muslims. This includes educational workshops, community outreach programs, and awareness campaigns to engage with individuals from various backgrounds. By providing accurate information and fostering dialogue, Manji aims to challenge existing biases and create a more informed and empathetic society.

Promoting Interfaith Dialogue

Interfaith dialogue is another essential tool in battling Islamophobia. Manji emphasizes the importance of creating platforms for open and respectful conversations between people of different faiths. By encouraging dialogue, shared experiences, and the recognition of common values, it becomes possible to bridge gaps and promote understanding between Muslim and non-Muslim communities.

Counteracting Negative Media Portrayals

Media plays a significant role in shaping public opinion and can perpetuate Islamophobic narratives. Manji actively works to counteract negative media portrayals of Islam and Muslims by advocating for accurate and nuanced representation. This includes engaging with media outlets, promoting diverse Muslim voices, and encouraging alternative narratives that challenge stereotypes and misinformation.

Fostering Community Alliances

Battling Islamophobia requires collective action and the formation of alliances across different communities. Manji actively builds connections and partnerships with individuals, organizations, and communities that share the goal of combating bigotry and promoting inclusivity. By working together, these alliances can challenge Islamophobia on multiple fronts and amplify their impact.

Engaging with Policy and Lawmakers

Political and legal systems play a crucial role in combating Islamophobia. Manji recognizes the importance of engaging with policymakers and advocating for inclusive policies that protect the rights and dignity of Muslim individuals. This includes challenging discriminatory practices, promoting religious freedom, and advocating for equitable treatment under the law.

Promoting Grassroots Activism

Grassroots activism is a powerful tool for challenging Islamophobia. Manji encourages individuals to take action within their own communities, empowering them to create change at the local level. This can involve organizing awareness campaigns, hosting community events, or supporting grassroots initiatives that promote interfaith dialogue and understanding.

Empowering Muslim Voices

Empowering Muslim voices is crucial in combating Islamophobia. Manji advocates for providing platforms and resources for Muslim individuals and communities to share their stories, perspectives, and experiences. By amplifying these voices, it becomes possible to challenge prevailing stereotypes and showcase the diversity and richness of Muslim identities.

Promoting Cultural Exchange

Cultural exchange programs can play a significant role in breaking down barriers and challenging Islamophobic attitudes. Manji supports initiatives that encourage people from different cultures to come together, fostering mutual understanding, respect, and appreciation. By facilitating cultural exchange, it becomes possible to build bridges and combat Islamophobia through shared experiences.

Addressing Institutional and Systemic Islamophobia

Institutional and systemic Islamophobia must also be addressed to achieve lasting change. Manji advocates for identifying and challenging discriminatory policies and practices within institutions such as schools, workplaces, and governmental bodies. By addressing these systemic issues, it becomes possible to create more inclusive and equitable spaces for Muslims and challenge the structures that perpetuate Islamophobia.

In conclusion, battling Islamophobia requires a multifaceted approach that addresses its root causes, fosters education and awareness, promotes interfaith dialogue, challenges negative media portrayals, builds alliances, engages with policymakers, empowers Muslim voices, encourages grassroots activism, promotes cultural exchange, and addresses institutional and systemic Islamophobia. Irshad Manji's work embodies these strategies, providing a blueprint for individuals and communities to effectively combat Islamophobia and promote a more inclusive and understanding society.

Threats and Outrage

In this section, we explore the various threats and outrage that LGBTQ activist Irshad Manji has faced throughout her journey. As an outspoken queer Muslim, Manji has been a target of hate and intolerance from both within her own community and outside it. However, she has bravely and resiliently confronted these challenges, using them as opportunities to educate, advocate, and promote change.

Facing Homophobia

One of the primary threats that Manji has encountered is homophobia, both from individuals and larger societal structures. Homophobia refers to the fear, discrimination, or prejudice against individuals who identify as LGBTQ. It manifests in various forms, including verbal abuse, physical violence, and exclusion from social spaces. Manji has experienced intense backlash due to her vocal support for LGBTQ rights, often receiving death threats and hate mail.

To address homophobia, Manji has been vocal in challenging societal norms and raising awareness about the rights and experiences of LGBTQ individuals. She emphasizes the importance of educating communities about sexual orientation and gender identity, debunking stereotypes, and fostering empathy and understanding. Through her advocacy work, Manji aims to break down stereotypes and foster inclusivity for all individuals, regardless of their sexual orientation or gender identity.

Confronting Religious Conservatism

As an openly queer Muslim activist, Manji has faced outrage and opposition from conservative religious groups who perceive her views as contradictory to Islamic teachings. These groups argue that homosexuality is incompatible with their interpretation of religious texts and often resort to quoting scripture to condemn LGBTQ individuals.

Manji firmly believes that it is possible to reconcile faith and queerness. She acknowledges that different interpretations of religious texts exist and encourages critical thinking within religious communities. By engaging in dialogue with religious scholars and promoting open discussions about LGBTQ issues in religious spaces, Manji aims to challenge conservative interpretations and promote acceptance and understanding.

To address the outrage and opposition she faces, Manji emphasizes the importance of highlighting the diversity of interpretations within religious communities. She believes that promoting inclusivity and challenging rigid beliefs can lead to a more compassionate and accepting environment for LGBTQ individuals within religious spaces.

Navigating Online Harassment

In the digital age, online harassment has become a significant threat to activists like Manji. This form of harassment often takes the form of cyberbullying, hate messages, and smear campaigns meant to intimidate and silence individuals advocating for LGBTQ rights. Manji has been subjected to cyberbullying and online harassment, including hate speech and threats on social media platforms.

To address online harassment, Manji emphasizes the importance of digital safety and self-care. She advocates for creating safe online spaces for LGBTQ individuals and encouraging active reporting of abusive content to social media platforms. Additionally, she stresses the significance of building a support network of allies who can provide emotional support and stand against online harassment.

Responding with Resilience

In the face of threats and outrage, Manji remains resilient and steadfast in her commitment to advocating for LGBTQ rights. She believes that responding to hate with hate only perpetuates the cycle of animosity and instead emphasizes the power of positive engagement and education. Manji's approach is to engage with empathy, compassion, and a willingness to listen to different perspectives, even when faced with aggression.

By responding with resilience, empathy, and knowledge, Manji has been able to dismantle stereotypes, educate communities, and inspire others to challenge their deeply-held beliefs. Her ability to navigate through outrage and threats serves as an inspiration for other activists and helps pave the way for a more inclusive and accepting world.

Example: Building Bridges through Dialogue

One example of Manji's response to threats and outrage is her commitment to engaging in dialogues with those who hold opposing views. She recognizes the value of dialogue in bridging divides and breaking down barriers. Manji has participated in panel discussions, debates, and public lectures, where she engages with individuals who may hold different beliefs or perspectives concerning LGBTQ issues.

By engaging in genuine conversations, even with those who oppose her views, Manji creates opportunities for mutual understanding and growth. These dialogues create a space for people to challenge their assumptions, learn from one another, and work towards common ground. Manji's commitment to constructive engagement highlights the importance of dialogue as a tool for change and encourages others to approach conversations with empathy and an open mind.

Conclusion

Threats and outrage pose significant challenges to LGBTQ activists like Irshad Manji. However, rather than succumbing to fear or responding with animosity, Manji has consistently demonstrated a spirit of resilience, empathy, and education. By addressing homophobia, confronting religious conservatism, navigating online harassment, and responding with resilience, Manji has paved the way for a more inclusive and accepting world. Her example serves as an inspiration for activists facing similar challenges, emphasizing the importance of engaging in dialogue, challenging norms, and cultivating empathy in the pursuit of equality.

Triumphs and Support

In the journey of LGBTQ activism, triumphs and support from various individuals and communities play a crucial role. This subsection explores some significant moments of triumph and the support that helped propel Irshad Manji's activism forward.

One of the first triumphs for Irshad Manji was finding acceptance within her immediate family and close friends. Coming out as queer and navigating her identity was a challenging process, but the unconditional love and support she received from her loved ones allowed her to embrace her true self and embark on her activism journey.

Another major triumph for Manji was finding acceptance and support in wider society. Through her activism and public speaking engagements, she was able to connect with individuals who shared her experiences or empathized with her struggles. These connections not only provided emotional support but also helped create a network of allies who were ready to contribute to the cause.

Support from allies and support networks played a vital role in Manji's journey. Allies, individuals who are not part of the LGBTQ community but support and advocate for LGBTQ rights, stood by her side and amplified her message. They used their privilege and platforms to raise awareness, challenge discriminatory practices, and promote inclusivity. The unwavering support and collaboration from these allies helped Manji reach a larger audience and spread her message of love and acceptance.

Additionally, finding support within the LGBTQ community itself was a significant triumph for Manji. She connected with fellow queer individuals who shared similar experiences and faced similar challenges. These connections fostered a sense of belonging and provided a safe space for her to share her struggles, gain insights, and engage in collective activism. The support and solidarity she found within the LGBTQ community strengthened her resolve to fight for equality and justice.

Triumphs and support were not limited to individuals. LGBTQ organizations and advocacy groups played a crucial role in empowering Manji and amplifying her message. These organizations provided resources, mentorship, and platforms for her to share her story and advocate for change. The collaboration and partnership with these groups facilitated larger campaigns and initiatives, showcasing the power of collective action in achieving tangible results.

One prominent triumph in Manji's journey was the tremendous impact of her book, "The Trouble with Islam Today". The publication of the book sparked global conversations on the intersection of LGBTQ rights, religion, and cultural traditions. The book not only resonated with queer Muslims but also reached a broader audience, challenging orthodox beliefs and encouraging critical thinking. The success of her book gave her a platform to engage with diverse communities and inspire dialogue on LGBTQ rights and religious inclusivity.

Support from academic institutions and universities also played a significant role in Manji's triumphs. Invitations to speak at universities and conferences provided her with opportunities to share her experiences, educate others, and influence future leaders. These events served as platforms for dialogue, debate, and the exchange of ideas, allowing Manji to challenge preconceived notions and create awareness about the complexities of LGBTQ identity and inclusion.

To sustain such triumphs and support, it is essential to create safe spaces for LGBTQ individuals, cultivate understanding, and work towards dismantling discriminatory systems.   Education and awareness initiatives are crucial in promoting inclusivity and equipping individuals with the necessary tools to challenge social norms and prejudices.

In conclusion, triumphs and support are instrumental in the LGBTQ activism journey. Irshad Manji experienced triumphs through finding acceptance within her family, receiving support from allies, and building connections within the LGBTQ community. Academic institutions, LGBTQ organizations, and advocacy groups also played a critical role in amplifying her message. The impact of her book and the opportunities to engage with diverse communities further fueled her triumphs. It is through these triumphs and continued support that Manji was able to make significant strides in promoting LGBTQ rights and challenging societal norms.

Dealing with Hateful Backlash

In every bold endeavor, there are those who oppose progress and cling to outdated beliefs. Irshad Manji, as a fierce advocate for LGBTQ rights within the Muslim community, has faced her fair share of hateful backlash. In this section, we will explore how she has bravely confronted and navigated such adversity, while inspiring others to do the same.

Hateful backlash can come in various forms, ranging from online harassment to physical threats. These attacks are often driven by fear, ignorance, and a refusal to accept the diverse realities of the world. For Irshad Manji, who advocates for the intersection of LGBTQ rights and Islam, the backlash has been particularly intense due to the deeply ingrained conservative beliefs within some Muslim communities.

Understanding the Roots of Hateful Backlash

To effectively deal with hateful backlash, it is crucial to understand its underlying roots. In the case of LGBTQ activism, backlash often stems from misconceptions about sexual orientation and gender identity, religious fundamentalism, and societal norms.

For Irshad, the backlash she has faced springs from the clash between her identity as a queer Muslim and traditional interpretations of Islam.   Some conservative interpretations of Islam condemn homosexuality, labeling it as sinful and incompatible with Islamic teachings. This discord between personal identity and religious teachings often fuels the fire of hateful backlash.

Maintaining Resilience in the Face of Adversity

Dealing with hateful backlash requires immense resilience.   Irshad Manji's unwavering commitment to her cause has enabled her to navigate these challenges with strength and grace.   Here are some strategies she uses to maintain her resilience:

+ **Building a Support Network:** Surrounding oneself with allies and a supportive community is crucial when facing hateful backlash. Irshad has cultivated a network of like-minded individuals, including other LGBTQ Muslims and activists, who provide emotional support and understanding.

+ **Self-Care:** Taking care of one's mental and emotional well-being is paramount in the face of adversity. Irshad practices self-care through activities such as meditation, therapy, and engaging in hobbies that bring her joy and peace.

+ **Finding Strength in Identity:** Embracing her identity as a queer Muslim has allowed Irshad to find strength and pride in who she is. By holding onto her true self, she is able to weather the storm of hateful backlash.

+ **Seeking Legal Protection:** In cases where hateful backlash escalates to threats or violence, legal protection becomes essential. Irshad has relied on legal measures to ensure her safety and discourage further harassment.

+ **Staying Educated:** Knowledge is power, especially when combatting ignorance. Irshad empowers herself through continuous learning, staying informed about LGBTQ rights, Islamic teachings, and the arguments against them. Armed with knowledge, she can effectively challenge hateful rhetoric.

Engaging in Constructive Dialogue

Irshad Manji firmly believes in the power of dialogue to challenge prejudice and ignorance. Instead of responding to hateful backlash with anger or hostility, she chooses to engage in constructive dialogue. By approaching conversations in a respectful and empathetic manner, she opens doors for understanding and bridges the divide between opposing perspectives.

Through her tireless efforts, Irshad has initiated dialogues with both LGBTQ activists and conservative religious leaders, seeking common ground and fostering empathy. These dialogues, although challenging at times, have often resulted in increased understanding and even small shifts in conservative attitudes towards LGBTQ rights.

Amplifying Positive Narratives

In the face of hateful backlash, it is essential to amplify positive narratives that counteract negative stereotypes and misconceptions. Irshad utilizes her platform and writing to highlight the accomplishments and stories of LGBTQ Muslims, showcasing their resilience, love, and commitment to their faith.

Through storytelling, Irshad emphasizes the compatibility of Islam and LGBTQ rights, breaking down barriers and inspiring others to challenge their own biases. By amplifying positive narratives, she not only counters the hateful rhetoric but also provides hope and validation to those who may feel marginalized.

Unconventional Wisdom: Embracing Love and Forgiveness

While it may seem counterintuitive, love and forgiveness can play a transformative role in dealing with hateful backlash. Rather than meeting hate with hate, Irshad encourages responding with compassion and empathy.

By demonstrating love and forgiveness towards those who project hate, she opens the opportunity for dialogue, growth, and change. This unconventional approach challenges the conventional thinking that confronts hate with more hate, offering a more compassionate alternative.

The Road Ahead

Dealing with hateful backlash is an ongoing battle, but Irshad Manji's resilience and determination provide a beacon of hope. As more individuals embrace their authentic selves and advocate for LGBTQ rights within traditional communities, the stigma and backlash will gradually diminish.

The key to overcoming hateful backlash lies in education, dialogue, empathy, and the amplification of positive narratives. By challenging prejudice and engaging in conversations with love and understanding, society can grow more inclusive and tolerant.

Whether it's through her writings, public speaking, or personal activism, Irshad Manji continues to pave the way for a future where LGBTQ individuals can be embraced and respected within all religious communities. Her journey serves as a reminder that progress is possible, even in the face of adversity. As we move forward, let her story inspire all of us to stand up against hateful backlash and fight for a world where love and acceptance prevail.

The Importance of Resilience

Resilience plays a crucial role in the life of any LGBTQ activist. It is the ability to bounce back from adversity, setbacks, and challenges. In the face of discrimination, violence, and hatred, resilience provides the strength to continue the fight for justice and equality. In this subsection, we will explore the importance of resilience in the context of LGBTQ activism, discuss strategies to cultivate resilience, and share stories of individuals who have demonstrated remarkable resilience in their journey.

Understanding Resilience

Resilience is not just about enduring hardships; it is about harnessing the lessons learned from these experiences to grow stronger and make a positive impact. LGBTQ activists often face immense adversity, including verbal and physical attacks, social exclusion, and legal obstacles. Without resilience, such challenges can easily discourage or demoralize individuals, hindering their ability to make lasting change. Resilience empowers activists to transform these obstacles into opportunities for growth and progress.

The Resilience Toolkit

Building resilience is an ongoing process that requires self-reflection, emotional intelligence, and the cultivation of certain skills. Here are some strategies to strengthen your resilience as an LGBTQ activist:

1. **Self-care and well-being:** Prioritize your mental and physical health. Engage in activities that bring you joy and relaxation, such as meditation, exercise, or spending time in nature. Taking care of yourself allows you to rejuvenate and approach activism from a place of strength.

2. **Cultivating a support network:** Surround yourself with supportive individuals who understand the challenges you face. Connect with other LGBTQ activists and allies who can provide emotional support, share experiences, and offer guidance. Building a strong network allows you to lean on others during difficult times.

3. **Mindfulness and self-awareness:** Practice mindfulness to develop a deeper understanding of your emotions, thoughts, and reactions. Being aware of your own triggers and stressors enables you to navigate them more effectively

and respond with resilience. Mindfulness techniques like deep breathing or journaling can help you maintain a sense of calm amidst adversity.

4. **Adapting to change:** LGBTQ activism is a constantly evolving landscape. Developing adaptability and flexibility allows you to navigate unexpected obstacles and adjust your strategies when needed. Embracing change as an opportunity rather than a setback fosters resilience and innovative thinking.

5. **Learning from setbacks:** View setbacks as learning experiences rather than failures. Reflect on the lessons you can glean from each situation and use them to refine your approach. Remember that resilience is not about avoiding difficulties but rather bouncing back stronger from them.

By incorporating these strategies into your activism journey, you can fortify your resilience and sustain your commitment to fighting for LGBTQ rights.

Stories of Resilience

Throughout history, countless LGBTQ activists have showcased remarkable resilience in the face of adversity. Their stories serve as inspiration and reminders of the power of resilience. Let's delve into the journeys of a few individuals who have embodied resilience in their activism:

1. **Marsha P. Johnson:** A leading figure in the LGBTQ rights movement, Marsha P. Johnson was a transgender woman of color who tirelessly fought for the rights of her community. Despite facing discrimination and violence, she remained resilient in her pursuit of justice. Marsha's resilience was evident in her pivotal role in the Stonewall uprising, which marked a turning point in LGBTQ history.

2. **Edie Windsor:** Edie Windsor was a prominent LGBTQ activist who played a vital role in the fight for marriage equality in the United States. After her spouse, Thea Spyer, passed away, Edie faced discriminatory inheritance taxes due to the Defense of Marriage Act (DOMA). With remarkable resilience, she challenged the law all the way to the Supreme Court and won, paving the way for the legalization of same-sex marriage.

3. **Gavin Grimm:** A transgender student from Virginia, Gavin Grimm became an advocate for transgender rights after facing discrimination in his school. Despite being denied access to the restroom aligned with his gender identity, Gavin showed incredible resilience by filing a lawsuit against his

school district. His case reached the Supreme Court, amplifying the conversation on transgender rights and inspiring other young activists.

These individuals embody the importance of resilience in the face of adversity. They serve as beacons of hope and motivation for LGBTQ activists worldwide, reminding us that one person's resilience can lead to transformative change.

Resilience in Action

To understand the practical application of resilience, let's consider a real-world example. Imagine an LGBTQ activist group facing opposition from conservative religious organizations. These organizations launch a widespread smear campaign to discredit and silence the group's efforts. In response, the group demonstrates resilience by using the following strategies:

+ **Maintaining focus:** The group stays true to its mission and remains focused on the ultimate goal – advocating for LGBTQ rights. They do not let the opposition divert them from their path.

+ **Seeking support:** The group reaches out to allies within and outside their community, forming partnerships with other social justice organizations. This network of support provides emotional and logistical assistance during challenging times.

+ **Turning adversity into opportunity:** The group leverages the opposition to raise awareness about their cause. They proactively engage with the media, sharing stories of resilience from their members and showcasing the positive impact of their work.

+ **Staying grounded in values:** The group remains rooted in their values, ensuring that their activism is guided by inclusivity, empathy, and respect for diverse perspectives. This commitment helps them navigate difficult discussions and maintain productive dialogue with their opponents.

Through these strategies, the activist group demonstrates resilience by refusing to be silenced and using adversity to strengthen their cause.

The Journey of Resilience

Resilience is not a destination but a continuous journey. LGBTQ activists must constantly adapt, grow, and learn from their experiences to maintain their resilience.   By incorporating self-care practices, cultivating support networks, practicing self-awareness, embracing change, and learning from setbacks, activists can build enduring resilience. They can serve as powerful catalysts for change, empowering themselves and inspiring others to join the fight for a more inclusive and equitable world.

Remember, resilience is not an innate trait but a skill that can be developed and nurtured. As you embark on your journey as an LGBTQ activist, embrace resilience as your greatest asset, knowing that it will allow you to overcome challenges and leave a lasting impact on the world.

Creating Safe Spaces for LGBTQ Muslims

Creating safe spaces for LGBTQ Muslims is crucial in fostering a sense of belonging, providing support, and promoting acceptance within religious communities. This subsection explores the challenges faced by LGBTQ Muslims and offers strategies for creating inclusive environments that prioritize their safety and well-being.

Understanding the Challenges

LGBTQ Muslims often experience unique challenges and face a multitude of intersecting forms of discrimination. Homophobia and transphobia within religious communities can lead to exclusion, isolation, and even violence. At the same time, they may also encounter Islamophobia within LGBTQ spaces, exacerbating their feelings of marginalization.

Additionally, some LGBTQ Muslims struggle with the conflict between their sexual or gender identity and their religious beliefs. The need to reconcile their faith with their authentic selves can be emotionally and psychologically taxing, sometimes leading to internalized homophobia or self-rejection.

Creating Inclusive Religious Spaces

To create safe spaces for LGBTQ Muslims within religious communities, it is important to challenge heteronormative and cisnormative assumptions and foster a spirit of inclusivity and acceptance. Here are some strategies to consider:

1. **Education and Awareness:** Organize workshops, seminars, and educational programs to raise awareness about LGBTQ rights, experiences, and identities within the context of Islam. This can help dispel misconceptions and promote understanding.

2. **Support Networks:** Establish support groups or LGBTQ-affirming organizations within religious communities to provide a safe and confidential space for individuals to share their experiences and find support from peers facing similar challenges.

3. **Advocacy and Dialogue:** Encourage open and respectful dialogue between LGBTQ individuals and religious leaders. Engaging in constructive conversations about LGBTQ rights and religious teachings can help foster an inclusive environment that acknowledges diverse identities and experiences.

4. **Inclusive Language and Practices:** Develop inclusive language and practices that recognize and honor LGBTQ individuals. This can include incorporating gender-neutral terminology and increasing visibility of LGBTQ-affirming resources in religious spaces.

5. **Accessible Religious Texts:** Promote interpretations of religious texts that affirm LGBTQ identities and challenge discriminatory viewpoints. Provide resources and scholarship that highlight progressive interpretations and encourage critical thinking.

Collaboration with LGBTQ Organizations

Collaborating with LGBTQ organizations is vital in creating safe spaces for LGBTQ Muslims. By forming alliances and working together, religious communities can benefit from the expertise and resources available within the LGBTQ movement. Here are some ways to foster collaboration:

1. **Partnerships:** Forge partnerships with LGBTQ organizations to organize joint events, share resources, and promote awareness and visibility of LGBTQ Muslims.

2. **Training and Workshops:** Engage LGBTQ organizations to provide training and workshops on LGBTQ cultural competency and inclusion to religious leaders and community members. This can help foster a deeper understanding and empathy towards LGBTQ Muslims.

3. **Mentorship and Guidance:** Connect LGBTQ Muslims with LGBTQ organizations that offer mentorship and guidance, allowing them to build supportive networks and access resources that address their specific needs.

4. **Advocacy and Activism:** Collaborate with LGBTQ organizations to advocate for policy changes and legislation that protect the rights of LGBTQ individuals. By joining forces, religious communities can amplify their impact and work towards greater societal acceptance.

Promoting Mental Health and Well-being

The mental health and well-being of LGBTQ Muslims should be a priority when creating safe spaces within religious communities. Here are some considerations for promoting mental health:

1. **Access to Mental Health Services:** Ensure LGBTQ-inclusive mental health services are accessible to individuals within religious communities. This can involve partnering with mental health professionals who specialize in LGBTQ-affirming therapy.

2. **Self-Care Resources:** Provide resources and information on self-care practices tailored to the needs of LGBTQ Muslims. This can include workshops on mindfulness, stress reduction, and coping strategies.

3. **Supportive Religious Counseling:** Train religious leaders to offer LGBTQ-affirming counseling, understanding the unique challenges faced by LGBTQ individuals and providing a compassionate and non-judgmental listening ear.

4. **Peer Support and Mentorship Programs:** Establish peer support groups and mentorship programs where LGBTQ Muslims can connect with others who have had similar experiences, fostering a sense of community and reducing feelings of isolation.

Examples and Resources

The following examples and resources can further aid in creating safe spaces for LGBTQ Muslims:

+ **The Inclusive Mosque Initiative** - A London-based organization that works towards creating inclusive and welcoming spaces for LGBTQ Muslims by challenging traditional gender norms and advocating for LGBTQ rights within an Islamic framework.

+ **The Muslim Alliance for Sexual and Gender Diversity (MASGD)** - MASGD provides resources, support, and advocacy for LGBTQ Muslims. Their website offers a range of educational materials, personal stories, and advice for LGBTQ Muslims and their allies.

+ **Zafigo** - An online platform that provides travel resources for LGBTQ individuals, including a specific section on LGBTQ-friendly Muslim destinations, which highlights places where LGBTQ Muslims can freely express their identities.

+ **"Living Out Islam: Voices of Gay, Lesbian, and Transgender Muslims"** by Scott Siraj al-Haqq Kugle - This book explores the experiences of LGBTQ

Muslims and offers insights into reconciling faith, sexuality, and gender identity.

Conclusion

Creating safe spaces for LGBTQ Muslims requires a collective effort from religious communities, LGBTQ organizations, and society as a whole. By fostering inclusivity, engaging in respectful dialogue, and addressing the unique challenges faced by LGBTQ Muslims, we can work towards a future where everyone feels affirmed, accepted, and valued within their faith communities. Remember, the journey towards creating safe spaces is ongoing, requiring continuous education, advocacy, and the willingness to challenge discriminatory beliefs and practices.

Empowering Others to Speak Out

In this empowering subsection, we delve into Irshad Manji's tireless efforts to empower others to speak out and share their stories. Through her work as an LGBTQ activist, she has inspired countless individuals to find their voices and fight for their rights. Let's explore the ways in which Manji has equipped others with the tools and confidence to advocate for change.

Lifting the Veil of Silence

One of the key aspects of empowering others to speak out is creating spaces where individuals feel safe and supported. Manji has been instrumental in establishing support networks and safe spaces for LGBTQ individuals, particularly within Muslim communities. She understands the importance of creating an environment where people can freely express their thoughts, concerns, and experiences without fear of judgment or backlash.

Manji's own vulnerability and openness in sharing her journey have served as a beacon of hope for others struggling with their identities. By breaking the silence and inviting others to do the same, she has paved the way for conversations about LGBTQ rights and acceptance.

Providing Resources and Education

In order to effectively empower others, knowledge and information are critical. Manji has dedicated herself to educating individuals on LGBTQ rights, intersectionality, and the importance of inclusive communities. Through her books, workshops, and training sessions, she equips individuals with the necessary tools to understand and articulate their experiences.

Manji also actively collaborates with LGBTQ organizations and allies to develop resources and toolkits that empower marginalized communities. These resources serve as guides for advocating for LGBTQ rights, navigating religious institutions, and addressing the challenges faced by queer Muslims.

Inspiring with Personal Stories

One of the most powerful ways to empower others is through storytelling. Manji has skillfully shared her own personal journey, triumphs, and challenges, demonstrating the strength and resilience required to overcome adversity. Her personal stories not only inspire individuals to embrace their own identities but also spark conversations, foster understanding, and challenge societal norms.

Moreover, Manji has amplified the voices of others within the LGBTQ community, elevating their stories and experiences. By sharing these stories, she empowers individuals who have historically been silenced to reclaim their narratives and advocate for change.

Cultivating Leadership and Advocacy Skills

Empowerment goes beyond just sharing stories; it also involves equipping individuals with the necessary skills to effect change. Manji recognizes the importance of cultivating leadership and advocacy skills within marginalized communities. She actively mentors LGBTQ youth, offering guidance and support as they navigate their own journeys.

Through workshops and programs, Manji has provided training in public speaking, community organizing, and advocacy. By imparting these skills, she empowers individuals to become effective advocates for their rights and the rights of others.

Supporting Mental Health and Well-being

Another crucial aspect of empowerment is addressing mental health and well-being. Manji understands the toll that activism and advocacy can take on individuals, particularly those from marginalized communities. She emphasizes the importance of self-care and offers strategies for maintaining mental and emotional balance.

Manji advocates for the destigmatization of mental health issues within LGBTQ communities and encourages seeking professional help when needed. By acknowledging the challenges and providing support, she ensures that individuals are equipped with the resilience and strength to continue their advocacy work.

Unconventional yet Relevant: The Power of Humor

In her quest to empower others, Manji often employs an unconventional yet effective tool: humor. She uses wit and satire to challenge societal norms and prejudices, creating a space for reflection and dialogue. By injecting humor into serious conversations, she disarms her audience, making them more receptive to challenging their own biases and reevaluating their beliefs.

Through her use of humor, Manji breaks down barriers, fosters connections, and empowers others to engage in meaningful conversations about LGBTQ rights and acceptance.

Exercises and Tips for Empowerment

1. Exercise: Write Your Story Take time to reflect on your own journey, struggles, and triumphs. Write your own personal story, focusing on moments of empowerment and self-discovery. Share this story within trusted circles or with organizations that support LGBTQ individuals. Your story has the power to inspire others and create change.

2. Tip: Seek Allies and Support Networks Surround yourself with allies and people who support your journey. Seek out support networks within your community or online platforms to connect with individuals who share similar experiences. Remember, empowerment is amplified through the strength of community.

3. Exercise: Public Speaking Practice Develop your public speaking skills by practicing in a safe and supportive environment. Join a public speaking club or participate in workshops that offer guidance and practice opportunities. By honing your communication skills, you will become a more effective advocate for yourself and others.

4. Tip: Prioritize Self-Care Balancing activism and personal well-being is crucial. Incorporate self-care practices into your daily routine, such as exercise, meditation, or spending time with loved ones. Recognize that self-care is not selfish, but rather a necessary component of effective and sustainable advocacy.

Remember, empowerment is a continuous journey. By empowering others to speak out, we create a ripple effect of change, fostering inclusive communities and promoting equality for all. Let the voices of the marginalized be heard and let their stories inspire generations to come.

The Impact of Personal Stories

Personal stories hold immense power in creating empathy, promoting understanding, and driving change. In the context of LGBTQ activism, personal stories play a crucial role in dismantling stereotypes, challenging biases, and inspiring others to embrace their authentic selves. In this subsection, we will explore the impact of personal stories in the LGBTQ community, highlighting their importance in creating a more inclusive society.

The Power of Narratives

Human beings are naturally drawn to stories. They have the ability to captivate our attention, evoke emotions, and challenge our perspectives. Personal narratives provide individuals with a platform to share their unique experiences, struggles, and triumphs. When it comes to LGBTQ activism, personal stories serve as powerful tools to humanize the movement, making it relatable to people from diverse backgrounds.

When individuals share their stories, they open themselves up to vulnerability. This vulnerability, in turn, opens up opportunities for connection and understanding. When people hear personal stories from LGBTQ individuals, it allows them to empathize with the challenges faced by the community. This empathy can lead to a shift in attitudes, breaking down prejudices, and fostering acceptance.

Normalization Through Personal Experiences

Personal stories help normalize LGBTQ identities, dispelling the notion that being queer is abnormal or deviant. By sharing personal experiences, individuals within the LGBTQ community can showcase the similarities they share with others, highlighting that their orientation or gender identity does not define them solely. This normalization helps challenge societal misconceptions and reduces stigmatization.

For example, a personal story shared by an LGBTQ individual can shed light on their everyday experiences, showcasing that they have the same desires, dreams, and emotions as anyone else. By sharing stories of love, family, and personal growth, individuals within the community help break the stereotypes and myths surrounding LGBTQ identities.

Breakdown of Stereotypes and Bias

Personal stories have the power to challenge stereotypes and biases associated with the LGBTQ community. By showcasing the diversity within the community, personal narratives dismantle the notion that all LGBTQ individuals are the same or fit into preconceived societal molds. This breakdown of stereotypes helps promote a more nuanced understanding of LGBTQ identities.

For instance, a personal story might highlight the intersecting identities of an LGBTQ individual, such as their race, religion, or socioeconomic background. This intersectionality challenges the perception that all LGBTQ individuals experience the world in the same way and highlights the existence of multiple narratives within the community.

Inspiration and Empowerment

Personal stories inspire and empower both LGBTQ individuals and allies. By sharing their struggles and overcoming societal barriers, LGBTQ individuals become role models and a source of hope for others who may still be navigating their own journeys of self-acceptance.

Through personal stories, individuals within the community can see themselves reflected, finding solace in the fact that they are not alone. These stories provide a sense of community, validating one's experiences and offering a source of support.

Effecting Societal Change

The impact of personal stories extends beyond the individual level and can lead to meaningful societal change. When personal narratives are shared widely, they have the potential to challenge oppressive systems, change public opinion, and influence policy decisions.

Stories of discrimination, resilience, and triumph can inspire activism and mobilize communities. They can galvanize support for LGBTQ causes, leading to the formation of advocacy groups, grassroots movements, and policy change. Personal stories ensure that LGBTQ voices are heard, amplifying their experiences and driving the conversation forward.

Resources and Support

Personal stories serve as valuable resources for LGBTQ individuals seeking support, guidance, and validation. These stories can provide a lifeline for those struggling with their identities, offering reassurance that they are not alone and that there is a community ready to embrace and support them.

In addition to providing emotional support, personal stories can also serve as practical resources. They can offer insights into navigating coming out, finding community resources, accessing healthcare, and dealing with discrimination. Personal narratives can also help LGBTQ individuals build resilience and develop strategies to overcome the challenges they may face.

The Digital Age and Personal Storytelling

With the advent of social media and digital platforms, personal stories have become more accessible and far-reaching. Online platforms such as YouTube, Instagram, and personal blogs have provided LGBTQ individuals with the opportunity to share their experiences with a global audience.

The digital age has empowered individuals to become storytellers, enabling them to control their narratives and shape public discourse. Through hashtags, viral campaigns, and online communities, personal stories have the potential to create a ripple effect, inspiring countless others and fostering a sense of shared humanity.

Exercising Caution and Ensuring Privacy

While personal stories are powerful tools for change, it is crucial to exercise caution and respect individuals' privacy. Sharing personal stories can be an intensely vulnerable experience, and consent must be obtained before sharing someone else's narrative. Respecting boundaries and ensuring the safety and well-being of storytellers is paramount.

Moreover, it is essential to create safe spaces and support networks for individuals sharing personal stories. The act of vulnerability in sharing one's experiences can be emotionally challenging, and it is vital to provide avenues for support, both online and offline.

Conclusion

Personal stories have the potential to challenge societal norms, dismantle stereotypes, and drive change. By sharing experiences, LGBTQ individuals and allies can foster empathy, inspire activism, and create a more inclusive society. However, it is essential to exercise caution, respect privacy, and provide support to individuals sharing their narratives. The impact of personal stories in the LGBTQ community is undeniable, and their continued sharing will play a crucial role in shaping a more accepting and equal world.

The Rise of a Rebel

Creating Dangerous Daughters

Establishing a Platform for Change

In this subsection, we delve into Irshad Manji's early efforts to establish a platform for change in the fight for LGBTQ rights within the Muslim community. Manji understood the power of visibility, storytelling, and grassroots activism in effecting meaningful change. Her pioneering work in this area serves as an inspiration for future activists seeking to spark social transformation.

The Power of Visibility

One of the key elements of Manji's strategy was the recognition of the power of visibility. By openly embracing her queer Muslim identity, she shattered societal expectations and challenged traditional beliefs within her community. Manji's visibility allowed her to connect with others facing similar struggles, and it also forced individuals and communities to confront their own biases and prejudices.

Manji utilized various platforms to amplify her voice, from public speaking engagements and documentary appearances to social media. She fearlessly shared her personal experiences, providing a relatable narrative that resonated with countless LGBTQ Muslims and non-Muslims alike. This visibility played a crucial role in breaking down barriers and fostering empathy and understanding.

Storytelling as a Catalyst for Change

Through her writing, speaking engagements, and media appearances, Manji harnessed the power of storytelling to ignite conversations and challenge entrenched attitudes. She artfully wove personal anecdotes with broader social and political contexts to highlight the urgent need for LGBTQ rights within the Muslim community.

Manji's stories humanized the struggles faced by LGBTQ Muslims, driving home the message that acceptance and inclusion were not only necessary but also integral to preserving the authenticity of Islamic teachings. By sharing these narratives, she created a sense of shared empathy and urgency among her audience, sparking critical dialogue and awakening communities to the importance of change.

Grassroots Activism

To establish a platform for change, Manji recognized the need for grassroots activism, as it provided a strong foundation for lasting transformation. She actively engaged with local LGBTQ organizations, leveraging their networks and resources to organize workshops, training sessions, and community dialogues on LGBTQ rights within the Muslim context.

By mobilizing individuals on a grassroots level, Manji was able to build a community of allies and advocates committed to challenging norms and effecting change within their respective communities. This bottom-up approach allowed for the cultivation of inclusive spaces and the promotion of LGBTQ rights at a grassroots level, ultimately leading to the broader acceptance of queer Muslims.

Harnessing Social Media

Manji understood the power of social media as a tool for activism and utilized it to its fullest potential. Through platforms like Twitter, Facebook, and YouTube, she amplified her message, reaching a global audience and connecting with LGBTQ Muslims worldwide.

Social media enabled Manji to not only disseminate her ideas but also engage in direct conversations with individuals, organizations, and communities. She used these platforms to initiate discussions, dispel misconceptions, and build bridges between various stakeholders. This digital activism allowed for the rapid dissemination of information and empowered individuals to challenge societal norms and demand change.

A Call to Action

Establishing a platform for change requires a multifaceted approach that encompasses visibility, storytelling, grassroots activism, and harnessing the power of social media. Manji's innovative strategies serve as a blueprint for future activists seeking to create lasting impact within their communities and effect positive change at a policy level.

It is essential for activists to embrace their personal narratives, as stories have the power to challenge deeply ingrained beliefs and foster understanding. By leveraging visibility and grassroots activism, individuals can build supportive communities and advocate for change from within.

In the next section, we explore how Manji took her platform for change even further by writing "The Trouble with Islam Today" and sparking a global movement for LGBTQ rights within the Muslim community.

Writing "The Trouble with Islam Today"

In this section, we explore Irshad Manji's courageous decision to write her groundbreaking book, "The Trouble with Islam Today." This bold endeavor marked a turning point in her activism, as she fearlessly confronted the challenges and contradictions within her own religion and community.

The Need for Critical Examination

As Manji delved deeper into her exploration of faith and identity, she began to question certain aspects of her Islamic upbringing. She witnessed firsthand the oppressive attitudes towards women, the lack of tolerance for diverse perspectives, and the suppression of free expression within her community. Recognizing that these issues were preventing progress and causing harm, Manji felt a deep sense of responsibility to ignite change.

Unearthing the Challenges

"The Trouble with Islam Today" was Manji's platform to shed light on the problematic aspects of her religion and to encourage a much-needed dialogue within the Muslim community. She eloquently articulated her concerns, addressing issues such as the lack of religious interpretation, the spread of extremist ideology, the denial of gender equality, and the marginalization of LGBTQ individuals.

Confronting Controversy

Unsurprisingly, the publication of "The Trouble with Islam Today" received intense scrutiny and triggered backlash from conservative factions within the Muslim community. Manji faced threats, accusations of blasphemy, and even calls for her death. However, she remained resolute in her quest for reform, refusing to be silenced by those who wished to maintain the status quo.

Empowering Muslims Worldwide

Despite the opposition, "The Trouble with Islam Today" struck a chord with many Muslims around the world who shared Manji's sentiments but lacked a platform to voice their concerns. The book became a catalyst for open discussion, encouraging individuals to critically examine their own beliefs and challenge the dominant narratives that hindered progress and inclusivity.

The Power of Courageous Writing

Manji's writing style in "The Trouble with Islam Today" was both engaging and thought-provoking. She eloquently expressed her frustrations while also providing thoughtful suggestions for positive change. By sharing her personal experiences and challenging conventional thinking, she successfully invited readers to question their own assumptions and join the conversation.

Navigating the Censorship Minefield

Manji's work faced significant challenges in countries where free speech is limited and censorship is prevalent. However, she refused to allow her message to be stifled and sought innovative ways to navigate these barriers. Through underground networks, digital platforms, and international support, she managed to push the boundaries of cultural and religious restrictions, amplifying her reach and impact.

Connecting Global Audiences

Thanks to the power of her words, "The Trouble with Islam Today" resonated not only within Muslim communities but also with individuals from diverse backgrounds. Manji's ability to bridge cultural and religious divides garnered attention and respect from audiences worldwide. Her book sparked conversations about the need for reform, not only within Islam but also within other faith traditions.

Expanding the Dialogue Through Social Media

In addition to her book, Manji leveraged the power of social media to expand her reach and engage with a global audience. She utilized platforms such as Twitter,

YouTube, and Facebook to share her ideas, connect with like-minded individuals, and build a community of activists dedicated to fostering change within Islam and promoting inclusivity.

Inspiring Others to Speak Up

"The Trouble with Islam Today" inspired a new generation of Muslim activists to find their voices and challenge the status quo. Manji's courageous stance encouraged individuals to speak up against injustice, advocate for equality, and demand a more inclusive interpretation of Islam. Through her writing, she planted the seeds of transformation and emboldened others to follow their own paths of activism.

Amplifying Marginalized Voices

One of the significant impacts of "The Trouble with Islam Today" was the spotlight it shone on marginalized communities within Islam, such as LGBTQ individuals, women, and religious minorities. By amplifying their voices and highlighting their struggles, Manji fostered empathy and solidarity among diverse groups, reinforcing the importance of intersectional activism.

The Lasting Impact of "The Trouble with Islam Today"

"The Trouble with Islam Today" marked a turning point in Irshad Manji's career and left an indelible impact on the Muslim community and beyond. Through her courageous writing and unwavering determination to challenge the status quo, she ignited a global conversation about the need for critical examination, reform, and inclusivity within Islam. Her work continues to inspire and empower individuals to question prevailing narratives and strive for a more just and equitable world.

The Birth of a Movement

The birth of a movement is often sparked by a single moment, an idea, or an individual's unwavering commitment to change. In the case of Irshad Manji, the birth of the movement can be traced back to a pivotal moment in her life and the intense desire to challenge the status quo.

At a young age, Manji recognized that the existing narrative surrounding Islam and its treatment of LGBTQ individuals was limited and often oppressive. This realization fueled her determination to initiate a much-needed dialogue within her community and ultimately shaped the birth of her movement.

1. The Awakening:

For Manji, the birth of her movement coincided with her own personal awakening. Recognizing her own identity as a queer Muslim, she confronted the discrepancies between her faith and her sexuality. This awakening propelled her towards a path of self-discovery and advocacy.

2. The Power of Words:

Manji harnessed the power of words by channeling her experiences and thoughts into writing. Through her book "The Trouble with Islam Today," she fearlessly confronted the deep-rooted discriminatory beliefs and practices within her community. This bold act of self-expression set the foundation for her movement and invited others to join the conversation.

3. Embracing Criticism:

The birth of a movement is often met with resistance and criticism. Manji faced backlash from conservative factions within the Muslim community, who viewed her unapologetic stance as sacrilegious. Rather than succumbing to discouragement, she saw this opposition as an opportunity to challenge the existing dogmas and encourage critical thinking within her community.

4. Global Impact:

The birth of Manji's movement had a ripple effect across the world. Her courage to question and challenge the status quo inspired individuals and communities, both within and outside the Muslim community, to explore the intersectionality of faith and LGBTQ rights. Manji's message resonated with countless people, sparking dialogue on the importance of inclusivity and promoting change.

5. Building an Alliance:

No movement can thrive without allies. Understanding the significance of collaboration, Manji reached out to LGBTQ and human rights organizations, building bridges and forming alliances. The collective strength of these alliances allowed the movement to grow, gain momentum, and create lasting change.

6. Harnessing Social Media:

In the digital age, the power of social media cannot be underestimated. Manji effectively leveraged various platforms to amplify her message and engage with a global audience. Through social media, she connected with individuals who felt marginalized and provided them with a platform to share their stories and experiences.

7. Shattering Silence:

The birth of a movement requires breaking the silence surrounding important issues. Manji fearlessly shared her own story and encouraged others to do the same. By shattering the silence surrounding LGBTQ rights within the Muslim community, she created a safe space for individuals to voice their experiences, ensuring that their stories were heard and acknowledged.

8. Inspiring Change:

The birth of Manji's movement ushered in a new era of hope for LGBTQ Muslims and their allies. As her message spread, it ignited hope in the hearts of those who had previously felt invisible or oppressed within their own communities. Through her advocacy and storytelling, Manji empowered individuals to embrace their own authentic identities and work towards a more inclusive future.

As we delve into the birth of this movement, it's important to recognize the transformative power of one individual's determination. Irshad Manji's unwavering commitment to challenging oppressive narratives inspired a movement that continues to evolve, bringing us closer to a world where faith and LGBTQ rights can coexist harmoniously. The next section will focus on the journey of this movement and its impact on LGBTQ Muslims worldwide.

Inspiring Queer Muslims Worldwide

Inspiring others is a crucial aspect of any activist's journey, and Irshad Manji has made a significant impact as a source of inspiration for queer Muslims worldwide. Through her powerful words and unwavering commitment to her cause, Manji has motivated countless individuals to embrace their identities, challenge societal norms, and advocate for their rights.

Understanding the Power of Representation

Representation is a powerful tool for inspiring marginalized communities to rise above societal constraints and embrace their authentic selves. Manji's visibility as a queer Muslim activist has provided a much-needed representation for queer Muslims who often feel isolated and unheard.

By openly speaking about her own experiences and struggles, Manji has shown queer Muslims that they are not alone in their journey. Her unwavering presence in the public eye has given hope and courage to those who have previously felt invisible or rejected by their own communities.

Highlighting the Intersectionality of Identities

One of the most profound ways Manji has inspired queer Muslims is by highlighting the intersectionality of identities. She recognizes that individuals can embody multiple marginalized identities that shape their experiences and challenges. In doing so, she encourages queer Muslims to embrace the totality of their identities and engage in activism that addresses the complexities of their lived experiences.

Manji's emphasis on intersectionality encourages queer Muslims to challenge not only homophobia but also other forms of discrimination, such as Islamophobia and racism. By acknowledging and addressing the interconnectedness of these issues, she inspires queer Muslims to fight for justice and equality on multiple fronts.

Sharing Personal Stories of Resilience

Stories have the power to educate, uplift, and empower. Manji has recognized this and has utilized the power of storytelling to inspire queer Muslims worldwide. By sharing her own journey, including the struggles she has faced and the progress she has made, she provides a roadmap for others to follow.

Manji's storytelling approach helps validate the experiences of queer Muslims who may be struggling to find acceptance within their communities. Through her personal anecdotes, she shows that resilience can lead to personal growth and positive change, encouraging others to persevere in their own battles.

Promoting Self-Acceptance and Self-Love

A crucial aspect of Manji's message is promoting self-acceptance and self-love within the queer Muslim community. She emphasizes the importance of embracing one's identity, regardless of societal expectations or religious teachings that may marginalize LGBTQ individuals.

By encouraging queer Muslims to love and accept themselves, Manji empowers them to navigate their own journey of self-discovery and authenticity. She encourages individuals to define their own path, rather than conforming to societal norms, and to celebrate their uniqueness.

Encouraging Global Solidarity and Collaboration

Manji's impact extends beyond inspiring individuals. She also fosters global solidarity and collaboration among queer Muslims and allies worldwide. By connecting diverse communities through her work, she encourages the exchange of ideas, experiences, and strategies for advocating LGBTQ rights within the Muslim world.

Her efforts to create inclusive spaces for dialogue and mutual understanding encourage queer Muslims and their allies to come together in pursuit of common goals. By bridging divides and fostering dialogue, Manji inspires global action and collective empowerment.

Unconventional but Relevant: Leveraging Technology

In today's digital age, technology plays a vital role in inspiring and mobilizing communities. Manji has utilized social media platforms, podcasts, and online platforms to amplify her message, reach a broader audience, and inspire queer Muslims worldwide.

By harnessing the power of technology, Manji has created spaces for dialogue, provided resources and support, and fostered virtual communities where individuals can connect and find inspiration. She has shown that technology is not only a tool for activism but also a valuable resource for inspiring growth and change within communities.

Example: The "Letters to a Young Muslim" Campaign

One remarkable example of Manji's inspiration in action is the "Letters to a Young Muslim" campaign. Through this initiative, she encourages queer Muslims to share their stories, experiences, and advice with young queer Muslims who may be struggling with their identities or facing discrimination.

This campaign not only validates the experiences of queer Muslims but also provides a platform for the voices and perspectives of diverse individuals within the community. By showcasing the resilience and wisdom of queer Muslims, Manji inspires hope and action in those who may be navigating their own paths.

Exercise: Sharing Your Story

Inspiring others begins with sharing one's own story. Take a moment to reflect on your personal journey as a queer Muslim or ally. Consider the challenges you have faced, the lessons you have learned, and the progress you have made.

Write a letter or create a social media post sharing your story and the insights you have gained along the way. Share it with your friends, family, or the broader community and encourage others to share their own stories.

By authentically sharing your experiences, you can inspire others to embrace their identities, navigate their own challenges, and become agents of change in their communities.

Additional Resources

1. "Letters to a Young Muslim" by Irshad Manji - In this book, Manji shares her personal journey and provides guidance to young Muslims navigating identity, faith, and activism.

2. The Moral Courage Project (www.moralcourage.com) - This project, founded by Manji, offers a platform for sharing stories of moral courage and inspiring individuals to challenge injustices.

3. "Becoming Visible: A Reader in Gay & Lesbian History for High School & College Students" by Kevin Jennings - This book offers a comprehensive overview of LGBTQ history, including stories of activists who have inspired change.

4. "We Have Always Been Here: A Queer Muslim Memoir" by Samra Habib - A memoir by Samra Habib detailing her experiences as a queer Muslim and the importance of finding acceptance and love within oneself.

Remember, inspiring others is an ongoing journey. Continue to learn, grow, and advocate for the rights and well-being of queer Muslims, as well as other marginalized communities. Your impact can create transformative change in the lives of individuals worldwide.

Global Impact and Recognition

Irshad Manji's bold activism and powerful message resonated far beyond the borders of Canada. Her relentless efforts to challenge homophobia and promote LGBTQ rights within Muslim communities garnered attention and recognition from around the world. This section explores the global impact she has had and the recognition she has received for her groundbreaking work.

Global Reach and Influence

Manji's advocacy work has reached people in various countries, transcending geographical and cultural boundaries. Through her books, public speaking engagements, and media appearances, she has been able to connect with individuals navigating similar struggles across the globe. Her message of inclusivity, religious freedom, and human rights has struck a chord with people from diverse backgrounds, fostering a sense of solidarity and empowerment within the LGBTQ community and the wider Muslim world.

Media Coverage and Speaking Engagements

As an outspoken activist, Manji has garnered extensive media coverage and has been invited to speak at numerous high-profile events and institutions worldwide. Her powerful TED Talks have reached millions of viewers, sparking important conversations about the intersection of faith and sexuality. Invitations to universities, conferences, and international forums have allowed her to share her experiences and insights, inspiring a new generation of activists and change-makers.

Example: One notable speaking engagement was at the United Nations Human Rights Council, where Manji delivered a compelling speech on the importance of LGBTQ rights as human rights. Her address garnered praise and sparked meaningful discussions among policymakers, diplomats, and human rights advocates, highlighting the significance of her global impact.

Recognition and Awards

Manji's exceptional contributions to LGBTQ activism and her efforts to promote understanding and inclusivity have earned her international recognition and prestigious awards. Her work has been acknowledged by influential organizations and institutions, solidifying her reputation as a trailblazer in the fight for LGBTQ rights.

Example: In 2016, Manji was honored with the Mosaic Barrier Breaker Award by the Council on American-Islamic Relations (CAIR). This award recognized her dedication to challenging stereotypes and breaking down barriers between the LGBTQ and Muslim communities. It symbolized the widespread recognition and respect she has earned for her tireless advocacy.

Global Movement Building

Manji's bold ideas and unwavering commitment have influenced a growing global movement aiming to reconcile faith and sexuality, particularly within Muslim communities. Through her writings and speaking engagements, she has inspired queer Muslims and their allies around the world to challenge oppressive social norms and advocate for equal rights.

Her principles of critical thinking, inclusivity, and respectful dialogue have served as a foundation for building bridges between LGBTQ individuals and religious communities. Manji's work has sparked important conversations within religious institutions and provided an impetus for progress, giving hope to those wrestling with their identities and seeking acceptance within their faith.

Online and Social Media Presence

Recognizing the power of technology and social media, Manji has leveraged these platforms to extend her advocacy's global reach. An active presence on platforms like Twitter, Facebook, and Instagram has allowed her to engage with a broad audience, disseminate information, share personal anecdotes, and provide support and resources for LGBTQ individuals and their allies.

Manji's online presence has fostered a sense of community among LGBTQ Muslims worldwide, creating safe spaces for dialogue, connection, and empowerment. Through these digital platforms, she continues to amplify marginalized voices, challenge misconceptions, and promote understanding on a global scale.

Unconventional Example: Using TikTok for Change

Manji's commitment to meeting people where they are includes embracing unconventional methods of activism. In line with this, she has embraced the use of TikTok, a popular short-form video platform, to engage with younger audiences and spread her message of inclusivity and empowerment.

By tapping into the creativity and accessibility of TikTok, Manji has been able to reach a new generation of individuals who may not engage with traditional media or attend academic conferences. Through humorous and informative videos, she tackles serious issues, sparks conversations, and challenges societal norms, all within the confines of a 60-second video.

Example: In one TikTok video, Manji performs a captivating lip-sync to a powerful and empowering song, using captions to highlight statistics and provide educational content about LGBTQ rights and acceptance within Muslim communities. The video goes viral, generating a wave of engagement, empathy, and support from viewers who may have otherwise been unaware of these issues.

Through her unconventional use of TikTok, Manji demonstrates her adaptability as a global activist and her willingness to explore new avenues to make a lasting impact.

Resources and Support Networks

Manji's global impact and recognition have also extended to the establishment of resources and support networks for LGBTQ individuals within Muslim communities. Understanding the importance of accessible and inclusive spaces, she has worked with like-minded organizations to develop programs, training materials, and toolkits that address the unique challenges faced by LGBTQ Muslims worldwide.

These resources provide guidance on reconciling faith and sexuality, navigating familial and community dynamics, and accessing mental health support. They act as invaluable tools for individuals, organizations, and religious leaders striving to create more inclusive and understanding environments within Muslim communities globally.

In conclusion, Irshad Manji's global impact and recognition as a queer Muslim activist have been instrumental in furthering the conversation on LGBTQ rights, religious tolerance, and social justice. Through media coverage, speaking engagements, recognition, and the use of online platforms, she has inspired individuals globally, fostered a sense of community, and paved the way for progress within marginalized communities. Manji's work serves as a testament to the power of personal stories, intersectionality, and the enduring legacy of LGBTQ activists in promoting equality and acceptance worldwide.

The Power of Courageous Writing

Courageous writing has the power to challenge norms, inspire change, and ignite movements. It is a tool that allows activists like Irshad Manji to communicate their message effectively, raise awareness, and reach a wider audience. In this subsection, we will explore the significance of courageous writing in the context of LGBTQ activism and how it has played a pivotal role in shaping the movement.

The Impact of Authenticity

One of the most powerful aspects of courageous writing is its ability to convey authenticity. When an activist shares their personal experiences and vulnerabilities through their writing, it creates a connection with readers and evokes empathy. In the case of queer Muslim activism, sharing personal stories and struggles can help break stereotypes and challenge misconceptions about LGBTQ Muslims.

By fearlessly exposing her own journey of self-discovery and embracing her queer Muslim identity, Irshad Manji has shown the world the importance of authenticity in creating change. Her writing invites readers to see the humanity in LGBTQ individuals, fostering understanding and acceptance.

Challenging the Status Quo

Courageous writing has the power to challenge the status quo and disrupt oppressive systems. By addressing the intersectionality of identities and highlighting the ways in which different forms of discrimination intersect, activists can provoke critical thinking and inspire action.

Through her writing, Manji challenges the conservative interpretations of Islam that contribute to the marginalization of LGBTQ individuals within Muslim communities. She fearlessly questions long-held beliefs and encourages a reevaluation of religious texts to be more inclusive and accepting. This courageous act of challenging deeply ingrained norms opens up space for dialogue and transformation.

Engaging with Different Audiences

Effective writing engages with diverse audiences, providing perspectives that resonate with a wide range of people. It sparks conversations, builds bridges, and invites individuals from different backgrounds to join the movement.

Manji's courageous writing has not only resonated within LGBTQ communities but has also reached audiences in the wider Muslim community, as well as non-Muslim allies. By sharing her personal experiences, she helps individuals outside the queer Muslim community understand the challenges faced by LGBTQ Muslims and inspires them to become allies. This inclusivity in her writing has been instrumental in creating spaces for dialogue, understanding, and solidarity.

Creating a Sense of Belonging

Courageous writing has the power to create a sense of belonging for individuals who may feel marginalized or isolated. By voicing their experiences, activists like Manji show that no one is alone in their struggle and provide a blueprint for resilience and self-acceptance.

Through her writing, Manji has empowered countless LGBTQ Muslims to embrace their identities and find their place within their faith communities. By sharing stories of personal growth and self-acceptance, she inspires others to embark on their own journeys of self-discovery and fosters a sense of belonging within the queer Muslim community.

Inspiring Future Activists

Courageous writing acts as an inspiration and catalyst for future activists. It provides a roadmap for those who are looking to make a difference and empowers them to use their voices to challenge injustice.

Manji's courageous writing has paved the way for queer Muslim activists and advocates to continue the fight for equality. By sharing her experiences and strategies, she equips future generations with the tools they need to navigate the challenges and setbacks of activism.

The Unconventional Power of Humor

While courageous writing often tackles serious topics, incorporating humor can be an effective and unconventional strategy. Humor allows activists to deliver their message in a relatable and accessible way, engaging readers who may otherwise be resistant.

Manji skillfully uses humor in her writing to disarm her audience and create a space for dialogue. By injecting wit and cleverness into her narratives, she captivates readers' attention and encourages them to consider perspectives they may have initially dismissed.

Understanding the Limits

It is important to acknowledge that courageous writing, while powerful, has certain limitations. Writing alone cannot dismantle systemic oppression or bring about widespread change. It serves as a tool, but it is the collective efforts of activists, organizations, and communities that drive lasting transformation.

Courageous writing must also navigate the complex dynamics of privilege and power. It is essential for activists to be aware of their own positionality and strive for inclusivity and intersectionality in their narratives.

Courageous Writing Exercise

To practice courageous writing, choose a topic related to LGBTQ rights or challenges faced by queer Muslims. Write a personal essay or creative piece that authentically explores the theme, incorporating humor and storytelling techniques. Consider how you can challenge norms, engage different audiences, and inspire change through your writing. Remember to be mindful of your own positionality and the need for inclusivity and intersectionality.

Additional Resources

1. Manji, Irshad. "The Trouble with Islam Today: A Muslim's Call for Reform in Her Faith." Random House, 2003.

2. Jenkins, Christine. "Writing to Change the World." North Atlantic Books, 2002.

3. Ahmed, Sabrina. "Queer Muslim Revolution: LGBTQ Activism in the Islamic World." Oneworld Publications, 2020.

4. TED Talk: Irshad Manji - "Faith Without Fear". Available at: `https://www.ted.com/talks/irshad_manji_faith_without_fear`.

5. Farsani, Sarah. "Courageous Writing: LGBTQ Voices from the Margins." GLAAD, 2019.

Overcoming Censorship and Opposition

One of the greatest challenges faced by queer Muslim activists like Irshad Manji is the prevalence of censorship and opposition. The intersectional nature of her work, tackling both LGBTQ rights and religious reform, has often made her a target for those who oppose her message. However, Manji's resilience and strategic approach have allowed her to navigate these obstacles and continue her fight for equality.

Understanding Censorship

Censorship is the suppression or control of information, ideas, or artistic expression by those in positions of power. In the context of Irshad Manji's work, censorship can take different forms. It can occur through the banning or restriction of her books, the blocking of her website or social media accounts, and even physical threats to her safety.

The Power of Courageous Writing

Irshad Manji's ability to articulate her ideas with clarity, passion, and intellectual rigor has been instrumental in overcoming censorship and opposition. Her influential book, "The Trouble with Islam Today," sparked a global conversation about the need for reform within Muslim communities. Through her writing, she fearlessly exposed cultural, religious, and political practices that perpetuate discrimination and hate.

Challenging Patriarchy and Conservative Interpretations

Opposition to Manji's work often stems from patriarchal and conservative interpretations of Islam, which view homosexuality as sinful and unacceptable. By engaging in dialogue and challenging these interpretations, Manji advocates for a more inclusive and progressive understanding of Islam. She emphasizes the importance of critical thinking, questioning, and reinterpreting sacred texts to promote LGBTQ rights and equality within religious spaces.

Building Alliances and Allieship

In the face of opposition, Manji has forged alliances with individuals and organizations that share her vision for equality. Collaborating with LGBTQ activists, human rights organizations, and intersectional social justice movements has provided crucial support and strength in overcoming censorship. Together, they amplify each other's voices, challenge oppressive systems, and create spaces for dialogue and understanding.

Utilizing Social Media and Technology

The advent of social media has provided a platform for activists like Irshad Manji to bypass traditional forms of censorship and reach a global audience. Through various social media channels, she has been able to share her ideas, connect with supporters, and counter opposition. Online platforms have enabled her to cultivate a community, mobilize collective action, and disseminate information freely.

Overcoming Hateful Backlash

Manji's work has not been without its share of hateful backlash. She has faced threats, personal attacks, and attempts to silence her voice. However, she remains resilient and steadfast in her commitment to creating change. Rather than allowing the negativity to deter her, she channels it as fuel to push her message further and embolden her activism.

The Importance of Resilience

Overcoming censorship and opposition requires a significant amount of resilience. It is essential for activists to prioritize self-care, mental well-being, and a support network. Engaging in mindfulness practices, seeking therapy or counseling, and connecting with likeminded individuals can help activists navigate the challenges they face and maintain their activism in the long run.

Creating Safe Spaces for LGBTQ Muslims

One of Manji's key strategies in overcoming opposition is the creation of safe spaces for LGBTQ Muslims. These spaces provide much-needed support, affirmation, and community for individuals who face discrimination and ostracism. By fostering safe spaces, Manji empowers LGBTQ Muslims to embrace their identities and advocate for their rights.

Empowering Others to Speak Out

Irshad Manji's work extends beyond her own activism; she actively seeks to empower others to speak out against censorship and opposition. Through mentorship programs, advocacy toolkits, and leadership training, Manji cultivates the next generation of activists who can carry the torch forward. By amplifying diverse voices and perspectives, she strengthens the overall movement for LGBTQ rights and religious reform.

The Impact of Personal Stories

In navigating censorship and opposition, personal stories have proven to be powerful tools. Manji highlights the importance of sharing individual narratives and experiences as a means to challenge stereotypes, build empathy, and dismantle prejudice. Personal stories humanize the struggles faced by LGBTQ Muslims and provide a counter-narrative to prevailing misconceptions.

The Legacy of Overcoming Censorship

By overcoming censorship and opposition, Irshad Manji has carved a path for future activists to follow. Her fearless pursuit of equality and justice inspires others to challenge oppressive systems and speak truth to power. The legacy she leaves behind serves as a reminder of the importance of fighting against censorship, cultivating resilience, and embracing one's authentic identity.

In conclusion, overcoming censorship and opposition is a significant hurdle for queer Muslim activists like Irshad Manji. By leveraging the power of courageous writing, building alliances, utilizing social media, prioritizing resilience, and creating safe spaces, Manji has paved the way for a more inclusive and accepting future. Her legacy continues to inspire and empower others to challenge censorship, fight for LGBTQ rights, and advocate for religious reform.

Connecting with Audiences Globally

In the age of technology and instant communication, activists like Irshad Manji have a unique opportunity to connect with audiences all around the world. By leveraging the power of the internet and social media platforms, Manji has been able to spread her message of LGBTQ rights and inclusive Islam to a global audience. In this subsection, we will explore some of the strategies and techniques that have allowed Manji to effectively connect with audiences globally.

Harnessing the Power of Social Media

Social media platforms such as Twitter, Facebook, Instagram, and YouTube have become powerful tools for activists to engage with their audiences. Irshad Manji has effectively utilized these platforms to share her message and connect with individuals from diverse backgrounds. Through her active presence online, she has been able to reach people across continents, who may have otherwise not been exposed to her work.

One of the key strategies in social media engagement is to create compelling and shareable content. Manji has been successful in using social media to amplify her message by creating content that is relatable, thought-provoking, and visually appealing. Whether it's sharing personal stories, highlighting the experiences of LGBTQ Muslims, or discussing intersectional issues, Manji ensures her posts are engaging and resonate with her global audience.

Facilitating Global Conversations

Another powerful way Manji connects with audiences globally is by facilitating global conversations on important topics. Through live webinars, online forums, and virtual conferences, she brings together individuals from different parts of the world to engage in meaningful discussions about LGBTQ rights and inclusion in the Muslim community.

These online platforms allow participants to share their experiences, ask questions, and learn from one another. Manji often invites experts, scholars, and activists to these conversations, enabling a diverse range of perspectives to be heard. By fostering an inclusive and respectful environment, Manji ensures that all participants, regardless of their geographical location, feel welcome and valued.

Creating Translated Content

Language barriers can often hinder effective communication and limit the reach of activists. To overcome this challenge, Manji recognizes the importance of creating content in multiple languages. By translating her books, articles, and social media posts into different languages, she can connect with audiences from a variety of cultural and linguistic backgrounds.

Manji also works with a team of translators to ensure the accuracy and cultural sensitivity of her content. This allows her message to reach individuals who may not be fluent in English but are passionate about LGBTQ rights and inclusive Islam. By broadening the accessibility of her work, Manji ensures that her message resonates with people from diverse language communities.

Engaging with Local Activists and Organizations

While global connectivity is important, Manji understands the significance of engaging with local activists and organizations to build strong networks and grassroots support. By collaborating with local LGBTQ organizations, Muslim community centers, and human rights groups, Manji can learn from their experiences, support their initiatives, and amplify their voices.

By actively participating in local events, conferences, and workshops, Manji demonstrates her commitment to understanding the unique challenges faced by different communities. This not only enriches her perspectives and knowledge but also enables her to connect with audiences on a more personal level. It is through these local connections that Manji can foster lasting change and inspire others to take action.

Unconventional Approach: Virtual Reality Experiences

In addition to traditional forms of communication, Manji has explored unconventional methods to connect with global audiences. One such approach is leveraging virtual reality (VR) technology to create immersive experiences that allow individuals to walk in the shoes of LGBTQ Muslims facing discrimination and prejudice.

Through VR storytelling, Manji takes her audience on a journey, providing a firsthand perspective of the challenges and triumphs of LGBTQ Muslims. By utilizing innovative technology, she creates empathy, fosters understanding, and encourages collective action. This unconventional approach not only captures the attention of audiences but also leaves a lasting impact on their perceptions and attitudes.

Conclusion

Irshad Manji's ability to connect with audiences globally has been instrumental in her mission to promote LGBTQ rights and inclusive Islam. By harnessing the power of social media, facilitating global conversations, creating translated content, engaging with local activists, and even exploring unconventional methods like virtual reality experiences, she has been able to reach people from all corners of the world.

In an increasingly interconnected world, it is essential for activists to utilize these strategies to engage with global audiences. By employing these techniques, activists can build bridges between communities, foster understanding, and inspire collective action towards a more inclusive and accepting world for all LGBTQ individuals, regardless of their cultural or religious backgrounds.

The Role of Social Media in Activism

In the digital era, social media has emerged as a powerful tool for LGBTQ activists like Irshad Manji to spread their message, build communities, and effect change. Social media platforms such as Facebook, Twitter, Instagram, and YouTube have transformed the way activists communicate, organize, and advocate for their causes. This subsection explores the role of social media in LGBTQ activism and highlights its impact on fostering inclusivity and amplifying marginalized voices.

Harnessing the Power of Online Communities

Social media enables activists to connect with like-minded individuals and create safe and inclusive communities. Online platforms provide a space where LGBTQ individuals can openly express their identities, share experiences, and find support. These virtual communities foster a sense of belonging, allowing individuals to build resilience and combat feelings of isolation. Moreover, social media platforms allow for the formation of global networks, enabling individuals from different backgrounds and cultures to come together and advocate for LGBTQ rights on a larger scale.

Amplifying Marginalized Voices

Social media has given a voice to individuals and communities whose experiences and perspectives have historically been marginalized and excluded. LGBTQ activists use platforms like Twitter and Instagram to share personal stories, educate others, and challenge societal norms. Through the power of storytelling, activists can humanize their experiences and generate empathy, ultimately leading to greater acceptance and understanding. By amplifying marginalized voices, social media acts as a catalyst for change and promotes inclusivity within society.

Advocacy and Awareness Campaigns

One of the most significant impacts of social media on LGBTQ activism is its ability to raise awareness about pressing issues and advocate for change. Activists leverage platforms like Facebook and YouTube to disseminate information, educate the public, and debunk myths and stereotypes surrounding LGBTQ individuals. Social media campaigns, such as hashtag movements and viral challenges, create a collective voice, generating momentum and influencing public opinion. Through these campaigns, activists can mobilize individuals, encourage participation, and drive action, ultimately leading to shifts in societal attitudes and policies.

Engaging with Decision-Makers

Social media has revolutionized the way activists engage with policymakers and decision-makers. Platforms like Twitter provide a direct line of communication to politicians, organizations, and celebrities, allowing activists to engage in real-time conversations and advocate for LGBTQ rights. By leveraging hashtags and tagging relevant stakeholders, activists can capture the attention of influential individuals and draw public support for their cause. Social media acts as a bridge between activists and decision-makers, fostering dialogue, and influencing policy discussions surrounding LGBTQ rights.

The Challenges and Opportunities of Social Media Activism

While social media presents numerous opportunities for LGBTQ activism, it is not without its challenges. The fast-paced nature of online platforms can make it difficult for activists to sustain long-term engagement and maintain allyship. Moreover, the proliferation of misinformation and the spread of hate speech pose threats to the safety and well-being of LGBTQ individuals. Activists must navigate these challenges by actively monitoring and moderating online spaces, utilizing privacy settings, and reporting instances of harassment or discrimination.

Despite these challenges, social media remains a powerful and accessible tool for LGBTQ activists. Its wide reach, low-cost nature, and ability to foster global connections make it an indispensable resource in the fight for LGBTQ rights. By harnessing the potential of social media, activists like Irshad Manji can create lasting change, amplify marginalized voices, and pave the way for a more inclusive and accepting world.

Engaging Exercise: Conducting a Social Media Campaign

To understand the impact of social media in activism, it is essential to engage in a hands-on exercise. Imagine you are an LGBTQ activist with a cause close to your heart. Develop a social media campaign that highlights the importance of LGBTQ inclusive education policies in schools. Create a hashtag, design engaging visual content, and craft compelling messages to raise awareness and advocate for change. Utilize different social media platforms to reach a diverse audience, engage with decision-makers, and amplify the voices of those affected. Evaluate the impact of your campaign by analyzing engagement metrics, responses from the public, and any policy changes that may result from your advocacy efforts.

Further Reading and Resources

1. "No Future Without Forgiveness" by Desmond Tutu: This book explores the importance of forgiveness and reconciliation in post-apartheid South Africa, providing valuable insights into how forgiveness can foster healing and social change.

2. "#MeToo: Beyond the Hashtag" by Mary Louise Adams: This article critically examines the global #MeToo movement and its impact on social media activism, shedding light on the potential and limitations of online activism.

3. "The Social Media Handbook for Activists" by Randy Stoecker: This practical guide offers tips and strategies for activists on effectively using social media for advocacy and creating meaningful online engagement.

4. LGBTQ+ Advocacy Organizations: Organizations like GLAAD, Human Rights Campaign, and the Trevor Project offer resources, toolkits, and support for LGBTQ activists looking to make a difference through social media activism.

Remember, social media is a powerful tool, but it is essential to use it responsibly and ethically. Be conscious of privacy settings, engage in healthy online discussions, and always prioritize the safety and well-being of yourself and others. Together, we can harness the potential of social media to create a more inclusive and accepting world for all LGBTQ individuals.

Amplifying Marginalized Voices

In the fight for equality and social justice, it is crucial to amplify the voices of marginalized communities. Those who are marginalized often face significant barriers in having their perspectives heard and their experiences understood. By amplifying these voices, we can create a more inclusive society that acknowledges the diverse experiences and challenges faced by different individuals.

Amplifying marginalized voices entails providing platforms and opportunities for individuals from marginalized communities to share their stories, ideas, and perspectives. It involves recognizing and addressing the systemic structures that contribute to their marginalization and actively working to dismantle these barriers.

One way to amplify marginalized voices is through storytelling. Sharing personal narratives and experiences can be a powerful tool in challenging stereotypes, debunking misconceptions, and fostering empathy. By giving individuals from marginalized communities a platform to speak their truth, we can humanize their experiences and increase understanding among wider audiences.

Additionally, grassroots movements and community organizing play a vital role in amplifying marginalized voices. These movements are often driven by individuals who are directly affected by systemic oppression. By organizing around shared goals and creating spaces for collective action, marginalized communities can come together, voice their concerns, and demand change.

Education and awareness are also critical in amplifying marginalized voices. It is important to provide accurate and inclusive education regarding the history, cultures, and experiences of marginalized communities. This can help build empathy and understanding among individuals who may have limited exposure to these perspectives.

Media representation is another essential avenue for amplifying marginalized voices. By promoting diversity in media and supporting content created by and for marginalized communities, we can challenge stereotypes, shift narratives, and create more inclusive storytelling.

Organizations and institutions can contribute to the amplification of marginalized voices by actively seeking out and supporting individuals from these communities. This can include providing funding, mentorship, and resources to help individuals share their stories, engage in advocacy work, and influence policy-making processes.

However, it is crucial to note that amplifying marginalized voices is not about speaking for or over these communities. It is vital to prioritize and center the voices and leadership of marginalized individuals themselves. Allies can play a supportive role by creating space, listening, and amplifying these voices, rather than assuming the role of spokesperson or decision-maker.

To effectively amplify marginalized voices, it is important to confront our own biases and privileges. We must be willing to examine and challenge the systems of power that perpetuate inequality. By doing so, we can contribute to creating a more equitable society where all individuals are heard, seen, and valued.

In conclusion, amplifying marginalized voices is a crucial aspect of promoting social justice and equality. It involves providing platforms for individuals from marginalized communities to share their experiences, challenging stereotypes and misconceptions, fostering empathy, and actively working to dismantle systemic barriers. Through storytelling, grassroots movements, education, media representation, and allyship, we can create a more inclusive society that recognizes and amplifies the voices of marginalized individuals.

Reformation Within Islam

Advocating for LGBTQ Rights

Advocating for LGBTQ rights is a crucial part of Irshad Manji's work and a key aspect of her activism. In this subsection, we will explore the principles and strategies behind her advocacy efforts, as well as the challenges she faced and the impact she made in the fight for LGBTQ equality.

Understanding LGBTQ Rights

Before delving into her advocacy work, it is important to understand the concept of LGBTQ rights. LGBTQ rights refer to the legal and social protections and freedoms that are granted to lesbian, gay, bisexual, transgender, and queer individuals. These rights encompass various aspects of life, including non-discrimination, marriage equality, access to healthcare, employment protection, and the right to live authentically without fear of persecution or violence.

LGBTQ individuals have historically faced systemic discrimination, marginalization, and violence due to their sexual orientation and gender identity. Advocacy for LGBTQ rights seeks to address these injustices and ensure equality and fair treatment for all individuals, regardless of their sexual orientation or gender identity.

Building Awareness and Visibility

Irshad Manji understands the power of visibility in advocating for LGBTQ rights. Visibility refers to the presence and representation of LGBTQ individuals in all aspects of society, including media, politics, and the public sphere. By being visible, LGBTQ individuals challenge societal norms, break down stereotypes, and foster empathy and understanding.

In her advocacy work, Manji emphasizes the importance of coming out and sharing personal stories. She encourages LGBTQ individuals to embrace their identity and be proud of who they are, despite potential challenges or backlash. By doing so, they inspire others and create a sense of community and belonging.

Additionally, Manji stresses the role of allies in supporting LGBTQ individuals. Allies are individuals who actively support and advocate for LGBTQ rights, even if they do not identify as LGBTQ themselves. Allies play a crucial role in amplifying LGBTQ voices, challenging discrimination, and creating inclusive spaces where all individuals can thrive.

Addressing Legal and Policy Changes

Advocacy for LGBTQ rights also involves challenging discriminatory laws and policies and pushing for progressive change. Irshad Manji recognizes the importance of legal protections and the role they play in ensuring equal rights for LGBTQ individuals.

She actively engages in lobbying efforts and collaborates with human rights organizations to advocate for LGBTQ-friendly legislation. This includes supporting measures such as non-discrimination laws, hate crime protections, marriage equality, and anti-conversion therapy legislation.

Manji also emphasizes the significance of influencing government decision-makers. Through direct communication, engagement with policymakers, and sharing personal stories, she aims to humanize the LGBTQ experience and create empathy and understanding among those in positions of power.

Creating Accepting and Inclusive Communities

Advocating for LGBTQ rights goes beyond legal and policy changes. It also involves creating accepting and inclusive communities where LGBTQ individuals can live authentic and fulfilling lives.

Irshad Manji promotes dialogue and education as powerful tools for social change. She speaks at universities and conferences, leads workshops and training sessions, and collaborates with LGBTQ organizations to raise awareness and promote LGBTQ inclusion. These efforts aim to challenge stereotypes, debunk myths, and foster empathy and understanding among diverse communities.

Additionally, Manji emphasizes the need for LGBTQ-inclusive religious spaces. She recognizes that religion plays a significant role in the lives of many individuals, and fostering acceptance within religious communities is crucial for creating social change. By engaging with religious scholars, revisiting sacred texts, and promoting critical thinking, Manji seeks to challenge anti-LGBTQ interpretations and create space for LGBTQ individuals within religious traditions.

Encouraging Global Solidarity

Irshad Manji's advocacy work extends beyond national borders. She actively engages in global solidarity efforts to support LGBTQ individuals worldwide, recognizing that LGBTQ rights are human rights and should be upheld universally.

Manji collaborates with international human rights organizations, participates in global conferences and forums, and advocates for LGBTQ rights on a global scale. She understands that addressing LGBTQ discrimination requires collective efforts and a united front.

Through her work, Manji seeks to create a global movement that celebrates diversity, challenges discrimination, and ensures equal rights and opportunities for all individuals, regardless of their sexual orientation or gender identity.

In conclusion, advocating for LGBTQ rights is a central aspect of Irshad Manji's activism. By building awareness and visibility, challenging discriminatory laws and policies, creating accepting communities, and fostering global solidarity, she has made a significant impact in the fight for LGBTQ equality. Her work serves as an inspiration for future generations of activists, who will continue to build on her foundation and strive for a more inclusive and equitable world.

Challenging Conservative Interpretations

In addition to advocating for LGBTQ rights within the Muslim community, Irshad Manji has been influential in challenging conservative interpretations of Islam. This subsection explores her efforts to push for a more inclusive and progressive understanding of the faith, breaking down barriers and promoting critical thinking.

Background

Conservative interpretations of Islam often marginalize and discriminate against LGBTQ individuals, perpetuating harmful beliefs and practices. These interpretations rely heavily on narrow interpretations of religious texts and outdated cultural norms. Irshad Manji recognized the need to challenge these interpretations in order to create a more inclusive and accepting environment for LGBTQ Muslims.

Principles of Progressive Interpretation

Progressive interpretation of religious texts involves a more contextual and holistic approach that recognizes the inherent diversity of interpretations. Irshad Manji argues that religious texts should be read with a critical lens, taking into account the historical, social, and cultural context, as well as the core principles of justice, compassion, and equality. This approach allows for a more nuanced understanding of Islamic teachings, one that can be adaptable to modern realities.

Critiques of Conservative Views

Irshad Manji identifies several problematic aspects of conservative interpretations and actively challenges them. She critiques the prevalent belief in the binary gender system, arguing that it oversimplifies human identity and excludes individuals who do not fit neatly into traditional gender categories. Manji also questions the rigid ideas of family structure and marriage, advocating for a broader understanding that encompasses various forms of love and companionship.

Promoting Gender Equality

One of the key issues Manji addresses is the unequal treatment of women within conservative interpretations of Islam. She challenges the restrictive gender roles imposed by patriarchy, emphasizing the importance of women's agency and empowerment. Manji encourages a reevaluation of religious texts to promote gender equality and women's rights.

Deconstructing Misconceptions

Through her work, Manji aims to break down the misconception that LGBTQ rights and Islam are inherently incompatible. She challenges the idea that being LGBTQ is a Western import or a result of moral degradation. Manji highlights the existence of LGBTQ individuals throughout Islamic history and their contributions to the faith, emphasizing that being queer does not make one any less Muslim.

Engaging with Scholars

Irshad Manji actively engages with Islamic scholars, both progressive and conservative, in promoting dialogue and fostering understanding. She encourages scholars to reexamine traditional interpretations and consider alternative viewpoints. Manji facilitates discussions and debates to challenge conservative perspectives and provide a platform for progressive voices within the Muslim community.

Creating a Space for Dialogue

One of the major challenges in challenging conservative interpretations is the resistance from conservative religious authorities. However, Manji remains undeterred and continues to create spaces for dialogue and critical engagement. She organizes conferences, workshops, and interfaith events that bring together LGBTQ Muslims, religious leaders, and activists to foster understanding and promote inclusivity.

Redefining Religious Authority

Manji's work also challenges the traditional understanding of religious authority. She encourages individuals to question and critically evaluate religious teachings, rather than blindly accepting them. Manji promotes the idea that religious authority should be inclusive and reflective of the diverse experiences and perspectives of the Muslim community.

The Role of Education

Education plays a crucial role in challenging conservative interpretations and fostering a more inclusive understanding of Islam. Manji emphasizes the importance of educating both LGBTQ individuals and the wider Muslim community about the principles of justice, compassion, and equality within the faith. She advocates for comprehensive sex education and the inclusion of LGBTQ-inclusive teachings in Islamic schools and seminaries.

Unconventional Example: Embracing LGBTQ Muslims in Worship Spaces

In challenging conservative interpretations, Manji has championed the importance of LGBTQ inclusion in worship spaces. She encourages mosques and other religious institutions to open their doors to LGBTQ Muslims, providing them a safe and welcoming environment to practice their faith. This unconventional example breaks the usual notion that conservative religious spaces are unwelcoming to LGBTQ individuals.

Conclusion

Irshad Manji's efforts in challenging conservative interpretations of Islam have been vital in promoting inclusivity and compassion within the Muslim LGBTQ community. By advocating for critical thinking, engaging with scholars, and fostering dialogue, she paves the way for a more progressive understanding of Islam that embraces the rights and dignity of all individuals, regardless of their sexual orientation or gender identity. Manji's work is an inspiration to others to question and challenge harmful interpretations, fostering a more inclusive future for LGBTQ Muslims.

Promoting Critical Thinking

Promoting critical thinking is crucial in any field or discipline, and LGBTQ activism is no exception. As Irshad Manji advocates for greater inclusion and acceptance of queer individuals within Islam, she also encourages the development of critical thinking skills among LGBTQ Muslims and their allies. This subsection will explore the importance of critical thinking in driving social change and provide strategies for promoting it within the LGBTQ Muslim community.

Understanding Critical Thinking

Critical thinking is the ability to objectively analyze and evaluate information, arguments, and beliefs in order to make reasoned judgments. It involves actively questioning assumptions, seeking evidence, considering alternative perspectives, and reaching independent conclusions. By fostering critical thinking skills, individuals can challenge and dismantle social norms that perpetuate discrimination and inequality.

In the context of LGBTQ Muslim activism, critical thinking plays a crucial role in challenging conservative interpretations of religious texts, addressing homophobia within Muslim communities, and advocating for inclusive religious spaces. It enables individuals to engage in thoughtful dialogue, question patriarchal and heteronormative structures, and navigate complex intersections of faith and sexuality.

Developing Critical Thinking Skills

Promoting critical thinking among LGBTQ Muslims can empower them to challenge oppressive systems and advocate for their rights. Here are some strategies to enhance critical thinking skills within the community:

1. Education and Awareness: Encourage LGBTQ Muslims to educate themselves about their religious teachings, as well as different interpretations and historical contexts. This knowledge will provide a foundation for critical analysis and empower them to challenge ingrained beliefs and prejudices.

2. Questioning Assumptions: Encourage individuals to critically examine their own beliefs, biases, and assumptions surrounding LGBTQ issues and Islam. This self-reflection aids in recognizing and challenging internalized homophobia, transphobia, and other biases.

3. Engaging with Diverse Perspectives: Encourage LGBTQ Muslims to actively seek out diverse voices and perspectives within their communities and beyond. By engaging with different viewpoints, individuals can broaden their understanding, challenge their own beliefs, and develop empathy for others' experiences.

4. Analyzing Religious Texts: Teach individuals to critically analyze religious texts, considering historical context, linguistic nuances, and alternative interpretations. This analysis can help LGBTQ Muslims reconcile their faith with their sexual orientation or gender identity and challenge homophobic interpretations.

5. Logical Reasoning: Promote the development of logical reasoning skills to evaluate arguments and identify fallacies. This enables individuals to construct well-reasoned arguments, contribute to discussions, and challenge discriminatory beliefs.

6. Encouraging Dialogue: Foster an environment that encourages open and respectful dialogue among LGBTQ Muslims and their allies. Dialogue enables the exchange of ideas, challenges assumptions, and promotes critical thinking through active listening and constructive criticism.

7. Media Literacy: Educate LGBTQ Muslims about media literacy to help them critically evaluate representations of LGBTQ individuals and Islam. This includes analyzing biases, stereotypes, and misinformation, which can be powerful tools in countering Islamophobia and promoting understanding.

Real-World Application

Applying critical thinking skills to real-world situations allows LGBTQ Muslims to advocate for their rights and challenge systems of injustice. Here is an example:

Case Study: Challenging Homophobic Stereotypes

Samira, a queer Muslim activist, notices recurring homophobic stereotypes about LGBTQ Muslims within her community. She decides to critically analyze the sources of these stereotypes and challenge their validity. Using her critical thinking skills, Samira:

1. Questions assumptions: Samira interrogates her own biases and questions the origins of the stereotypes she encounters. She acknowledges the importance of critical thinking in breaking free from these harmful narratives.

2. Engages with diverse perspectives: Samira seeks out LGBTQ Muslims with different experiences and engages in conversations to understand their realities, challenges, and beliefs. This allows her to challenge the one-dimensional stereotypes perpetuated within her community.

3. Analyzes religious texts: Samira critically analyzes religious texts, exploring alternative interpretations that promote LGBTQ inclusion. She engages with scholars who reinterpret scripture through an inclusive lens and learns from their insights.

4. Constructs well-reasoned arguments: Armed with knowledge and critical thinking skills, Samira constructs well-reasoned arguments to challenge the homophobic stereotypes within her community. She disseminates this information through speeches, online platforms, and community events.

By promoting critical thinking, Samira helps debunk harmful stereotypes, fosters dialogue in her community, and creates a more inclusive environment for LGBTQ Muslims.

Conclusion

Promoting critical thinking within the LGBTQ Muslim community is essential for driving social change, challenging oppressive norms, and advocating for greater inclusivity. By developing critical thinking skills, individuals can challenge discriminatory beliefs, engage with diverse perspectives, and construct well-reasoned arguments. Emphasizing critical thinking not only strengthens the LGBTQ Muslim activist movement but also promotes a more inclusive and understanding world.

Reconciling Faith and Queerness

The journey of reconciling faith and queerness is an often complex and deeply personal one. It involves exploring the intersections of one's religious beliefs and their sexual orientation or gender identity. In this subsection, we will delve into the challenges faced by LGBTQ individuals within religious communities and the approaches taken to find harmony and acceptance.

Understanding Religious Doctrine

Reconciliation begins by understanding the religious doctrines that may have contributed to the negative attitudes towards queerness within certain faiths. By studying the scriptures, traditions, and teachings, individuals can gain a deeper understanding of the historical and cultural context in which these beliefs were formed. It is important to note that interpretations vary, and not all religious followers hold a prejudiced view towards the LGBTQ community.

Questioning and Critical Thinking

Reconciling faith and queerness often involves questioning long-held beliefs and engaging in critical thinking. LGBTQ individuals may ask themselves: Do the teachings of my faith condemn same-sex relationships? Are these teachings timeless, or are they influenced by cultural biases? By critically examining these beliefs and seeking alternative interpretations, individuals can challenge heteronormative and cisnormative interpretations that may exist within their religious traditions.

Seeking Inclusive Interpretations

Many progressive faith communities have emerged that offer inclusive interpretations of religious texts, affirming the validity and dignity of LGBTQ individuals. These interpretations highlight the core teachings of love, compassion, and acceptance, emphasizing the inherent worth of all individuals. Inclusive faith leaders and scholars play a vital role in providing interpretive frameworks that validate the existence and experiences of LGBTQ individuals.

Engaging in Dialogue

Open and respectful dialogue is essential in reconciling faith and queerness. By engaging in conversations with religious leaders, fellow congregants, and academics, LGBTQ individuals can advocate for understanding and inclusion. Dialogue allows for the exploration of diverse perspectives and challenges preconceived notions about the incompatibility of faith and queerness.

Building Supportive Communities

Creating or joining supportive communities is crucial in the reconciliation process. LGBTQ-affirming faith communities provide safe spaces where individuals can freely express their queerness without fear of judgment or rejection. These communities offer support, guidance, and spiritual nourishment while encouraging individuals to cultivate a positive relationship with their faith.

Embracing Personal Spirituality

For some LGBTQ individuals, organized religion may not provide the acceptance they seek. In such cases, redefining and embracing personal spirituality becomes a powerful tool for reconciliation. Exploring alternative spiritual practices, connecting with nature, and engaging in mindfulness and meditation can nurture a deep sense of spirituality that aligns with one's queerness.

Balancing Different Identities

Reconciling faith and queerness often involves navigating the complexities of multiple identities. It requires finding a balance between one's religious identity, LGBTQ identity, and other aspects of individuality. Embracing intersectionality and recognizing how different aspects of identity shape one's experiences can provide insights into forging a harmonious and authentic existence.

Seeking Guidance and Support

Reconciling faith and queerness can be challenging, and seeking guidance from LGBTQ-inclusive religious organizations, counselors, and support groups is essential. These resources offer advice, emotional support, and affirmation for individuals on their journey towards reconciliation. The support and guidance provided by these communities create a space for healing, growth, and self-acceptance.

Advocacy and Activism

Individuals who have successfully reconciled their faith and queerness often become advocates and activists within their religious communities. Through education, awareness campaigns, and promoting LGBTQ-inclusive policies, they work towards creating a more accepting environment for LGBTQ individuals within their faith traditions.

Celebrate Diversity Within Faith Communities

In reconciling faith and queerness, it is important to amplify the voices and experiences of diverse LGBTQ individuals within faith communities. By celebrating their stories, struggles, and achievements, we foster understanding, compassion, and acceptance among all members of the community.

In conclusion, reconciling faith and queerness requires an individualized and deeply introspective journey. It involves critical thinking, engaging in dialogue, seeking inclusive interpretations, building supportive communities, and embracing personal spirituality. Through these steps, individuals can reconcile their faith and queerness, forging a path towards self-acceptance, spiritual fulfillment, and a harmonious existence.

Gaining Muslim Support

Gaining support within Muslim communities is crucial for the success of LGBTQ activism. It requires engaging in dialogue, promoting understanding, and challenging conservative interpretations of Islamic teachings. In this subsection, we will explore effective strategies to gain Muslim support for LGBTQ rights.

Understanding Islamic Teachings

To gain Muslim support, it is important to have a deep understanding of Islamic teachings. This involves recognizing the diversity within the Muslim community and the different interpretations of the Quran and Hadiths (sayings of Prophet Muhammad). It is essential to approach discussions with empathy, respect, and an open mind.

Promoting Inclusive Interpretations

One effective strategy to gain Muslim support is to promote inclusive interpretations of Islamic teachings. Highlighting alternative interpretations that affirm LGBTQ identities can help challenge the prevailing conservative views. This requires engaging with progressive Muslim scholars and activists who advocate for LGBTQ rights within an Islamic framework.

Sharing Personal Stories

Sharing personal stories is a powerful way to gain support and create empathy. By sharing the experiences of LGBTQ Muslims, we can humanize the struggle for acceptance within Muslim communities. These stories help challenge stereotypes, break down barriers, and encourage compassionate understanding.

Building Alliances with Progressive Muslim Organizations

Collaborating with progressive Muslim organizations is essential in gaining Muslim support. These organizations often have a better understanding of the cultural and religious context and can help bridge the gap between LGBTQ activists and Muslim communities. Through education, dialogue, and joint advocacy efforts, we can make significant progress towards achieving acceptance and equality.

Engaging Religious Leaders

Religious leaders hold significant influence within Muslim communities. Engaging with them and seeking their support for LGBTQ rights is crucial. This can be done through open dialogues, conferences, and workshops. By addressing their concerns, providing theological justifications, and showcasing the importance of inclusivity, we can gradually change their attitudes towards LGBTQ individuals.

Promoting Dialogue and Education

Education is a potent tool for change. By organizing workshops and seminars on LGBTQ issues within Islamic contexts, we can promote dialogue and foster understanding. These platforms allow for open discussions, dispelling misconceptions, and answering questions. Creating spaces for Muslims to learn and ask questions helps in gaining support for LGBTQ rights.

Emphasizing Common Values

To gain Muslim support, it is crucial to emphasize the common values shared between Islam and LGBTQ rights, such as justice, compassion, and respect for human dignity. By framing LGBTQ rights as an extension of these shared values, we can find common ground and foster acceptance among Muslim communities.

Addressing Concerns and Misconceptions

Many Muslims have concerns and misconceptions about LGBTQ individuals and their rights. Addressing these concerns openly and honestly can help break down barriers and gain support. Providing accurate information, challenging stereotypes, and offering resources for further education can contribute to changing attitudes and gaining acceptance.

Creating Inclusive Spaces

Creating inclusive spaces within Muslim communities is essential to gain support for LGBTQ individuals. This involves working towards inclusive policies in mosques, community centers, and Islamic organizations. By advocating for LGBTQ-affirming spaces that are welcoming and accepting, we can foster a sense of belonging and build support within Muslim communities.

Highlighting Intersectionality

Gaining Muslim support for LGBTQ rights also involves recognizing the intersectionality of oppression. By highlighting the experiences of LGBTQ Muslims who face multiple forms of discrimination, we can build solidarity and foster empathy within Muslim communities. Recognizing the interconnectedness of struggles can help Muslims understand the importance of standing up for LGBTQ rights.

In conclusion, gaining Muslim support for LGBTQ rights requires engaging in dialogue, promoting inclusive interpretations of Islamic teachings, sharing personal stories, building alliances with progressive Muslim organizations, and engaging with religious leaders. By emphasizing common values, addressing concerns and misconceptions, creating inclusive spaces, and highlighting intersectionality, we can create a more accepting and supportive environment within Muslim communities. It is through these efforts that we can achieve true equality and justice for LGBTQ individuals.

Engaging with Religious Scholars

Engaging with religious scholars is a crucial aspect of Irshad Manji's activism, as she seeks to challenge conservative interpretations of Islam and promote inclusivity within the faith. By fostering dialogue and collaboration with religious leaders, Manji works towards reformation within Islam and creates spaces for queer Muslims to reconcile their faith and sexuality. In this subsection, we will explore the strategies and principles behind engaging with religious scholars and the impact it has on the LGBTQ Muslim community.

Background on Interactions with Religious Scholars

Engaging with religious scholars requires a delicate balance of respect, knowledge, and open-mindedness. It involves challenging deeply ingrained beliefs while maintaining a respectful and productive conversation. It is crucial to approach these interactions with a genuine desire for dialogue, understanding, and the improvement of religious interpretations regarding LGBTQ rights.

The Role of Critical Thinking and Scholarship

Critical thinking plays a significant role in engaging with religious scholars. It involves questioning and critically examining existing interpretations of religious texts and traditions, while also grounding arguments in scholarly research and scriptural evidence. By fostering critical thinking skills, Manji encourages scholars to re-evaluate traditional interpretations of Islam that marginalize LGBTQ individuals.

Promoting Bridge-Building and Common Ground

Engaging with religious scholars necessitates finding common ground and establishing a basis for productive conversations. By emphasizing shared values, such as compassion, justice, and social harmony, Manji encourages religious scholars to consider LGBTQ rights within an inclusive framework of Islam. Highlighting these shared values helps create a space for genuine dialogue and understanding.

Using Personal Stories and Narratives

Personal stories and narratives play a powerful role in engaging with religious scholars. They humanize LGBTQ experiences and challenge stereotypes, allowing scholars to connect on an emotional level and gain insight into the struggles faced by queer Muslims. Manji's use of personal stories helps to dispel misconceptions and foster empathy towards LGBTQ individuals, ultimately leading to more informed and inclusive discussions.

Addressing Misinterpretations and Misunderstandings

Engaging with religious scholars involves addressing misinterpretations and misunderstandings about LGBTQ issues within Islam. By providing accurate information, backed by scriptural analysis and scholarly research, Manji challenges the misconceptions that often underlie homophobia within religious communities. This helps to correct mischaracterizations and promote a more nuanced understanding of LGBTQ identities within the faith.

Promoting Inclusivity and LGBTQ-Affirming Spaces

Engaging with religious scholars also aims to promote inclusivity and LGBTQ-affirming spaces within mosques and religious communities. Manji advocates for the creation of safe spaces where queer Muslims can fully embrace their identities without fear of prejudice or discrimination. By fostering dialogue and collaboration between scholars and LGBTQ Muslims, Manji seeks to encourage the development of LGBTQ-affirming practices and policies within religious institutions.

Understanding Cultural and Historical Contexts

Engaging with religious scholars requires a deep understanding of the cultural and historical contexts in which interpretations of Islam have developed. By appreciating the diversity of interpretations across different times and regions, Manji creates opportunities for scholars to challenge rigid interpretations and consider alternative perspectives that are more inclusive of LGBTQ individuals.

Promoting Resources and Education

Engaging with religious scholars involves providing resources and educational materials that promote a better understanding of LGBTQ issues within Islam. Manji works to create toolkits, books, and online resources that scholars can access to deepen their knowledge of LGBTQ rights and engage in informed discussions. These resources serve as valuable references and tools for scholars seeking to broaden their understanding of the intersection of faith and queerness.

Examples and Case Studies

Engaging with religious scholars often involves sharing examples and case studies that highlight the challenges faced by LGBTQ Muslims. These examples can include personal stories, research findings, and real-life experiences that demonstrate the need for a more inclusive interpretation of Islam. By presenting concrete examples, Manji encourages scholars to confront the lived realities of queer Muslims and the urgency for change.

Challenges and Caveats

Engaging with religious scholars is not without its challenges and caveats. It requires patience, persistence, and the ability to navigate sensitive topics without causing division or animosity. It is essential to approach these conversations with humility, acknowledging that change takes time and may not happen immediately. Additionally, not all religious scholars may be open to dialogue or receptive to LGBTQ rights; thus, it is crucial to focus efforts on those willing to engage in constructive discussions.

The Power of Engaging with Religious Scholars

Engaging with religious scholars holds the power to promote change from within religious communities. By challenging outdated interpretations and fostering dialogue, activists like Manji work towards a more inclusive and accepting understanding of Islam. These efforts contribute to the creation of LGBTQ-affirming spaces and a reformation within the faith that aligns with the values of compassion, justice, and equality.

In conclusion, engaging with religious scholars is an essential component of Irshad Manji's activism. By fostering dialogue, promoting critical thinking, and challenging misinterpretations, she aims to create a more inclusive and understanding religious space for LGBTQ Muslims. Through respectful engagement, personal narratives, and an emphasis on shared values, Manji inspires scholars to reconsider their positions and work towards an interpretation of Islam that embraces LGBTQ individuals.

The Importance of Inclusivity in Islam

Inclusivity is a fundamental aspect of Islam, promoting compassion, understanding, and equality among believers. It is essential to recognize that the teachings of Islam embrace diversity and emphasize the importance of inclusivity for all individuals, regardless of their sexual orientation or gender identity. In this subsection, we will explore why inclusivity is crucial in Islam and how it contributes to building a more harmonious and accepting society.

Promoting Compassion and Understanding

One of the core principles of Islam is the promotion of compassion and understanding towards fellow human beings. The Qur'an teaches Muslims to be kind, just, and compassionate to all people, regardless of their background or identity. Inclusivity in Islam means acknowledging and respecting the inherent worth and dignity of all individuals, including LGBTQ members of the community.

By embracing inclusivity, Muslims can foster an environment of empathy, where everyone feels valued and accepted. This promotes a sense of unity and encourages the development of genuine relationships and understanding between diverse individuals. Inclusivity helps Muslims fulfill their duty to treat others with kindness, as stated in the Qur'an: "And We have certainly honored the children of Adam and carried them on the land and sea and provided for them of the good things and preferred them over much of what We have created" (Qur'an 17:70).

Challenging Societal Stigma

In many societies, including some Muslim-majority countries, societal stigma and discrimination against LGBTQ individuals persist. However, it is crucial to recognize that these prejudices are not inherent to Islam itself. Rather, they arise from cultural, historical, and societal factors that have been conflated with religious teachings.

By embracing inclusivity in Islam, Muslims can challenge and rectify these misconceptions, dismantling the barriers that prevent LGBTQ individuals from fully participating in religious and community life. Inclusive practices and attitudes affirm the rights and dignity of all individuals, regardless of their sexual orientation or gender identity, empowering them to be equal participants in society.

Recognizing the Diversity of Human Experience

Islam recognizes the inherent diversity of the human experience and emphasizes the importance of unity within this diversity. The concept of inclusivity in Islam encourages Muslims to embrace and appreciate the diversity of sexual orientations, gender identities, and expressions within the community.

Inclusive practices and attitudes create room for individuals to authentically express their identities and be fully included in religious worship, social gatherings, and community activities. By recognizing and valuing the unique experiences of LGBTQ Muslims, Islamic communities can foster a sense of belonging, where everyone can fully participate without fear of judgment or exclusion.

Addressing Misinterpretations and Providing Education

Unfortunately, misinterpretations of religious texts have contributed to the marginalization of LGBTQ individuals in Muslim communities. However, it is essential to remember that interpretations of religious texts are subject to human biases and limitations. Embracing inclusivity requires Muslims to engage in critical thinking, reexamine traditional interpretations, and challenge harmful narratives that perpetuate discrimination.

Education plays a vital role in addressing misinterpretations and fostering inclusivity. By providing resources, hosting workshops, and engaging in open dialogue, Islamic scholars and leaders can help Muslims understand the diverse interpretations of religious texts and promote a more inclusive understanding of Islam. Education empowers Muslims to challenge existing biases, foster empathy, and create a safe space for LGBTQ individuals within the Muslim community.

Reconciliation of Faith and Queerness

For LGBTQ Muslims, reconciling their faith with their sexual orientation or gender identity can be a complex and deeply personal journey. Inclusivity in Islam means supporting individuals on this journey, affirming their identities, and providing spiritual guidance that embraces their whole selves.

By fostering inclusivity, Islamic communities can create opportunities for LGBTQ Muslims to explore their faith on their terms, engaging in meaningful dialogue, and seeking spiritual guidance without fear of rejection. This inclusive approach acknowledges that faith and queerness are not mutually exclusive, providing a holistic foundation for LGBTQ Muslims to have a strong sense of belonging in their religious community.

Conclusion

Inclusivity is not only compatible with Islam, but it is also a vital aspect of the religion. Embracing inclusivity promotes compassion, challenges societal stigma, recognizes the diversity of human experience, addresses misinterpretations, and reconciles faith with queerness. It allows Muslims to uphold principles of justice, equality, and empathy, creating a more harmonious, accepting, and loving community. By truly embracing inclusivity in Islam, Muslims can foster an environment where all individuals, regardless of their sexual orientation and gender identity, can thrive and experience a sense of belonging within their religious community.

Revisiting Sacred Texts

Revisiting sacred texts is a crucial aspect of the ongoing discussions surrounding LGBTQ rights within Islam. It involves reevaluating traditional interpretations of religious texts and exploring alternative interpretations that are more inclusive and affirming of queer individuals. This process of reinterpretation allows for a deeper understanding of the relationship between faith and sexuality, opening up new possibilities for acceptance and equality.

Understanding Traditional Interpretations

Traditional interpretations of sacred texts, such as the Quran and Hadiths, have often been interpreted in ways that condemn same-sex relationships and non-conforming gender identities. These interpretations have led to the marginalization and discrimination of LGBTQ individuals within Muslim communities.

However, it is important to note that these interpretations are not fixed or universally agreed upon. They are subject to historical and cultural contexts, as well as the biases of interpreters. Revisiting sacred texts requires acknowledging the multifaceted nature of their interpretations and examining the underlying assumptions and perspectives that have shaped these interpretations.

Exploring Alternative Interpretations

Revisiting sacred texts involves engaging with alternative interpretations that challenge the traditional understanding of LGBTQ issues. These alternative interpretations take into account the principles of justice, compassion, and inclusivity, which are central to Islamic teachings. By examining the broader message of the Quran and exploring different scholarly opinions, new perspectives emerge that promote acceptance and understanding of queer individuals.

For example, some scholars argue that the Quranic verses that are often used to condemn homosexuality can be interpreted in a more nuanced manner. They suggest that these verses should be understood within their historical and cultural context, taking into consideration the specific societal practices that were being addressed, such as exploitative forms of same-sex relationships or non-consensual acts.

Unconventional Approaches

In the journey of revisiting sacred texts, creativity and unconventional approaches can play a significant role. One such approach involves exploring the concept of ijtihad, which refers to independent reasoning and interpretation. This allows room for scholars to apply their critical thinking skills and develop new understandings of religious texts, particularly when it comes to issues that were not explicitly addressed during the time of revelation.

Additionally, drawing on the principles of maqasid al-shariah, which refers to the objectives or higher purposes of Islamic law, provides a framework for reevaluating interpretations of sacred texts. By focusing on the overarching goals of justice, equity, and human welfare, one can argue for more inclusive readings of religious texts that affirm the rights and dignity of LGBTQ individuals.

Examples of Reinterpretation

There are numerous examples of scholars and activists who have engaged in the process of revisiting sacred texts to foster inclusivity and acceptance of LGBTQ individuals. For instance, Scott Kugle, a professor of South Asian and Islamic studies, has developed an interpretation of Islamic texts that supports the existence of same-sex relationships and advocates for their acceptance within Muslim communities.

Another example is the work of the inclusive mosque movement, which seeks to create spaces that are welcoming to individuals of all sexual orientations and gender identities. These mosques challenge traditional interpretations through their practices and teachings, emphasizing the need for empathy, understanding, and support for LGBTQ Muslims.

Resources and Tools for Reinterpretation

In the journey of revisiting sacred texts, it is essential to have access to resources and tools that facilitate a deeper understanding of the texts and their interpretations. This includes translations of the Quran, as well as commentaries and works by scholars who have explored alternative approaches to LGBTQ issues within Islam.

Online platforms, such as the Muslim Alliance for Sexual and Gender Diversity, provide a wealth of resources, including articles, books, and educational materials, that assist individuals in navigating the process of reinterpretation. These resources not only support individuals in their personal journeys but also serve as valuable tools for creating dialogue and promoting greater understanding within Muslim communities.

Challenges and Controversies

Revisiting sacred texts and engaging in alternative interpretations is not without its challenges and controversies. Such efforts can be met with resistance from conservative religious authorities, who may view any departure from traditional interpretations as a threat to religious orthodoxy.

There is also the challenge of balancing the need for reinterpretation with respect for religious traditions and the rights of those who hold conservative beliefs. It is important to foster dialogue and engagement that is respectful and empathetic, recognizing that change takes time and requires a multipronged approach that includes education, advocacy, and respectful engagement with religious scholars and communities.

Conclusion

Revisiting sacred texts is a critical step in the process of promoting LGBTQ rights within Islam. By challenging traditional interpretations and engaging with alternative perspectives, it is possible to foster a more inclusive and accepting understanding of LGBTQ individuals within Muslim communities. This process requires creativity, critical thinking, and a commitment to justice and compassion. It is through the reevaluation of sacred texts that the path to reconciling faith and sexuality becomes clearer, paving the way for a more inclusive and equal future.

Pushing for Progressive Change

In this subsection, we explore the proactive efforts made by Irshad Manji to bring about progressive change within the Muslim community and beyond. Manji's unwavering commitment to challenging regressive interpretations of Islam and advocating for LGBTQ rights has had a significant impact on promoting acceptance and inclusivity. Let's delve into the strategies she employed and the influence she exerted in pushing for progressive change.

One of the key ways in which Manji pushed for progressive change was through education and raising awareness. She recognized the power of knowledge and aimed to dismantle misconceptions and stereotypes about LGBTQ individuals within the Muslim community. Manji addressed these issues by conducting workshops, leading training sessions, and speaking at universities and conferences. By engaging with diverse audiences and sharing personal stories, she fostered understanding and empathy, fighting against prejudice and discrimination.

To further her cause, Manji collaborated with LGBTQ organizations and forged alliances with individuals and groups sympathetic to her goals. This strategic approach allowed her to amplify her voice and extend her reach beyond traditional platforms. By building bridges with like-minded influencers, Manji expanded the conversation on LGBTQ rights and challenged conservative interpretations of Islam.

Manji also played a pivotal role in engaging with religious scholars and challenging discriminatory beliefs within Muslim communities. She encouraged critical thinking and provided alternative interpretations of sacred texts that upheld LGBTQ rights. Through dialogue and open-mindedness, Manji facilitated conversations that pushed the boundaries of religious traditions and paved the way for more inclusive interpretations.

Advocacy and lobbying efforts were a central part of Manji's strategy to effect change at the policy level. She actively campaigned for LGBTQ rights and sought collaborations with human rights organizations. By influencing decision-makers and policymakers, Manji aimed to bring about legislative reforms that protected LGBTQ individuals from discrimination. Her tireless efforts expanded the conversation on LGBTQ rights globally and contributed to the advancement of equality.

Manji's work in pushing for progressive change extended beyond advocating for LGBTQ rights. She recognized the intersections of various social justice issues and actively contributed to conversations on gender equality, racial justice, and religious tolerance. Through her activism, she challenged discriminatory practices and fostered collaborations across different communities.

To sustain the momentum of the LGBTQ rights movement, Manji focused on empowering the next generation of activists. She mentored LGBTQ youth, empowered queer Muslims, and supported youth-led initiatives. Recognizing the power of mentorship and leadership development, she cultivated young voices, ensuring a legacy of continuing progress and advocacy.

In pushing for progressive change, Irshad Manji exemplified the limitless possibilities that arise from questioning traditional interpretations and championing inclusivity and acceptance. Her efforts to redefine faith and identity, engage in dialogue and education, and impact policies and legislation propelled the LGBTQ rights movement forward. Manji's inspiring journey reminds us of the importance of challenging societal norms, reimagining faith practices, and advocating for marginalized communities.

The Global Impact of Reformation

Religion has long played a significant role in shaping societies and individuals' lives, and within the scope of LGBTQ activism, the impact of religious reformation cannot be overstated. In this subsection, we will explore the global impact of the reformation within Islam and its profound implications for LGBTQ rights and acceptance. We will delve into the key principles and strategies driving this movement, the challenges it faces, and the potential it holds for creating a more inclusive and equitable world for LGBTQ individuals.

Evolution and Intellectual Rigor

One of the fundamental aspects of reformation within any religion is an evolution in the understanding of sacred texts and theological interpretations. Reformation endeavors intend to foster open dialogue and critical thinking, questioning established norms and beliefs that perpetuate discrimination and bigotry.

Within Islam, this intellectual rigor involves engaging with religious scholars, academics, and community leaders to deconstruct traditional interpretations that condemn homosexuality. Scholars who challenge the status quo emphasize the importance of revisiting sacred texts in their historical and cultural contexts, considering the evolution of human knowledge, and embracing a more compassionate and inclusive understanding of Islam.

Promoting Inclusivity and Equality

The reformation within Islam seeks to challenge and dismantle patriarchal structures and attitudes that perpetuate discrimination against LGBTQ individuals. It encourages initiatives that actively advocate for LGBTQ rights and facilitate acceptance within Muslim communities.

Education plays a pivotal role in this process. The movement emphasizes the need for inclusive curriculum in Islamic educational institutions and mosques, which promotes understanding, empathy, and acceptance of diverse sexual orientations and gender identities. By engaging with religious leaders, educators, and parents, the reformation movement addresses the misconceptions surrounding LGBTQ issues and highlights the essence of compassion and justice within Islamic teachings.

Interfaith Engagement and Global Solidarity

The impact of religious reformation within Islam extends beyond the boundaries of the Muslim community. Engaging in interfaith dialogue and collaboration allows for the establishment of common ground and provides an opportunity to build alliances with other faith-based movements advocating for LGBTQ rights.

Solidarity among diverse religious communities amplifies the voices calling for social justice and equality. By sharing experiences, challenging homophobia, and advocating for LGBTQ rights collectively, the reformation movement strengthens the global fight against discrimination and fosters a more inclusive and accepting world.

Addressing Cultural Sensitivities

The reformation within Islam faces unique challenges due to the diverse cultural contexts in which Muslims reside. While theological arguments are essential, addressing these cultural sensitivities is equally crucial to ensure progress toward LGBTQ acceptance.

Culturally sensitive strategies include framing LGBTQ rights and inclusion within Islamic values and narratives, using local examples and stories that resonate with the specific cultural backgrounds of Muslim communities. It also involves engaging with cultural influencers, artists, and media personalities to promote positive representations of LGBTQ individuals within their respective societies.

Empowering the Vulnerable and Marginalized

Reformation within Islam recognizes the various intersecting identities that individuals embody and advocates for the empowerment of those who face multiple forms of discrimination and marginalization. This includes addressing the challenges faced by LGBTQ Muslims who are also racial or ethnic minorities, immigrants, refugees, or living in countries where LGBTQ rights are suppressed.

By centering the experiences and voices of the most vulnerable, the reformation movement aims to create a more equitable and inclusive society. It prioritizes initiatives that provide resources, support, and safe spaces for LGBTQ Muslims, enabling them to live authentically and thrive in their faith communities.

The Need for Continued Advocacy

Despite significant progress made through the reformation movement within Islam, the journey towards full LGBTQ acceptance is far from over. It requires continuous advocacy, both within Muslim communities and in collaboration with other LGBTQ movements worldwide.

The reformation movement must navigate complex political landscapes, cultural resistances, and deep-rooted prejudices. To sustain its momentum and effect lasting change, it must adapt to emerging challenges, engage with policymakers, and push for legislative reforms that protect LGBTQ rights globally.

Unconventional yet Relevant: Queer Theology

An unconventional yet relevant aspect of the reformation movement within Islam is the emergence of queer theology. Queer theology offers a critical examination of religious texts and traditions from LGBTQ perspectives, challenging heteronormative and cisnormative interpretations.

This interdisciplinary field draws from various academic disciplines, including religious studies, queer theory, and gender studies, to explore the intersections between faith, sexuality, and gender identity. It strives to reconcile LGBTQ experiences with religious teachings and traditions, fostering a deeper understanding and recognition of LGBTQ individuals' spiritual journeys.

Conclusion

The global impact of reformation within Islam is immense, offering hope and possibilities for LGBTQ Muslims worldwide. Through intellectual rigor, promotion of inclusivity and equality, interfaith engagement, cultural sensitivity, empowerment of the marginalized, and continued advocacy, the reformation movement aims to challenge discriminatory beliefs and create a more welcoming and accepting environment within Muslim communities.

It is essential to recognize that the journey towards full LGBTQ acceptance is ongoing. By taking unconventional yet relevant approaches, such as queer theology, and fostering global solidarity, the reformation within Islam contributes to the broader LGBTQ rights movement, shaping a future where all individuals can live authentically and flourish, regardless of their sexual orientation or gender identity.

Engaging in Dialogue and Education

Speaking at Universities and Conferences

Speaking at universities and conferences is a crucial aspect of Irshad Manji's activism, allowing her to engage with diverse audiences and share her experiences and insights. It provides a platform to spread awareness, challenge stereotypes, and encourage meaningful conversations about the intersection of LGBTQ rights and Islam. In this subsection, we will explore the importance of speaking at universities and conferences and highlight the strategies that Irshad Manji employs to engage her audience effectively.

The Significance of Universities and Conferences

Universities and conferences serve as hubs of knowledge and ideas, attracting individuals from different backgrounds and disciplines. They provide an environment conducive to critical thinking, where attendees are open to new perspectives and eager to engage in meaningful discussions. By speaking at universities and conferences, Irshad Manji can reach a wide range of individuals, including students, academics, and professionals, all of whom play a vital role in shaping society's attitudes and policies.

Furthermore, universities and conferences often host panels, workshops, and discussions on social justice issues, making them ideal platforms to address the challenges faced by LGBTQ Muslims. These events provide opportunities for networking and collaboration, allowing activists like Irshad Manji to share experiences and learn from others who are working towards similar goals.

Engaging the Audience

To ensure her message resonates with the audience, Irshad Manji employs various strategies when speaking at universities and conferences. Firstly, she emphasizes the power of storytelling. By sharing her personal journey as a queer Muslim activist, she captivates the audience and helps them relate to her experiences on a human level. This approach fosters empathy and encourages individuals to question their preconceived notions.

Secondly, Irshad Manji uses interactive methods to engage the audience actively. For instance, she incorporates thought-provoking discussion questions, group activities, and Q&A sessions during her talks. This participatory approach encourages attendees to reflect on their own beliefs and challenge societal norms, creating an open dialogue that fosters learning and growth.

Addressing Key Issues

When speaking at universities and conferences, Irshad Manji addresses key issues that impact LGBTQ Muslims. She discusses the importance of religious acceptance and inclusivity, highlighting the need for reform within Islamic communities. By navigating the complex intersection of sexual identity, faith, and culture, she encourages individuals to critically evaluate their beliefs and challenge oppressive traditions.

Moreover, Irshad Manji sheds light on the challenges faced by LGBTQ Muslim youth, who may feel caught between their sexual orientation and religious identity. She explores the impact of societal stigma, emphasizing the need for safe spaces and support systems within educational institutions. Her talks provide solace and guidance to individuals struggling with their identity, empowering them to embrace their authentic selves.

Resources and Toolkits

In addition to her speaking engagements, Irshad Manji develops resources and toolkits to support universities and conferences in fostering LGBTQ inclusivity. These resources provide valuable information on LGBTQ rights, intersectionality, and strategies for creating safe and supportive environments. By providing tangible resources, Irshad Manji enables educational institutions to take concrete steps towards promoting inclusion and dismantling discriminatory practices.

An Unconventional Approach

To engage the audience in a thought-provoking manner, Irshad Manji occasionally employs unconventional approaches during her talks. For example, she uses humor to challenge stereotypes and break down barriers. By infusing her speeches with wit and light-heartedness, she captures the attention of the audience and creates a welcoming atmosphere, conducive to productive discussions.

Furthermore, Irshad Manji shares real-world examples and case studies, illustrating the diverse experiences of LGBTQ Muslims globally. These stories humanize the issues at hand, making them relatable and showcasing the richness and diversity within LGBTQ Muslim communities.

Exercises: Fostering Inclusive Spaces

To promote active engagement and reflection among the audience, here are some exercises that can be incorporated into Irshad Manji's speaking engagements at universities and conferences:

1. Divide the audience into small groups and assign each group a specific scenario related to LGBTQ Muslim inclusion. Ask them to brainstorm strategies and solutions to address the challenges presented in the scenario. Afterwards, facilitate a group discussion to share their ideas and insights.

2. Conduct a "myth-busting" activity where participants write down common misconceptions about LGBTQ Muslims. Collect the responses and address each myth, providing accurate information and debunking stereotypes. Encourage participants to ask questions and engage in dialogue to deepen their understanding.

3. Use storytelling as a tool for empathy-building. Have individuals in the audience share personal narratives or stories of LGBTQ Muslims they

know. This exercise helps create empathy and humanizes the experiences of LGBTQ Muslims, fostering a greater understanding of their challenges.

By incorporating these exercises, Irshad Manji encourages audience members to actively participate, reflect on their beliefs, and challenge societal norms, fostering a more inclusive and empathetic environment.

Conclusion

Speaking at universities and conferences allows Irshad Manji to engage with a diverse audience, challenge stereotypes, and encourage dialogue surrounding LGBTQ rights and Islam. By employing various strategies, engaging the audience, and addressing key issues, she creates spaces for reflection, learning, and transformation. Through her unconventional approach and resource development, she supports educational institutions in creating inclusive environments for LGBTQ Muslims. With her inspiring words and thought-provoking exercises, Irshad Manji paves the way for a more compassionate and accepting future.

Leading Workshops and Training Sessions

Leading workshops and training sessions plays a crucial role in empowering individuals and fostering inclusivity within the LGBTQ community. Irshad Manji, as a renowned LGBTQ activist, understands the significance of creating safe spaces for learning, growth, and support. In this subsection, we delve into the principles, strategies, and impact of leading workshops and training sessions.

The Importance of Workshop Facilitation

Workshop facilitation is an art that requires both knowledge and skills to effectively engage participants and create a transformative learning experience. As a workshop leader, Irshad Manji understands the importance of setting the right tone, establishing an inclusive environment, and enabling meaningful discussions. Here are some key principles of workshop facilitation:

1. **Creating a Safe Space:** Facilitators must establish an atmosphere of trust and respect where participants feel comfortable sharing their experiences, thoughts, and emotions. Emphasizing confidentiality and ensuring confidentiality can foster an environment conducive to open dialogue.

2. **Setting Clear Objectives:** Workshops should have specific goals and outcomes. Clearly articulating these objectives helps participants understand what

they can expect from the session and keeps the facilitator focused on delivering key messages.

3. **Interactive and Participatory Approach:** Engaging participants through interactive activities, group discussions, and experiential exercises enhances their learning experience. Facilitators should encourage active participation to promote knowledge exchange, critical thinking, and personal reflection.

4. **Cultivating Inclusivity:** Workshop facilitators should ensure that all participants, regardless of their background or identities, feel valued and included. By being mindful of the language used, facilitating respectful discussions, and challenging discriminatory behavior, facilitators can create a space that embraces diversity.

Designing Effective Workshop Content

Effective workshop content is crucial for engaging participants, promoting learning, and driving positive change. Irshad Manji incorporates various elements into her workshops to create an impactful experience for participants. Here are some key components to consider when designing workshop content:

1. **Educational Materials:** Workshop sessions often include educational materials such as handouts, slides, or multimedia presentations. These resources can provide participants with foundational knowledge, relevant case studies, and resources for further exploration.

2. **Sharing Personal Stories:** Personal stories have a profound impact on individuals, fostering empathy and understanding. Irshad Manji shares her own experiences as a Queer Muslim activist, inspiring participants to reflect on their own identities and journeys.

3. **Group Activities:** Engaging participants in group activities promotes collaboration, builds connection, and offers practical opportunities for participants to apply the concepts they've learned. These activities may include role-playing, problem-solving tasks, or interactive exercises.

4. **Guest Speakers and Panel Discussions:** Inviting guest speakers or organizing panel discussions allows participants to hear diverse perspectives and engage with experts in the field. This helps broaden their understanding and challenges preconceived notions.

5. **Skill-Building Exercises:** Workshops often include skill-building exercises to enhance participants' abilities to advocate for LGBTQ rights and foster inclusive spaces. These exercises may focus on active listening, conflict resolution, or effective communication.

Addressing Challenges and Ensuring Participant Growth

Leading workshops and training sessions may present challenges that require careful consideration and proactive strategies. Irshad Manji acknowledges these challenges and offers solutions to ensure participant growth and engagement. Here are some common challenges facilitators may encounter and ways to address them:

1. **Resistance or Opposition:** Some participants may hold discriminatory beliefs or be resistant to change. Facilitators can address this by creating a safe environment, using evidence-based arguments, and encouraging open dialogue.

2. **Overcoming Fear and Shame:** Participants might feel hesitant to share their personal experiences due to fear or shame. Facilitators can alleviate these concerns by sharing their own vulnerability and demonstrating empathy, thereby creating a supportive environment.

3. **Dealing with Emotional Reactions:** Workshops may bring forth intense emotions from participants. Facilitators should be trained to handle emotional reactions and provide appropriate support resources, such as mental health professionals or support groups.

4. **Lack of Diversity in Workshops:** Facilitators should actively work towards creating diverse and inclusive spaces. This can be achieved by intentionally reaching out to underrepresented communities and collaborating with local LGBTQ organizations.

Unconventional Approach: The Power of Storytelling and Creativity

An unconventional yet powerful approach in workshop facilitation is utilizing the power of storytelling and creativity. Irshad Manji encourages participants to embrace their authentic selves by sharing personal narratives and utilizing creative mediums. Here are some innovative strategies to consider:

1. **Story Circles:** Participants gather in small groups and share personal stories related to their LGBTQ experiences, faith, and activism. This promotes a sense of community, empathy, and empowerment.

2. **Artistic Expression:** Facilitators can incorporate art-based activities, such as painting, writing, or poetry, to encourage participants to express their feelings and experiences through creative outlets. This allows for catharsis and promotes self-discovery.

3. **Using Technology:** Integrating technology, such as multimedia storytelling platforms or virtual reality, can offer unique opportunities for participants to share their stories and amplify their voices on a global scale.

Remember, leading workshops and training sessions is an ongoing learning process. Facilitators should continuously seek feedback, reflect on their practice, and adapt their approach to ensure the best possible experience and outcomes for participants. By embracing diversity, fostering inclusivity, and empowering individuals, workshops can be powerful tools for change within the LGBTQ community and beyond.

Collaboration with LGBTQ Organizations

In this subsection, we will explore the importance of collaboration between LGBTQ activists and organizations. Collaboration plays a vital role in advancing the rights and well-being of the LGBTQ community. By joining forces and leveraging the strengths of different organizations, activists can create a powerful collective voice that is better equipped to tackle the complex challenges faced by LGBTQ individuals around the world.

The Power of Collaboration

Collaboration with LGBTQ organizations enables activists to pool their resources, share expertise, and maximize their impact. By working together, organizations can leverage their unique strengths to create a more comprehensive and effective approach to advocating for LGBTQ rights.

One benefit of collaboration is the ability to amplify messages and increase visibility. When multiple organizations come together, they can collectively raise awareness about LGBTQ issues and attract a wider audience. This collaborative effort ensures that important messages reach a broader range of people, leading to greater understanding and support.

Furthermore, collaboration allows activists to tap into a wider network of connections. By partnering with LGBTQ organizations, activists gain access to existing networks and communities, which can help promote their cause and mobilize supporters. These connections can also facilitate knowledge sharing and the exchange of best practices, enabling activists to learn from each other and enhance their strategies.

Challenges and Solutions

While collaboration offers numerous benefits, it also comes with its own set of challenges. One common challenge is coordinating and aligning the goals and priorities of multiple organizations. Each organization may have its own focus areas and strategies, making it essential to find common ground and establish shared objectives. Effective communication and open dialogue are key to ensure that all parties are working towards a collective vision.

Another challenge is managing conflicts and differences of opinion that may arise during collaborative efforts. Disagreements over strategy, messaging, or decision-making can hinder progress and create divisions within the coalition. It is crucial to foster an environment of respect, diversity, and inclusivity, allowing for constructive discussions and finding compromise when necessary.

To overcome these challenges, organizations can establish clear guidelines and structures for collaboration. This may involve developing shared values and principles, establishing decision-making processes, and setting up mechanisms for addressing conflicts. Regular communication and evaluation of the collaboration can also help identify and address issues in a timely manner.

Examples of Successful Collaborations

Collaboration between LGBTQ organizations has led to significant progress in advancing LGBTQ rights worldwide. Here are some inspiring examples:

1. The Global Equality Caucus: This international network of parliamentarians, supported by the LGBTQ organization Equality Rights Group, advocates for LGBTQ rights on a global scale. By collaborating with organizations, the caucus has been able to mobilize lawmakers and drive legislative change in support of LGBTQ rights.

2. The Pride Fund: This initiative, established by several LGBTQ justice organizations, provides financial support to local LGBTQ organizations and initiatives. By pooling resources and funding, the Pride Fund strengthens grassroots movements and empowers local communities to effect change.

3. The LGBTQ+ Peace Coalition: This coalition brings together LGBTQ organizations and peacebuilding organizations to address the unique challenges faced by LGBTQ individuals in conflict-affected areas. By combining their expertise, these organizations work towards promoting peace, reconciliation, and equality for LGBTQ communities in regions affected by conflict.

These examples demonstrate the power of collaboration in making a tangible impact on LGBTQ rights. By working together, organizations can achieve more significant advancements in policy changes, legal protections, and societal acceptance.

Unconventional Approach: Guerrilla Activism

Guerrilla activism is an unconventional approach that challenges societal norms and engages the public in unexpected ways. This form of activism relies on surprise, creativity, and disruption to raise awareness and create change. Collaborating with LGBTQ organizations can support guerrilla activists by providing resources, expertise, and a wider platform to amplify their message.

For example, LGBTQ organizations can collaborate with guerrilla activists to plan and execute impactful actions, such as flash mobs, public art installations, or performances. By combining their skills and knowledge, these collaborations can generate significant media attention, spark conversations, and challenge societal norms related to LGBTQ issues.

However, it's important to note that guerrilla activism should be approached with caution, ensuring that it is respectful, safe, and aligned with the goals and values of LGBTQ organizations. Collaboration in these cases plays a crucial role in guiding and supporting guerrilla activists to ensure their actions have a positive and lasting impact.

Resources and Support

Collaboration with LGBTQ organizations offers access to valuable resources and support networks. These organizations often provide a range of services, including legal aid, counselling, advocacy training, and community engagement programs. By partnering with LGBTQ organizations, activists can tap into these resources to strengthen their advocacy efforts and support the LGBTQ community.

In addition, LGBTQ organizations offer opportunities for networking and building relationships with like-minded individuals. These connections can lead to mentorship, collaboration on projects, and the exchange of ideas, further enhancing the effectiveness of activism.

Exercises

1. Research and identify three LGBTQ organizations in your country or region. Explore their mission, activities, and initiatives. Identify potential areas of collaboration that could further advance LGBTQ rights in your community.

2. Imagine you are a grassroots LGBTQ activist seeking to collaborate with an established LGBTQ organization. Develop a proposal outlining the benefits of collaboration, the areas in which you could contribute, and the potential impact of the collaboration on advancing LGBTQ rights.

3. Reflect on the challenges and benefits of collaboration with LGBTQ organizations. Write a brief essay discussing how collaboration can enhance the effectiveness of LGBTQ activism and overcome common obstacles faced by individual activists.

Key Takeaways

- Collaboration with LGBTQ organizations allows activists to pool resources and expertise, amplifying their impact on LGBTQ rights. - Effective communication and alignment of goals are crucial for successful collaboration. - Examples of successful collaborations include global advocacy networks, grassroots funding initiatives, and peacebuilding coalitions. - Collaboration can also support unconventional forms of activism, such as guerrilla activism, when approached in a respectful and safe manner. - LGBTQ organizations provide valuable resources, support networks, and opportunities for networking and mentorship. - Exercises provide opportunities to explore collaboration with LGBTQ organizations, reflect on the challenges and benefits, and develop proposals for collaboration.

Advocacy Through Social Media

In today's digital age, social media has become a powerful tool for activism. It offers a platform for individuals and organizations to communicate, engage, and mobilize communities on a global scale. This subsection explores the ways in which Irshad Manji utilizes social media as a means of LGBTQ advocacy and the impact it has on promoting change and fostering inclusivity.

Harnessing the Power of Social Media

Social media platforms such as Twitter, Facebook, Instagram, and YouTube have revolutionized the way information is shared and consumed. Irshad Manji recognized early on the potential of these platforms in reaching audiences and sparking conversations about LGBTQ rights and inclusion. By leveraging the power of social media, she has been able to amplify her message and connect with individuals and organizations worldwide.

Through engaging posts, thought-provoking tweets, and visually captivating images, Manji creates content that resonates with her diverse audience. She understands the importance of crafting messages that are relatable, informative, and shareable to maximize their impact. By using concise and compelling language, she captures people's attention and encourages them to take part in the dialogue surrounding LGBTQ issues.

Building Online Communities

One of the most significant advantages of social media is its ability to unite people and create online communities centered around a shared cause or interest. Irshad Manji uses various social media platforms to build and nurture communities of LGBTQ individuals, allies, and activists.

These communities provide a safe space for individuals to share their experiences, seek support, and engage in meaningful discussions. Manji fosters an environment where people can connect with one another, exchange ideas, and find solace in their shared struggles and triumphs. By cultivating these communities, she empowers individuals to find their voice and stand up for their rights.

Engaging in Conversation and Education

Social media has fundamentally changed the way we communicate and learn. It offers an accessible and inclusive platform for discussions on a range of topics, including LGBTQ rights and acceptance. Irshad Manji harnesses social media's potential to engage in conversations and educate her audience.

She uses her platforms to facilitate dialogue by asking thoughtful questions, sharing personal stories, and highlighting the experiences of marginalized communities. Through live streams, webinars, and Q&A sessions, she encourages open and honest discussions about the intersection of faith, sexuality, and gender identity. Manji's approach to advocacy through social media focuses on fostering empathy, promoting understanding, and challenging preconceived notions.

Amplifying Diverse Perspectives

One of the core strengths of social media is its ability to amplify diverse voices and perspectives. Irshad Manji leverages her platform to highlight the stories and experiences of LGBTQ individuals from various backgrounds and cultures.

Through guest posts, interviews, and collaborations, she gives a voice to those who are often overlooked or marginalized. By amplifying these diverse perspectives, Manji broadens the understanding of LGBTQ issues and promotes inclusivity within the broader societal discourse.

Creating Call-to-Action Campaigns

Social media platforms offer a unique opportunity to mobilize individuals and generate real-world action. Irshad Manji consistently uses her online presence to launch call-to-action campaigns that inspire her followers to take part in advocacy efforts.

These campaigns may involve signing petitions, supporting LGBTQ-friendly legislation, attending rallies, volunteering, or donating to relevant organizations. By providing clear instructions and resources, Manji empowers her followers to become active participants in creating change. Through the power of social media, she has mobilized thousands of individuals to rally behind important causes.

The Power of Authenticity

In a world of carefully curated online personas, authenticity stands out. Irshad Manji's approach to social media advocacy revolves around being genuine and unapologetically herself. By being authentic and vulnerable in sharing her own journey and struggles, she creates a space for others to do the same.

Authenticity fosters trust, facilitates meaningful connections, and makes the advocacy message more relatable and impactful. Manji's commitment to being true to herself serves as an inspiration for others to embrace their identities and share their stories on their own terms.

Conclusion

Social media has transformed the landscape of LGBTQ activism, creating unprecedented opportunities for individuals like Irshad Manji to advocate and drive change. Through harnessing the power of social media, Manji builds communities, engages in conversations, amplifies diverse perspectives, and mobilizes action. By leveraging the authenticity of these platforms, she empowers individuals to find their voice, challenge societal norms, and foster inclusivity on a global scale.

As technology continues to advance, it is essential for activists to adapt and utilize social media tools effectively. By leveraging these platforms strategically, future LGBTQ advocates can continue to promote dialogue, generate empathy, and push for greater equality and acceptance. The power of social media lies in its ability to connect people, amplify voices, and inspire collective action, and the potential for change is limitless.

Promoting LGBTQ+ Inclusion in Mosques

Mosques are not only places of worship for Muslims, but also community centers where individuals seek guidance, support, and a sense of belonging. It is essential to promote LGBTQ+ inclusion within these spaces, creating a more welcoming and inclusive environment for all individuals, regardless of their sexual orientation or gender identity. In this subsection, we will explore the importance of LGBTQ+ inclusion in mosques, discuss the challenges faced, and provide strategies to foster acceptance and understanding.

Understanding the Need for LGBTQ+ Inclusion

Recognizing the need for LGBTQ+ inclusion in mosques requires an understanding of the experiences faced by LGBTQ+ individuals within Islamic communities. Historically, many Muslim societies have been less accepting of homosexuality and transgender identities, basing their beliefs on conservative interpretations of religious texts. Consequently, LGBTQ+ Muslims often face ostracism, discrimination, and even violence within their own communities.

Considering the significant role mosques play in the lives of Muslims, it is crucial to promote inclusion and acceptance for all individuals, including those who identify as LGBTQ+. By doing so, mosques can become safe spaces where LGBTQ+ Muslims can practice their faith authentically and without fear of judgment or exclusion.

Challenges and Solutions

Promoting LGBTQ+ inclusion in mosques presents several challenges, including deep-rooted cultural and religious beliefs, lack of understanding, and resistance to change. However, with empathetic dialogue and education, these challenges can be addressed effectively. Here are some strategies to overcome these barriers and foster a more inclusive environment:

1. **Education and Awareness:** Misunderstandings about LGBTQ+ identities often stem from a lack of knowledge. Mosques can take the initiative to provide educational resources, workshops, and guest speakers who can address common misconceptions and build empathy. By fostering understanding, mosques can bridge the gap between communities and promote acceptance.

2. **Opening Dialogues:** Creating spaces for open and respectful discussions is crucial for fostering LGBTQ+ inclusion in mosques. Mosques can organize panel discussions, community forums, or support groups for LGBTQ+ individuals and their allies to share their experiences and challenges. These dialogues allow for building connections and breaking down barriers.

3. **Inclusive Sermons and Khutbahs:** Friday sermons and khutbahs provide an opportunity for mosque leaders to address LGBTQ+ inclusion from an Islamic perspective, emphasizing the values of compassion, love, and acceptance. By incorporating inclusive messaging into religious teachings, mosques can promote a more supportive environment.

4. **Inclusive Policies and Practices:** Mosques can adopt inclusive policies that explicitly state their commitment to LGBTQ+ inclusion. These policies can address issues such as inclusive language, restroom facilities, and safe spaces within the mosque. By implementing these practices, mosques can send a clear message of acceptance and support to LGBTQ+ individuals.

5. **Supportive Imams and Religious Leaders:** Imams and religious leaders play a critical role in influencing the attitudes and behaviors of mosque attendees. Mosques should encourage their imams to engage in training programs or workshops that focus on LGBTQ+ issues, religious acceptance, and inclusive teachings. By equipping religious leaders with knowledge and empathy, mosques can promote positive change within their communities.

6. **Collaboration and Partnerships:** Mosques can collaborate with LGBTQ+ organizations and community groups to foster understanding and support. By building relationships and working together, mosques can demonstrate their commitment to inclusivity and create a broader network of support for LGBTQ+ individuals.

Case Study: Al-Fatiha Foundation

One organization that has played a significant role in promoting LGBTQ+ inclusion in mosques is the Al-Fatiha Foundation. Founded in 1997, Al-Fatiha provided LGBTQ+ Muslims with a platform to connect, share their experiences, and promote dialogue within Muslim communities.

The organization organized retreats, conferences, and support groups that created a safe space for LGBTQ+ Muslims. These initiatives allowed individuals to openly discuss their experiences, seek guidance from religious scholars, and build networks of support.

Through these efforts, the Al-Fatiha Foundation challenged the prevailing narrative and fostered a more inclusive environment within mosques and Islamic communities. While the organization closed its doors in 2011, its impact on LGBTQ+ inclusion in mosques continues to resonate.

Further Resources and Recommendations

Promoting LGBTQ+ inclusion in mosques requires ongoing education, dialogue, and engagement. Here are some additional resources and recommendations:

+ **Books:** "Queer Muslim Revolution" by Faisal Alam and "Radical Love: An Introduction to Queer Muslim Activism" by Junaid Jahangir offer valuable insights into the intersectionality of LGBTQ+ and Muslim identities.

+ **Online Platforms:** Organizations such as Muslims for Progressive Values (MPV), The Inner Circle, and the Inclusive Mosque Initiative provide resources, support, and community-building opportunities for LGBTQ+ Muslims.

+ **Training Programs:** Mosques can benefit from educational programs and workshops provided by organizations like Muslims for Progressive Values and the Human Rights Campaign Foundation. These programs offer guidance on fostering LGBTQ+ inclusion in Muslim communities.

+ **Community Engagement:** Mosques can engage with local LGBTQ+ organizations and activists to foster understanding, support, and collaboration. By participating in Pride events or initiatives, mosques can demonstrate their commitment to inclusivity.

Conclusion

Promoting LGBTQ+ inclusion in mosques is vital for creating a sense of belonging, acceptance, and support for LGBTQ+ Muslims. While the journey may pose challenges, it is essential to engage in open dialogue, education, and collaboration to foster a more inclusive environment. By embracing LGBTQ+ inclusion, mosques can play a significant role in fostering acceptance, understanding, and spiritual growth for all individuals, regardless of their sexual orientation or gender identity.

Remember, the fight for LGBTQ+ rights and inclusion is an ongoing process. By continuing to learn, support, and advocate, we can pave the way for a more inclusive future within mosques and Islamic communities.

The Power of Education in Breaking Barriers

Education has always been a powerful tool for societal change, and in the context of LGBTQ activism, it plays a crucial role in breaking down barriers and challenging stereotypes. In this section, we will explore how education can empower individuals, promote understanding, and foster acceptance, ultimately contributing to a more inclusive and egalitarian society.

Promoting LGBTQ+ Awareness and Acceptance

One of the primary goals of education in LGBTQ activism is to increase awareness and understanding of LGBTQ+ issues, identities, and experiences. By incorporating LGBTQ+ history, literature, and perspectives into curricula, educators can provide students with a broader and more accurate representation of the diversity of human experiences. This can help challenge harmful stereotypes, debunk myths, and dispel the ignorance that often underlies discrimination and prejudice.

Educational institutions can also provide comprehensive sexuality education that includes LGBTQ+ topics. This is essential because it helps foster a culture of acceptance, respect, and inclusion from an early age. By teaching students about different sexual orientations and gender identities, educators can cultivate an environment where all students feel seen, valued, and supported.

Example: One effective approach is to incorporate LGBTQ+ literature into English classes. By reading and analyzing works by LGBTQ+ authors, students can gain insights into their experiences and challenges. This not only expands students' cultural understanding but also helps them develop empathy and compassion.

Addressing Bullying and Discrimination

Education plays a crucial role in preventing and addressing bullying and discrimination against LGBTQ+ individuals. By implementing anti-bullying policies and providing training for educators, schools can create safe and inclusive spaces for all students. Educators can be trained to recognize and address instances of bullying, while also promoting empathy, respect, and understanding among students.

Moreover, LGBTQ+-inclusive education can also benefit the wider student population by challenging traditional gender stereotypes and encouraging healthy relationships based on consent and respect. By teaching about LGBTQ+ issues, students are exposed to the importance of equality and fairness, promoting a more inclusive society for all.

Example: Schools can implement peer support programs where older students act as mentors and allies to younger LGBTQ+ students. This support system helps create a sense of belonging, reduces isolation, and fosters a welcoming school culture.

Empowering LGBTQ+ Students

Education equips LGBTQ+ students with the knowledge and tools needed to advocate for their rights and navigate the challenges they may face. By offering LGBTQ+-specific support groups and counseling services, educational institutions can provide a crucial lifeline for LGBTQ+ students, helping them develop resilience and self-confidence.

In addition, promoting LGBTQ+ representation in various fields can inspire and empower LGBTQ+ students to pursue their passions and break through barriers. When LGBTQ+ individuals are visible as successful professionals, scientists, artists, and leaders, it helps challenge the notion that queerness and success are mutually exclusive.

Example: LGBTQ+ student organizations and clubs provide spaces for activism, peer support, and community-building. These groups offer educational resources, social events, and opportunities to organize awareness campaigns and advocacy initiatives.

Engaging Parents and Families

Education not only encompasses formal schooling but also extends to families and communities. Engaging parents in dialogues around LGBTQ+ issues is essential for promoting acceptance and support. Parent-teacher associations and community workshops can provide a platform to address misconceptions, answer questions, and share resources that help parents understand the experiences and identities of LGBTQ+ individuals.

By fostering open and inclusive conversations, parents can become important allies in breaking down barriers and challenging societal norms. Creating supportive environments at home can be a significant factor in the overall well-being and success of LGBTQ+ students.

Example: Hosting community-wide events, such as panel discussions or film screenings, that bring together LGBTQ+ individuals, parents, and educators can facilitate productive conversations and promote understanding.

Teacher Training and Inclusivity

Effective education in LGBTQ+ issues requires educators to be knowledgeable, inclusive, and sensitive to the needs of LGBTQ+ students. Teacher training programs should incorporate LGBTQ+-inclusive pedagogies, teaching strategies, and classroom management techniques.

Training should focus on equipping educators with the tools to create a safe and supportive environment, address biases, respond to discrimination, and offer inclusive resources. By fostering inclusivity both inside and outside the classroom, educators can set powerful examples and create a positive ripple effect among their students and colleagues.

Example: Workshops and seminars can be organized to provide educators with an understanding of LGBTQ+ identities, terminology, and experiences. These sessions can facilitate open discussions, share best practices, and address concerns raised by educators.

Making Education Accessible for LGBTQ+ Youth

Education is most effective when it is accessible to all. However, LGBTQ+ youth often face unique challenges that can hinder their access to education. Homelessness, family rejection, and bullying in schools are just a few barriers that LGBTQ+ students may encounter.

To ensure inclusivity, educational institutions and policymakers must actively work towards eliminating these barriers. This can involve securing funding for LGBTQ+ support services, establishing safe housing options for homeless LGBTQ+ youth, and implementing policies that protect against discrimination based on sexual orientation and gender identity.

Example: Collaborations between educational institutions, LGBTQ+ organizations, and social services can offer comprehensive support systems for LGBTQ+ youth, including access to secure housing, mental health resources, and educational scholarships.

In conclusion, education is a powerful tool that can break down barriers, challenge prejudices, and foster inclusivity. By promoting LGBTQ+ awareness and acceptance, addressing discrimination, empowering LGBTQ+ students, engaging families, providing comprehensive teacher training, and making education accessible for all, we can harness education's transformative power in the fight for LGBTQ+ rights and equality.

Sure! Here's a detailed and engaging section on "Bridging Divides through Dialogue":

Bridging Divides through Dialogue

Bridging the divides between different communities is essential for fostering understanding, empathy, and ultimately creating a more inclusive society. Dialogue plays a crucial role in this process, enabling individuals from diverse backgrounds to come together, discuss their differences, and find common ground. In this section, we explore the power of dialogue in bridging divides and building bridges of understanding.

The Importance of Dialogue

Dialogue is the art of sincere and open conversation, where individuals actively listen to each other's perspectives without judgment or prejudice. It allows for the exchange of ideas, encourages empathy, and promotes mutual respect. In the context of LGBTQ activism and Muslim communities, dialogue becomes a powerful tool for breaking down stereotypes, challenging biases, and fostering positive change.

By engaging in dialogue, LGBTQ activists and Muslim communities can address misperceptions, debunk myths, and build authentic connections. It provides an opportunity to humanize the experiences of marginalized individuals and address misconceptions that may hinder acceptance and inclusion. Additionally, dialogue enables both sides to learn from one another and promote social progress.

Creating Safe Spaces for Dialogue

Creating safe spaces is vital when engaging in dialogue between LGBTQ activists and Muslim communities. These spaces should encourage open and respectful conversations, where participants feel comfortable expressing their opinions and experiences. Safe spaces foster empathy, allowing individuals to share their stories without fear of judgment or reprisal.

Organizations and community groups can play a pivotal role in facilitating safe dialogue spaces. They can organize moderated discussion panels, interfaith gatherings, or even informal meet-ups where individuals from different backgrounds can interact in a supportive environment.

It's important to emphasize that safe spaces should be inclusive and accessible to all. This means taking into account the intersecting identities of individuals, such as race, gender, and socioeconomic status, and ensuring that everyone's voice is heard and respected.

Active Listening and Empathy

Active listening is a fundamental aspect of effective dialogue. It involves giving our full attention to what others are saying, suspending judgment, and seeking to understand their perspective. Through active listening, we demonstrate respect and validate the experiences of others.

Empathy plays a crucial role in dialogue, allowing participants to step into each other's shoes and understand the challenges they face. It requires setting aside our own biases and preconceptions to truly comprehend the struggles and experiences of others. Cultivating empathy helps build bridges of understanding and lays the foundation for productive dialogue.

Breaking the Ice: Strategies for Dialogue

Initiating dialogue between LGBTQ activists and Muslim communities may seem daunting, particularly given the sensitive nature of the topics involved. However, with proper planning and respectful approaches, meaningful conversations can be fostered. Here are some strategies for breaking the ice:

1. Start with common ground: Identifying shared values and common goals helps establish a foundation of understanding. Recognizing the mutual desire for dignity, respect, and justice builds trust and paves the way for fruitful dialogue.

2. Use inclusive language: When initiating dialogue, it is crucial to use inclusive language that respects the identities and experiences of all participants. Avoid assumptions and generalizations that may alienate or offend.

3. Organize joint initiatives: Collaborative projects, such as interfaith events, LGBTQ-Muslim conferences, or community service activities, can create opportunities for dialogue in a more relaxed and inclusive setting.

4. Engage with community leaders: Building relationships with influential community figures, both within the LGBTQ and Muslim communities, can help bridge divides and promote dialogue at a broader scale.

5. Seek common goals: Identifying shared goals, such as combating discrimination or promoting acceptance, helps unite individuals across different communities and fosters dialogue toward achieving these objectives.

Challenges and Caveats

While dialogue is a powerful tool for bridging divides, it is not without its challenges and caveats. Some individuals may be resistant to engaging in conversations that challenge their beliefs or go against societal norms. It is essential to approach dialogue with patience, understanding, and a long-term perspective.

Additionally, cultural and language barriers may hinder effective dialogue. In such cases, translators or cultural mediators can play a crucial role in facilitating mutual understanding and ensuring that all participants can actively engage in the conversation.

Furthermore, it is important to acknowledge power dynamics that may exist between different groups. Inadequate representation or power imbalances within dialogue spaces can hinder authentic conversations. Efforts must be made to ensure that marginalized voices are centered and that power is distributed equitably.

Examples and Resources

Numerous organizations and resources focus on promoting dialogue between LGBTQ activists and Muslim communities. These initiatives provide valuable platforms for discussion, learning, and collaboration:

1. The Muslim Alliance for Sexual and Gender Diversity (MASGD): MASGD works to promote dialogue and inclusion within Muslim communities by organizing conferences, workshops, and support networks.

2. The Salam Project: The Salam Project aims to foster dialogue and understanding between LGBTQ individuals and Muslims through storytelling, education, and advocacy work.

3. The Trevor Project: The Trevor Project provides crisis intervention and suicide prevention services to LGBTQ youth, offering resources and support networks for individuals in need.

4. "I Am Your Protector": This global campaign encourages people from diverse faith communities to stand up against hate, fostering dialogue and promoting understanding.

5. "Living Out Loud: A History of the Gay and Lesbian Community in Australia": This book by Graham Willett chronicles the history of the LGBTQ community in Australia, highlighting the power of dialogue in overcoming discrimination and adversity.

Exercise: Facilitating a Dialogue Session

To practice facilitating a dialogue session, imagine you are organizing an event aiming to bridge divides between LGBTQ activists and Muslim communities. Design an agenda for the session, including icebreaker activities, discussion topics, and strategies to ensure inclusivity and respectful dialogue. Consider the challenges and caveats discussed in this section and provide solutions to overcome them.

Remember, effective dialogue requires creating an atmosphere of trust, empathy, and respect, allowing participants to openly share their perspectives and experiences.

In conclusion, dialogue is a powerful tool for bridging divides and creating understanding between LGBTQ activists and Muslim communities. By actively listening, practicing empathy, and fostering safe spaces, individuals can engage in meaningful conversations that challenge biases, break down stereotypes, and lay the groundwork for a more inclusive society. Through dialogue, we can bridge divides, promote empathy, and work towards a future of acceptance and equality.

Empowering LGBTQ Muslims Globally

In this subsection, we will explore the various ways in which activists and organizations are working to empower LGBTQ Muslims globally. By establishing support systems, promoting inclusivity, and advocating for equal rights, these initiatives aim to address the unique struggles faced by LGBTQ individuals within Muslim communities.

Support Networks and Resources

One of the key steps in empowering LGBTQ Muslims is the creation of support networks and resources. These platforms provide a safe space for individuals to connect, share experiences, and seek guidance. Online communities, such as forums, social media groups, and websites, play a crucial role in enabling LGBTQ Muslims to find solace and support, especially in areas where physical LGBTQ-friendly spaces are limited.

Organizations and initiatives like the Muslim Alliance for Sexual and Gender Diversity (MASGD) and the LGBTQ Muslim Retreat provide a supportive environment for LGBTQ Muslims to come together, discuss their intersecting identities, and foster a sense of belonging. These platforms empower individuals by validating their experiences, normalizing their identities, and offering them a community that understands their unique challenges.

Education and Awareness

Empowering LGBTQ Muslims globally also involves education and awareness campaigns. It is crucial to dispel misconceptions and challenge stereotypes surrounding both Islam and LGBTQ identities. By promoting inclusive literature, organizing workshops, and conducting awareness events, activists strive to educate Muslim communities and create spaces of acceptance.

Organizations like Muslims for Progressive Values (MPV) are dedicated to promoting LGBTQ-inclusive interpretations of Islamic teachings. They provide resources, engage in interfaith dialogue, and encourage critical thinking about religion and sexuality. These initiatives empower LGBTQ Muslims by creating an understanding that faith and sexual orientation are not mutually exclusive, fostering a more inclusive and tolerant environment.

Advocacy for Legal and Social Change

Empowering LGBTQ Muslims globally requires advocacy for legal and social change. Activists work diligently to challenge discriminatory laws and policies that inflict harm on LGBTQ individuals within Muslim-majority countries. This advocacy involves partnering with human rights organizations, engaging in public awareness campaigns, and lobbying governments to protect the rights of LGBTQ Muslims.

The Global LGBT Muslim Network is an example of a collaborative effort to advocate for change. This network brings together activists, organizations, and individuals to promote LGBTQ rights and challenge oppressive practices. By sharing knowledge, resources, and strategies, they aim to empower LGBTQ Muslims globally by advocating for their legal protections and equal recognition.

Interfaith Dialogue and Collaboration

Another crucial aspect of empowering LGBTQ Muslims globally is engaging in interfaith dialogue and collaboration. By fostering understanding and building relationships with individuals from different religious backgrounds, activists work towards creating a more inclusive society for all.

Interfaith LGBTQ Pride events, such as the LGBTQ Muslim Pride Parade in Toronto, bring together people from diverse faith communities to celebrate inclusivity and challenge prejudices. These events offer a platform for individuals to share their stories, bridge divides, and foster a greater sense of empathy and understanding.

Initiatives like the Inner Circle provide a space for LGBTQ individuals from different faiths, including Islam, to come together and engage in dialogue. This dialogue encourages the exploration of intersectional identities and helps LGBTQ Muslims realize that they are not alone in their experiences.

Addressing Mental Health and Well-being

Empowering LGBTQ Muslims globally also involves addressing mental health and well-being challenges faced by individuals within these communities. Discrimination, stigma, and the sense of not fitting into societal expectations can lead to mental health issues. Thus, it is essential to provide resources, support, and mental health services tailored to the specific needs of LGBTQ Muslims.

Organizations such as the Muslim Youth Helpline offer confidential support, counseling, and resources to LGBTQ Muslims who may be struggling with their mental well-being. They provide a safe and non-judgmental space for individuals to explore their feelings, receive guidance, and access professional help if needed.

Additionally, promoting self-care practices and raising awareness about mental health within Muslim communities helps to reduce the stigma associated with seeking therapy or counseling. LGBTQ Muslim activists play a crucial role in advocating for the importance of mental health, thus empowering individuals to prioritize their well-being.

Unconventional Yet Relevant: Art and Expression

Art and expression have long been powerful tools for empowerment and social change. Creativity allows marginalized voices to be heard and serves as a catalyst for societal transformation. LGBTQ Muslim artists and writers are using their talents to challenge stereotypes, explore identities, and advocate for acceptance.

Through visual arts, literature, music, and performances, LGBTQ Muslim artists express their unique experiences, dismantling stereotypes and fostering empathy. These creative endeavors empower LGBTQ individuals by providing a platform to reclaim narratives, challenge societal norms, and inspire others to embrace their identities.

For instance, the work of artist Samra Habib, who identifies as a queer Muslim, beautifully captures the intersectional experiences of being both LGBTQ and Muslim. Her photography project, "Just Me and Allah," showcases the strength, resilience, and diversity within LGBTQ Muslim communities.

In conclusion, empowering LGBTQ Muslims globally requires the establishment of support networks, education and awareness campaigns, advocacy for legal and social change, interfaith dialogue, addressing mental health challenges, and the promotion of artistic expression. By embracing these approaches, activists and organizations are working towards a more inclusive world where LGBTQ Muslims can live authentically and fully participate in their communities.

Creating Resources and Toolkits

Creating resources and toolkits is a crucial aspect of LGBTQ activism, as they provide valuable information, guidance, and support for individuals navigating their identities and advocating for their rights. These resources and toolkits serve as a comprehensive guide, aiding both activists and individuals seeking to understand and support the LGBTQ community. In this subsection, we will explore the key components and considerations in developing effective resources and toolkits.

Understanding the target audience

To create resources and toolkits that effectively cater to the needs of the LGBTQ community, it is crucial to thoroughly understand the target audience. This includes considering factors such as age, gender identity, sexual orientation, cultural background, and level of knowledge about LGBTQ issues. It is essential to recognize the diverse experiences and challenges faced by different demographics within the community and tailor the content accordingly.

Engaging with community members through surveys, focus groups, and interviews can provide valuable insights into the specific needs and preferences of the target audience. This feedback can help ensure that the resources and toolkits address their concerns, provide relevant information, and offer practical guidance.

Comprehensive information and support

Resources and toolkits should provide comprehensive information about LGBTQ identities, experiences, and rights. This includes explaining key terminology, debunking common misconceptions, and addressing the intersectionality of LGBTQ identities with other aspects such as race, religion, and disability. It is essential to provide accurate and up-to-date information, drawing from credible sources, research, and lived experiences.

In addition to information, resources should offer practical support and guidance. This can include providing tips for coming out, dealing with discrimination, navigating legal systems, accessing healthcare, and understanding mental health issues. It is important to include resources for support services, helplines, and organizations specializing in LGBTQ issues, ensuring individuals have access to the help and support they may need.

Inclusive and diverse representation

Creating resources and toolkits that reflect the diversity of the LGBTQ community is crucial. Representation matters, and individuals from all backgrounds within the community should be included and celebrated. This means showcasing diverse experiences, identities, and stories from various cultural, ethnic, and religious backgrounds.

Inclusive representation helps individuals feel seen, heard, and validated. It also aids in challenging stereotypes and promoting understanding among allies and those outside the LGBTQ community. Including personal stories and narratives from a range of individuals helps humanize the experiences of LGBTQ individuals and fosters empathy and connection.

Interactive and engaging content

To effectively engage the target audience, resources and toolkits should use interactive and engaging content formats. This can include videos, infographics, quizzes, interactive worksheets, and storytelling. Multimedia content helps to convey information in a dynamic and accessible manner, catering to different learning styles and preferences.

Gamification elements can also be incorporated to make the learning process enjoyable and memorable. This can include creating activities, challenges, and quizzes that encourage active participation and reinforce key concepts. Interactive content not only enhances the learning experience but also encourages individuals to share the resources with others, extending their impact and reach.

Collaboration and partnerships

Developing resources and toolkits is a collaborative effort. It is important to involve individuals from the LGBTQ community, including activists, educators, psychologists, and community leaders, in the creation process. Their insights, expertise, and lived experiences can help ensure the resources are relevant, accurate, and inclusive.

Collaborating with LGBTQ organizations, human rights groups, and educational institutions can also strengthen the development of resources and toolkits. These collaborations can provide access to additional expertise, resources, and platforms for dissemination. It also helps build a network of support and collaboration, fostering a unified and impactful approach to LGBTQ activism.

Evaluation and updating

Regular evaluation and updating of resources and toolkits are essential to ensure their relevance, accuracy, and effectiveness. This involves seeking feedback from users, monitoring changes in legislation and societal attitudes, and staying updated on emerging LGBTQ issues.

Evaluation can be conducted through user surveys, focus groups, and analyzing website analytics to assess engagement and impact. This feedback helps identify areas for improvement, updates, and additions to the resources to better serve the LGBTQ community.

Additionally, resources should be designed in a modular and flexible manner, allowing for easy updates and customization. This ensures that new information and emerging issues can be easily incorporated into existing resources without the need for a complete overhaul.

Follow-up and support

Creating resources and toolkits is just the beginning. Ongoing support is crucial for individuals accessing the resources. This can include follow-up communication, providing access to online communities or support groups, and offering personalized guidance.

Connecting individuals to existing LGBTQ support networks, helplines, and counseling services can ensure that they have continued support beyond the resources. It is essential to emphasize the importance of self-care, mental health, and seeking professional help when needed.

Unconventional approach: The power of art

An unconventional approach to creating resources and toolkits is harnessing the power of art. Artistic mediums, such as visual arts, literature, and performance, have the ability to create emotional connections, challenge norms, and foster empathy.

Incorporating art into resources and toolkits can involve showcasing artwork, poetry, and stories from LGBTQ artists. It can also involve encouraging individuals to express their own experiences and emotions through art. Artistic activities, such as drawing, painting, or storytelling, can serve as therapeutic tools, helping individuals explore their identities and connect with others.

Artistic expressions can transcend language and cultural barriers, making it a powerful tool to reach diverse audiences globally. By combining art with educational content, resources and toolkits can evoke emotions, create memorable experiences, and inspire action.

Example: Toolkit for LGBTQ-inclusive workplaces

To illustrate the application of the principles mentioned above, let's consider the creation of a toolkit for LGBTQ-inclusive workplaces.

The toolkit would include:

+ Comprehensive information on LGBTQ identities, workplace discrimination, legal protections, and best practices for creating an inclusive environment.

+ Personal stories from LGBTQ individuals who have navigated workplace challenges and found success.

+ Interactive quizzes and worksheets to help employers assess their current practices and develop strategies for improvement.

+ Infographics and visual guides illustrating key concepts and dispelling myths or misconceptions about LGBTQ individuals.

+ Case studies showcasing successful LGBTQ-inclusive workplace initiatives and their positive impact.

+ Links to resources, organizations, and support services specializing in LGBTQ workplace inclusion.

+ Tips for creating employee resource groups, providing LGBTQ-inclusive benefits and policies, and promoting allyship within the organization.

+ Guidance on addressing and preventing LGBTQ-related discrimination, including specific strategies for HR departments and managers.

+ An evaluation form to gather feedback from employers who have used the toolkit, allowing for continuous improvement and customization.

+ Follow-up webinars or virtual workshops to support employers in implementing inclusive practices and addressing challenges.

By following the guidelines outlined in this subsection, the toolkit can provide employers with the knowledge, resources, and practical guidance necessary to create LGBTQ-inclusive workplaces.

Conclusion

Creating resources and toolkits is a powerful means of supporting and advocating for the LGBTQ community. By considering the target audience, providing comprehensive information, embracing inclusive representation, utilizing interactive content, fostering collaboration, evaluating and updating materials, offering ongoing support, and exploring unconventional approaches, these resources can have a profound impact on individuals and society as a whole.

As LGBTQ activism continues to evolve, it is vital to adapt and innovate resource creation processes, leveraging technology and diverse perspectives. By doing so, we can ensure that resources and toolkits are effective, relevant, and accessible, creating a more inclusive and accepting world for all.

Fostering Understanding and Empathy

In the journey towards creating a more inclusive and empathetic society, fostering understanding and empathy is crucial. It allows individuals to transcend their biases, recognize shared humanity, and actively engage in dismantling barriers that perpetuate discrimination based on sexual orientation and religious beliefs. In this subsection, we will explore various strategies and approaches to foster understanding and empathy among diverse communities, with a particular focus on LGBTQ individuals and Muslims.

Creating Safe Spaces for Dialogue

Safe spaces provide an environment where people feel comfortable expressing their opinions, sharing their experiences, and engaging in open and honest dialogue. Establishing safe spaces for dialogue between LGBTQ individuals and Muslim communities can foster understanding and empathy by creating opportunities for mutual learning and collaboration.

One effective approach is to organize moderated panel discussions or community forums where LGBTQ activists and Muslim leaders can engage in respectful conversations. These events allow participants to ask questions, challenge stereotypes, and gain a deeper understanding of each other's experiences and perspectives. By providing a platform for dialogue, we can break down barriers, challenge prejudices, and stimulate empathy.

Promoting Cultural Exchange Programs

Cultural exchange programs have proven to be powerful tools for fostering understanding and empathy between different communities. Through these programs, LGBTQ individuals and Muslims can interact, share their stories, and build meaningful connections.

For instance, organizing LGBTQ-Muslim alliances where individuals from both communities can engage in activities such as workshops, art exhibitions, and storytelling sessions can create opportunities for personal connections and empathy-building. Such exchanges can help dispel misconceptions, bridge divides, and foster a sense of compassion and unity.

Supporting LGBTQ-Muslim Collaborative Projects

Collaborative projects that bring together LGBTQ individuals and Muslim communities have the potential to foster understanding and empathy while creating positive change. By working on joint initiatives, participants can find common ground, challenge stereotypes, and explore shared values.

One way to support LGBTQ-Muslim collaborative projects is through the establishment of grants and funding opportunities. These resources can help facilitate the development of joint initiatives, such as LGBTQ-Muslim art exhibits, film festivals, or community service projects. By providing the necessary resources, we can encourage collaboration and promote understanding between these communities.

Promoting LGBTQ-Inclusive Education

Education plays a crucial role in fostering understanding and empathy. By promoting LGBTQ-inclusive education, we can challenge stereotypes, provide accurate information, and cultivate empathy among students.

Educational institutions can incorporate inclusive curriculum that covers a wide range of LGBTQ experiences and perspectives, including those of LGBTQ Muslims. By integrating LGBTQ-related topics into various subjects, such as literature, history, and social sciences, students can develop a deeper understanding of diverse identities and promote empathy.

Additionally, workshops and training sessions for teachers and school administrators can help create LGBTQ-inclusive school environments. These sessions can focus on addressing biases, promoting LGBTQ acceptance, and developing strategies for creating safe spaces for all students.

Using Storytelling and Media for Empathy-Building

Storytelling and media have the power to humanize experiences, challenge stereotypes, and foster empathy. By sharing personal narratives and promoting diverse representation, we can create platforms for LGBTQ individuals and Muslim communities to be heard and understood.

Platforms such as podcasts, documentaries, and social media campaigns can amplify the voices of LGBTQ individuals and Muslims, allowing them to share their stories, challenges, and aspirations. By showcasing the diversity within these communities, we can challenge stereotypes, combat homophobia and Islamophobia, and foster a greater sense of empathy among broader audiences.

Challenging Queerphobia and Islamophobia Together

To foster understanding and empathy, it is essential to address and challenge both queerphobia and Islamophobia. By acknowledging the unique struggles faced by LGBTQ individuals within Muslim communities and the discrimination faced by Muslims within the LGBTQ community, we can create a more inclusive environment for all.

Creating allyship between LGBTQ individuals and Muslims involves actively listening, learning, and supporting each other's journeys. It requires challenging stereotypes, advocating for the rights of both groups, and working together to combat discrimination. By building bridges and developing mutual respect, we can foster understanding, empathy, and solidarity.

Embracing Intersectionality

Understanding the intersections of identities is vital to fostering empathy. LGBTQ Muslims have unique experiences that result from their intersecting identities and face specific challenges within their communities and broader society.

To foster understanding and empathy, we must acknowledge and address the particular struggles faced by LGBTQ Muslims. This involves recognizing and validating their experiences, supporting LGBTQ Muslim organizations and initiatives, and amplifying their voices. By centering their experiences, we can create a more inclusive dialogue that promotes mutual understanding and empathy.

In conclusion, fostering understanding and empathy is crucial for creating an inclusive society for LGBTQ individuals and Muslims. By creating safe spaces for dialogue, promoting cultural exchange programs, supporting collaborative projects, promoting LGBTQ-inclusive education, using storytelling and media, challenging queerphobia and Islamophobia, and embracing intersectionality, we can bridge divides and create a world characterized by empathy and acceptance. It is through these efforts that we can pave the way for a more inclusive future for all.

Unapologetically Authentic

Personal Evolution and Growth

Overcoming Internalized Homophobia

Internalized homophobia is a pervasive issue faced by many LGBTQ individuals, including Irshad Manji. It refers to the negative feelings, beliefs, and attitudes that queer individuals internalize due to societal messages and prejudices against homosexuality. In this subsection, we will explore the phenomenon of internalized homophobia, its impact on individuals, and strategies for overcoming it.

Understanding Internalized Homophobia

Internalized homophobia often stems from growing up in a society that stigmatizes and marginalizes LGBTQ individuals. Queer individuals may internalize these negative societal messages, leading to feelings of self-hatred, shame, and denial of their own identities. This internalized homophobia can manifest in various ways, such as:

- Self-loathing: Feeling unworthy or disgusted with one's own sexuality.

- Fear of rejection: Believing that one will be rejected or ostracized by family, friends, or community if their sexual orientation is known.

- Self-denial: Suppressing or denying one's own same-sex attractions or gender identity.

- Overcompensation: Engaging in hypermasculine or hyperfeminine behaviors to conform to societal expectations.

Internalized homophobia can have detrimental effects on an individual's mental health, self-esteem, and overall well-being. It can lead to internal conflict, depression, anxiety, and a sense of isolation. Overcoming internalized homophobia is a complex and deeply personal journey that requires self-reflection, education, and support.

Challenging Internalized Homophobia

1. Self-acceptance and self-compassion: The first step in overcoming internalized homophobia is to cultivate self-acceptance and self-compassion. This involves recognizing that there is nothing inherently wrong with being LGBTQ and that one deserves love, respect, and happiness. Engaging in positive self-affirmations and practicing self-care can be helpful in building self-acceptance.

2. Educating oneself: Knowledge is a powerful tool in challenging internalized homophobia. Learning about LGBTQ history, rights, and contributions to society can help develop a sense of pride and belonging. Reading books, attending workshops, and engaging in conversations with other queer individuals can provide valuable insights and support.

3. Seeking support: It is crucial to surround oneself with a supportive network of friends, family, and LGBTQ organizations. Finding a safe space where one can share experiences, fears, and doubts without judgment can be immensely helpful in combatting internalized homophobia. Support groups, online forums, and LGBTQ community centers provide valuable resources and connections.

4. Counseling and therapy: Seeking professional help through counseling or therapy can assist in addressing deep-rooted issues related to internalized homophobia. Therapists specialized in LGBTQ issues can guide individuals through the process of self-discovery and help develop coping strategies to deal with internalized homophobia.

5. Building resilience: Overcoming internalized homophobia requires resilience, as the journey may involve facing external prejudice and discrimination. Building resilience involves developing a strong sense of self, setting boundaries, and finding ways to cope with adversity. Engaging in activities that promote self-growth and self-expression, such as art, writing, or sports, can also foster resilience.

6. Empowering others: As one progresses on their journey of overcoming internalized homophobia, they can become advocates for other LGBTQ individuals who are still struggling. By sharing their own stories, offering support, and challenging societal norms, individuals can help create a more inclusive and accepting world.

Embracing Authenticity and Identity

Overcoming internalized homophobia is an ongoing process, and it is important to remember that progress can take time. Each individual's journey will be unique, and it is crucial to honor one's own pace and experiences. Embracing authenticity and identity is a continuous process that allows individuals to live their lives authentically and unapologetically.

By challenging internalized homophobia, queer individuals like Irshad Manji are breaking the chains of societal expectations, embracing their true selves, and inspiring others to do the same. Their stories serve as beacons of hope and reminders that it is possible to overcome internalized homophobia and live a life full of love, acceptance, and pride.

In conclusion, overcoming internalized homophobia is a deeply personal and transformative journey. By cultivating self-acceptance, educating oneself, seeking support, and building resilience, individuals can challenge and overcome the negative effects of internalized homophobia. Embracing authenticity and identity paves the way for a more inclusive and accepting world, where LGBTQ individuals can live their lives without fear or shame.

Finding Love and Acceptance

In the journey of queer Muslims, one of the most significant challenges is finding love and acceptance, both within themselves and from the people around them. Irshad Manji's own experiences and insights shed light on this complex and personal aspect of the LGBTQ Muslim identity.

Love is a universal human need, and for LGBTQ Muslims, it can be particularly challenging to navigate due to the intersection of religious and cultural beliefs. Subsection 2 explores the different aspects of finding love and acceptance in the context of being a queer Muslim.

Understanding Personal Worth and Self-Acceptance

For many queer Muslims, acceptance starts with self-acceptance. Coming to terms with one's sexuality while holding onto faith can be a daunting task. The intersectional identity of being both queer and Muslim often requires individuals to confront internalized homophobia and reconcile their religious beliefs with their sexual orientation.

Irshad Manji provides inspiring examples of individuals who have journeyed towards self-acceptance, encouraging others to embrace their authentic selves. Through her own personal growth, Manji emphasizes the importance of understanding one's personal worth and choosing self-acceptance as a foundation for building a fulfilling life.

Exploring Supportive Communities

Finding love and acceptance often involves seeking out supportive communities that understand and embrace the complex identities of queer Muslims. LGBTQ support groups, queer Muslim organizations, and inclusive mosques are crucial spaces that provide a sense of belonging and acceptance.

These spaces allow individuals to connect with others who have shared experiences, exchange stories, and find solace and understanding. Irshad Manji highlights the role of such communities in helping LGBTQ Muslims navigate their identity while fostering a sense of belonging and support, ultimately leading to self-acceptance and empowerment.

Building Relationships and Navigating Cultural Expectations

Navigating relationships can be challenging for LGBTQ Muslims due to cultural expectations and traditional norms surrounding love and marriage. Irshad Manji acknowledges these challenges and offers insights into forging meaningful relationships while challenging societal expectations.

She encourages individuals to actively engage in open and honest conversations with their partners, exploring the ways in which faith and sexuality intersect. By challenging cultural expectations and fostering mutual understanding, queer Muslims can build relationships based on mutual respect, love, and acceptance.

Supporting Mental and Emotional Well-being

The journey of finding love and acceptance can take a toll on mental and emotional well-being. It is important for queer Muslims to prioritize self-care and seek professional help, if needed. Irshad Manji emphasizes the importance of mental health advocacy and offers resources and strategies for LGBTQ Muslims to maintain their well-being.

Cultivating self-love, practicing mindfulness, and seeking therapy are some of the strategies that Manji highlights. By prioritizing mental and emotional well-being, queer Muslims can navigate the challenges of finding love and acceptance in a healthier and more balanced way.

Reconciling Faith and Love

For many queer Muslims, reconciling their faith with their desire for love and acceptance can be a deeply personal struggle. Irshad Manji provides insights into her own journey of reconciling faith with her queer identity, acknowledging that the path is unique for each individual.

She encourages queer Muslims to engage with progressive interpretations of religious texts and seek out scholars and religious leaders who promote inclusivity. By challenging traditional narratives and reclaiming their faith, queer Muslims can find love and acceptance while staying true to their religious beliefs.

Understanding the Importance of Allies

Allies play a crucial role in supporting LGBTQ Muslims in their quest for love and acceptance. Irshad Manji stresses the significance of allies from within the Muslim community as well as from external sources.

She highlights the importance of allies who actively challenge homophobia and transphobia within their communities and who advocate for the inclusion and acceptance of LGBTQ Muslims. By standing together with allies, queer Muslims can find strength and forge a path towards love and acceptance.

Takeaways

In this subsection, we explored the journey of finding love and acceptance for queer Muslims. Through self-acceptance, building supportive communities, navigating cultural expectations, prioritizing well-being, reconciling faith and love, and recognizing the importance of allies, queer Muslims can embark on a path towards love, acceptance, and self-empowerment. The stories and insights shared by Irshad Manji provide invaluable guidance and inspiration for queer Muslims seeking to navigate their identities and thrive in a world that celebrates and accepts them. Remember, the journey to finding love and acceptance is unique for each individual, and it is essential to prioritize self-care and authenticity throughout the process.

Embracing Self-Care and Well-being

In the journey of fighting for LGBTQ rights and challenging societal norms, it is easy to forget the importance of self-care and well-being. Activism can be emotionally and mentally draining, often leaving individuals feeling overwhelmed and burnt out. Irshad Manji understands the significance of embracing self-care and well-being and recognizes that taking care of oneself is crucial in sustaining the energy needed for long-term activism.

The Importance of Self-Care

Self-care is the practice of taking deliberate actions to promote physical, mental, and emotional well-being. For activists like Manji, who are constantly engaged in challenging conversations and fighting for justice, self-care becomes a necessary tool to navigate through the hardships of activism. It allows activists to rejuvenate, recenter their focus, and continue their work with renewed energy.

Prioritizing Mental Health

Mental health is a vital aspect of self-care, and it is essential for activists to prioritize their mental well-being. The pressures and challenges faced by activists can take a toll on their mental health, leading to burnout, depression, and anxiety. It is crucial for activists to recognize the signs of mental distress and proactively seek support.

Solution-focused therapy is a psychological approach that can be particularly helpful for activists. This approach focuses on identifying solutions and developing strategies to address specific challenges or stressors. Activists can work with a therapist to develop effective coping mechanisms, enhance their resilience, and maintain their mental well-being.

The Power of Physical Self-Care

Engaging in physical self-care practices is equally important for activists. Regular exercise, a balanced diet, and sufficient rest are all essential components of physical well-being. Physical activity not only improves overall health but also releases endorphins, which provide a natural boost to mood and energy levels.

Moreover, incorporating mindfulness techniques such as **yoga** and **meditation** into one's routine can help manage stress and promote inner calm. These practices allow activists to be present in the moment, connect with their bodies, and cultivate inner strength.

Finding Balance and Setting Boundaries

Creating boundaries is essential for maintaining well-being amidst the demands of activism. Activists often find themselves inundated with requests for support or involvement in various initiatives. While it is important to be engaged, setting boundaries helps prevent burnout.

Practicing saying "no" when necessary and prioritizing self-care activities is an act of self-preservation and empowerment. By setting realistic expectations and boundaries, activists can ensure they have the time and energy to focus on their well-being.

Community and Support Networks

Building a strong support system is crucial for activists. Surrounding oneself with like-minded individuals who understand the challenges faced in the fight for LGBTQ rights provides a sense of belonging and support. These communities can offer emotional support, guidance, and validation.

Additionally, seeking professional support through therapy or counseling can provide a safe space for activists to process their experiences, explore their emotions, and navigate the complexities of activism.

Unconventional Approach: Laughter Therapy

One unconventional yet effective method of self-care that activists can consider is laughter therapy. Laughter has been shown to have numerous physical and mental health benefits, including reducing stress, boosting the immune system, and increasing happiness levels.

Engaging in activities that bring joy and laughter, such as watching comedy shows, engaging in playful interactions, or practicing laughter yoga, can serve as an effective stress-reliever for activists. Laughter therapy allows individuals to release tension, connect with their inner child, and find humor even in challenging situations.

Reflection and Recharging

Taking time for reflection and recharging is essential for sustaining long-term activism. Engaging in activities such as journaling or spending time in nature can provide a space for self-reflection, introspection, and personal growth. This time away from the demands of activism allows activists to reconnect with their values, reassess their goals, and recharge their energy.

Exercise: Cultivating a Self-Care Routine

To develop a personalized self-care routine, activists can follow these steps:

1. Reflect on your current self-care habits and identify areas that need improvement.

2. Identify self-care activities that bring you joy, calmness, or energy.

3. Prioritize these activities and set aside dedicated time for them regularly.

4. Experiment with different self-care practices, such as meditation, exercise, or creative hobbies, to find what works best for you.

5. Seek support from your community of activists and consider joining or creating a support group.

6. Practice setting boundaries that prioritize your well-being and learn to say "no" when necessary.

7. Keep a self-care journal to track your progress and adjust your routine as needed.

Remember, self-care is not selfish; it is a necessary tool for sustaining long-term activism. By embracing self-care and well-being, activists like Irshad Manji can continue their fight for equality with resilience and determination.

Exploring Intersectionality

Intersectionality, a concept coined by Kimberlé Crenshaw, is the recognition that individuals can experience multiple forms of oppression and discrimination simultaneously, and that the intersections of these identities are important to consider in understanding and addressing social inequalities. In the case of Irshad Manji, exploring intersectionality is crucial as it helps shed light on the unique challenges faced by LGBTQ Muslims, highlighting the need for a comprehensive approach to activism that addresses the complexities of their experiences.

Understanding Intersectionality

Intersectionality acknowledges that our identities are not discrete or separate, but rather interconnected and overlapping. It recognizes that social categories such as race, gender, sexuality, religion, and disability are not experienced in isolation, but rather interact with and shape one another. For instance, being both LGBTQ and Muslim means that one's experience of prejudice and discrimination is not solely due to either their sexual orientation or religious affiliation, but rather the convergence of these identities.

Challenges Faced by LGBTQ Muslims

Exploring intersectionality enables us to understand how the experiences of LGBTQ Muslims are shaped by multiple forms of marginalization and exclusion. LGBTQ Muslims often face challenges related to their sexual orientation and gender identity, such as prejudice, stigma, and discrimination within both LGBTQ and Muslim communities. On top of this, they may also experience Islamophobia and racism, creating a complex web of oppression.

Colliding Identities: Navigating Double Discrimination

One of the challenges faced by LGBTQ Muslims is the tension between their sexual orientation or gender identity and their religious beliefs and practices. Some conservative interpretations of Islam view homosexuality as sinful or deviant, exacerbating the struggles that LGBTQ Muslims face in reconciling their faith and sexuality. This collision of identities can lead to a sense of isolation, shame, and internalized homophobia.

Building Inclusive Spaces

To address the unique challenges faced by LGBTQ Muslims, it is essential to create safe and inclusive spaces that recognize and embrace intersectionality. This involves engaging in dialogue with both LGBTQ and Muslim communities, challenging their prejudices and misconceptions, and fostering acceptance and understanding. It also requires promoting LGBTQ-inclusive interpretations of religious texts and advocating for the recognition of LGBTQ rights within religious frameworks.

Embracing Diversity and Collaboration

Exploring intersectionality encourages us to celebrate and embrace the diversity within LGBTQ Muslim communities. It highlights the importance of uplifting the voices and experiences of those at the intersections of multiple identity markers, recognizing that their struggles and perspectives are unique. Collaboration with other marginalized communities and social justice movements becomes crucial in addressing overlapping forms of discrimination and working towards a more equitable society.

Combating Stereotypes and Stereotyping

Intersectionality challenges us to question and dismantle stereotypes associated with both LGBTQ identities and religious affiliations. It requires us to move beyond narrow or monolithic understandings of these identities and recognize the diverse experiences and perspectives within LGBTQ Muslim communities. By doing so, we can challenge the assumptions and biases that fuel discrimination and create space for the full expression of selfhood and authenticity.

Example: Discrimination Faced by LGBTQ Muslim Women

Intersectionality can be illustrated by examining the experiences of LGBTQ Muslim women. They face not only discrimination based on their gender, but also Islamophobia, homophobia, and transphobia. This intersectionality compounds their struggles and places them at greater risk of violence, harassment, and marginalization. However, the unique experiences of LGBTQ Muslim women also provide them with a distinct perspective and the potential for powerful activism that addresses multiple social justice issues.

Resources for Exploring Intersectionality

There are various resources available to delve deeper into understanding intersectionality and its relevance to LGBTQ Muslims. Books like "Intersectionality" by Patricia Hill Collins and Kimberlé Crenshaw and "Living Out Islam: Voices of Gay, Lesbian, and Transgender Muslims" edited by Scott Siraj al-Haqq Kugle provide insightful analyses and personal narratives. Non-profit organizations, such as the Muslim Alliance for Sexual and Gender Diversity and the Trevor Project, actively work towards supporting LGBTQ Muslims and promoting intersectional perspectives.

Unconventional Approach: Arts as a Tool for Intersectional Exploration

An unconventional yet effective approach to exploring intersectionality is through the use of art. Artistic mediums, such as poetry, storytelling, and visual arts, can become powerful tools for individuals to express their intersectional identities and experiences. By engaging with art, both as creators and viewers, we can cultivate empathy, challenge stereotypes, and foster dialogue that goes beyond theoretical frameworks. Art creates spaces for the imagination and reflection necessary to understand the complexities of intersectional identities.

In conclusion, exploring intersectionality is vital in understanding the challenges faced by LGBTQ Muslims and developing comprehensive approaches to activism. By recognizing the intersecting dimensions of oppression and embracing diverse identities, we can work towards creating inclusive spaces that honor the full humanity and experiences of LGBTQ Muslims.

Inspiring LGBTQ Muslims to Thrive

In this section, we will explore the ways in which Irshad Manji inspires LGBTQ Muslims to thrive, embracing their identities and finding support within their communities. Manji's courageous activism and personal journey provide valuable guidance and encouragement for those navigating the intersection of faith, sexuality, and identity.

Creating LGBTQ-Inclusive Muslim Spaces

One of the key ways Manji inspires LGBTQ Muslims is by advocating for the creation of inclusive spaces within the Muslim community. She emphasizes the importance of mosques, Islamic organizations, and community centers being welcoming and accepting of all individuals, regardless of their sexual orientation or gender identity.

Manji encourages LGBTQ Muslims to challenge stereotypes and break down barriers by actively engaging with and educating their communities. By sharing their stories and experiences, LGBTQ Muslims can inspire positive change and foster empathy within their communities. Manji provides guidance on how to approach these conversations respectfully and effectively, emphasizing the significance of dialogue and understanding.

Amplifying LGBTQ Muslim Voices

Manji believes in the power of amplifying the voices of LGBTQ Muslims, ensuring their stories and perspectives are heard. She emphasizes the importance of creating platforms for LGBTQ Muslims to share their experiences and engage in meaningful dialogue.

Through public speaking engagements, workshops, and conferences, Manji encourages LGBTQ Muslims to step into the spotlight and share their unique journeys. She provides resources and support for individuals to develop their public speaking skills and build their confidence as advocates for LGBTQ rights within the Muslim community.

Supporting Mental Health and Well-being

Thriving as an LGBTQ Muslim requires prioritizing mental health and well-being. Manji acknowledges the challenges faced by LGBTQ Muslims, who often experience higher rates of mental health issues due to the intersection of multiple identities.

To inspire LGBTQ Muslims to thrive, Manji emphasizes the importance of self-care and self-acceptance. She highlights the value of seeking professional support, such as therapy or counseling, to navigate the complexities of identity. Manji provides recommendations for LGBTQ-friendly mental health resources and encourages the development of support networks within the community.

Fostering Mentorship and Role Models

Manji believes strongly in the power of mentorship and the positive impact role models can have on LGBTQ Muslims. She encourages LGBTQ individuals within the Muslim community to seek out mentors who can support them emotionally and guide them on their journey.

Manji also emphasizes the importance of LGBTQ Muslims becoming mentors themselves, sharing their experiences and providing support to those who may be struggling. By fostering mentorship relationships, LGBTQ Muslims can inspire and empower each other to embrace their identities and thrive.

Promoting Self-Expression and Authenticity

A core aspect of inspiring LGBTQ Muslims to thrive is encouraging self-expression and authenticity. Manji advocates for individuals to embrace their true selves, challenging societal expectations and norms that may restrict their freedom.

Through storytelling and personal anecdotes, Manji demonstrates the power of living authentically. By showcasing her own journey of self-discovery and self-acceptance, she inspires LGBTQ Muslims to embrace their identities, celebrate their diversity, and thrive in all aspects of their lives.

In conclusion, Irshad Manji's unwavering activism and personal journey provide invaluable inspiration for LGBTQ Muslims seeking to thrive within their faith communities. By advocating for inclusive spaces, amplifying voices, supporting mental health, fostering mentorship, and promoting self-expression, Manji empowers LGBTQ Muslims to embrace their identities and live authentic, fulfilling lives. Her work challenges societal norms and encourages individuals to create a more inclusive and accepting world.

Navigating Relationships and Vulnerability

In this subsection, we delve into the intricacies of navigating relationships and vulnerability, specifically within the context of LGBTQ individuals. Building and maintaining healthy relationships can be challenging for anyone, but when you add the complexities of being queer and vulnerable in a society that can be intolerant, it can become even more daunting. In this subsection, we explore the unique dynamics and experiences faced by LGBTQ individuals as they navigate relationships, and we provide insights and strategies for fostering healthy connections.

Understanding Vulnerability in LGBTQ Relationships

Vulnerability is an essential aspect of any relationship, as it involves opening oneself up emotionally and being honest and authentic with a partner. However, for LGBTQ individuals, vulnerability can be particularly challenging due to the stigma and discrimination they may face. Many LGBTQ individuals have experienced rejection, shame, or even violence because of their sexual orientation or gender identity. As a result, they may develop mechanisms to protect themselves, such as building emotional walls or being cautious about disclosing their true selves to others.

To navigate vulnerability in LGBTQ relationships, it is crucial to create a safe and affirming environment where partners can express themselves without fear of judgment or discrimination. This entails fostering open communication, actively listening to one another, and cultivating an atmosphere of acceptance and understanding. By creating a space where vulnerability is valued and respected, partners can support each other's growth and emotional well-being.

Overcoming Fear and Shame

Fear and shame are common emotions experienced by LGBTQ individuals in relationships, particularly when it comes to societal expectations and the pressure to conform to heteronormative ideals. Many LGBTQ individuals have grown up in environments that taught them their identities were immoral or wrong. These beliefs can manifest as internalized homophobia, biphobia, or transphobia, which can erode self-esteem and hinder their ability to engage fully in relationships.

Overcoming fear and shame requires self-reflection, self-compassion, and support from partners and the larger LGBTQ community. It is essential for individuals to challenge societal norms and embrace their identities unapologetically. Engaging in therapy, attending LGBTQ support groups, and seeking out queer-affirming resources can also play a vital role in fostering self-acceptance and healing.

Developing Trust and Intimacy

Trust and intimacy are fundamental components of any successful relationship. However, for LGBTQ individuals who have experienced rejection or betrayal based on their sexual orientation or gender identity, developing trust can be challenging. Additionally, the lack of LGBTQ representation in media and society can create a sense of isolation and make it difficult to find relatable role models for healthy LGBTQ relationships.

To foster trust and intimacy, it is important for partners to communicate their needs and concerns openly and honestly. Both individuals should make an effort to listen attentively and validate each other's experiences. Building trust takes time, and it is crucial to approach the process with patience, empathy, and understanding.

Cultivating intimacy in LGBTQ relationships involves creating shared experiences and connections. This can be achieved through activities such as traveling, exploring common interests, or engaging in open and vulnerable conversations. By fostering a strong emotional connection, partners can deepen their intimacy and create a foundation of trust.

Navigating Intersectionality in Relationships

Intersectionality plays a significant role in LGBTQ relationships, as individuals navigate the complexities of their multiple identities. LGBTQ individuals may also identify as members of different racial or ethnic minority groups, have diverse cultural backgrounds, or possess varying abilities. These intersecting identities can influence relationship dynamics and vulnerabilities.

Acknowledging and understanding intersectionality is crucial for fostering inclusivity and creating a supportive environment in relationships. Partners should actively educate themselves about the unique challenges faced by LGBTQ individuals with intersecting identities and actively work to dismantle systems of oppression that may affect their relationship.

It is important to have open and respectful conversations about cultural differences, privilege, and the impact of societal structures on individuals with varied identities. By embracing intersectionality, partners can better navigate the complexities of their relationship and work together to promote inclusivity and social justice within their broader communities.

Seeking Support and Community

Navigating relationships, particularly as an LGBTQ individual, can be both fulfilling and challenging. Seeking support from the LGBTQ community and allies can provide a crucial network of understanding and validation. LGBTQ-inclusive support groups, online communities, and LGBTQ organizations can offer resources, guidance, and a sense of belonging.

Additionally, couples counseling or therapy can provide a safe and neutral space for partners to address any relationship challenges, strengthen their connection, and develop valuable communication and problem-solving skills.

Remember, vulnerability in relationships is a journey that requires patience, self-reflection, and constant growth. By embracing your authentic self, finding support, and cultivating open and honest communication with your partner, you can navigate the complexities of vulnerability and foster a relationship built on trust, intimacy, and mutual respect.

Conclusion

In this section, we explored the intricacies of navigating relationships and vulnerability, specifically within the context of LGBTQ individuals. We discussed the challenges faced by LGBTQ individuals when it comes to vulnerability in relationships, including fear, shame, and trauma. We provided strategies for overcoming these challenges, such as creating safe and affirming spaces, challenging societal norms, and seeking support from the LGBTQ community.

We also highlighted the importance of trust and intimacy in LGBTQ relationships and provided suggestions for building these foundations. Additionally, we discussed the significance of intersectionality in relationships and the need to embrace diverse identities and experiences.

By fostering open communication, supporting one another's growth, and seeking resources and support from the LGBTQ community, individuals can navigate the complexities of vulnerability in relationships and cultivate healthy, loving connections. Remember, the journey towards authentic and fulfilling relationships requires ongoing effort, self-reflection, and a commitment to growth.

Discovering Self-Love and Authenticity

Discovering self-love and authenticity is a transformative journey that allows individuals to embrace their true identities and find happiness in their lives. In this subsection, we will explore the importance of self-love, strategies for cultivating authenticity, and the positive impact it can have on mental health and overall well-being.

Understanding Self-Love

Self-love is the foundation of a healthy and fulfilling life. It involves accepting and nurturing oneself, embracing one's strengths and weaknesses, and practicing self-compassion. Many individuals struggle with self-love due to societal pressures, internalized negativity, or past trauma. However, it is important to recognize that self-love is not selfish or narcissistic but rather a necessary component of overall well-being.

Negative Self-Talk

Negative self-talk is a common obstacle to self-love. It involves internalizing critical thoughts and beliefs about oneself, leading to low self-esteem and limited self-acceptance. To counter negative self-talk, individuals can practice positive affirmations, challenge negative thoughts, and surround themselves with supportive and uplifting people.

Self-Care Practices

Self-care plays a fundamental role in cultivating self-love. It involves engaging in activities that promote physical, emotional, and mental well-being. Self-care practices can include regular exercise, healthy eating, pursuing hobbies, setting boundaries, practicing mindfulness, and seeking professional support when needed. By prioritizing self-care, individuals can enhance their self-worth and create a positive relationship with themselves.

Embracing Authenticity

Authenticity refers to living in alignment with one's true self, values, and beliefs. When individuals embrace authenticity, they let go of societal expectations and embrace their unique identities. This process can be empowering, as it allows individuals to live a life that is true to themselves, rather than conforming to societal norms or expectations.

Self-Reflection

Self-reflection is a crucial component of embracing authenticity. It involves exploring one's values, passions, and desires to gain a deeper understanding of oneself. Through self-reflection, individuals can identify their authentic selves and make choices that align with their true identity.

Embracing Vulnerability

Embracing vulnerability is an essential aspect of authenticity. It involves being open and honest about one's thoughts, feelings, and experiences, even in the face of potential judgment or rejection. By embracing vulnerability, individuals can build genuine and meaningful connections with others and foster self-acceptance.

Setting Boundaries

Setting boundaries is vital in maintaining authenticity. It involves establishing limits on what is acceptable or comfortable for oneself and communicating these boundaries to others. Setting boundaries allows individuals to prioritize their own needs, values, and well-being, and ensures that they are not compromising their authenticity for the sake of others.

The Impact on Mental Health and Well-being

Discovering self-love and embracing authenticity has a profound impact on mental health and overall well-being. By cultivating self-love and living authentically, individuals experience increased self-esteem, improved mental resilience, and a greater sense of happiness. The ability to be true to oneself and confidently navigate life's challenges contributes to improved mental health outcomes.

Positive Self-Image

Self-love fosters a positive self-image, enabling individuals to appreciate their unique qualities and strengths. Developing a healthy self-image enhances confidence and self-assurance, which positively impacts mental health and overall well-being.

Resilience

Embracing authenticity and loving oneself cultivates resilience. When individuals are secure in their identity, they are better equipped to handle setbacks, criticism, and adversity. They develop the inner strength to navigate challenges and bounce back from hardships, leading to improved mental resilience.

Authentic Relationships

Living authentically attracts genuine and meaningful connections with others. By being true to oneself, individuals attract like-minded individuals who appreciate and accept them for who they are. Authentic relationships provide support, understanding, and validation, contributing to overall well-being.

Practical Strategies for Discovering Self-Love and Authenticity

Discovering self-love and embracing authenticity is a lifelong journey that requires commitment and self-reflection. Here are some practical strategies to facilitate this process:

Journaling

Journaling is a powerful tool for self-discovery and self-reflection. Through writing, individuals can explore their thoughts, emotions, and experiences, gaining clarity about their true desires and values. Setting aside time for regular journaling allows for deeper self-exploration and self-acceptance.

Seeking Support

Seeking support from trusted individuals can be instrumental in cultivating self-love and authenticity. Friends, family, and mentors who provide unconditional support can offer guidance, validation, and perspectives that contribute to personal growth and self-acceptance.

Mindfulness Practices

Practicing mindfulness helps individuals develop self-awareness and acceptance. Mindfulness involves being present in the moment, non-judgmentally observing one's thoughts and emotions. Mindfulness practices, such as meditation or deep breathing exercises, can promote self-compassion and acceptance.

Engaging in Self-Expression

Engaging in self-expression allows individuals to embrace their authenticity and celebrate their unique identities. This can take various forms, such as creative arts, writing, fashion, or participating in advocacy work. By expressing themselves authentically, individuals reinforce their self-love and inspire others to do the same.

Embracing Self-Love and Authenticity: Key Takeaways

Discovering self-love and embracing authenticity is a transformative journey that requires self-reflection, self-acceptance, and the courage to be vulnerable. By prioritizing self-care, setting boundaries, and practicing self-compassion, individuals can cultivate self-love and create a positive relationship with themselves. Embracing authenticity allows individuals to live in alignment with their true selves, fostering resilience, and attracting genuine connections. The impact on mental health and overall well-being is profound, leading to increased self-esteem, improved mental resilience, and a greater sense of happiness. By incorporating practical strategies such as journaling, seeking support, practicing mindfulness, and engaging in self-expression, individuals can embark on a path of self-discovery, self-acceptance, and lasting personal growth. Embracing self-love and authenticity not only benefits the individual but also paves the way for a more accepting and inclusive world.

The Importance of Mental Health Advocacy

Mental health advocacy plays a crucial role in creating an inclusive and supportive society. It involves promoting awareness, understanding, and action to address mental health challenges faced by individuals, including members of the LGBTQ community. In this subsection, we will explore the importance of mental health advocacy and its significance in supporting the well-being and resilience of LGBTQ individuals.

Understanding Mental Health in the LGBTQ Community

Mental health challenges are prevalent among LGBTQ individuals due to the unique experiences and societal pressures they face. Discrimination, stigma, and social exclusion can contribute to increased rates of anxiety, depression, substance abuse, self-harm, and suicide within this community. It is essential to recognize and address these mental health disparities to ensure the overall well-being of LGBTQ individuals.

Creating Safe Spaces and Support Networks

One of the primary goals of mental health advocacy is to create safe spaces for LGBTQ individuals to seek support and access mental health services. These safe spaces can include LGBTQ-specific support groups, community centers, and online platforms that provide a sense of belonging, understanding, and validation. By connecting individuals with shared experiences, these spaces reduce isolation and foster a supportive network.

Promoting LGBTQ-Inclusive Mental Health Services

Mental health advocacy also emphasizes the importance of LGBTQ-inclusive mental health services. This means ensuring mental healthcare professionals receive education and training in understanding the unique mental health needs and experiences of LGBTQ individuals. The development of specialized LGBTQ-affirmative therapy practices can help address specific challenges and promote better mental health outcomes within the community.

Combating Stigma and Prejudice

Mental health advocacy for the LGBTQ community involves challenging and dismantling the stigma and prejudice that contribute to mental health disparities.

This includes raising awareness, educating the general public, and addressing the harmful stereotypes and misconceptions associated with LGBTQ individuals. By combating these prejudices, mental health advocacy helps promote acceptance, understanding, and empathy.

Supporting LGBTQ Youth Mental Health

Advocacy efforts must prioritize supporting the mental health of LGBTQ youth, as they are particularly vulnerable to mental health challenges. It is crucial to create safe and inclusive environments within schools, families, and communities to mitigate the negative impact of stigma, bullying, and rejection. Advocacy can also involve implementing mental health programs specifically tailored to LGBTQ youth needs.

Addressing Intersectionality of Mental Health

Mental health advocacy within the LGBTQ community must recognize and address the intersectionality of identities. LGBTQ individuals may also face discrimination and mental health challenges related to their race, ethnicity, socioeconomic status, or disability. Advocacy efforts should aim to create inclusive spaces that acknowledge and support the complex experiences of individuals at the intersections of multiple identities.

Promoting Self-Care and Well-being

Mental health advocacy encourages self-care practices and promotes overall well-being among LGBTQ individuals. This can involve promoting healthy coping mechanisms, stress management techniques, and self-compassion. Advocacy efforts should also highlight the importance of seeking professional help when needed and destigmatizing the use of therapy and medication as forms of support.

Raising Awareness and Destigmatizing Mental Health

Raising awareness about mental health challenges faced by the LGBTQ community is a key aspect of mental health advocacy. By destigmatizing conversations around mental health, we can create an environment that encourages open dialogues and facilitates access to appropriate support and resources. This includes challenging harmful societal narratives that undermine the validity of LGBTQ individuals' mental health concerns.

The Role of Education and Research

Education and research play a vital role in mental health advocacy. By promoting research on LGBTQ mental health, we can better understand the unique challenges and develop evidence-based interventions. Education initiatives can help foster empathy, understanding, and allyship among healthcare professionals, educators, and the general public. This knowledge serves as a foundation for effective mental health advocacy.

Advocacy in Policy and Legislation

Mental health advocacy within the LGBTQ community also extends to policy and legislation. Advocacy efforts focus on lobbying for equal access to mental health services, developing policies that support LGBTQ-inclusive mental healthcare, and challenging discriminatory practices. By shaping policies, mental health advocacy can create a legal framework that protects the rights and well-being of LGBTQ individuals.

Unconventional Approach: The Power of Art Therapy

In addition to traditional advocacy methods, utilizing unconventional approaches such as art therapy can be effective in supporting the mental health of LGBTQ individuals. Art therapy provides a creative outlet for self-expression, allowing individuals to explore and process their emotions. It can serve as a therapeutic tool, promoting healing, self-discovery, and resilience within the LGBTQ community.

Conclusion: A Call to Action

Mental health advocacy within the LGBTQ community is a crucial endeavor that requires ongoing commitment and collaboration. By creating safe spaces, promoting LGBTQ-inclusive mental health services, combating stigma, supporting youth, addressing intersectionality, and employing various approaches, we can strengthen the mental health outcomes for members of the LGBTQ community. Through education, research, policy change, and the unyielding dedication of advocates, we can build a more inclusive society that values and protects the mental health and well-being of all individuals, regardless of their sexual orientation or gender identity.

In this subsection, we discussed the importance of mental health advocacy within the LGBTQ community. We explored various aspects, including creating safe spaces, promoting LGBTQ-inclusive mental health services, combating stigma, supporting LGBTQ youth, considering intersectionality, promoting self-care, raising awareness, fostering education and research, advocating for policy change, and utilizing unconventional approaches such as art therapy. By addressing these areas, mental health advocates can help improve the well-being and resilience of LGBTQ individuals, creating a more inclusive and supportive society. Remember, mental health matters, and everyone deserves access to quality care and support.

Balancing Activism and Personal Life

In the quest for social justice and equality, activists often find themselves consumed by their work, dedicating countless hours to their cause. While this level of commitment is commendable, it is crucial for activists, like Irshad Manji, to strike a balance between their activism and personal life. Balancing activism and personal life is not only vital for the overall well-being of the individual but also ensures the sustainability and effectiveness of their advocacy efforts. In this subsection, we will explore strategies and considerations for achieving this balance.

The Importance of Self-Care

One of the fundamental aspects of balancing activism and personal life is practicing self-care. Activism can be emotionally and physically draining, often exposing activists to traumatic experiences, constant criticism, and burnout. To maintain resilience and effectiveness, activists must prioritize self-care. This includes engaging in activities that promote physical, mental, and emotional well-being, such as regular exercise, meditation, therapy, and connecting with loved ones. By taking care of themselves, activists can prevent burnout and better cope with the challenges they face.

Setting Boundaries and Prioritizing

Balancing activism and personal life necessitates establishing clear boundaries and priorities. Activists often have a long list of tasks and demands, but it is important to set realistic expectations and recognize personal limitations. Prioritizing projects and commitments ensures that time and energy are allocated appropriately. By setting clear boundaries, activists can create space for their personal lives, relationships, and hobbies, which are essential for maintaining balance and avoiding a sense of constant urgency.

Delegating and Collaborating

Recognizing that activism is a collective effort is crucial for balancing personal life. Activists should learn to delegate tasks and collaborate with others. This not only lightens the workload but also allows for shared responsibility and a diversity of perspectives. By building relationships and partnerships, activists can create a support network that enables them to step back when necessary without compromising the progress of their cause.

Time Management and Organization

Effective time management and organization are essential skills for activists seeking to balance their personal and activist commitments. Creating a structured schedule, setting aside dedicated time for personal activities, and actively managing tasks can help maintain a healthy balance. Utilizing productivity tools and techniques, such as goal-setting, prioritization, and time-tracking, can enhance efficiency and ensure that important personal aspects of life receive the attention they deserve.

Maintaining Perspective and Celebrating Achievements

In the midst of activism, it is easy to focus solely on the challenges and losses. However, it is crucial to maintain perspective and celebrate achievements, no matter how small. Recognizing progress and victories reinforces motivation and provides a sense of fulfillment, contributing to overall well-being and maintaining the drive to continue the fight for equality.

Unconventional Wisdom

In the process of balancing activism and personal life, it is essential to remember that self-care does not equate to selfishness. Prioritizing personal well-being does not diminish the importance of the work being done; rather, it ensures that activists can sustain their commitment and make a lasting impact. Activists should embrace the idea that taking care of themselves is just as important as advocating for others.

Real-World Example

To illustrate the importance of balancing activism and personal life, let us consider the example of an LGBTQ rights activist working tirelessly to advance transgender rights. While their dedication and passion are commendable, they find themselves constantly overwhelmed, neglecting their personal relationships and hobbies. As a result, their energy and motivation begin to dwindle, leading to decreased effectiveness in their advocacy efforts.

Realizing the need for balance, the activist starts incorporating self-care practices into their routine. They set aside time each day for meditation, exercise, and quality time with loved ones. Additionally, they start delegating tasks and collaborating with other activists, cultivating a strong support network. With improved self-care and time management, the activist finds renewed energy and motivation, leading to more impactful and sustainable advocacy. They also serve as an inspiration to other activists on the importance of balance and self-care.

Resources and Tools

To assist activists in balancing their activism and personal life, various resources and tools are available:

- "Activism and Well-being: A Guide for Social Justice Advocates" by The Tzedek Social Justice Fund provides practical advice and strategies for maintaining well-being while engaging in activism.

- The book "The Burnout Cure: Learning to Love Stress" by Dr. Christie Ford offers insights on preventing and recovering from burnout, with tips and techniques for self-care.

- Online platforms, such as Trello and Google Calendar, can help with managing tasks, setting goals, and organizing one's schedule effectively.

- Community organizations and support groups focused on activism and self-care provide spaces for activists to share experiences, resources, and strategies for balancing personal and activist commitments.

- Professional therapists or counselors experienced in working with activists can provide guidance and support in maintaining balance and managing the emotional challenges of activism.

Summary

Balancing activism and personal life is essential for the overall well-being, sustainability, and effectiveness of activists. Prioritizing self-care, setting boundaries, delegating tasks, and managing time diligently are just a few strategies that can help activists create a healthy balance. By acknowledging the importance of personal well-being alongside their activism, activists like Irshad Manji can continue making a meaningful impact while leading fulfilling lives. Remember, self-care and balance are not selfish; they are vital for long-term and impactful activism.

Embracing Self-Expression

In this subsection, we delve into the importance of embracing self-expression as an integral aspect of LGBTQ activism and personal growth. Self-expression allows individuals to authentically showcase their true selves, challenge societal norms, and cultivate a sense of empowerment. It plays a vital role in advocating for LGBTQ rights and fostering understanding and acceptance within society.

Understanding Self-Expression

Self-expression refers to the unique and individual ways in which people communicate their identities, beliefs, and emotions to the world. It involves using various forms of artistic and creative expression, such as writing, painting, music, fashion, and performance, to convey personal experiences and perspectives.

For LGBTQ individuals, self-expression often plays a crucial role in navigating their identities and overcoming societal and cultural expectations. It offers a platform for individuals to embrace their queerness, celebrate their diverse identities, and challenge the heteronormative constraints imposed by society.

Self-Expression in Activism

Self-expression is a powerful tool in LGBTQ activism, enabling individuals to raise awareness, break barriers, and spark conversations about queer issues. Through artistic mediums and creative endeavors, activists effectively communicate their stories and advocate for LGBTQ rights.

Art exhibits, poetry slams, spoken-word performances, and music concerts are just a few examples of how self-expression is harnessed to foster inclusivity and promote social change. These platforms allow LGBTQ activists to share their experiences, educate others, and build bridges of empathy and understanding.

The Role of Fashion and Style

Fashion and personal style are forms of self-expression often utilized by LGBTQ individuals to challenge gender norms and express their unique identities. LGBTQ activists have long used fashion as a means of political statement, reclaiming spaces and advocating for acceptance.

From Harvey Milk's iconic rainbow flag to the contemporary fashion movements like gender-neutral clothing and queer fashion shows, the LGBTQ community has continuously challenged the status quo through style. Fashion can serve as a powerful visual symbol, allowing individuals to embrace their authentic selves and encourage others to do the same.

The Intersection of Self-Expression and Mental Health

Embracing self-expression is not only essential for external advocacy but also for internal well-being. It provides a channel for LGBTQ individuals to express their emotions, explore their identities, and enhance their mental health.

Studies have shown that engaging in creative self-expression, such as journaling, painting, or dancing, can reduce stress, increase self-awareness, and foster self-acceptance. By engaging in self-expression, LGBTQ individuals can find solace, build resilience, and embrace their identities with confidence and pride.

Promoting Self-Expression in LGBTQ Spaces

Creating safe and inclusive spaces that foster self-expression is paramount in supporting the mental health and well-being of LGBTQ individuals. LGBTQ organizations, community centers, and support groups should actively encourage and provide platforms for individuals to express themselves authentically.

Organizing art workshops, open mic nights, and storytelling events can empower LGBTQ individuals to share their experiences, connect with others, and celebrate their identities. These spaces ensure that self-expression becomes a central component of the community and allow for growth, healing, and empowerment.

Challenges and Opportunities

While self-expression is liberating, it is important to recognize the unique challenges that LGBTQ individuals may face. Societal prejudice, discrimination, and fear of judgment can hinder self-expression and restrict individual freedoms.

Addressing these challenges requires collective effort from both LGBTQ activists and allies. By promoting inclusivity, educating society, and challenging harmful stereotypes, we can create an environment that allows for diverse forms of self-expression to thrive.

Unlocking the Power of Self-Expression

To fully unlock the power of self-expression, it is essential to encourage creativity, celebrate diversity, and amplify marginalized voices. This can be achieved through: 1. Providing access to creative resources and education for all individuals, regardless of their socioeconomic background. 2. Actively promoting LGBTQ artists, musicians, and performers who use their platforms to defy norms and advocate for change. 3. Engaging in collaborations between LGBTQ and mainstream artists, fostering dialogue and bridging gaps between communities. 4. Supporting LGBTQ-focused art and creative centers that prioritize inclusivity, diversity, and self-expression. 5. Recognizing the intersectionality of identities and experiences within the LGBTQ community and amplifying underrepresented voices.

By embracing self-expression as a fundamental aspect of LGBTQ activism, we not only fuel personal growth and well-being but also create a world that embraces diversity, equality, and self-acceptance. Let us celebrate individuality, encourage creative freedom, and inspire future generations to confidently express their authentic selves. Together, we can build a more inclusive and vibrant world where everyone's voice is heard and valued.

Impacting Policies and Legislation

Lobbying for LGBTQ Rights

Lobbying is a crucial aspect of any social movement, including the fight for LGBTQ rights. It involves advocating for policy changes, influencing lawmakers, and raising awareness about the issues faced by the LGBTQ community. Lobbying can be done by individuals, organizations, or groups, and is aimed at creating legal and societal changes that promote equality and acceptance.

1. Understanding the Importance of Lobbying

Lobbying plays a significant role in promoting LGBTQ rights because it helps shape legislative agendas, influences public opinion, and pushes for necessary policy reforms. By engaging in lobbying efforts, activists can exert pressure on lawmakers and decision-makers to ensure that the rights and needs of LGBTQ individuals are recognized and protected.

2. Building Advocacy Networks

Successful lobbying requires building strong advocacy networks within the LGBTQ community and beyond. Collaboration with other organizations, activists, and allies can amplify the voices of marginalized individuals and create a unified front for change. These networks provide support, share resources, and coordinate efforts to lobby for LGBTQ rights effectively.

3. Identifying Target Policies and Legislation

To lobby effectively, it is essential to identify specific policies and legislation that need to be addressed or implemented. These may include laws related to anti-discrimination, hate crimes, marriage equality, healthcare access, employment, and housing. By focusing on specific issues, activists can develop targeted strategies for change and have a greater impact on policymakers.

4. Engaging with Lawmakers

Lobbying involves engaging with lawmakers and key decision-makers to advocate for LGBTQ rights. This can be done through meetings, hearings, public testimonies, and written communications. Effective communication skills, persuasive arguments, and a deep understanding of the issues at hand are crucial when engaging with policymakers. Personal stories and experiences can be powerful tools in conveying the urgency and importance of LGBTQ rights.

5. Leveraging Public Opinion and Media

Public opinion and media play a significant role in lobbying efforts. By working strategically with media outlets, activists can raise awareness about LGBTQ issues, challenge stereotypes and misinformation, and shape public opinion. It is essential to develop relationships with journalists, use social media platforms to disseminate information, organize awareness campaigns, and leverage popular support to influence policymakers.

6. Coalition Building and Grassroots Mobilization

Lobbying is not just about working with policymakers; it also involves grassroots mobilization and building coalitions with other social justice movements. By forming alliances with feminist, racial justice, disability rights, and other groups, LGBTQ activists can create a more inclusive and powerful movement. Collaborative efforts broaden the scope of advocacy and increase the chances of legislative success.

7. Fundraising and Resource Mobilization

Lobbying requires financial resources to support advocacy efforts, organize events, and sustain campaigns. Fundraising and resource mobilization play a crucial role in ensuring the sustainability and effectiveness of lobbying initiatives. Activists can seek funding from individual donors, foundations, and corporate sponsors who are aligned with their cause. Additionally, organizing fundraising events and leveraging social media platforms can also generate financial support for lobbying activities.

8. Overcoming Challenges and Opposition

Lobbying for LGBTQ rights is not without its challenges. Activists may face opposition from conservative groups, religious organizations, and lawmakers who hold prejudiced views or oppose equality measures. It is important to anticipate and address these challenges by building coalitions, countering misinformation, and engaging in respectful and evidence-based dialogue. Flexibility, resilience, and persistence are key in navigating these obstacles and continuing the fight for justice.

9. Evaluating the Impact of Lobbying Efforts

Regular evaluation of lobbying efforts is crucial to measure impact and adjust strategies accordingly. Monitoring changes in policies, assessing the public's perception, and tracking improvements in institutional practices provide valuable insights into the effectiveness of lobbying initiatives. These evaluations help activists identify areas for improvement, celebrate successes, and ensure that efforts are aligned with the evolving needs of the LGBTQ community.

10. Continuing the Fight for LGBTQ Rights

Lobbying for LGBTQ rights is an ongoing process that requires long-term commitment and dedication. The fight for equality and acceptance will continue to evolve as new challenges and issues emerge. Activists must remain vigilant and adapt their strategies to respond to changing political landscapes, societal attitudes, and legal frameworks. By staying informed, connected, and committed, those lobbying for LGBTQ rights will contribute to a more inclusive and accepting world for all.

Collaborating With Human Rights Organizations

Collaborating with human rights organizations is a crucial aspect of Irshad Manji's work as a queer Muslim activist. Through partnerships with various organizations, Manji has been able to amplify her message, advocate for change, and create a global impact. In this subsection, we will explore the importance of collaboration with human rights organizations, the benefits it brings, and the strategies and challenges involved.

The Importance of Collaboration

Collaboration with human rights organizations allows for collective strength in advocating for LGBTQ rights and promoting inclusivity within Muslim communities. By joining forces, activists and organizations can pool their resources, expertise, and influence to drive meaningful change on a broader scale.

One key benefit of collaboration is the ability to tap into a wider network of allies and supporters. Human rights organizations often have established connections with politicians, policymakers, and influencers, which can help amplify the message and create a larger platform for advocacy. By working together, activists can leverage these networks to push for policy changes, legislative reforms, and societal acceptance.

Moreover, collaboration allows for the sharing of knowledge, best practices, and strategies. Human rights organizations often have extensive experience in navigating legal frameworks, organizing campaigns, and implementing effective advocacy initiatives. Working alongside these organizations provides valuable insights and guidance, enabling activists like Manji to more effectively tackle the complex challenges they face.

Strategies and Approaches

Collaboration with human rights organizations can take various forms, depending on the specific goals and contexts of the advocacy work. Here are some strategies and approaches that have been successful in the collaboration between Irshad Manji and human rights organizations:

1. **Partnerships and Alliances:** Building partnerships and alliances with established human rights organizations that share a common vision and goals. This allows for the pooling of resources, expertise, and networks, creating a stronger collective voice for change.

2. **Joint Campaigns and Advocacy:** Collaborating on campaigns and advocacy efforts to raise awareness about LGBTQ rights within Muslim communities and advocate for policy reforms. By working together, activists and organizations can reach a broader audience, create a larger impact, and put greater pressure on decision-makers.

3. **Capacity Building:** Collaborating on capacity-building initiatives, such as training programs and workshops, to equip activists with the necessary skills and knowledge to navigate the complexities of LGBTQ rights activism. Human rights organizations can provide valuable guidance and support in areas such as strategic planning, media engagement, and fundraising.

4. **Information Sharing and Research:** Collaborating on research projects and information sharing to generate data and evidence that supports the advocacy work. Human rights organizations often have access to research resources and expertise that can strengthen the evidence base of the movement, thereby increasing its credibility and influence.

5. **International Solidarity**: Collaborating with international human rights organizations to foster global solidarity and support for LGBTQ rights in Muslim-majority countries. This can include participation in international forums, conferences, and campaigns, as well as leveraging international human rights frameworks to hold governments accountable.

Challenges and Considerations

While collaboration with human rights organizations brings numerous benefits, it is not without its challenges. It is important to navigate these challenges effectively to ensure a successful partnership. Here are some considerations to keep in mind:

1. **Maintaining Authenticity**: It is crucial for activists like Irshad Manji to maintain their authenticity and independence while collaborating with organizations. Ensuring that the partnership aligns with their values, goals, and principles is essential to avoid dilution of the advocacy message.

2. **Power Dynamics**: Power dynamics within collaborations can pose challenges. Activists must be mindful of potential imbalances in authority, resources, and decision-making. Fostering open and transparent communication, and establishing shared decision-making processes, can mitigate these challenges.

3. **Cultural Sensitivity**: Collaborating with human rights organizations from different cultural contexts requires a deep understanding of local customs, sensitivities, and nuances. It is important to approach collaborations with cultural humility and respect, ensuring that the voices and experiences of marginalized communities within Muslim-majority countries are centered and respected.

4. **Legal and Safety Concerns**: Collaborating with human rights organizations in countries with repressive laws and limited freedoms can pose legal and safety challenges. Activists must be diligent in assessing the risks and taking measures to ensure the safety of themselves and their collaborators.

Case Study: Collaboration for LGBTQ Rights in Malaysia

A notable example of collaboration between Irshad Manji and human rights organizations is their work in Malaysia, where same-sex relationships are criminalized and LGBTQ individuals face significant discrimination and marginalization.

Manji collaborated with local human rights organizations, such as Sisters in Islam and Justice for Sisters, to advocate for LGBTQ rights and challenge discriminatory laws and policies. Together, they organized workshops, public forums, and campaigns, engaging with diverse stakeholders, including religious leaders, policymakers, and the media.

Through their collaboration, they were able to bring attention to the plight of LGBTQ individuals in Malaysia, challenge societal norms, and influence public opinion. They worked together to highlight the intersections of religious freedom, human rights, and LGBTQ rights, aiming to create a more inclusive and accepting society.

While progress has been slow, the collaboration between Irshad Manji and Malaysian human rights organizations continues to inspire activism and provide hope for a future where LGBTQ individuals can live free from discrimination and persecution.

Conclusion

Collaborating with human rights organizations is a vital strategy for LGBTQ activists like Irshad Manji to drive meaningful changes within Muslim communities. Through partnerships and alliances, activists can leverage resources, expertise, and networks to amplify their message, advocate for policy reforms, and create a global impact. However, collaboration also presents challenges that must be navigated, including power dynamics, cultural sensitivities, and legal and safety concerns. By addressing these challenges and fostering effective collaborations, activists can create a more inclusive and accepting world for LGBTQ individuals.

Influencing Government Decision-Makers

Influencing government decision-makers plays a crucial role in advancing LGBTQ rights and achieving legal reforms. By engaging with key stakeholders, activists can shape policies and legislations that effectively address the needs and rights of the LGBTQ community. This subsection will explore strategies and approaches to effectively influence government decision-makers to promote equality and champion LGBTQ rights.

Understanding the Political Landscape

Before engaging with government decision-makers, it is essential to understand the political landscape and dynamics that influence policy-making. This involves studying political parties, their positions on LGBTQ rights, and key decision-makers within those parties. By identifying the political allies and opponents, activists can develop targeted advocacy strategies.

One effective method is to conduct a political analysis, which involves researching politicians' voting records, public statements, and party platforms. This analysis helps in identifying supportive legislators and building alliances with like-minded individuals. It also helps identify potential allies within government bureaucracies, such as human rights commissions or LGBTQ rights committees.

Building Relationships and Alliances

Building relationships and alliances with government decision-makers is a critical step in influencing policy outcomes. This involves reaching out to policymakers through various channels, including meetings, letters, and public engagements. The goal is to establish a dialogue and build trust based on shared values and interests.

One effective approach is to organize advocacy days or events where LGBTQ activists and community members can meet with government representatives to discuss issues, share personal stories, and provide evidence-based arguments. These events create opportunities for decision-makers to better understand the challenges faced by the LGBTQ community and the importance of policy reforms.

Additionally, building alliances with other advocacy groups and civil society organizations can amplify the impact of LGBTQ advocacy efforts. By collaborating with organizations working on human rights, gender equality, and social justice, activists can leverage collective resources and expertise to influence decision-makers effectively.

Policy Research and Evidence-Based Advocacy

To effectively influence government decision-makers, it is crucial to back advocacy efforts with robust research and evidence. Policymakers are more likely to consider proposals supported by credible data and research. Activists should engage in policy research to understand the specific issues affecting the LGBTQ community and develop evidence-based policy recommendations.

For example, conducting surveys, studies, and collecting data on discrimination, violence, health disparities, and economic inequalities faced by LGBTQ individuals can provide a strong evidence base for advocating for policy changes. Presenting this data in a clear and compelling manner through reports, infographics, and presentations can have a significant impact on decision-makers.

Moreover, developing policy briefs that outline the problem, proposed solutions, and anticipated benefits can help policymakers understand the importance of legislative reforms. These briefs should include case studies, real-life examples, and success stories from jurisdictions that have implemented similar reforms to highlight the positive outcomes.

Engaging in Lobbying and Advocacy

Lobbying and advocacy are powerful tools to influence government decision-making processes. Lobbying involves direct communication with policymakers to promote legislative changes and garner support for LGBTQ rights. Activists can engage in individual or collective lobbying efforts to meet with lawmakers, present their arguments, and advocate for specific policy reforms.

When engaging in lobbying, it is crucial to tailor communication strategies to the specific needs and interests of decision-makers. This may involve framing arguments in a way that highlights economic benefits, public opinion support, or alignment with human rights principles. Communicating key messages effectively and using persuasive techniques, such as storytelling, can leave a lasting impact on decision-makers.

Public Awareness Campaigns

Public awareness campaigns are an essential component of influencing government decision-makers. By raising awareness and rallying public support for LGBTQ rights, activists can create pressure on politicians to prioritize and act on these issues. Public campaigns can include media engagements, social media campaigns, rallies, and protests that highlight the importance of legislative reforms.

To make public campaigns effective, activists should employ strategic messaging and storytelling techniques that resonate with diverse audiences. This involves crafting messages that are relatable, empathetic, and focused on shared values, such as equality, fairness, and human rights. Engaging public figures and celebrities who support LGBTQ rights can also help reach a wider audience and generate public attention.

Taking Legal Action

In certain situations, taking legal action can be an effective strategy to influence government decision-makers. Litigation can highlight the discriminatory nature of existing laws and policies, and create legal precedents that push for legal reforms. By challenging discriminatory laws in courts, activists can raise public awareness and put pressure on governments to reconsider their positions.

When considering legal actions, activists should collaborate with legal experts, human rights organizations, and LGBTQ advocacy groups to develop strategic litigation plans. This involves identifying suitable test cases, gathering evidence, and mobilizing resources to support the legal process. Legal actions can have a lasting impact on government decision-makers, fostering a legal environment conducive to LGBTQ rights.

Conclusion

Influencing government decision-makers is a complex but essential undertaking in the fight for LGBTQ rights. By understanding the political landscape, building relationships and alliances, conducting policy research, engaging in lobbying and advocacy, launching public awareness campaigns, and strategically taking legal actions, activists can effectively shape policies and legislation that promote equality and safeguard the rights of the LGBTQ community. Persistent efforts and collaboration with like-minded individuals and organizations are vital to making a lasting impact on government decision-makers and advancing the cause of LGBTQ rights.

Progress and Setbacks

In the journey towards achieving equality and dismantling discriminatory practices, progress is often accompanied by setbacks. This subsection explores the strides made in LGBTQ activism, as well as the challenges faced along the way.

Recognizing Milestones

Over the years, LGBTQ activists have achieved significant milestones in the fight for equal rights. Marriage equality has been a major triumph, with many countries legalizing same-sex marriage and recognizing the importance of love and commitment regardless of sexual orientation. This progress has been essential in dismantling discriminatory laws and societal beliefs.

Another milestone is the increasing visibility and acceptance of transgender individuals. The transgender rights movement has gained significant momentum, resulting in greater recognition and protection of gender identity. This has led to policy changes in areas such as healthcare, education, and employment, ensuring transgender individuals have the same rights as their cisgender counterparts.

Furthermore, LGBTQ representation in media and popular culture has grown, allowing for greater visibility and understanding. Television shows, movies, and books featuring LGBTQ characters and narratives have helped challenge stereotypes and foster empathy and acceptance.

Challenges and Resistance

Despite the progress made, LGBTQ activists continue to face numerous challenges and setbacks. Advocacy for LGBTQ rights is met with staunch resistance from conservative individuals and religious institutions that hold anti-LGBTQ beliefs. This resistance often leads to legal battles, regressive policy changes, and systemic discrimination.

In some countries, LGBTQ individuals still face persecution, imprisonment, or even the death penalty. These oppressive laws and practices are deeply rooted in cultural norms, religious doctrines, and political ideologies that perpetuate discrimination and prejudice.

Additionally, discrimination and violence against LGBTQ individuals remain prevalent in various aspects of life, including education, employment, healthcare, and housing. Homophobia, transphobia, and biphobia create barriers to equality and hinder progress.

Addressing Backlash and Pushing Forward

To counter setbacks and continue making progress, LGBTQ activists adopt various strategies. Advocacy organizations work tirelessly to challenge discriminatory laws and policies through legal action, lobbying, and grassroots mobilization. They collaborate with allies and human rights organizations to amplify their message and build coalitions for a united front against discrimination.

One effective approach is public education and awareness campaigns that aim to challenge stereotypes and dismantle prejudices. By showcasing the diverse experiences and contributions of LGBTQ individuals, these campaigns foster empathy and understanding, gradually shifting societal attitudes.

LGBTQ activists also emphasize the importance of inclusive education that acknowledges and celebrates diverse sexual orientations and gender identities. They advocate for comprehensive sexual education that covers LGBTQ topics and promotes lessons of acceptance, consent, and healthy relationships.

Additionally, activists push for workplace equality, demanding non-discrimination policies and inclusive practices. This involves educating employers and employees about LGBTQ issues and creating safe and welcoming environments for everyone.

Unconventional Solution: Allyship and Intersectionality

One unconventional yet highly effective solution lies in the power of allyship and intersectionality. Allies, who may not identify as LGBTQ themselves, play a crucial role in advocating for equal rights. They use their privilege to uplift marginalized voices, challenge discrimination, and create more inclusive spaces.

Moreover, recognizing the intersections between different forms of discrimination is vital for comprehensive activism. LGBTQ individuals often experience discrimination simultaneously based on their sexual orientation, gender identity, race, religion, or disability. By understanding and addressing these intersections, activists can better advocate for the rights of individuals facing overlapping systems of oppression.

Real-World Example: Progress in LGBTQ Healthcare

A concrete example of progress in the LGBTQ rights movement is the advancement of LGBTQ healthcare. In the past, LGBTQ individuals often faced discrimination, unequal access to care, and insensitivity from healthcare providers. However, in recent years, there has been an increased focus on LGBTQ-inclusive healthcare practices.

Healthcare organizations have implemented policies to ensure that LGBTQ individuals receive culturally competent and affirming care. This includes staff training on LGBTQ health issues, using inclusive language, and creating supportive environments.

Additionally, some healthcare systems now offer specialized services such as hormone replacement therapy for transgender individuals, sexual health resources tailored to LGBTQ populations, and mental health support for LGBTQ youth.

While there is still work to be done to achieve full equality in healthcare, this progress showcases the power of advocacy efforts in combating discrimination and improving the quality of care for LGBTQ individuals.

Conclusion

Progress in LGBTQ activism is undeniable, with advancements in marriage equality, transgender rights, media representation, and increased visibility. However, setbacks persist, fueled by resistance, discrimination, and oppressive laws. By addressing challenges head-on, embracing allyship and intersectionality, and highlighting real-world examples of progress, the LGBTQ rights movement can forge ahead towards a more inclusive and accepting future.

Leaving a Lasting Legacy

Leaving a lasting legacy is not just about making a name for oneself, but rather about creating a positive and long-lasting impact on society. In this subsection, we will explore how Irshad Manji, the queer Muslim activist, has left a lasting legacy through her tireless advocacy for LGBTQ rights and her fearless pursuit of social justice.

The Power of Visibility

One of the most significant ways in which Irshad Manji has left a lasting legacy is through her visibility as a queer Muslim activist. By openly sharing her personal story and experiences, she has shattered stereotypes and challenged societal norms, inspiring countless individuals to embrace their true identities.

Through her visibility, Manji has shown that it is possible to reconcile one's faith with one's sexual orientation, and that being true to oneself is essential for personal growth and happiness. Her courage to live authentically has empowered LGBTQ individuals, especially queer Muslims, to embrace their own identities and strive for acceptance and inclusion within their communities.

Empowering Others to Speak Out

Another way in which Manji has left a lasting legacy is by empowering others to speak out and share their stories. Through her work, she has encouraged marginalized individuals, particularly LGBTQ Muslims, to find their voice and challenge societal and religious barriers.

Manji's mentorship programs and advocacy initiatives have provided a platform for LGBTQ individuals to share their experiences, express their concerns, and advocate for change. By amplifying their voices, she has helped create a supportive network of activists who continue to push for LGBTQ rights and challenge discrimination within their communities.

Creating Safe Spaces for LGBTQ Muslims

Manji's legacy also lies in her work towards creating safe spaces for LGBTQ Muslims. Recognizing the struggles faced by queer individuals within religious communities, she has established organizations and initiatives that provide support, resources, and counseling to those in need.

These safe spaces serve as havens where individuals can freely express themselves, discuss their challenges, and find acceptance and understanding. By fostering dialogue and empathy, Manji has paved the way for a more inclusive and compassionate culture, where LGBTQ Muslims can navigate their identities without fear or prejudice.

Promoting LGBTQ+ Inclusion in Mosques

One of Manji's remarkable achievements is her advocacy for LGBTQ+ inclusion within mosques. Recognizing the importance of religious spaces in the lives of many individuals, she has worked tirelessly to challenge heteronormativity and create acceptance within Muslim communities.

Manji has engaged in dialogue with religious leaders, highlighting the need for revisiting traditional interpretations of Islamic teachings and reimagining a more inclusive understanding of sexuality and gender. By creating resources, leading workshops, and organizing training sessions, she has provided tools for mosques to become more inclusive and welcoming, supporting LGBTQ+ individuals in their spiritual journeys.

Cultivating Empathy Through Storytelling

Storytelling has been a powerful tool in Manji's legacy, as it allows for the cultivation of empathy and understanding. Through her writing, speaking engagements, and media presence, she has shared stories that humanize LGBTQ+ individuals, dispel ignorance, and challenge stereotypes.

By sharing personal narratives and highlighting the diversity within the LGBTQ+ community, Manji has encouraged others to view queer individuals as complex human beings with shared hopes, dreams, and struggles. This storytelling approach has helped break down barriers, fostered compassion, and ultimately contributed to a more inclusive and accepting society.

In conclusion, Irshad Manji has left a lasting legacy through her work as a queer Muslim activist. As a visible and unapologetic advocate for LGBTQ+ rights, she has inspired others to embrace their true identities and strive for acceptance. Through her efforts, Manji has empowered marginalized individuals, created safe spaces, promoted inclusivity within religious communities, and cultivated empathy through storytelling. Her legacy serves as a reminder of the importance of standing up for justice and creating a more inclusive world for future generations.

Advocacy for Legislative Change

In this subsection, we delve into the crucial role of advocacy for legislative change in advancing LGBTQ rights. Irshad Manji's journey as an activist is characterized by her tireless efforts to challenge discriminatory laws and promote legal reforms.

Through her advocacy strategies, Manji has been instrumental in influencing government decision-makers and shaping policies that protect and promote the rights of the LGBTQ community.

Understanding the Importance of Legislative Change

Legislative change plays a pivotal role in dismantling systemic discrimination and ensuring that the LGBTQ community enjoys equal rights and protections under the law. By advocating for legal reforms, activists like Manji work towards creating a more inclusive society that respects and upholds the rights of all individuals, regardless of their sexual orientation or gender identity.

Through legislation, activists can address a range of issues that impact LGBTQ individuals, such as marriage equality, nondiscrimination protections, healthcare access, and the criminalization of homosexuality. Legislative change is a powerful tool in challenging discriminatory practices and promoting a more inclusive society.

Identifying Problematic Laws and Policies

Advocacy for legislative change begins with identifying and challenging problematic laws and policies that infringe upon the rights of the LGBTQ community. Manji's expertise lies in meticulously examining legal frameworks, both within her own community and globally, to identify discriminatory laws and advocate for their revision or repeal.

For example, Manji has drawn attention to the oppressive laws that criminalize homosexuality in many countries, leading to harassment, violence, and persecution of LGBTQ individuals. By shedding light on these discriminatory laws, she has been able to mobilize support and advocate for legal reforms that protect the rights and safety of LGBTQ people.

Collaborating with Human Rights Organizations

Effective advocacy for legislative change often requires collaboration with human rights organizations that share the same goals. By partnering with these organizations, activists like Manji can leverage their collective expertise, resources, and networks to amplify their efforts and advocate for legislative reforms at a larger scale.

Collaboration with organizations such as Amnesty International, Human Rights Watch, and the International Gay and Lesbian Human Rights Commission enables activists to access crucial legal expertise, engage in strategic lobbying efforts, and utilize international mechanisms to press for legislative change.

Through these partnerships, activists can navigate complex legal systems and mobilize support from various stakeholders, including policymakers, legal professionals, and civil society.

Influencing Government Decision-Makers

Advocacy for legislative change involves engaging with government decision-makers to express the need for legal reforms that advance LGBTQ rights. Influencing policymakers requires skillful communication, evidence-based arguments, and building relationships of trust and respect.

Manji has actively engaged with politicians, policymakers, and government officials to educate them about the issues affecting the LGBTQ community. Through dialogues, meetings, and public engagement, she has been able to convey the urgency and importance of legislative change, highlighting the need for policies that protect LGBTQ rights, promote equality, and challenge discriminatory practices.

Tackling Challenges and Setbacks

Advocacy for legislative change is not without its challenges and setbacks. Pushing for legal reforms often meets with resistance from conservative groups and individuals who oppose LGBTQ rights. Activists like Manji face significant barriers, including political opposition, cultural biases, and deep-rooted prejudices, which can impede progress.

To address these challenges, effective advocacy strategies involve building broad-based coalitions, mobilizing public support, and countering misinformation. Activists must also be resilient in the face of setbacks, adapting their approaches and strategies to navigate the political landscape, and continuing to push for legislative change through innovative means.

The Role of International Human Rights Law

International human rights law provides a powerful framework for advocacy for legislative change. It sets out universal principles and standards that all governments should uphold, including the rights of LGBTQ individuals.

By highlighting the international commitments and obligations that governments have entered into, activists can hold them accountable for protecting LGBTQ rights. Manji has effectively utilized international human rights law to advocate for legislative change, drawing attention to the discrepancies between national laws and international standards.

Creating Policy Recommendations

Advocacy for legislative change involves developing policy recommendations that address the specific needs and concerns of the LGBTQ community. Manji's expertise in researching and analyzing complex issues allows her to propose practical and evidence-based policy solutions to advance LGBTQ rights.

Policy recommendations must be comprehensive, addressing a wide range of issues ranging from healthcare and education to employment and family rights. They should be guided by principles of inclusivity, equal protection, and respect for human rights.

Strengthening LGBTQ Rights Globally

Advocacy for legislative change is not limited to national borders. Activists like Manji work towards strengthening LGBTQ rights globally by engaging with international organizations, forging alliances with activists from different countries, and promoting dialogue and collaboration across regions.

By sharing experiences, strategies, and lessons learned, activists can build a global movement that amplifies the voices of LGBTQ individuals and advocates for legislative change worldwide. Strengthening international solidarity is integral to advancing LGBTQ rights and fostering a more inclusive and accepting world.

In conclusion, advocacy for legislative change is a vital component of LGBTQ activism. Through identifying problematic laws, collaborating with human rights organizations, engaging with government decision-makers, and utilizing international human rights law, activists like Irshad Manji are able to shape policies that protect and promote the rights of LGBTQ individuals. While challenges and setbacks may arise, sustained efforts in advocacy for legislative change play a pivotal role in building a more inclusive and equitable society for all.

The Role of International Human Rights Law

In the fight for LGBTQ rights, international human rights law plays a crucial role in shaping global policies, advocating for equality, and protecting the rights of marginalized communities. This subsection explores the significance of international human rights law in promoting and protecting the rights of LGBTQ individuals and communities worldwide. We will delve into the principles, mechanisms, and challenges associated with international human rights law and its impact on LGBTQ activism.

Principles of International Human Rights Law

International human rights law is based on the fundamental principles of equality, non-discrimination, and dignity for all individuals, irrespective of their sexual orientation or gender identity. The Universal Declaration of Human Rights (UDHR), adopted by the United Nations General Assembly in 1948, enshrines the principles of human rights and serves as the foundation for international human rights law.

The UDHR, along with subsequent international treaties, such as the International Covenant on Civil and Political Rights (ICCPR) and the International Covenant on Economic, Social and Cultural Rights (ICESCR), recognizes and protects a wide range of human rights, including the right to life, liberty, privacy, freedom of expression, and non-discrimination. These rights form the basis for addressing the different aspects of LGBTQ discrimination and ensuring equal protection for all individuals, regardless of their sexual orientation or gender identity.

Mechanisms of International Human Rights Law

International human rights law operates through a range of mechanisms that monitor and enforce compliance with human rights standards. These mechanisms include international treaties, regional human rights systems, treaty bodies, and special rapporteurs.

International Treaties: The adoption and ratification of international treaties, such as the ICCPR and the ICESCR, create legal obligations for states to respect, protect, and fulfill the rights enshrined in these instruments. These treaties provide a framework for addressing LGBTQ rights within the broader context of human rights.

Regional Human Rights Systems: Regional human rights systems, such as the European Convention on Human Rights (ECHR), the Inter-American Commission on Human Rights, and the African Charter on Human and Peoples' Rights, play a vital role in promoting and protecting human rights at the regional level. These systems complement and reinforce international human rights standards, providing additional avenues for LGBTQ individuals and communities to seek redress for human rights violations.

Treaty Bodies: Treaty bodies are committees of independent experts established under specific international treaties to monitor the implementation of these treaties by states parties. For example, the Human Rights Committee oversees the implementation of the ICCPR. LGBTQ activists can engage with these treaty bodies by submitting shadow reports, participating in hearings, and advocating for robust interpretations of human rights standards that protect LGBTQ rights.

Special Rapporteurs: Special rapporteurs are independent experts appointed by the United Nations Human Rights Council to examine and address specific human rights issues. There are various special rapporteurs who focus on issues related to sexual orientation and gender identity, such as the Special Rapporteur on Violence against Women and the Independent Expert on Sexual Orientation and Gender Identity. These rapporteurs play a critical role in raising awareness, documenting violations, and making recommendations to states on LGBTQ rights.

Challenges and Progress

Despite the progress made in recognizing LGBTQ rights within international human rights law, significant challenges persist. Many states maintain conservative attitudes and cultural or religious beliefs that contribute to discrimination against LGBTQ individuals. These challenges often impede the effective enforcement of LGBTQ rights at the international level.

Limited Recognition: While international human rights law recognizes the importance of LGBTQ rights, not all states have ratified or fully implemented international treaties that protect these rights. In some cases, states may have reservations when ratifying or implementing these treaties, leading to limited legal protections for LGBTQ individuals.

Cultural and Religious Objections: LGBTQ rights often clash with deeply held cultural or religious beliefs in many societies, leading to resistance and opposition to the recognition and protection of these rights. Striking a balance between respecting cultural and religious diversity while upholding human rights principles remains a complex challenge in advancing LGBTQ rights through international human rights law.

Enforcement and Compliance: Ensuring the enforcement and compliance of international human rights standards, especially regarding LGBTQ rights, can be a significant hurdle. Some states fail to investigate and prosecute human rights violations against LGBTQ individuals, while others lack the necessary legal frameworks and institutions to protect these rights effectively.

Despite these challenges, international human rights law has made significant strides in advancing LGBTQ rights globally. Landmark decisions by regional human rights courts, such as the European Court of Human Rights and the Inter-American Court of Human Rights, have affirmed the rights of LGBTQ individuals, debunking discriminatory laws and practices. The work of treaty bodies and special rapporteurs continues to shed light on the violations faced by LGBTQ communities and drive conversations and legal reforms.

Case Study: The Yogyakarta Principles

An important example of the impact of international human rights law on LGBTQ activism is the Yogyakarta Principles. Developed in 2006 by human rights experts from around the world, these principles provide a comprehensive framework for addressing human rights violations based on sexual orientation and gender identity.

The Yogyakarta Principles draw on existing international human rights law to articulate the rights of LGBTQ individuals and the corresponding state obligations. They cover a wide range of issues, including non-discrimination, protection from violence and torture, access to justice, freedom of expression and association, and the right to health.

While the Yogyakarta Principles are not legally binding, they have influenced the interpretation and application of human rights standards concerning LGBTQ rights. They provide a valuable tool for activists, legal professionals, and policymakers to guide their advocacy efforts and promote legal reforms that align with international human rights law.

Resources for LGBTQ Activists

LGBTQ activists can leverage a range of resources to navigate the complexities of international human rights law. Here are some key resources and organizations that provide valuable support:

1. International Lesbian, Gay, Bisexual, Trans, and Intersex Association (ILGA): ILGA is a global federation of LGBTQ rights organizations that advocates for the rights of LGBTQ individuals and communities at the international level. They provide resources, reports, and advocacy tools to support activists worldwide.

2. United Nations Human Rights Council: The United Nations Human Rights Council is an intergovernmental body that promotes and protects human rights globally. LGBTQ activists can engage with the council by submitting reports, participating in sessions, and accessing relevant publications on LGBTQ rights.

3. Human Rights Watch: Human Rights Watch is a non-governmental organization dedicated to researching and advocating for human rights worldwide.

Their reports, policy briefs, and advocacy work shed light on human rights abuses, including those faced by LGBTQ individuals.

4. International Service for Human Rights (ISHR): ISHR works to protect and promote human rights defenders, providing resources, training, and advocacy support. They engage with the United Nations human rights system, including treaty bodies and special rapporteurs, to advance human rights globally.

5. OutRight Action International: OutRight Action International focuses on advancing LGBTQ rights globally. They provide resources, conduct research, and advocate for policy changes that promote LGBTQ rights within international human rights frameworks.

These resources, along with local LGBTQ organizations that are well-versed in international human rights law, can offer valuable guidance and support to activists addressing LGBTQ rights at the international level.

Conclusion

The role of international human rights law in promoting and protecting LGBTQ rights cannot be overstated. International treaties, regional human rights systems, treaty bodies, and special rapporteurs form a comprehensive framework for advocating for equality, non-discrimination, and dignity for all individuals, regardless of their sexual orientation or gender identity.

While challenges persist, progress has been made in recognizing LGBTQ rights within international human rights law. Landmark decisions, advocacy efforts, and the development of guiding principles like the Yogyakarta Principles have shaped the legal landscape, providing essential tools for activists fighting for equality and justice.

As LGBTQ activists continue their advocacy, it is crucial to foster collaboration, engage with international human rights mechanisms, and leverage available resources and organizations to drive positive change and create a more inclusive world for LGBTQ individuals and communities.

Acknowledgments

I would like to express my gratitude to Irshad Manji for her tireless work in advancing LGBTQ rights and inspiring the next generation of activists. Her courage, leadership, and commitment to inclusive and equitable societies have paved the way for meaningful change. I would also like to thank the LGBTQ activists, organizations, and advocates worldwide who continue to fight for justice and equality. Your resilience and determination are shaping a better future for all.

Creating Policy Recommendations

Creating effective policy recommendations is crucial in advancing LGBTQ rights and ensuring equal treatment and protection for all individuals, regardless of their sexual orientation or gender identity. In this subsection, we will explore the key principles and strategies involved in developing impactful policy recommendations that promote inclusivity and address the unique challenges faced by LGBTQ individuals.

Understanding the Context

Before formulating policy recommendations, it is essential to understand the specific contextual factors that influence LGBTQ rights and experiences. Considerations such as the legal and social landscape, cultural norms, and the level of acceptance or discrimination faced by LGBTQ individuals play a significant role in shaping effective policy recommendations.

Identifying Key Areas for Policy Change

To create impactful policy recommendations, it is essential to identify and prioritize the key areas where change is needed. This can include legislation, regulations, institutional practices, and social norms that impede LGBTQ individuals' rights and well-being. Some key areas commonly addressed in LGBTQ policy recommendations include:

- Legal protections against discrimination in employment, housing, education, healthcare, and public services.

- Recognition and legal rights for same-sex partnerships, including marriage equality and adoption rights.

- Inclusive gender identity recognition laws that allow for legal recognition of non-binary, transgender, and intersex individuals.

- Education policies that promote LGBTQ-inclusive curricula, teacher training, and anti-bullying measures.

- Healthcare policies that ensure access to gender-affirming care, mental health support, and HIV prevention and treatment.

- Criminal justice reforms to address disproportionately high rates of violence, harassment, and incarceration faced by LGBTQ individuals.

✦ Immigration policies that protect LGBTQ asylum seekers and refugees fleeing persecution based on their sexual orientation or gender identity.

Evidence-Based Approach

Policy recommendations should be based on robust evidence and research to ensure their effectiveness and credibility. It is important to gather data on the specific challenges faced by LGBTQ individuals in various domains, such as healthcare, education, employment, and criminal justice. This evidence can come from academic studies, surveys, focus groups, and personal testimonies. The data should be analyzed in a rigorous and objective manner to inform policy recommendations that address the root causes of discrimination and inequality.

Engaging Stakeholders

Involving a range of stakeholders in the policy development process is crucial for creating recommendations that are inclusive, realistic, and implementable. This includes policymakers, LGBTQ organizations, human rights groups, community members, and experts from relevant fields such as law, psychology, sociology, and economics. Engaging various stakeholders ensures diverse perspectives are considered, increasing the likelihood of achieving consensus and garnering support for the proposed policy recommendations.

Building Alliances

Creating policy recommendations in isolation may limit their impact. Building alliances with other social justice movements allows for a broader understanding of intersecting identities and shared struggles. Collaborating with organizations advocating for women's rights, racial justice, disability rights, and other marginalized groups can strengthen policy recommendations by fostering a more holistic and inclusive approach.

Clear and Realistic Goals

Policy recommendations should articulate clear and achievable goals. It is important to outline specific outcomes or changes desired within a realistic timeframe. For instance, recommendations could aim to amend existing legislation, develop new policies, or advocate for the inclusion of LGBTQ rights in international human rights standards. Clarity around goals facilitates effective advocacy and helps measure progress towards desired outcomes.

Advocacy and Implementation Strategies

Policy recommendations should be accompanied by well-thought-out advocacy and implementation strategies. This involves identifying key decision-makers, leveraging public opinion and media support, mobilizing grassroots activism, and utilizing legal avenues to create pressure for change. Building diverse coalitions and alliances strengthens advocacy efforts, amplifying the voices of LGBTQ individuals, and increasing the likelihood of successful implementation.

Tracking Progress and Evaluation

It is crucial to monitor and evaluate the implementation of policy recommendations to track progress and identify areas for improvement. This includes holding decision-makers accountable, collecting data on the impact of policy changes, and assessing outcomes against the original goals. Regular evaluation informs iterative adjustments, ensuring that policy recommendations remain responsive to evolving needs and challenges in the LGBTQ community.

Unconventional Approach: Creative Campaigning

To capture attention and generate public support, creative campaigning can be a powerful tool alongside traditional policy recommendations. Artistic expressions such as music, poetry, theater, visual arts, and social media can help raise awareness, challenge stereotypes, and humanize LGBTQ experiences. By fostering empathy and building connections between diverse audiences, creative campaigns can break down barriers and foster dialogue towards policy change.

Conclusion

Creating effective policy recommendations requires a comprehensive understanding of the context, evidence-based approaches, stakeholder engagement, and strategic advocacy efforts. By prioritizing key areas for policy change, building alliances, and setting clear goals, we can advance LGBTQ rights and work towards a more inclusive and equitable society. Through ongoing evaluation and innovative approaches, policymakers and advocates can drive positive change and ensure the protection and dignity of all LGBTQ individuals. Remember, the fight for equality continues, and your contributions matter.

Strengthening LGBTQ Rights Globally

In this subsection, we will explore the importance of strengthening LGBTQ rights globally and the various strategies and initiatives that can be employed to achieve this goal. We will examine the significance of international cooperation, legal reforms, and advocacy efforts in creating a more inclusive and accepting world for LGBTQ individuals.

The Global Landscape of LGBTQ Rights

The status of LGBTQ rights varies greatly across different countries and regions. While some countries have made significant strides in recognizing and protecting the rights of LGBTQ individuals, many others still lag behind, with discriminatory laws and social attitudes prevailing. In order to strengthen LGBTQ rights on a global scale, it is crucial to understand the existing challenges and opportunities in different contexts.

International Cooperation and Advancement

One of the key strategies in strengthening LGBTQ rights globally is international cooperation. Collaboration between governments, organizations, and activists worldwide can have a powerful impact on driving progress and fostering change. By sharing best practices, resources, and knowledge, countries can work together to create a more inclusive and equitable society.

Promoting intergovernmental dialogue and cooperation can lead to the establishment of international frameworks and agreements that protect LGBTQ rights. For example, the United Nations' Universal Declaration of Human Rights and the International Covenant on Civil and Political Rights explicitly protect the rights of all individuals, regardless of their sexual orientation or gender identity. Advocacy efforts to ensure the implementation and enforcement of these agreements are crucial in advancing LGBTQ rights globally.

Legal Reforms and Policy Advocacy

Another essential aspect of strengthening LGBTQ rights globally is the pursuit of legal reforms and policy advocacy. Legislation plays a vital role in safeguarding the rights of LGBTQ individuals and creating an inclusive legal framework. Advocacy efforts focused on promoting anti-discrimination laws, decriminalizing same-sex relationships, and recognizing gender identity can lead to significant improvements in the lives of LGBTQ people.

Legal reform and policy advocacy should also aim to address other intersecting forms of discrimination, such as those based on race, ethnicity, religion, or disability. Intersectionality recognizes that individuals may face multiple forms of discrimination and that their experiences are shaped by the intersection of various identities. By addressing these intersecting forms of discrimination, legal reforms can create a more inclusive and equitable society for all marginalized groups.

Empowering Local LGBTQ Movements

Local LGBTQ movements play a crucial role in driving change and advocating for equal rights in their respective countries and communities. Strengthening and empowering these movements is essential to achieving lasting progress. This can be accomplished through capacity-building initiatives, leadership development programs, and providing resources and support to grassroots organizations.

Supporting local LGBTQ movements also involves amplifying their voices and creating platforms for them to share their experiences and advocate for their rights. Collaboration between local and international LGBTQ organizations can facilitate the exchange of knowledge, resources, and strategies, ultimately strengthening the collective movement for LGBTQ rights.

The Role of Education and Awareness

Education and awareness-building initiatives are vital in promoting LGBTQ rights globally. By challenging stereotypes, dispelling myths, and providing accurate information, these initiatives can foster empathy, understanding, and acceptance. Comprehensive sexuality education that includes LGBTQ-inclusive content can help reduce stigma and discrimination and provide support to LGBTQ youth.

Furthermore, integrating LGBTQ perspectives and resources into existing educational curricula can promote inclusivity and create safer learning environments for LGBTQ students. Sensitizing healthcare professionals, teachers, and other service providers to LGBTQ issues can also contribute to the overall well-being and acceptance of LGBTQ individuals.

Challenges and Opportunities

Although progress has been made in advancing LGBTQ rights globally, significant challenges persist. Cultural and religious beliefs, political resistance, and deep-rooted biases often hinder efforts to create inclusive societies. However, these challenges can also present opportunities for dialogue, engagement, and change.

Engaging with religious leaders and communities, for example, can help challenge misconceptions and promote acceptance. By highlighting the principles of empathy, love, and compassion within religious texts, advocates can demonstrate that LGBTQ rights are not in conflict with religious values. This approach can facilitate dialogue and foster greater understanding between religious communities and LGBTQ individuals.

Conclusion

Strengthening LGBTQ rights globally requires a multi-faceted approach that combines international cooperation, legal reforms, policy advocacy, empowering local movements, and education and awareness-building initiatives. By addressing the challenges while capitalizing on the opportunities, we can create a more inclusive and accepting world for LGBTQ individuals. It is through collective action, unwavering determination, and ongoing dialogue that we can continue to make progress and ensure that LGBTQ rights are protected and respected on a global scale.

In the fight for equality, every step forward matters, and as we strengthen LGBTQ rights globally, we pave the way for a more inclusive and compassionate future. Let us embrace the task at hand and work together to create lasting change.

Challenging Discriminatory Laws

In this subsection, we explore the critical role of challenging discriminatory laws in the fight for LGBTQ rights. Discriminatory laws can have a devastating impact on the lives of LGBTQ individuals, perpetuating inequality and denying them basic human rights. To advocate for change, activists must understand the legal barriers they face and employ strategic methods to challenge these laws effectively.

Understanding Discriminatory Laws

Discriminatory laws can take various forms, including criminalization of consensual same-sex relationships, denial of marriage rights, restrictions on gender identity recognition, and limitations on LGBTQ individuals' access to healthcare, employment, and housing. These laws not only infringe upon basic human rights but also foster environments that breed discrimination, prejudice, and violence.

In order to effectively challenge these laws, activists must have a solid understanding of legal frameworks, both domestic and international, that protect and promote human rights. This entails familiarizing themselves with constitutional law, anti-discrimination legislation, and international human rights instruments such as the Universal Declaration of Human Rights, the International Covenant on Civil and Political Rights, and the Yogyakarta Principles.

Strategies for Challenging Discriminatory Laws

Challenging discriminatory laws requires a multifaceted approach that combines legal advocacy, grassroots organizing, public outreach, and strategic litigation. Here are some strategies that activists can employ:

1. Legal Advocacy: Activists can engage in legal advocacy to lobby for the repeal or amendment of discriminatory laws. This involves working with lawmakers, influencing public policy, and presenting legal arguments highlighting the violation of human rights principles. By generating public support, activists can exert pressure on legislators to effect legal change.

2. Grassroots Organizing: Building a strong grassroots movement is essential for challenging discriminatory laws. Activists can mobilize communities, form alliances with LGBTQ organizations, hold public demonstrations, and engage in awareness campaigns to shift public opinion and garner support.

3. Strategic Litigation: Strategic litigation plays a crucial role in challenging discriminatory laws. Activists can identify key legal cases that have the potential to set legal precedents and bring about systemic change. By strategically selecting cases, developing strong legal arguments, and partnering with skilled lawyers, activists can challenge discriminatory laws in courtrooms and use legal victories as catalysts for broader change.

4. International Advocacy: International advocacy is vital for challenging discriminatory laws, especially in countries where legal systems may not be receptive to LGBTQ rights. Activists can collaborate with international human rights organizations, engage with UN mechanisms, and participate in global platforms to put pressure on governments and advocate for change on an international scale.

Real-World Examples

To illustrate the impact of challenging discriminatory laws, let's consider two real-world examples:

Example 1: Decriminalization of Homosexuality in India: The legal battle for decriminalization of homosexuality in India provides an inspiring example of challenging discriminatory laws. In 2009, the Delhi High Court ruled that Section 377 of the Indian Penal Code, which criminalized consensual same-sex relationships, was unconstitutional. This landmark judgment was the result of years of legal advocacy, grassroots mobilization, and strategic litigation led by LGBTQ activists and organizations. However, in 2013, the Supreme Court overturned the ruling. Undeterred, activists persisted, and in 2018, the Supreme Court revisited the issue and struck down Section 377, decriminalizing homosexuality. This victory demonstrated the power of persistence and strategic legal action in challenging discriminatory laws.

Example 2: Marriage Equality in the United States: The fight for marriage equality in the United States showcases the power of strategic litigation in challenging discriminatory laws. The case of Obergefell v. Hodges, which was decided by the Supreme Court in 2015, legalized same-sex marriage nationwide. This outcome was the result of decades of legal advocacy, grassroots organizing, and a strategic approach to litigation. Activists strategically selected cases that would challenge discriminatory marriage laws in different states, building a compelling legal argument rooted in the principles of equality and fundamental rights. By securing a landmark legal victory, activists paved the way for marriage equality and set a precedent for future LGBTQ rights cases.

Resources and Further Reading

Here are some resources and further reading material for activists and individuals interested in challenging discriminatory laws:

- The Yogyakarta Principles: Principles on the Application of International Human Rights Law in Relation to Sexual Orientation and Gender Identity

- International Lesbian, Gay, Bisexual, Trans and Intersex Association (ILGA) – ilga.org

- Human Rights Watch – hrw.org/category/topic/lgbt-rights

- American Civil Liberties Union (ACLU) – aclu.org/issues/lgbt-rights

- Lambda Legal – lambdalegal.org

- The Center for Constitutional Rights – ccrjustice.org

Conclusion

Challenging discriminatory laws is a critical aspect of LGBTQ activism. By understanding the legal landscape, employing strategic methods, and using legal advocacy, grassroots organizing, and strategic litigation, activists can effectively challenge discriminatory laws that perpetuate inequality and deny basic human rights. Through real-world examples, we have seen how persistence and strategic action can lead to significant legal victories. As the fight for LGBTQ rights continues, it is crucial to build on the progress made and rally collective efforts to create a world free from discriminatory laws.

Building Bridges Between Communities

Interfaith Dialogue and Understanding

In the journey of LGBTQ activism, one of the most important aspects is fostering interfaith dialogue and understanding. It is through conversations and empathy that bridges are built between different religious communities, paving the way for greater acceptance and inclusion. In this subsection, we will explore the significance of interfaith dialogue, its benefits, and how it can contribute to the advancement of LGBTQ rights.

The Importance of Interfaith Dialogue

Religion plays a significant role in the lives of millions of people around the world. It often shapes beliefs, values, and attitudes towards various social issues, including LGBTQ rights. Interfaith dialogue seeks to bring together individuals from different religious backgrounds to engage in meaningful conversations and foster understanding. This dialogue recognizes the diversity of religious practices and beliefs, creating space for respectful exchange and collaboration.

By engaging in interfaith dialogue, LGBTQ activists can build bridges of understanding and work towards dismantling harmful stereotypes and prejudices. It allows for the exploration of shared values and common ground, facilitating cooperation and advocacy across different religious communities.

Challenges and Solutions

Engaging in interfaith dialogue comes with its own set of challenges. Religious teachings and interpretations may vary, and some individuals may hold deeply ingrained prejudices against LGBTQ individuals. However, overcoming these challenges is vital to creating a more inclusive and accepting society.

One way to address these challenges is by promoting education and awareness within religious communities. By providing resources, organizing workshops, and inviting guest speakers, individuals can gain a better understanding of LGBTQ experiences and the intersectionality of identities. It is essential to emphasize that accepting LGBTQ individuals aligns with the principles of love, compassion, and respect that are often at the core of many religious teachings.

Additionally, interfaith dialogue can help highlight the commonalities between diverse faith traditions regarding justice, equality, and human rights. By focusing on these shared values, individuals can transcend differences and foster a sense of unity in advocating for LGBTQ rights. It is crucial to create safe and inclusive spaces for dialogue where all participants can express their beliefs and share their experiences openly.

Real-World Examples

To illustrate the impact of interfaith dialogue, let's consider a real-world example. In the aftermath of the tragic shooting at the Pulse nightclub in Orlando, Florida, in 2016, members of various religious communities came together to show support for the LGBTQ community. Interfaith vigils were organized, where people of different faiths gathered to mourn the victims and express solidarity.

These interfaith gatherings demonstrated the power of dialogue in fostering mutual understanding and empathy. It allowed LGBTQ individuals to see that not all religious individuals held homophobic views, and it helped religious communities recognize the importance of supporting and affirming LGBTQ rights.

Resources and Tools

To promote interfaith dialogue and understanding, there are several resources and tools available that can assist activists and community organizers.

1. Interfaith Network for Equality and Solidarity (INES): INES is an international organization that connects LGBTQ activists, religious leaders, and communities committed to promoting dialogue and fostering LGBTQ inclusivity within religious spaces. They provide resources, organize conferences, and facilitate discussions on LGBTQ rights from an interfaith perspective.

2. Religions for Peace: Religions for Peace is an interfaith organization that works towards promoting peace, justice, and social cohesion. Their LGBTQ task

forces and working groups actively engage in LGBTQ-inclusive discussions and initiatives within religious communities.

3. Interfaith Youth Core: The Interfaith Youth Core focuses on building interfaith relationships among young people. They offer educational resources and training programs that equip youth with the skills and knowledge to engage in interfaith dialogue effectively.

4. Believe Out Loud: Believe Out Loud is a platform that aims to empower LGBTQ Christians and their allies. They provide diverse resources, stories, and tools for individuals and communities seeking to reconcile their faith with LGBTQ inclusion.

5. Local Interfaith Organizations: Many cities and regions have interfaith organizations working towards fostering dialogue and understanding. These organizations often hold events, workshops, and outreach programs that promote inclusivity and dialogue.

Tricks of the Trade

Engaging in successful interfaith dialogue requires patience, empathy, and active listening. Here are a few tricks to facilitate constructive conversations:

1. Establish a safe and respectful environment: Create spaces where individuals feel comfortable expressing their beliefs and experiences without fear of judgment or backlash.

2. Emphasize shared values: Highlight values that promote justice, love, and compassion, reminding participants of the common ground they share.

3. Use storytelling: Personal stories can be powerful tools to foster understanding and empathy. Encourage participants to share their experiences and listen actively to one another.

4. Seek partnership and collaboration: Develop partnerships with religious leaders, organizations, and communities to create lasting change. Collaboration allows for a broader reach and impact.

Exercises

1. Role-Playing: Organize a role-playing exercise where participants take on different religious perspectives and engage in dialogue surrounding LGBTQ rights. This exercise helps individuals understand different viewpoints and challenges prejudices.

2. Panel Discussions: Host panel discussions featuring individuals from diverse religious backgrounds who support LGBTQ rights. Encourage open and

respectful dialogue, allowing participants to address challenging questions and misconceptions.

Unconventional Approach

Comic book storytelling: Create a comic book or graphic novel that showcases various religious characters coming together to support LGBTQ rights. This unconventional approach combines art and narratives to capture attention and reach a broader audience.

In conclusion, interfaith dialogue and understanding are crucial in advancing LGBTQ rights. By fostering respectful conversations, promoting education, and emphasizing shared values, interfaith dialogue allows for collaboration, empathy, and the dismantling of harmful prejudices. It is through these efforts that bridges can be built, leading to a more inclusive and accepting society for LGBTQ individuals.

Allies in the LGBTQ and Muslim Communities

In this subsection, we will explore the crucial role of allies in supporting the LGBTQ and Muslim communities. Allies play a significant part in promoting acceptance, understanding, and equality for marginalized groups. Let's delve into the importance of allyship and ways in which individuals can become effective allies.

Understanding Allyship

Allyship is the practice of individuals, who are not part of a marginalized community, actively supporting and advocating for the rights and well-being of that community. In the context of LGBTQ and Muslim communities, allies are individuals who recognize the struggles faced by queer Muslims and actively stand up against discrimination and prejudice.

To become an effective ally, it is essential to educate oneself about the unique challenges faced by the LGBTQ and Muslim communities. This includes understanding the intersectionality of identities and the complexities of navigating multiple marginalized identities simultaneously. By learning about the history, experiences, and aspirations of queer Muslims, allies can better support and uplift their voices.

Building Bridges of Understanding

One of the fundamental aspects of allyship is building bridges of understanding between the LGBTQ and Muslim communities. Allies can initiate and engage in respectful dialogues that promote empathy, compassion, and mutual respect.

By fostering open and meaningful conversations, allies can address misconceptions, challenge stereotypes, and promote acceptance. This can be done through various platforms, such as community events, workshops, and educational initiatives. Allies can invite LGBTQ individuals and Muslim leaders to share their experiences, allowing for a better understanding of the intersectionality of queer and Muslim identities.

Supporting LGBTQ Muslims' Well-being

Allies have a crucial role to play in supporting LGBTQ Muslims' mental health and overall well-being. Discrimination, internalized homophobia, and religious conflicts can significantly impact the emotional and psychological state of queer Muslims. Allies can provide emotional support, resources, and create safe spaces for LGBTQ Muslims to express themselves without fear of judgment or rejection.

Mental health advocacy is an essential aspect of allyship, as it acknowledges the unique challenges faced by individuals navigating intersectional identities and provides resources and support to address these challenges. Allies can promote mental health awareness within the LGBTQ and Muslim communities and work towards reducing stigma and barriers to accessing mental health services.

Challenging Homophobia and Islamophobia

To be effective allies, individuals must actively challenge homophobia and Islamophobia in their personal and professional spheres. This includes calling out discriminatory behavior, language, and attitudes. Allies should use their privilege and influence to create inclusive spaces and promote tolerance and acceptance within their communities.

By addressing and dismantling homophobia and Islamophobia, allies contribute to creating an environment where LGBTQ Muslims feel safe, valued, and accepted. This can be done through raising awareness, advocating for policies that protect LGBTQ and Muslim rights, and fostering a culture of respect and inclusion.

Becoming Advocates for Change

Allies have the power to amplify the voices of LGBTQ Muslims and advocate for their rights. This can be done through active participation in protests, social media campaigns, and lobbying efforts. By standing alongside members of the LGBTQ and Muslim communities, allies create a united front against discrimination and inequality.

Supporting LGBTQ-led organizations, initiatives, and events is another crucial way in which allies can contribute to positive change. This support can come in the form of financial contributions, volunteering time and expertise, or amplifying the work of these organizations through social media and personal networks.

Promoting Inclusive Education and Resources

Allies can make a significant impact by advocating for inclusive education and resources that address the needs of LGBTQ Muslims. This can involve partnering with educational institutions, community organizations, and religious leaders to develop curricula, workshops, and resources that foster a better understanding of queer Muslim experiences and promote inclusivity.

Creating materials that highlight the narratives and contributions of LGBTQ Muslims can help challenge stereotypes, break down barriers, and foster greater acceptance. Allies can also advocate for the inclusion of LGBTQ-inclusive education in school curricula and the availability of resources that support LGBTQ Muslims in their spiritual journeys.

Conclusion

Allies play a crucial role in supporting, uplifting, and advocating for the rights and well-being of the LGBTQ and Muslim communities. By building bridges of understanding, challenging discrimination, and promoting inclusive practices, allies contribute to creating a more accepting and equitable society.

Becoming an ally requires education, empathy, and a commitment to continuous learning and growth. By embracing allyship, individuals contribute to the empowerment and liberation of LGBTQ Muslims, fostering a world where everyone can thrive regardless of their sexual orientation, gender identity, or religious beliefs.

Remember, allyship is an ongoing journey that requires active engagement, listening, and amplifying marginalized voices. Together, we can create a future where queer Muslims can live authentically and without fear, while being embraced and celebrated for the richness of their identities.

Encouraging Empathy and Compassion

In this subsection, we delve into the importance of encouraging empathy and compassion in the LGBTQ and Muslim communities. Creating spaces of understanding and fostering empathy are crucial for building connections, promoting acceptance, and dismantling harmful stereotypes and prejudices. Let's explore the strategies and practical steps that can be taken to cultivate empathy and compassion within these communities.

Building Bridges of Understanding

Empathy is the ability to understand and share the feelings of another person. It is a fundamental aspect of building bridges of understanding between different individuals and communities. Encouraging empathy involves actively seeking to understand and relate to the experiences of others, even if they may be different from our own.

One effective strategy for fostering empathy is through open dialogue and active listening. By engaging in meaningful conversations and actively listening to diverse perspectives, we can develop a deeper understanding of the challenges and experiences faced by LGBTQ individuals within the Muslim community. This can help break down barriers, bridge divides, and create a space for empathy to flourish.

Promoting Dialogue and Communication

Promoting dialogue and communication is another crucial step in encouraging empathy and compassion. By creating safe and inclusive spaces for open discussions, individuals from both the LGBTQ and Muslim communities can come together to share their stories, struggles, and aspirations.

Workshops and training sessions can be organized to facilitate dialogue and communication. These sessions can provide education, promote understanding, and foster empathy by bringing together individuals with diverse backgrounds and experiences. Through open and honest conversations, stereotypes can be challenged, misconceptions can be corrected, and empathy can be nurtured.

Sharing Personal Stories

Personal stories have the power to change hearts and minds. By sharing personal experiences, LGBTQ Muslims can help others understand the challenges they face and the unique journeys they undertake in reconciling their faith and sexuality.

Platforms such as social media, blogs, and public speaking engagements can be used to amplify personal stories. By providing a platform for authentic voices to be heard, a greater sense of empathy and compassion can be cultivated within and beyond these communities. Personal stories help humanize the struggles, triumphs, and aspirations of LGBTQ Muslims, fostering connection, empathy, and understanding.

Education and Awareness

Education plays a vital role in encouraging empathy and compassion. By providing accurate information about LGBTQ issues and Islam, both communities can gain a deeper understanding and appreciation for each other's experiences.

Educational resources, workshops, and training programs can be developed to promote awareness and understanding of LGBTQ identities and Islam's teachings on inclusivity and compassion. By dispelling myths and fostering knowledge, empathy can grow, and stereotypes can be dismantled.

Allieship and Support

Allies and support networks play a crucial role in fostering empathy and compassion within and between LGBTQ and Muslim communities. Allies are individuals who stand in solidarity with LGBTQ Muslims, actively working to challenge discrimination, biases, and harmful stereotypes.

Organizations and individuals can actively engage in allyship by creating safe spaces, offering support, and advocating for LGBTQ rights within Muslim communities. Allies can play a crucial role in promoting empathy by listening, learning, and amplifying the voices of LGBTQ Muslims.

The Power of Art and Media

Art and media have the power to transcend boundaries and foster empathy. Films, literature, music, and visual arts can be vehicles for sharing the experiences and stories of LGBTQ Muslims, promoting empathy, and enhancing understanding.

Encouraging the creation and promotion of LGBTQ Muslim art and media can help humanize their experiences, bridging divides and creating opportunities for empathy to flourish. Through art, viewers and audiences can connect on an emotional level, fostering empathy, and challenging preconceived notions.

Exercise: Empathy and Compassion Reflection

Reflect on a time when you felt empathy and compassion towards someone from a different background or community. What factors contributed to your ability to empathize with them? How did this experience influence your perceptions and attitudes towards that community? Share your reflections with a partner and discuss how empathy and compassion can be nurtured within your own lives and communities.

By encouraging empathy and compassion within LGBTQ and Muslim communities, we can foster a culture of understanding, acceptance, and respect. Through open dialogue, personal storytelling, education, allieship, and the power of art and media, empathy can be nurtured to build bridges between communities. Empathy and compassion are powerful catalysts for positive change, and by nurturing these qualities, we can create a more inclusive and equitable world.

Promoting Religious Tolerance

In this subsection, we delve into the importance of promoting religious tolerance within the context of LGBTQ activism. As Irshad Manji has exemplified throughout her career, bridging divides and fostering understanding between religious communities and the LGBTQ community is essential for creating inclusive spaces. By promoting dialogue, empathy, and compassion, we can work towards building a more accepting and tolerant society for all.

Understanding Religious Diversity

Religious diversity is a fundamental aspect of the human experience, with a wide array of faith traditions and beliefs practiced around the world. As LGBTQ activists, it is crucial to acknowledge and respect the diverse religious identities within our communities. This includes recognizing that many LGBTQ individuals hold religious beliefs and values that are integral to their identities.

Promoting Dialogue and Understanding

Promoting religious tolerance requires open and respectful dialogue between the LGBTQ community and religious communities. It is important to create spaces where individuals can engage in meaningful conversations, share personal stories, and explore the intersections between faith, sexuality, and gender identity.

By fostering understanding and empathy, we can break down stereotypes, challenge misconceptions, and bridge the gap between different communities. It is crucial to approach these conversations with a willingness to listen and learn from one another, fostering a sense of mutual respect and understanding.

Encouraging Empathy and Compassion

Empathy and compassion are at the heart of promoting religious tolerance. As LGBTQ activists, it is essential to cultivate these qualities within ourselves and encourage others to do the same. This includes actively seeking to understand the religious perspectives and experiences of others, even if they may differ from our own.

By acknowledging the struggles faced by LGBTQ individuals within religious communities and offering support, we can foster an environment of empathy and compassion. This involves creating safe spaces where individuals can share their experiences, offer guidance, and provide emotional support to one another.

Promoting Religious Freedom

Promoting religious tolerance goes hand in hand with advocating for religious freedom. LGBTQ activists should work to ensure that individuals have the right to practice their religion free from discrimination or harm, regardless of their sexual orientation or gender identity.

By challenging discriminatory practices and legislation that restrict religious freedom for LGBTQ individuals, we can advance both LGBTQ rights and religious tolerance. This requires engaging with policymakers, advocating for inclusive policies, and collaborating with organizations that champion religious liberty.

Fostering Inclusive Spaces

One of the key ways to promote religious tolerance is by fostering inclusive spaces within religious communities. This involves challenging anti-LGBTQ attitudes and fostering dialogue within religious institutions to create welcoming environments for LGBTQ individuals.

By advocating for LGBTQ-inclusive practices, such as officiating same-sex marriages, offering LGBTQ-inclusive religious education, and providing support for LGBTQ individuals and their families, we can promote religious tolerance and acceptance from within.

Combating Xenophobia and Racism

Promoting religious tolerance also requires addressing xenophobia and racism within and outside religious communities. LGBTQ activists should work to challenge stereotypes, combat prejudice, and foster solidarity across different racial and ethnic backgrounds within religious spaces.

By highlighting the intersections between LGBTQ identities and racial or ethnic identities, we can build bridges and promote understanding. This involves supporting initiatives that challenge racism and xenophobia, promoting diversity and inclusivity, and uplifting marginalized voices within religious communities.

Engaging in Global Solidarity

Promoting religious tolerance is not limited to specific regions or communities. LGBTQ activists have a responsibility to engage in global solidarity and support efforts to promote religious tolerance around the world.

This may involve partnering with international LGBTQ and human rights organizations, collaborating with activists from different religious backgrounds, and leveraging social media and digital platforms to amplify voices advocating for religious tolerance.

Creating Safe Spaces for LGBTQ Youth

Promoting religious tolerance also means creating safe spaces for LGBTQ youth within religious communities. LGBTQ activists should work with religious leaders and organizations to develop policies and programs that address the unique needs of LGBTQ youth.

By providing resources, support groups, and educational opportunities, we can ensure that LGBTQ youth feel accepted and valued within their religious communities. This includes challenging harmful practices such as conversion therapy and promoting comprehensive LGBTQ-inclusive sex education.

Cultivating Empathy Through Storytelling

Storytelling plays a powerful role in promoting religious tolerance. By sharing personal stories of LGBTQ individuals who have found acceptance within their religious communities, we can challenge stereotypes and inspire positive change.

LGBTQ activists can utilize various mediums, such as books, documentaries, social media campaigns, and public speaking engagements, to amplify these narratives. This enables individuals to connect on a deeper level, fostering empathy and understanding across religious divides.

Embracing Inclusivity and Diversity in Faith Communities

Ultimately, promoting religious tolerance requires actively embracing inclusivity and diversity within faith communities. LGBTQ activists should encourage religious leaders to adopt LGBTQ-affirming teachings and practices, ensuring that LGBTQ individuals feel respected, supported, and welcomed.

This includes challenging harmful interpretations of religious texts that perpetuate discrimination and working towards a more inclusive understanding of religion. By embracing diversit

Fostering Inclusive Spaces

Creating inclusive spaces is vital for ensuring that LGBTQ individuals, including those from Muslim backgrounds, feel safe, accepted, and supported. In this subsection, we will explore various strategies and practices that can be employed to foster inclusive spaces within communities, organizations, and religious institutions.

Understanding Inclusion

Inclusion is not merely about tolerance or acceptance; it goes beyond that. It involves actively embracing and valuing the diversity of identities and experiences within a space. Inclusive spaces provide equal opportunities, respect, and support for all individuals, regardless of their sexual orientation, gender identity, or religious affiliation.

Building Awareness and Education

One of the first steps in fostering inclusive spaces is to promote awareness and education about LGBTQ issues within the community. This can be achieved through workshops, training sessions, and guest speakers who can share their experiences and knowledge. By providing accurate information and dispelling misconceptions, we can create a more informed and empathetic environment.

Establishing LGBTQ+ Support Groups

Support groups specifically designed for LGBTQ individuals can be instrumental in providing spaces where people can connect, share their stories, and find support. These groups can be organized within religious institutions, community centers, or online platforms, allowing individuals to navigate the intersectionality of their identities and find solace in others who have similar experiences.

Creating Safe Spaces

Safe spaces are physical or virtual environments where LGBTQ individuals can freely express themselves without fear of discrimination or judgment. They should be designated as spaces free from hate speech, harassment, and intolerance. Creating safe spaces involves establishing clear guidelines and policies to protect the rights and dignity of all individuals.

Promoting Dialogue and Understanding

Encouraging open and respectful dialogue is crucial in fostering inclusive spaces. This can be achieved through facilitated discussions, panel debates, or interfaith dialogues. Creating opportunities for people to engage in meaningful conversations and learn from diverse perspectives helps break down barriers and promote understanding.

Supporting LGBTQ-Inclusive Policies

Inclusive spaces require the adoption of LGBTQ-inclusive policies and practices. Organizations and religious institutions should ensure that they have non-discrimination policies that explicitly protect LGBTQ individuals. Additionally, equal opportunity and anti-bullying policies should be in place to prevent any form of discrimination based on sexual orientation or gender identity.

Amplifying LGBTQ Voices

Inclusive spaces should actively uplift and amplify the voices of LGBTQ individuals. This can be done by providing platforms for them to share their stories, experiences, and expertise. Organizing LGBTQ cultural events, art exhibitions, or film screenings can showcase the diversity of the community and create opportunities for LGBTQ voices to be heard.

Celebrating LGBTQ Affirmation and Inclusion

Inclusive spaces should celebrate LGBTQ affirmation and inclusion as important values. This can be done through LGBTQ Pride events, awareness campaigns, or initiatives that highlight the contributions of LGBTQ individuals. By actively celebrating diversity and affirming LGBTQ identities, inclusive spaces become nurturing environments for all.

Engaging with Faith Leaders

Engaging with faith leaders and religious institutions is essential in fostering inclusive spaces within religious communities. Working collaboratively, religious leaders play a vital role in challenging discriminatory beliefs and practices. By engaging with them in dialogue, sharing resources, and encouraging LGBTQ acceptance within religious teachings, inclusive spaces can be created within faith spaces.

Providing Resources and Support

Inclusive spaces need to provide resources and support to LGBTQ individuals who may be facing challenges or seeking guidance. This can include mental health support services, counseling, information on LGBTQ-friendly organizations, and resources on reconciling faith and sexuality. Accessible resources and support networks are crucial in creating inclusive environments.

Unconventional Approach: LGBTQ-Inclusive Sermons

A potential unconventional approach to fostering inclusive spaces is for religious leaders to deliver LGBTQ-inclusive sermons. This involves addressing LGBTQ issues from a faith perspective, debunking misconceptions, and promoting acceptance and understanding. By incorporating LGBTQ topics into sermons, religious leaders can positively influence their congregations and open up conversations about LGBTQ inclusivity.

Overall, fostering inclusive spaces requires a collective effort and a commitment to continuous learning and growth. By building awareness, providing support, and promoting dialogue, we can create environments where LGBTQ individuals can live authentically and thrive within their respective communities and religious institutions.

Intersections of LGBTQ and Racial Identities

In the fight for equality, it is essential to recognize and address the intersections of LGBTQ and racial identities. LGBTQ individuals come from diverse racial and ethnic backgrounds, and their experiences are shaped by both their sexual orientation and their racial identity. Understanding these intersections is crucial to creating inclusive spaces and fighting against discrimination and prejudice.

Acknowledging the Diversity within the LGBTQ Community

The LGBTQ community is not homogeneous; it consists of individuals from various racial, ethnic, and cultural backgrounds. Recognizing and celebrating this diversity is important for building an inclusive movement. By acknowledging and promoting the voices and experiences of racial minority LGBTQ individuals, we can create a more comprehensive understanding of the challenges they face.

Intersectionality Theory

Intersectionality theory, developed by Kimberlé Crenshaw, provides a framework for analyzing how various aspects of identity, such as race, gender, and sexuality, intersect and interact to shape individuals' experiences. This theory emphasizes the interconnectedness of marginalized identities and recognizes that individuals may experience different forms of discrimination simultaneously.

For example, LGBTQ individuals who are also racial minorities might face unique challenges such as racial profiling, xenophobia, and the fetishization of their identities. Intersectionality theory allows us to understand these complex experiences and work towards addressing the multiple layers of discrimination they face.

Racial Disparities in the LGBTQ Community

While progress has been made in the fight for LGBTQ rights, racial disparities persist within the community. Racial minority LGBTQ individuals often face higher rates of homelessness, unemployment, and healthcare disparities compared to their white counterparts. They may also encounter challenges in finding acceptance within their own racial and ethnic communities.

To address these disparities, it is crucial to uplift and amplify the voices of racial minority LGBTQ individuals. This can be done through inclusive representation in media, leadership positions, and community organizations. By fostering spaces that prioritize racial equity, we can work towards dismantling the barriers that prevent equal access to rights and resources.

Fighting Racism Within the LGBTQ Community

In the fight for LGBTQ equality, it is imperative to confront and address the racism that exists within the community. Racism can manifest in various ways, including stereotypes, microaggressions, and exclusionary practices. These harmful behaviors undermine the inclusive and intersectional ideals that the LGBTQ movement strives for.

Challenging racism within the LGBTQ community requires active allyship, education, and confronting one's own biases. By creating safe spaces for dialogue and promoting anti-racist practices, we can work towards building a community that is truly inclusive and supportive of all its members.

Promoting Intersectional Advocacy

Intersectional advocacy is essential in addressing the needs and experiences of LGBTQ individuals with diverse racial identities. This involves recognizing that the fight for LGBTQ rights intersects with other social justice movements, such as racial justice and immigration reform.

By collaborating with organizations and individuals working towards racial justice, advocating for policies that address the needs of racial minority LGBTQ individuals, and engaging in intercommunity dialogue, we can build stronger coalitions and create lasting change.

Case Study: LGBTQ Refugees of Color

An example of the intersection of LGBTQ and racial identities is the experience of LGBTQ refugees of color. These individuals face unique challenges as they navigate the process of seeking asylum or resettlement in a new country.

LGBTQ refugees of color often encounter racism, homophobia, and transphobia not only in their countries of origin but also within the LGBTQ communities in their host countries. They may struggle to find culturally competent support and face barriers to accessing essential services.

Creating a safe and inclusive environment for LGBTQ refugees of color requires a comprehensive approach that addresses their intersecting identities. This can involve providing cultural competency training to service providers, advocating for LGBTQ-inclusive refugee policies, and fostering community support networks that are sensitive to the unique needs of this population.

Resources and Further Reading

To gain a deeper understanding of the intersections of LGBTQ and racial identities, explore the following resources:

+ "This Bridge Called My Back: Writings by Radical Women of Color" edited by Cherríe Moraga and Gloria E. Anzaldúa

+ "Black on Both Sides: A Racial History of Trans Identity" by C. Riley Snorton

+ "Queer Brown Voices: Personal Narratives of Latina/o LGBT Activism" edited by Uriel Quesada, Letitia Gomez, and Salvador Vidal-Ortiz

+ "Sister Outsider: Essays and Speeches" by Audre Lorde

By engaging with these resources, we can deepen our understanding of the experiences of LGBTQ individuals with diverse racial identities and contribute to the ongoing fight for equality and justice. Remember, true progress can only be achieved when we recognize and address the intersections of LGBTQ and racial identities.

Combating Xenophobia and Racism

Xenophobia and racism are deeply rooted issues that continue to plague societies across the globe. In this subsection, we will explore strategies to combat these forms of discrimination, with a specific focus on fostering understanding, empathy, and inclusivity.

Understanding Xenophobia and Racism

Xenophobia refers to the fear, mistrust, or hatred of foreigners or individuals from different cultural backgrounds. Racism, on the other hand, is the belief in the inherent superiority or inferiority of certain races, leading to discrimination and prejudice. Both xenophobia and racism have detrimental effects on individuals and communities, perpetuating social division and hindering progress towards equality.

To combat xenophobia and racism effectively, it is essential to understand their root causes. Often, these prejudiced attitudes stem from ignorance, stereotypes, and a lack of exposure to diverse cultures and perspectives. It is important to recognize the impact of systemic structures that perpetuate these biases, such as discriminatory policies, socio-economic inequalities, and media representations.

Educating for Empathy and Inclusion

One of the most powerful ways to combat xenophobia and racism is through education. By incorporating inclusive curricula, promoting intercultural exchange programs, and encouraging dialogue, we can cultivate empathy and understanding among individuals. Schools, universities, and community organizations play a crucial role in fostering a inclusive environment.

Teachers should strive to incorporate diverse voices and experiences into the classroom, offering opportunities for students to learn about different cultures, religions, and histories. This can include guest speakers, multicultural events, and resource materials that challenge stereotypes and biases. Additionally, promoting anti-bullying and anti-discrimination campaigns in educational institutions can help create safer spaces for students from marginalized communities.

Promoting Intercultural Dialogue

Engaging in intercultural dialogue is key to combating xenophobia and racism. By bringing individuals from various backgrounds together, we can facilitate meaningful conversations, break down stereotypes, and build bridges between communities. This can be achieved through community forums, workshops, and cultural festivals that celebrate diversity and encourage dialogue.

In these spaces, it is important to create an atmosphere of respect and active listening. Participants should be encouraged to share their experiences, challenges, and aspirations, fostering mutual understanding and empathy. Promoting collaboration and cooperation between different cultural and ethnic groups can help break down barriers and create stronger, more inclusive communities.

Advocating for Policy Changes

To combat xenophobia and racism on a broader scale, it is crucial to advocate for policy changes that address systemic discrimination. This may include advocating for laws against hate speech, supporting equal opportunity initiatives, and promoting inclusive immigration policies. By actively engaging with lawmakers and policymakers, we can work towards dismantling discriminatory systems and creating more just and inclusive societies.

Furthermore, it is important to tackle the issue of racial profiling by law enforcement agencies and to support accountability mechanisms. Police departments should emphasize community policing and cultural sensitivity training to foster positive interactions between officers and minority communities.

Promoting Media Representation

Media plays a significant role in shaping public opinion and perpetuating stereotypes. To combat xenophobia and racism, it is important to promote diverse and accurate media representation. Journalists, filmmakers, and content creators have a responsibility to challenge biases and accurately reflect the diversity of our societies.

Media entities should actively seek out stories and perspectives from underrepresented communities, providing platforms for marginalized voices to be heard. By doing so, we can humanize individuals from different backgrounds, challenging stereotypes and fostering empathy among audiences.

Unconventional Approach: Community Exchanges

An unconventional yet effective approach in combating xenophobia and racism is facilitating community exchanges. This involves organizing cultural immersion programs where individuals from different communities live and work together for a period of time. By experiencing each other's daily lives, participants can develop a deeper understanding and appreciation for diverse cultures and combat prejudice head-on.

These community exchanges can take the form of home-stays, volunteer programs, or collaborative projects. By encouraging genuine connections and fostering relationships, this approach can break down barriers and bridge divides on a personal level.

Conclusion

Combating xenophobia and racism requires a multi-faceted approach involving education, dialogue, policy changes, media representation, and unconventional strategies. By fostering understanding, empathy, and inclusivity, we can dismantle the deeply ingrained biases that perpetuate discrimination. It is our collective responsibility to create a world where individuals are valued for their unique contributions, regardless of their cultural or racial background. The fight against xenophobia and racism is an ongoing endeavor, and it requires the commitment and efforts of individuals, communities, and institutions worldwide. Let us strive for unity and embrace the beauty of our diversity.

Engaging in Global Solidarity

Engaging in global solidarity is a crucial aspect of LGBTQ activism, as it allows for the creation of strong networks and alliances that transcend national borders. By working together, activists can amplify their voices, share resources, and support one another in their collective fight for LGBTQ rights around the world. In this subsection, we will explore the importance of global solidarity, strategies for engaging in international activism, and the power of collaboration on a global scale.

Understanding the Importance of Global Solidarity

Global solidarity is essential in the LGBTQ movement because it recognizes the interconnectedness of struggles faced by LGBTQ individuals across different countries and cultures. It acknowledges the shared experiences of discrimination, violence, and marginalization that LGBTQ individuals face, regardless of their geographic location. By standing in solidarity with each other, activists can work together to address common issues and advocate for change on a global level.

Solidarity also allows activists to break the isolation and build a sense of community, providing emotional support and fostering a sense of belonging. When activists from different countries come together, they gain strength from each other's stories, resilience, and determination. By collaborating, they create a united front against discrimination and injustice.

Strategies for Engaging in International Activism

Engaging in international activism requires strategic planning and effective collaboration. Here are some strategies for successfully engaging in global solidarity:

1. **Information sharing and knowledge exchange:** International activists should establish networks and platforms for sharing information, experiences, and best practices. This can be done through regular meetings, conferences, webinars, or online forums. By learning from one another, activists can gain insights into successful strategies, innovative approaches, and emerging challenges in LGBTQ activism.

2. **Partnerships and coalitions:** Building partnerships and coalitions with organizations and activists around the world is crucial for effective international activism. By forming alliances, activists can amplify their impact and exert more pressure on governments, institutions, and other stakeholders. These partnerships can focus on specific issues, such as advocating for legal reforms or combating violence against LGBTQ individuals.

3. **Campaign coordination:** Coordinating global campaigns can be a powerful tool for raising awareness, mobilizing support, and pressuring decision-makers. Through coordinated actions, such as synchronized demonstrations, social media campaigns, or letter-writing campaigns, activists can demonstrate their collective strength and demand change.

4. **Leveraging international platforms and mechanisms:** International platforms, such as the United Nations or regional human rights bodies, provide opportunities for advocates to raise LGBTQ issues on a global stage. By utilizing these platforms, activists can bring attention to the human rights violations faced by LGBTQ individuals in different countries and put pressure on governments to take action.

5. **Supporting grassroots movements:** Supporting grassroots LGBTQ organizations and activists in different countries is crucial for building sustainable change. International activists can provide financial support, capacity-building resources, and technical assistance to grassroots movements, empowering them to create positive change within their communities.

The Power of Global Collaboration

Collaborating on a global scale has the potential to bring about significant change and advance LGBTQ rights around the world. Here are some examples of successful global collaborations:

+ The **International LGBTQI Youth and Student Organization (IGLYO)** is an alliance of LGBTQ youth and student organizations working together to promote LGBTQ rights in education and society. By sharing experiences and organizing joint advocacy efforts, IGLYO has successfully influenced policies and practices in education, leading to more inclusive environments for LGBTQ youth.

+ The **Global Interfaith Network for LGBTQ+ People (GIN)** is a network of LGBTQ individuals, allies, and organizations working within faith communities to promote LGBTQ inclusion and acceptance. GIN brings together activists, religious leaders, and scholars from different religious traditions to engage in dialogue, education, and advocacy. By collaborating across faith traditions, GIN has helped foster more inclusive and accepting attitudes towards LGBTQ individuals within religious communities.

+ The **International Lesbian, Gay, Bisexual, Trans and Intersex Association (ILGA)** is a global federation of LGBTQ organizations that advocates for the rights of LGBTQ individuals worldwide. Through its global network, ILGA has played a vital role in promoting legal reforms, challenging discriminatory laws, and raising awareness of LGBTQ issues on an international scale.

These examples demonstrate the power of collaboration and the impact it can have on advancing LGBTQ rights globally. By working together and engaging in global solidarity, activists can create lasting change and pave the way for a more inclusive and accepting world.

Challenges and Considerations

Engaging in global solidarity is not without its challenges. Activists must navigate cultural differences, language barriers, and varying political landscapes when collaborating across borders. Understanding the context and complexities of different countries is essential to ensure effective advocacy.

Moreover, activists must be mindful of power dynamics and privilege within global collaborations. It is crucial to center the voices and experiences of the most marginalized individuals and communities, as they often bear the brunt of discrimination and violence.

Additionally, when engaging in international activism, activists must be aware of and respect local leadership and expertise. It is essential to avoid imposing Western-centric approaches and instead support local movements in their strategies and priorities.

Conclusion

Engaging in global solidarity is a fundamental aspect of LGBTQ activism, as it allows activists to address common challenges, share resources, and advocate for change on a global level. By forming strategic partnerships, coordinating campaigns, and leveraging international platforms, activists can amplify their impact and create lasting change. Collaboration and solidarity are powerful tools that can bring about a more inclusive and accepting world for LGBTQ individuals everywhere. The fight for equality continues, and through global solidarity, the LGBTQ movement can build on past achievements and forge a path toward a more just and inclusive future.

Creating Safe Spaces for LGBTQ Youth

In this section, we will explore the importance of creating safe spaces for LGBTQ youth and discuss strategies for fostering inclusivity and support. It is crucial to provide a nurturing environment where these young individuals can express their true selves without fear of judgment or discrimination.

Understanding the Challenges Faced by LGBTQ Youth

LGBTQ youth often face unique challenges in their journey of self-discovery and self-acceptance. They may experience bullying, rejection from family and friends, mental health issues, and a lack of understanding within their communities.

To better support these youth, it is essential to understand the specific challenges they face. This includes educating ourselves about the struggles they may encounter, such as the coming-out process, navigating gender identity, and dealing with societal prejudices.

Creating LGBTQ-Inclusive Policies and Practices

To establish safe spaces for LGBTQ youth, organizations, educational institutions, and community centers must prioritize the implementation of LGBTQ-inclusive policies and practices. This includes:

- Developing anti-discrimination policies that explicitly protect LGBTQ individuals from harassment and bullying.

- Ensuring the inclusion of LGBTQ perspectives in educational curricula to promote understanding and empathy.

- Offering gender-neutral restrooms and facilities to accommodate the diverse needs of LGBTQ youth.

- Providing comprehensive sex education that includes LGBTQ-inclusive content, covering topics such as consent, healthy relationships, and LGBTQ health.

- Establishing LGBTQ support groups, clubs, and alliances within schools and community centers.

- Encouraging staff and volunteers to undergo LGBTQ sensitivity training to create an inclusive and welcoming environment.

By implementing these policies and practices, organizations can help create environments where LGBTQ youth feel safe, valued, and supported.

Mentoring and Peer Support Programs

Mentoring and peer support programs play a vital role in creating safe spaces for LGBTQ youth. These programs connect experienced individuals, such as LGBTQ adults or older LGBTQ youth, with younger individuals who may benefit from guidance, empathy, and encouragement.

Mentoring programs provide LGBTQ youth with role models who have successfully navigated similar struggles. They offer emotional support, advice, and guidance, helping young individuals build resilience and develop a stronger sense of self.

Peer support programs allow LGBTQ youth to connect with others who share similar experiences. These programs facilitate the formation of friendships, provide a sense of belonging, and offer a space where young individuals can openly discuss their challenges and triumphs.

Promoting Mental Health and Well-being

Supporting the mental health and well-being of LGBTQ youth is crucial in creating safe spaces. LGBTQ individuals are at an increased risk of experiencing mental health issues such as depression, anxiety, and suicidal ideation due to the challenges they face.

Organizations should prioritize mental health services tailored to the needs of LGBTQ youth. This includes providing access to counseling services with professionals who are knowledgeable about LGBTQ issues and fostering a culture that destigmatizes seeking help.

Furthermore, it is essential to educate LGBTQ youth about self-care practices, coping mechanisms, and stress management techniques. This knowledge empowers them to prioritize their well-being and equips them with the tools to navigate the complexities of their identity.

Community Engagement and Advocacy

Creating safe spaces for LGBTQ youth requires community engagement and advocacy at all levels. It is crucial to involve community members, parents, educators, and policymakers in the conversation to foster a collective commitment to inclusivity.

Community engagement can include organizing workshops, seminars, and awareness campaigns that promote acceptance, challenge stereotypes, and provide education about LGBTQ issues. These initiatives aim to create more understanding within the community and reduce stigma.

Advocacy efforts should focus on pushing for policy changes that protect the rights and well-being of LGBTQ youth. This can involve lobbying for LGBTQ-inclusive anti-discrimination laws, comprehensive sex education, mental health support, and LGBTQ-affirming healthcare services.

An Unconventional Approach: The Power of Art

In addition to more traditional strategies, incorporating art and creative expression can be a powerful tool in creating safe spaces for LGBTQ youth. Art allows youth to explore and express their identity, emotions, and experiences in a unique and cathartic manner.

Organizing art workshops, open mic nights, and exhibitions can provide a platform for LGBTQ youth to share their stories and perspectives. Through these creative outlets, they can find validation, build connections, and foster a sense of community.

Art can also be a powerful advocacy tool, raising awareness about LGBTQ issues and challenging societal norms. By encouraging LGBTQ youth to use their creativity to create social change, we empower them to become active participants in their own liberation.

Conclusion

In conclusion, creating safe spaces for LGBTQ youth requires a multi-faceted approach. It involves implementing inclusive policies and practices, providing mentoring and peer support programs, prioritizing mental health and well-being, engaging the community, and exploring unconventional avenues such as art.

By fostering an environment that celebrates diversity, educates, supports, and advocates for LGBTQ youth, we empower the next generation to thrive, contribute to society, and lead the charge towards a more inclusive future. It is our collective responsibility to ensure that no LGBTQ youth faces a world devoid of safe spaces and opportunities for growth.

Cultivating Empathy Through Storytelling

Storytelling has long been a powerful tool for cultivating empathy and fostering understanding. Through sharing personal narratives and experiences, individuals can connect on a deeper level, breaking down barriers and creating a sense of shared humanity. In the context of LGBTQ activism, storytelling plays a crucial role in challenging stereotypes, combating discrimination, and encouraging empathy within communities.

The Power of Personal Stories: Personal stories have the ability to evoke emotions and challenge preconceived notions. By sharing their own experiences, LGBTQ individuals can humanize their struggles, hopes, and dreams, allowing others to connect with their journey on a personal level. These stories serve as a reminder that LGBTQ individuals are not just statistics or abstract concepts, but real people with unique stories and perspectives.

Combatting Stereotypes and Ignorance: Storytelling is a powerful tool in combatting stereotypes and ignorance faced by the LGBTQ community. By sharing diverse narratives, encompassing different identities and experiences, stereotypes can be challenged and dismantled. Personal stories can break down misconceptions, generate empathy, and create a more inclusive and accepting society.

For example, a transgender individual sharing their story of self-discovery, transition, and acceptance can dispel myths, misconceptions, and ignorance surrounding trans identities. Their story humanizes the transgender experience, allows others to develop a deeper understanding, and fosters empathy and acceptance.

Building Bridges and Encouraging Dialogue: Storytelling creates a platform for dialogue and understanding between LGBTQ individuals and the wider community. By sharing their stories, individuals provide an opportunity for others to ask questions, engage in meaningful conversations, and challenge their own biases and assumptions.

Through dialogue, misconceptions can be addressed, and a sense of empathy can be fostered. This dialogue allows for genuine connections to be formed, breaking down barriers and creating space for mutual respect and acceptance.

Empowering Others to Share Their Stories: Storytelling not only empowers the storyteller but also encourages others to share their own stories. When individuals see the impact and power of personal narratives, they are inspired to speak up and share their own experiences.

By creating a safe and supportive environment for individuals to tell their stories, the LGBTQ community can amplify marginalized voices and provide a platform for their narratives to be heard. This not only fosters inclusivity but also enriches the collective understanding of the diverse LGBTQ experience.

Embracing Digital Platforms and Social Media: In today's digital age, storytelling has found a new home on social media platforms. Through blogs, vlogs, podcasts, and social media campaigns, personal stories can reach a wider audience and have a greater impact.

Digital storytelling allows for creativity and accessibility, enabling individuals to share their experiences in various formats. These platforms also provide opportunities for collaboration and amplification of voices, creating a sense of community and support.

Unleashing the Power of Art and Creativity: Storytelling is not limited to written or spoken narratives. Art and creativity can play a powerful role in sharing personal stories and nurturing empathy.

Photography, visual arts, theater, dance, and music can all be used as mediums for LGBTQ individuals to express their experiences. These creative forms of storytelling evoke emotions, provoke thought, and engage the audience in a unique and visceral way. They can transcend language barriers and cultural differences, allowing for a universal understanding and connection.

Caveats and Challenges: While storytelling is a powerful tool for cultivating empathy, challenges and caveats must be considered. It is essential to respect the autonomy and boundaries of individuals sharing their stories. Consent, privacy, and the emotional well-being of storytellers should always be prioritized.

Another challenge is the potential for selective listening, where some individuals may dismiss or disregard narratives that do not align with their beliefs or biases. To mitigate this, it is crucial to foster an environment of openness, respect, and active listening, ensuring that all stories are heard and valued.

Conclusion: In the realm of LGBTQ activism, storytelling acts as a catalyst for empathy, understanding, and change. Personal narratives have the power to humanize experiences, challenge stereotypes, build bridges, and empower individuals to speak their truth. By cultivating empathy through storytelling, we create a world where inclusivity, acceptance, and understanding thrive.

The Future of LGBTQ Activism

Inspiring the Next Generation

Mentoring LGBTQ Youth

Mentoring LGBTQ youth is a vital component of creating a supportive and inclusive environment for this marginalized community. As a mentor, you have the power to make a positive impact on the lives of young LGBTQ individuals, helping them navigate the challenges they may face and empowering them to embrace their authentic selves. In this subsection, we will explore the importance of mentoring LGBTQ youth, discuss strategies for effective mentorship, and provide resources for both mentors and mentees.

Why Mentoring Matters

Mentoring plays a crucial role in the personal and social development of LGBTQ youth. Many face unique challenges, such as discrimination, rejection, and mental health issues, which can greatly impact their self-esteem and overall well-being. By providing mentorship, you can offer guidance, support, and empowerment to LGBTQ youth, helping them build resilience and navigate the complexities of their identities.

    1.1.1 Problem: LGBTQ youth often struggle with self-acceptance and understanding their place in the world. Without guidance and support, they may experience feelings of isolation, anxiety, and depression. How can mentors help LGBTQ youth develop self-confidence and a positive self-image?

    1.1.1 Solution: Mentors can inspire and guide LGBTQ youth by sharing their own experiences and providing a safe space for open discussions. They can help youth explore their identities, challenge self-doubt, and celebrate their unique qualities. By offering unconditional support and affirming their worth, mentors can help build the self-confidence and positive self-image of their mentees.

1.1.2 Problem: LGBTQ youth often face discrimination and bullying, which can lead to social isolation and a lack of peer support. How can mentors help LGBTQ youth build strong social connections and find a sense of belonging?

1.1.2 Solution: Mentors can assist LGBTQ youth in finding supportive communities, such as LGBTQ organizations, youth groups, or online platforms. They can help connect mentees with positive role models and facilitate opportunities for them to develop friendships with other LGBTQ individuals. By nurturing social connections, mentors can help LGBTQ youth find a sense of belonging and create supportive networks.

1.1.3 Problem: LGBTQ youth may struggle with their mental health due to societal pressures, discrimination, and internalized homophobia or transphobia. How can mentors support the mental well-being of their mentees?

1.1.3 Solution: Mentors can provide a listening ear, offer guidance, and help LGBTQ youth access mental health resources. They can encourage open conversations about mental health, normalize seeking help, and provide coping strategies for dealing with stress and anxiety. By being a supportive presence in their mentees' lives, mentors can help them navigate the challenges of mental health and promote overall well-being.

Effective Mentorship Strategies

Being an effective mentor requires patience, empathy, and a willingness to listen and learn. Here are some strategies for cultivating a positive and impactful mentorship relationship with LGBTQ youth:

1. Establish trust and create a safe space: Building trust is essential for a successful mentorship relationship. Create a safe and confidential environment where mentees feel comfortable opening up and expressing their thoughts and concerns.

2. Practice active listening: Give your full attention to your mentees and actively listen to their experiences, emotions, and needs. Validate their feelings and provide non-judgmental support.

3. Provide guidance and resources: Offer guidance based on your own experiences while recognizing that every LGBTQ individual's journey is unique. Provide information and resources that can help mentor youth navigate LGBTQ-specific challenges, such as coming out, finding affirming healthcare providers, or understanding their legal rights.

4. Encourage self-advocacy: Empower mentees to advocate for themselves and their needs. Teach them important life skills, such as effective communication,

self-care strategies, and how to navigate systems and institutions that may not be LGBTQ-inclusive.

5. Foster resilience: Help mentees develop resilience by encouraging positive coping strategies, promoting self-care, and reinforcing the importance of self-compassion and self-acceptance. Support them in setting and achieving their goals, both personal and professional.

6. Be an ally: Educate yourself about LGBTQ issues and be an ally in promoting equality and inclusivity. Stand up against discrimination, challenge stereotypes and biases, and show your mentees that you are committed to creating a more accepting society.

7. Seek guidance and support: Recognize that you may not have all the answers and be willing to seek guidance from LGBTQ organizations, mental health professionals, or other mentors. Reach out to other mentors for advice and share best practices with fellow mentors.

Resources for Mentors and Mentees

There are several resources available to both mentors and mentees that can provide guidance, support, and additional information on mentoring LGBTQ youth:

1. LGBTQ youth organizations: Connect with local LGBTQ youth organizations and see if they offer mentorship programs or resources for mentors. Examples include The Trevor Project, GLSEN, and PFLAG.

2. LGBTQ-inclusive literature: Familiarize yourself with literature that explores LGBTQ experiences and issues. Books like "This Book is Gay" by Juno Dawson and "The ABC's of LGBT+" by Ashley Mardell can provide valuable insights and serve as conversation starters.

3. Online platforms: Explore online platforms and communities that cater to LGBTQ youth, such as the It Gets Better Project, Queer Youth Advice, and LGBTQchat.net. These platforms often provide resources, support forums, and opportunities for mentorship connections.

4. LGBTQ cultural centers: Many cities have LGBTQ cultural centers that offer various programs, workshops, and events. Check if they have mentorship initiatives or networking opportunities for LGBTQ youth.

5. Mental health resources: Familiarize yourself with mental health resources specifically tailored for LGBTQ youth, such as The Trevor Project's TrevorSpace, LGBT National Help Center, and GLBTNearMe.

Remember, as a mentor, your commitment and dedication to the positive growth of LGBTQ youth can have a lasting impact. By offering guidance, support, and acceptance, you can help shape a more inclusive and equitable future for all.

Empowering Queer Muslims

Empowering queer Muslims is a crucial aspect of advancing LGBTQ rights within the Muslim community. It requires a comprehensive approach that addresses the unique challenges faced by individuals who navigate the intersection of their faith and sexuality. This subsection explores key strategies for empowering queer Muslims and creating a more inclusive and accepting society.

Challenging Stigma and Discrimination

To empower queer Muslims, it is essential to challenge the stigma and discrimination they face within their communities. Education plays a vital role in dispelling misconceptions and fostering understanding. Workshops, seminars, and awareness campaigns can be organized to provide accurate information about LGBTQ identities, experiences, and rights in Islam. These initiatives should include discussions on the diversity of sexual orientations and gender identities found within Muslim communities, emphasizing that being queer does not conflict with being Muslim.

Additionally, it is crucial to highlight the positive contributions and achievements of queer Muslims. Sharing success stories and showcasing LGBTQ Muslim role models can break down stereotypes and demonstrate the potential for harmonious coexistence.

Advocacy and Support Networks

Creating advocacy platforms and support networks specifically tailored to the needs of queer Muslims is essential. These networks can provide a safe space for individuals to share their experiences, seek guidance, and connect with others who share similar journeys. They can offer emotional support, resources, and advice on navigating challenges such as coming out to family, dealing with discrimination, and reconciling faith and sexuality.

Organizations and individuals can advocate for LGBTQ rights within Muslim communities and work towards policy changes that embrace inclusivity and protection of LGBTQ individuals. Lobbying for LGBTQ-inclusive policies and legislation, engaging with religious leaders, and encouraging dialogue are all powerful tools in empowering queer Muslims.

Promoting Self-Acceptance and Self-Care

Empowering queer Muslims involves promoting self-acceptance and self-care. Many queer Muslims struggle with internalized homophobia and guilt due to societal and religious pressures. Providing resources and support for mental health and well-being is essential. This can be done through counseling services, peer support groups, and access to LGBTQ-affirming therapists who understand the unique challenges faced by queer Muslims.

Encouraging self-expression and celebrating diverse identities is also crucial for empowerment. Events that promote queer Muslim art, literature, and culture can provide a platform for self-expression and help validate the identities and experiences of queer Muslims. Promoting self-acceptance also includes addressing the intersectionality of identities, recognizing that queer Muslims face additional layers of discrimination based on race, ethnicity, gender, and socioeconomic status.

Education and Dialogue

Education and dialogue are fundamental in empowering queer Muslims. By engaging with religious scholars, community leaders, and educational institutions, conversations around LGBTQ rights and acceptance can be fostered. Initiatives such as curriculum reform, training programs for educators, and interfaith dialogues can play a significant role in challenging homophobic narratives and promoting inclusivity.

Promoting inclusive religious spaces is essential for empowering queer Muslims. It involves advocating for LGBTQ-inclusive sermons, providing LGBTQ-affirming spaces within mosques, and supporting religious leaders who are allies for queer Muslims. Additionally, resources such as guidelines for LGBTQ-inclusive worship can be developed to facilitate the creation of inclusive prayer spaces.

Encouraging Leadership and Activism

Empowering queer Muslims requires nurturing leadership and providing opportunities for activism. Mentorship programs can pair emerging queer Muslim activists with experienced individuals who have made significant strides in the LGBTQ and Muslim advocacy landscape. These programs can provide guidance, support, and foster the development of new strategies to empower queer Muslims.

Youth-led activism is also crucial in empowering queer Muslims. By supporting and amplifying the voices of young activists, perspectives and experiences from this demographic can drive change within Muslim communities.

Providing training and resources for grassroots organizing, public speaking, and online activism can empower queer Muslim youth to advocate for their rights.

Unconventional yet Relevant: Addressing Online Hate

With the rise of social media, addressing online hate and cyberbullying has become increasingly important in empowering queer Muslims. Creating campaigns that promote respectful online discourse, combating hate speech, and providing guidance on reporting and blocking abusive individuals can help create safer digital spaces for queer Muslims. Online resources and toolkits can equip individuals with strategies for dealing with online harassment and protecting their mental well-being.

In conclusion, empowering queer Muslims necessitates a multifaceted approach that challenges stigma, provides support networks, promotes self-acceptance, fosters education and dialogue, encourages leadership and activism, and addresses the unique challenges posed by online hate. By employing these strategies, we can build a more inclusive and accepting society where queer Muslims can thrive.

Youth-Led Activism

Youth-led activism plays a vital role in driving social change and shaping the future of LGBTQ rights. Irshad Manji recognizes the importance of empowering young activists and fostering their leadership skills to create a sustainable movement. In this section, we will explore the ways in which youth-led activism contributes to the fight for equality, highlighting the challenges they face and the strategies they employ to make a difference.

The Power of Youth Activism

Youth activists bring a fresh perspective and unwavering dedication to the table. Their energy, passion, and fearlessness are essential in pushing for change, breaking down barriers, and challenging oppressive systems. Engaging young activists is crucial as they hold the potential to mobilize their peers, influence societal attitudes, and create lasting impact.

Recognizing Intersectional Identities

One of the key strengths of youth-led activism is its ability to embrace intersectionality. Young activists understand that LGBTQ rights intersect with other struggles, such as racial justice, gender equality, and economic justice. They actively work towards creating an inclusive movement that addresses the unique experiences of individuals with multiple marginalized identities.

Understanding the interconnections between different forms of oppression allows youth-led activists to build bridges and collaborate with diverse communities. By centering intersectionality, they ensure that the fight for LGBTQ rights is not disconnected from broader struggles for social justice.

Tools and Strategies

Youth-led activists leverage various tools and strategies to amplify their voices and effect change. Social media platforms like Instagram, Twitter, and TikTok provide a space for young activists to share their stories, educate others, and mobilize support. Hashtags and online campaigns create visibility and facilitate global solidarity.

Taking inspiration from past movements, youth activists organize protests, marches, and rallies to draw attention to LGBTQ issues. They utilize art, music, and creative expressions to communicate their messages effectively, engaging a wide audience. By harnessing the power of technology and creativity, they transcend geographical boundaries and connect with LGBTQ communities worldwide.

Challenges Faced by Youth Activists

Despite their enthusiasm and commitment, youth activists encounter various challenges in their advocacy work. They often face resistance from conservative sectors of society, including religious institutions, policymakers, and even within their own families. Overcoming stereotypes and facing discrimination can be emotionally and mentally draining.

Additionally, youth activists grapple with the lack of experience and resources compared to more established organizations. Funding, mentorship, and opportunities for skill development are essential for youth activists to sustain their work and amplify their impact. Building a strong support network and connecting with experienced activists can help address these challenges.

Building Alliances and Mentorship

Youth-led activism thrives when there is collaboration among different generations of activists. Building alliances with established LGBTQ organizations and activists provides mentorship, guidance, and a platform to amplify their voices. Mentorship programs connect youth activists with experienced leaders who provide support, resources, and insights gained through years of activism.

Establishing mentorship programs also benefits the LGBTQ community as a whole. It ensures a transfer of knowledge, sustains the momentum of the movement, and empowers the next generation of leaders. By fostering intergenerational collaboration, youth activists can learn from the struggles and successes of their predecessors, creating a more impactful and sustainable movement.

Education and Empowerment

Empowering young activists through education is crucial for their personal and professional development. Workshops, training sessions, and skill-building programs equip them with the tools needed to effectively advocate for LGBTQ rights. These programs can focus on public speaking, community organizing, advocacy tactics, and media literacy.

By investing in the education of youth activists, we create a generation of informed advocates who can challenge oppressive systems and work towards building a more inclusive society. Empowering youth also ensures the continuation of the LGBTQ movement, driving progress for generations to come.

Embracing Diversity of Tactics

Youth-led activism embraces a wide range of tactics, recognizing that different approaches are necessary to effect change. Some activists engage in direct action, staging protests and demonstrations to raise awareness and disrupt oppressive systems. Others focus on community organizing, creating safe spaces and support networks for LGBTQ youth.

By embracing the diversity of tactics, youth activists effectively cater to the needs of their communities. They understand that change happens both at the grassroots level and through legislative reforms. This flexibility ensures that the movement remains dynamic, responsive, and adaptable to emerging challenges.

Unconventional Strategies: Artivism

Artivism, the fusion of art and activism, is an unconventional yet powerful strategy employed by youth activists. It utilizes the transformative power of art to challenge social norms, provoke thought, and create empathy. Artistic expressions, such as paintings, poetry, music, and performance art, offer an emotional and compelling way to engage with audiences and foster understanding.

Through artivism, youth activists tap into the universal language of creativity to dismantle stereotypes, humanize the LGBTQ experience, and celebrate diverse identities. Art has the ability to transcend barriers and evoke empathy, making it a potent tool for sparking conversations and driving societal change.

Conclusion

Youth-led activism is a driving force in the fight for LGBTQ rights. Empowering young activists, nurturing their leadership skills, and embracing their intersectional identities are crucial to building a sustainable movement. By recognizing and addressing the challenges they face, providing mentorship and resources, and embracing diverse tactics, we can create a future where equality is realized for all. Let us continue to invest in the potential of youth-led activism and work towards a more inclusive and just society.

Recognizing Intersectional Identities

In the fight for LGBTQ rights, it is crucial to recognize and address the unique challenges faced by individuals who belong to intersecting marginalized communities. The concept of intersectionality acknowledges that forms of oppression, such as racism, sexism, classism, and ableism, are interconnected and cannot be separated from one another. In this subsection, we will explore the significance of recognizing intersectional identities within the LGBTQ community and discuss strategies for promoting inclusivity and equality.

Understanding Intersectionality

Intersectionality originated from the work of Black feminist scholar Kimberlé Crenshaw, who highlighted that the experiences of Black women faced forms of discrimination that were unique to their intersecting identities. This concept has since been expanded to understand the overlapping systems of oppression faced by individuals who belong to multiple marginalized groups.

Recognizing intersectional identities is crucial because it acknowledges that individuals do not experience discrimination or prejudice solely based on their LGBTQ identity. For example, a queer person of color may face discrimination based on both their race and sexual orientation. Ignoring these intersecting identities can lead to the erasure of experiences and perpetuate further discrimination.

Addressing Intersectionality in LGBTQ Activism

To create an inclusive and intersectional movement, we must actively address the experiences and needs of individuals who hold intersectional identities within the LGBTQ community. Here are some strategies to promote inclusivity and equality:

1. **Amplifying Voices**: Ensure that the experiences and perspectives of intersectional individuals are given visibility and are at the forefront of conversations within the LGBTQ movement. This can be accomplished by featuring diverse voices in media, conferences, and panel discussions.

2. **Collaboration and Solidarity**: Encourage collaboration and alliance-building between various marginalized communities. By working together, LGBTQ activists can address shared struggles and create a stronger, more united movement.

3. **Education and Awareness**: Promote education and awareness about intersectionality within the LGBTQ community. This can be achieved through workshops, training sessions, and educational resources that provide a deeper understanding of the interconnections between various forms of discrimination.

4. **Policy and Advocacy**: Advocate for policies and legislation that address the specific needs and concerns of individuals with intersectional identities. This includes fighting for anti-discrimination laws that consider the overlapping identities and experiences of marginalized individuals.

5. **Supportive Spaces**: Create safe and inclusive spaces for individuals with intersecting identities within the LGBTQ community. It is essential to ensure that these spaces acknowledge and affirm the various identities and provide support that is sensitive to their unique needs.

Case Study: LGBTQ Muslims of Color

An example of intersectionality within the LGBTQ community is the experience of LGBTQ Muslims of color. They face overlapping forms of discrimination based on their religion, race, and sexual orientation. LGBTQ Muslims of color may encounter exclusion within Muslim communities, racism within LGBTQ spaces, and Islamophobia in wider society. Recognizing the particular challenges faced by this group is crucial in creating an inclusive LGBTQ movement that represents all individuals.

To address the needs of LGBTQ Muslims of color, initiatives such as LGBTQ-affirming mosques, interfaith dialogues, and support groups specifically tailored to their experiences have emerged. These initiatives provide spaces where individuals can reconcile their varied identities and fight against the multiple forms of discrimination they face.

Conclusion

Recognizing intersectional identities is vital for creating an inclusive LGBTQ movement that addresses the needs and experiences of individuals who face multiple forms of discrimination. By amplifying voices, fostering collaboration, promoting education and awareness, advocating for policy change, and creating supportive spaces, we can work towards a more inclusive and equitable society for all LGBTQ individuals, regardless of their intersecting identities. Remember, acknowledging intersectionality strengthens our fight for equality and justice. Together, we can build a more diverse and inclusive LGBTQ movement that leaves no one behind.

Sustaining the Movement's Momentum

Sustaining the momentum of the LGBTQ rights movement is crucial for effecting lasting change in society. It requires ongoing activism, community engagement, and strategic planning. In this subsection, we will explore the key strategies and initiatives that can help sustain the movement's momentum.

Understanding the Challenges

Before delving into sustaining the movement's momentum, it's important to understand the challenges that LGBTQ activists face. Discrimination, prejudice, and ignorance continue to impact the lives of LGBTQ individuals worldwide. Moreover, societal attitudes and legal frameworks vary across countries, making it necessary to address region-specific challenges.

One of the key challenges is to combat the rise of anti-LGBTQ movements and organizations. These groups often spread misinformation, stigmatize the LGBTQ community, and lobby against LGBTQ rights. Sustaining the momentum requires countering this opposition through education, awareness campaigns, and by amplifying voices of marginalized individuals within the LGBTQ community.

Education and Awareness

Education and awareness campaigns play a crucial role in sustaining the movement's momentum. By teaching individuals about LGBTQ history, rights, and issues, we can foster empathy, understanding, and support. Educational initiatives can include awareness programs in schools and universities, workshops for professionals, and public campaigns that challenge stereotypes and promote inclusivity.

To make education more effective, it is essential to incorporate diverse voices and experiences. This can be done through inclusive curriculum development, where LGBTQ perspectives are integrated across various subjects. Giving LGBTQ individuals the opportunity to share their stories and lived experiences can help create a more inclusive society.

Building Alliances and Coalitions

Sustaining the movement's momentum requires building alliances and coalitions with other social justice movements. LGBTQ activists can collaborate with feminist organizations, racial justice groups, disability rights activists, and other marginalized communities to fight intersecting forms of discrimination.

By recognizing the interconnectedness of various struggles for liberation, the LGBTQ movement can harness collective power, advocate for more comprehensive policies, and amplify marginalized voices. Building strong alliances and coalitions is key to challenging societal structures that perpetuate discrimination and inequality.

Political Engagement and Advocacy

Political engagement and advocacy at local, national, and international levels are essential for sustaining the movement's momentum. LGBTQ activists can collaborate with politicians, lawmakers, and government bodies to shape progressive legislation and policies. This includes advocating for LGBTQ-inclusive anti-discrimination laws, gender recognition rights, and comprehensive sex education.

Engaging with political processes can also involve supporting LGBTQ candidates for elected positions, conducting voter education campaigns, and mobilizing communities to participate in elections. By actively participating in political processes, the movement can exert influence and ensure that LGBTQ rights remain a priority on the political agenda.

Supporting LGBTQ Youth

Sustaining the movement's momentum necessitates providing support and resources for LGBTQ youth. Many young individuals face rejection, bullying, and discrimination due to their sexual orientation or gender identity. Empowering LGBTQ youth is crucial for building a strong foundation for the movement's future.

Community organizations and activists can establish support groups, counseling services, and safe spaces specifically tailored for LGBTQ youth. These initiatives can provide mentorship programs, mental health support, and leadership training, emphasizing the importance of self-acceptance and resilience. By providing a nurturing environment, we can help LGBTQ youth embrace their identities and become future leaders in the movement.

Using Social Media and Technology

In the digital era, social media and technology have become powerful tools for sustaining the movement's momentum. Social media platforms, online campaigns, and digital storytelling allow activists to reach a global audience, share personal narratives, and mobilize support.

Utilizing social media platforms effectively involves creating engaging content, fostering online communities, and employing digital advocacy strategies. Online petitions, hashtags, and virtual events can help drum up public support and create a sense of solidarity among LGBTQ individuals worldwide.

Embracing Art and Culture

Art and culture offer unique avenues for sustaining the movement's momentum. LGBTQ artists and creatives can use their platforms to challenge societal norms, push boundaries, and convey powerful messages of inclusivity and diversity. By embracing art and culture, the movement can engage with a broader audience, sparking conversations, and fostering empathy.

Supporting LGBTQ artists, hosting art exhibitions, and promoting LGBTQ-centric literature, music, and films can create spaces for dialogue and reflection. Artistic expressions can evoke emotions, challenge prejudices, and inspire change, making it an invaluable tool for sustaining the movement's momentum.

Inclusive Policy Advocacy

Sustaining the movement's momentum requires continued advocacy for inclusive policies and institutions. LGBTQ activists can work towards implementing policies that protect LGBTQ rights in various domains. This includes pushing for LGBTQ-inclusive healthcare services, employment protections, and housing policies.

Moreover, inclusive policy advocacy must also address the unique needs of intersectional identities within the LGBTQ community. Recognizing the experiences of LGBTQ individuals who also belong to other marginalized groups is essential for creating truly inclusive policies.

Partnering with Corporations

Partnering with corporations can be a powerful strategy for sustaining the movement's momentum. Companies that support LGBTQ rights can use their influence and resources to advance LGBTQ equality. By implementing inclusive workplace policies, promoting diverse representation, and engaging in corporate social responsibility initiatives, corporations can contribute to societal change.

LGBTQ activists can collaborate with corporate entities through partnerships, sponsorships, and advocacy campaigns. These collaborations can promote awareness, fund initiatives, and demonstrate the economic benefits of LGBTQ-inclusive practices.

International Solidarity

Lastly, sustaining the movement's momentum requires international solidarity. The fight for LGBTQ rights is a global struggle, and supporting activists in different countries is essential. Organizations dedicated to LGBTQ equality can provide resources, funding, and expertise to grassroots movements worldwide.

Moreover, activists can engage in international advocacy efforts, urging governments and international bodies to prioritize LGBTQ rights. By fostering connections and amplifying voices from diverse regions, the movement can build a stronger and more inclusive global LGBTQ community.

In conclusion, sustaining the momentum of the LGBTQ rights movement involves a multifaceted approach. It requires education, building alliances, political engagement, supporting youth, utilizing technology, embracing art, advocating for inclusive policies, partnering with corporations, and promoting international solidarity. By employing these strategies, the movement can ensure long-term progress and create a more inclusive and equitable world for all LGBTQ individuals.

The Impact of Mentorship Programs

Mentorship programs play a crucial role in the lives of LGBTQ youth, providing guidance, support, and opportunities for personal and professional growth. In this subsection, we will explore the profound impact of mentorship programs on the lives of LGBTQ individuals, highlighting the benefits and long-lasting effects they have on their personal development, sense of belonging, and overall well-being.

Fostering Personal Growth and Development

Mentorship programs provide LGBTQ youth with valuable role models who can guide them through the challenges and complexities of navigating their identities. Mentors share their own experiences, provide advice and encouragement, and help mentees develop important life skills, such as self-confidence, resilience, and decision-making.

For example, a mentor may help a young LGBTQ person overcome internalized homophobia or transphobia, empowering them to embrace their true selves and fostering a sense of self-acceptance. By having a mentor who has gone through similar experiences, LGBTQ youth can gain the confidence to navigate their identities with pride and authenticity.

Furthermore, mentorship programs often offer opportunities for educational and professional development. Mentors can provide guidance on academic choices, career paths, and job search strategies. By connecting LGBTQ youth with relevant resources, networks, and opportunities, mentorship programs help to level the playing field and increase their chances of success.

Creating a Sense of Belonging and Community

Feeling a sense of belonging and having a supportive community is crucial for the mental and emotional well-being of LGBTQ individuals. Mentorship programs provide a safe and inclusive environment where LGBTQ youth can find acceptance, understanding, and a sense of community.

Mentors act as advocates and allies, offering a listening ear, emotional support, and encouragement during challenging times. They create a space where mentees can openly discuss their concerns, fears, and aspirations without judgment. By fostering a sense of belonging, mentorship programs help LGBTQ youth develop a positive self-image and a strong support network.

In addition to the mentor-mentee relationship, mentorship programs often include group activities and events where LGBTQ individuals can connect with peers who share similar experiences and identities. These opportunities for socialization and networking help to combat feelings of isolation and create a sense of solidarity within the LGBTQ community.

Building Resilience and Empowerment

Mentorship programs empower LGBTQ youth by teaching them resilience and equipping them with the tools to navigate the challenges they may face. Mentors offer guidance on how to handle discrimination, bullying, and societal pressures, empowering mentees to stand up for themselves and advocate for their rights.

Through the mentor-mentee relationship, LGBTQ youth learn valuable life skills such as problem-solving, effective communication, and self-advocacy. They gain the confidence to confront adversity head-on and overcome obstacles they may encounter along their journey.

Moreover, mentors often introduce mentees to other LGBTQ individuals who have successfully navigated similar challenges and achieved personal and professional success. By seeing real-life examples of thriving LGBTQ individuals who have overcome adversity, youth gain hope and inspiration for their own futures.

Addressing Intersectionality

Intersectionality, the interconnection of social categories such as race, gender, and sexuality, is a crucial consideration in mentorship programs. LGBTQ individuals, particularly those from marginalized communities, often face multiple forms of discrimination, and their unique experiences must be acknowledged and addressed.

Mentorship programs that prioritize intersectionality ensure that the needs and experiences of LGBTQ individuals from diverse backgrounds are understood and validated. They foster an environment where mentees feel comfortable discussing the intersectional challenges they face and help them build resilience and advocate for themselves in all aspects of their lives.

An Unconventional Approach: Reverse Mentorship

While traditional mentorship models involve experienced adults guiding young individuals, reverse mentorship offers a unique and valuable approach. In reverse mentorship, LGBTQ youth become mentors to older adults, sharing their perspectives, insights, and experiences.

Reverse mentorship challenges age-based power dynamics and helps break down generational biases and stereotypes. LGBTQ youth can enlighten older adults about the contemporary LGBTQ experience, creating empathy, understanding, and a deeper sense of intergenerational connection.

By creating opportunities for reverse mentorship, mentorship programs further empower LGBTQ youth, allowing them to take on leadership roles, contribute to their communities, and effect positive change.

Further Reading and Resources

1. "The Mentoring Effect: Young People's Perspectives on the Outcomes and Availability of Mentoring" by MENTOR National. This research report explores the impact of mentoring on youth in various domains, highlighting the importance of mentorship programs.

   2. "Mentoring LGBTQ Youth: A Guide to Supporting Kindness, Resilience, and Empowerment" by Dr. Elizabeth C. McCallum. This book offers practical guidance for mentors working with LGBTQ youth, providing insights into their unique needs and experiences.

   3. "Connections Matter: How Youth Relationships and Mentoring Help Shape Identity Development and Spiritual Growth" by Belle Rose Ragins. This article emphasizes the importance of relationships and mentoring in shaping identity development and spiritual growth among LGBTQ youth.

   4. TrevorSpace.org - An online community for LGBTQ youth ages 13-24, offering peer support, resources, and mentorship opportunities.

   5. It Gets Better Project (itgetsbetter.org) - A global LGBTQ youth support network that aims to uplift and inspire LGBTQ youth through personal stories and mentorship.

   Remember, mentorship programs are not a one-size-fits-all solution, and their impact can vary depending on individual circumstances. However, by prioritizing the needs of LGBTQ youth, providing inclusive and intersectional support, and fostering a sense of belonging, mentorship programs can have a transformative effect on the lives of LGBTQ individuals, empowering them to thrive and make a lasting impact on their communities.

Supporting LGBTQ Youth Mental Health

Mental health is a crucial aspect of overall well-being, and it is no different for LGBTQ youth. In this subsection, we will explore the unique challenges faced by LGBTQ youth in terms of mental health and discuss strategies and resources for supporting and promoting their mental well-being.

Understanding the Challenges

LGBTQ youth often face distinct challenges that can negatively impact their mental health. Discrimination, stigma, and social rejection can lead to increased rates of anxiety, depression, and suicidal ideation. The added burden of navigating their sexual and gender identities in an often unsupportive environment can exacerbate these mental health struggles.

Example: Emily, a 16-year-old transgender girl, is constantly bullied at school because of her gender identity. The constant harassment takes a toll on her mental health, leading to anxiety and depression.

Creating Safe Spaces

Creating safe and inclusive spaces is crucial for supporting LGBTQ youth mental health. Schools, community organizations, and mental health professionals all have a role to play in ensuring these spaces are available and accessible.

Example: The Rainbow Youth Center in the city has partnered with local schools to create safe spaces where LGBTQ students can connect with supportive peers and access mental health resources.

Providing Culturally Competent Support

To effectively support LGBTQ youth, mental health professionals must receive appropriate training to understand the unique experiences and challenges faced by this population. Culturally competent therapists can provide empathetic and effective care tailored to the specific needs of LGBTQ youth.

Example: A local counseling center offers specialized training for therapists to enhance their understanding of LGBTQ youth mental health and ensure they are equipped to provide inclusive care.

Promoting Resilience and Coping Strategies

Building resilience and teaching effective coping strategies are essential for LGBTQ youth to navigate the challenges they face. Psychoeducation, support groups, and therapy can all play a role in helping LGBTQ youth develop resilience and learn positive coping mechanisms.

Example: The local LGBTQ youth organization hosts workshops on resilience-building and coping strategies, providing youth with an opportunity to develop valuable skills and connect with others who share similar experiences.

Addressing the Intersectionality of Identities

It is crucial to acknowledge that LGBTQ youth may have intersectional identities that can further complicate their mental health challenges. Intersectionality considers how multiple aspects of a person's identity, such as race, ethnicity, or disability, overlap and influence their experiences.

Example: A counseling center collaborates with community organizations that focus on racial justice and disability advocacy to ensure that LGBTQ youth with intersecting identities receive comprehensive and culturally responsive mental health support.

Empowering LGBTQ Youth

Empowering LGBTQ youth involves providing them with the tools, resources, and support they need to advocate for themselves and create positive change in their communities. Encouraging their involvement in activism and fostering leadership skills can contribute to improved mental well-being.

Example: The LGBTQ youth center organizes workshops on self-advocacy and leadership, empowering young individuals to amplify their voices and advocate for their rights.

Seeking Professional Help

In some cases, LGBTQ youth may require professional mental health support beyond what is available in their immediate environment. It is essential to connect them with licensed therapists who specialize in LGBTQ youth mental health.

Example: The LGBTQ helpline provides youth with access to confidential support from trained professionals who can offer guidance, resources, and referrals to LGBTQ-friendly mental health providers.

Resources and Helplines

There are various resources and helplines available for LGBTQ youth seeking support or information about mental health. These resources can provide a lifeline for those who may not have access to immediate support in their local communities.

Example: The Trevor Project, a national LGBTQ youth helpline, offers 24/7 support through phone, chat, and text for LGBTQ youth in crisis or seeking someone to talk to about their mental health.

Conclusion

Supporting LGBTQ youth mental health requires a comprehensive approach that considers their unique challenges, provides safe spaces, and offers culturally competent care. By creating inclusive environments, providing resources, and empowering LGBTQ youth, we can contribute to their overall mental well-being and help them thrive.

Remember, your voice matters! If you or someone you know is struggling with mental health, don't hesitate to reach out to the available resources and supportive communities. Together, we can create a world where LGBTQ youth can grow, flourish, and lead fulfilling lives.

Cultivating Leadership Skills

Leadership is an essential skill for activists who aim to bring about positive change in society. Cultivating leadership skills requires a combination of self-reflection, communication, collaboration, and strategic thinking. In this subsection, we will explore the key principles and practices that can help individuals develop and enhance their leadership abilities.

Understanding Leadership

Before diving into developing leadership skills, it's crucial to have a clear understanding of what leadership entails. Leadership is not about having power or control over others; it's about inspiring and motivating individuals to work towards a common goal. Genuine leadership is based on respect, empathy, and the ability to influence others positively.

Self-Reflection and Awareness

Self-reflection is fundamental to developing leadership skills. It involves examining one's values, strengths, weaknesses, and areas for growth. Taking the time to understand oneself better can lead to improved decision-making, effective communication, and building strong relationships with others.

To cultivate self-reflection and awareness, individuals can engage in practices such as journaling, meditation, or seeking feedback from trusted mentors or peers. These practices help in identifying personal biases, understanding different perspectives, and developing a growth mindset.

Effective Communication

Effective communication is a cornerstone of effective leadership. Leaders must be able to clearly articulate their ideas, listen actively, and adapt their communication style to different audiences. They should be empathetic, open-minded, and respectful in their interactions.

To enhance their communication skills, individuals can practice active listening, asking clarifying questions, and providing constructive feedback. Additionally, developing nonverbal communication skills, such as body language and facial expressions, can significantly improve the effectiveness of their message delivery.

Collaboration and Team Building

Leadership is not a solo endeavor; it involves working collaboratively with others towards a shared vision. Cultivating leadership skills necessitates the ability to build and maintain high-performing teams.

To develop collaboration and team-building skills, individuals can engage in activities that foster trust, promote active participation, and encourage diverse perspectives. Encouraging open communication, recognizing and appreciating the strengths of team members, and creating an inclusive and supportive environment are crucial aspects of effective team building.

Strategic Thinking and Decision-making

Leaders must possess strategic thinking abilities to navigate complex challenges and make informed decisions. Strategic thinking involves the ability to analyze situations, identify opportunities, anticipate potential obstacles, and develop appropriate plans of action.

To cultivate strategic thinking skills, individuals can engage in activities such as scenario planning, problem-solving exercises, and critical analysis of real-world issues. Developing a broader understanding of the social, political, and cultural landscapes can also contribute to effective decision-making as a leader.

Leading by Example

Leadership is not only about words; it is also about actions. Leading by example is a powerful way to inspire and influence others. When leaders embody the values they advocate for, they create a sense of authenticity and credibility.

To lead by example, individuals can demonstrate ethical behavior, act with integrity, and consistently uphold the values they believe in. They can also prioritize self-care and well-being, showing the importance of balancing personal and professional commitments.

Identifying and Nurturing Potential Leaders

Cultivating leadership skills also involves identifying and nurturing potential leaders within communities. Developing a new generation of leaders ensures the sustainability of the movement and expands the impact of the LGBTQ activism.

To identify potential leaders, organizations and individuals can create mentorship programs, leadership development workshops, and networking opportunities. Providing platforms for voice and visibility, encouraging participation in decision-making processes, and offering ongoing support and guidance are essential for nurturing emerging leaders.

Tricks and Unconventional Strategies

In the journey of cultivating leadership skills, it is important to be open to unconventional strategies and creative approaches. Sometimes, thinking outside the box can lead to breakthroughs and innovative solutions.

One unconventional strategy is promoting reverse mentoring, where younger or less experienced individuals mentor senior or more experienced leaders. This approach allows for knowledge exchange, fresh perspectives, and breaking hierarchical barriers within organizations and movements.

Another trick is embracing failure as a learning opportunity. Leaders should develop resilience and learn from their mistakes. The ability to adapt and grow from failure can strengthen leadership skills and inspire others to persevere despite challenges.

Exercises and Practice

Developing leadership skills requires consistent practice. Here are a few exercises that individuals can engage in to enhance their leadership abilities:

1. Role-Playing: Simulate challenging situations and practice effective communication, decision-making, and problem-solving techniques.

2. Team-Building Activities: Engage in activities that foster collaboration, trust-building, and problem-solving within teams.

3. Case Studies: Analyze real-world case studies related to LGBTQ activism and develop strategic plans of action.

4. Public Speaking: Take opportunities to speak in public, whether at local events, conferences, or university settings, to enhance confidence and communication skills.

5. Reflection and Feedback: Regularly reflect on personal actions and seek feedback from mentors, peers, and team members to identify areas for improvement.

Resources and Further Reading

To further develop leadership skills, individuals can explore the following resources:

1. "Leadership on the Line: Staying Alive Through the Dangers of Change" by Ronald A. Heifetz and Marty Linsky.

2. "Dare to Lead: Brave Work. Tough Conversations. Whole Hearts." by Brené Brown.

3. "The Leadership Challenge" by James M. Kouzes and Barry Z. Posner.

4. Online courses and workshops on leadership development offered by organizations such as Coursera, EdX, and LinkedIn Learning.

5. Attending leadership conferences, seminars, and networking events within the LGBTQ advocacy community.

Remember, cultivating leadership skills is an ongoing process that requires dedication, self-reflection, and continuous learning. As leaders, individuals have the power to make a significant impact on the LGBTQ community and beyond.

Creating Advocacy Toolkits for Youth

In the fight for LGBTQ rights and equality, it is essential to engage and empower the next generation of activists. Young people possess a unique perspective and energy that can drive significant change. To support and equip them, it is crucial to provide advocacy toolkits specifically designed to meet their needs.

Understanding the Needs of LGBTQ Youth

LGBTQ youth face numerous challenges, including discrimination, bullying, and social isolation. To create effective advocacy toolkits, it is vital to understand their unique needs and tailor resources accordingly.

One of the primary challenges for LGBTQ youth is the lack of knowledge about their rights and available support systems. Advocacy toolkits should include comprehensive information about laws, policies, and resources available at local, regional, and national levels. This information will empower young people to navigate challenging situations with confidence.

Additionally, these toolkits should address mental health concerns, as LGBTQ youth often experience higher rates of anxiety, depression, and suicidal ideation.

Resources such as helpline numbers, counseling services, and strategies for self-care should be included to promote overall well-being.

Building Advocacy Skills

Empowering youth requires equipping them with the necessary skills to advocate for their rights effectively. Advocacy toolkits should provide guidance on how to communicate their needs and concerns, engage with policymakers, and create grassroots movements.

Effective communication skills are pivotal in driving change. Toolkits should offer tips on public speaking, persuasive writing, and social media engagement. By honing these skills, youth can effectively articulate their message, mobilize their peers, and influence broader audiences.

The toolkits should also emphasize the importance of collaboration and coalition-building. Encouraging youth to work together with other advocacy groups and individuals strengthens their impact and fosters a sense of solidarity. Strategies for organizing rallies, workshops, and awareness campaigns can be included to support youth-led movements.

Promoting Intersectionality

Youth advocacy should center on intersectionality, acknowledging the interconnected nature of different forms of oppression. LGBTQ youth often face discrimination based not only on their sexual orientation or gender identity but also due to other aspects of their identity, such as race, ethnicity, religion, or disability.

Advocacy toolkits should educate youth about intersectionality and inclusivity, emphasizing the importance of understanding and addressing various forms of discrimination. This understanding will help young activists build alliances and promote solidarity with other marginalized groups.

Including real-life case studies and stories of individuals who have experienced intersectional discrimination can provide powerful examples and inspire youth to fight for justice and equality.

Utilizing Technology and Digital Platforms

In the digital age, technology plays a crucial role in advocacy efforts. Advocacy toolkits should provide guidance on utilizing digital platforms effectively to raise awareness, mobilize support, and challenge discriminatory practices.

To maximize impact, toolkits should offer practical tips on leveraging social media platforms, creating engaging content, and reaching a wider audience. Additionally, information on online safety and dealing with online harassment should be included to ensure young activists can navigate the digital landscape confidently.

Mentorship and Support Networks

Youth advocacy is nurtured through mentorship and support networks. Advocacy toolkits should highlight the importance of finding mentors who can provide guidance, offer advice, and share their own experiences.

Toolkits can include resources for finding mentorship programs, connecting with experienced activists, and building support networks. Encouraging the participation of LGBTQ allies as mentors can provide diverse perspectives and contribute to a more inclusive movement.

Moreover, the toolkits should emphasize the significance of peer support. Creating spaces for LGBTQ youth to connect and share experiences can foster a sense of belonging and strengthen the collective power of the movement. Online forums, support groups, and networking platforms can be recommended as safe and inclusive spaces for LGBTQ youth to find support.

Exercises and Activities

Advocacy toolkits should incorporate interactive exercises and activities to engage youth and reinforce their learning. These activities can range from role-playing scenarios to group discussions and creative projects.

For example, role-playing activities can help youth practice advocacy skills in a safe environment. They can simulate conversations with policymakers, confrontational situations, or public speaking engagements. By immersing themselves in these scenarios, young activists can gain confidence and refine their strategies.

Creative projects, such as art exhibitions, spoken word performances, or short films, can serve as powerful tools for raising awareness and promoting empathy. Toolkits can provide guidance on conceptualizing and executing these projects, empowering youth to leverage their creativity for social change.

Unconventional Approach: Gamification

To captivate and engage youth, an unconventional approach to advocacy toolkits could involve gamification. Creating interactive games or challenges that explore

LGBTQ rights and advocacy can make the learning experience enjoyable and immersive.

Gamification can involve quizzes, puzzles, or virtual reality experiences that allow youth to navigate real-life scenarios. By gamifying the learning process, advocacy toolkits can foster active participation and enhance retention of information.

Resources and Further Reading

To ensure the efficacy and relevance of advocacy toolkits, providing resources for further reading and ongoing education is crucial. Toolkits should include a curated list of books, articles, documentaries, and online platforms that delve deeper into LGBTQ rights, activism, and intersectionality.

Additionally, toolkits should direct youth to existing organizations, both local and global, that specialize in LGBTQ youth advocacy. These organizations can offer ongoing support, mentorship opportunities, and advocacy campaigns for youth to get involved in.

Conclusion

Creating advocacy toolkits for LGBTQ youth is an essential component of promoting their activism and ensuring a brighter future of equality. These toolkits should equip youth with knowledge, skills, and resources, empowering them to navigate challenges, amplify their voices, and drive positive change. By cultivating the next generation of activists, we can continue the fight for LGBTQ rights and create a more inclusive world for all.

Amplifying Young Voices

In the fight for LGBTQ rights, amplifying the voices of young activists is crucial. They bring fresh perspectives, innovative ideas, and the energy needed to drive social change. This subsection explores ways to empower and amplify these young voices, ensuring their contributions are heard and valued.

Creating Safe Spaces for Expression

A key step in amplifying young voices is creating safe spaces where they can express themselves without fear of judgment or discrimination. Schools, community centers, and online platforms play a vital role in providing these spaces. Educators and community leaders should foster inclusive environments that encourage open dialogue, empathy, and respect for diverse identities.

Online platforms, such as social media, can be powerful tools for young activists to share their experiences and engage with a wider audience. Organizations and communities should actively promote digital spaces where LGBTQ youth can connect, learn, and organize for change.

Supporting Youth-Led Initiatives

To amplify young voices, it's essential to provide support and resources for youth-led initiatives. Many young activists have innovative ideas and the drive to make a difference, but they often face barriers like lack of funding or mentorship. Organizations should create grants, scholarships, and mentorship programs specifically designed to support LGBTQ youth in their advocacy work.

Mentorship programs connect young activists with experienced leaders who can provide guidance, share knowledge, and offer support. These relationships foster personal and professional growth, ensuring that their voices are heard and their impact is maximized.

Engaging with Mainstream Media

Amplifying young voices requires reaching a broader audience, and engaging with mainstream media is an effective avenue to achieve this. Media outlets should actively seek out and feature young LGBTQ activists, providing them with a platform to share their stories, experiences, and perspectives.

When young activists are given the opportunity to speak on mainstream media channels, it challenges stereotypes and educates the public about the issues facing the LGBTQ community. This exposure helps to normalizing LGBTQ identities and promotes acceptance and understanding.

Promoting Intersectionality

An inclusive movement is one that fully embraces intersectionality, acknowledging the interconnected nature of different identities and experiences. Amplifying young voices means recognizing the unique challenges faced by LGBTQ individuals who also belong to marginalized communities based on race, ethnicity, socio-economic status, disability, or religion.

Organizations should actively seek out and support LGBTQ youth from diverse backgrounds, ensuring their voices are amplified and their experiences are included in the broader narrative. Intersectionality should be a guiding principle in all aspects of LGBTQ activism, both in policy advocacy and in grassroots movements.

Digital Activism and Online Tools

In the digital age, young activists are leveraging technology to amplify their voices and effect change. Online tools such as petitions, social media campaigns, and viral videos have become powerful vehicles for spreading awareness and mobilizing support.

Organizations should provide resources and training to help young activists leverage digital platforms effectively. This includes workshops on digital activism, online safety, and using social media as a tool for advocacy. By harnessing the power of technology, young activists can amplify their messages and reach a global audience.

Unconventional Approach: Virtual Reality Storytelling

One unconventional but highly impactful approach to amplifying young voices is through virtual reality (VR) storytelling. VR technology allows users to immerse themselves in the lived experiences of others, creating a deep sense of empathy and understanding.

By partnering with young activists and content creators, organizations can develop VR experiences that showcase the challenges faced by LGBTQ youth. These immersive narratives can break down barriers, humanize the struggle for equality, and inspire action among viewers.

Exercise: Creating an LGBTQ Youth Mentorship Program

Designing an LGBTQ youth mentorship program is an excellent way to amplify young voices. Develop a framework for a mentorship program that connects experienced LGBTQ activists with passionate and driven young individuals. Consider the structure, goals, and potential outcomes of the program. How will you ensure the program is accessible and inclusive for diverse communities? How will you measure the impact and success of the program?

Conclusion

Amplifying young voices is crucial for creating lasting change in the fight for LGBTQ rights. By creating safe spaces, supporting youth-led initiatives, engaging with mainstream media, promoting intersectionality, leveraging online tools, and exploring unconventional approaches like VR storytelling, we can ensure that the valuable contributions of young activists are recognized and amplified. Together, we can empower the next generation and work towards a more inclusive and equitable future.

Continuing the Fight for Equality

Addressing Global LGBTQ Issues

Addressing global LGBTQ issues is a crucial aspect of LGBTQ activism. It involves recognizing the challenges faced by LGBTQ individuals across different countries and cultures and working towards creating a more inclusive and accepting world. In this subsection, we will explore some of the key global LGBTQ issues and discuss strategies for addressing them.

Understanding the Global LGBTQ Landscape

To effectively address global LGBTQ issues, it is crucial to have a comprehensive understanding of the diverse challenges faced by LGBTQ individuals worldwide. In many countries, homosexuality is still criminalized, with severe penalties including imprisonment and even the death penalty. Discrimination, violence, and harassment against LGBTQ individuals are prevalent in various forms, impacting their safety, well-being, and access to healthcare, education, and employment.

Advocacy for LGBTQ Rights

Advocacy plays a vital role in addressing global LGBTQ issues. It involves raising awareness, pushing for legislative changes, and promoting equality and inclusivity. LGBTQ activists and organizations work tirelessly to influence policy-making, engage with governments and international bodies, and collaborate with human rights organizations to promote the rights of LGBTQ individuals.

Collaboration with Human Rights Organizations

Collaborating with human rights organizations is instrumental in addressing global LGBTQ issues. These organizations possess expertise in human rights advocacy and can provide invaluable support, resources, and guidance to LGBTQ activists. By working together, they can amplify their voices, mobilize resources, and push for systemic changes to ensure the protection and promotion of LGBTQ rights.

Pushing for Legal Reforms

Legal reforms are crucial for advancing LGBTQ rights globally. Advocacy efforts should focus on challenging discriminatory laws and supporting the enactment of comprehensive anti-discrimination laws that protect LGBTQ individuals from violence, discrimination, and harassment. Additionally, advocating for the decriminalization of homosexuality and the recognition of same-sex relationships is an essential goal in many countries.

Overcoming Discrimination in the Workplace

Discrimination against LGBTQ individuals in the workplace is a significant issue globally. Activists and organizations work to promote equal employment opportunities for LGBTQ individuals by advocating for non-discrimination policies and fostering inclusive work environments. This includes supporting initiatives that raise awareness about LGBTQ rights in the workplace, providing sensitivity training, and encouraging employers to adopt inclusive policies and practices.

Solidarity and Collaboration

Addressing global LGBTQ issues requires solidarity and collaboration among activists and organizations worldwide. By joining forces, sharing knowledge and resources, and supporting each other's efforts, the LGBTQ community can create a unified front against discrimination and advocate for change at both local and international levels. Solidarity also includes supporting LGBTQ movements in countries where activism is difficult or confronted with resistance.

Fighting for Marriage Equality

Marriage equality remains a significant global LGBTQ issue. While progress has been made, many countries still deny same-sex couples the right to marry or recognize their marriages performed in other jurisdictions. Advocacy efforts should focus on legalizing same-sex marriage and promoting recognition and acceptance of diverse family structures.

Tackling LGBTQ Conversion Therapy

LGBTQ conversion therapy, which aims to change an individual's sexual orientation or gender identity, is a harmful practice that persists globally. Activists work towards banning and criminalizing conversion therapy, advocating for legislation that protects LGBTQ individuals from these harmful practices, and raising awareness about the severe physical and psychological consequences.

Promoting Inclusive Education Policies

Inclusive education policies are essential in addressing global LGBTQ issues. Activists strive to include LGBTQ-inclusive curriculum and support programs in schools to promote understanding, respect, and acceptance of diverse sexual orientations and gender identities. Additionally, advocating for the implementation of policies that protect LGBTQ students from bullying and discrimination is crucial.

Protecting Transgender Rights

Transgender individuals face specific challenges and discrimination globally. Activists focus on advocating for legal recognition of gender identity, promoting access to healthcare, fighting against discrimination in various spheres of life, and raising awareness about transgender rights and issues. Additionally, transgender activists play a critical role in empowering the transgender community and amplifying their voices.

Adapting to Emerging Challenges

Addressing global LGBTQ issues requires continuously adapting to emerging challenges. Activists must remain vigilant about new forms of discrimination, such as online harassment and cyberbullying, and develop strategies to combat them effectively. Staying informed about advancements in technology, exploring new avenues for advocacy, and leveraging social media platforms are essential in reaching a wider audience and effecting change.

In summary, addressing global LGBTQ issues requires a multifaceted approach that includes advocacy, collaboration, legal reforms, solidarity, and adaptation to emerging challenges. By working together across borders, LGBTQ activists can create a world that celebrates and respects the rights and dignity of LGBTQ individuals everywhere.

Pushing for Legal Reforms

In this subsection, we will delve into the crucial aspect of pushing for legal reforms to promote LGBTQ rights. The fight for equality goes beyond cultural and social acceptance. It requires systemic change that can only be achieved through legislative action. Advocating for legal reforms is central to dismantling discriminatory laws and ensuring the protection and rights of the LGBTQ community.

Understanding the Legal Landscape

Before embarking on the journey of legal reforms, it is imperative to comprehend the existing legal landscape. Laws regarding LGBTQ rights vary greatly across jurisdictions, with some countries having progressive legislation while others retain regressive and discriminatory laws. Therefore, understanding the legal context in a specific region is paramount to identify areas in need of reform.

Different legal aspects should be considered, such as anti-discrimination laws, hate crime legislation, gender recognition, marriage equality, adoption rights, employment protection, and access to healthcare. Each of these areas plays a vital role in securing the rights and dignity of LGBTQ individuals.

Identifying Key Issues

To effectively push for legal reforms, it is crucial to identify the key issues and prioritize the areas in need of immediate attention. This process involves conducting comprehensive research, engaging with local LGBTQ organizations, and consulting legal experts specializing in human rights and LGBTQ law.

Some of the key issues that require attention include:

1. **Criminalization and decriminalization:** In many countries, consensual same-sex sexual activities are still criminalized. Advocacy efforts should focus on decriminalizing such activities and protecting individuals from prosecution and discrimination based on their sexual orientation or gender identity.

2. **Anti-discrimination laws:** Strengthening anti-discrimination laws is crucial to protect LGBTQ individuals from discrimination in various domains, including employment, healthcare, housing, and public accommodations. Advocates need to push for comprehensive legislation prohibiting discrimination based on sexual orientation and gender identity.

3. **Gender recognition and legal documentation:** Many transgender and non-binary individuals face significant challenges in obtaining legal recognition of their gender identity. Advocating for gender recognition laws and ensuring access to legal documentation reflecting individuals' affirmed gender is essential for their rights and wellbeing.

4. **Marriage equality and partnership recognition:** Marriage equality is a cornerstone of LGBTQ rights, granting same-sex couples the same legal rights and recognition as opposite-sex couples. Advocates should work towards legalizing same-sex marriage and establishing legal provisions for partnership recognition.

5. **Parental rights and adoption:** LGBTQ individuals and same-sex couples often face challenges when it comes to parental rights, adoption, and assisted reproductive technologies. Advocacy efforts should aim to remove barriers and ensure equal access to parenting rights and adoption processes.

6. **Healthcare access:** LGBTQ individuals often encounter barriers in accessing appropriate healthcare that caters to their specific needs. Advocacy for legal reforms in healthcare should focus on addressing these disparities and ensuring inclusive and non-discriminatory healthcare practices.

Advocacy Strategies

Advocacy for legal reforms requires strategic planning and execution. The following strategies can be effective in pushing for change:

1. **Public awareness campaigns:** Raising public awareness is crucial to generate support for legal reforms. Engaging in campaigns that highlight the importance of LGBTQ rights and the need for legal equality can help garner public support and put pressure on lawmakers.

2. **Coalition building:** Collaboration with other human rights organizations, social justice advocates, and allies is vital to strengthen the advocacy efforts. Building coalitions amplifies the collective voice and increases the chances of successful legal reforms.

3. **Engaging policymakers:** Building relationships with policymakers is essential to influence legislative processes. Engaging in dialogues, providing research-based evidence, and proposing draft legislation can help facilitate legal reforms.

4. **Litigation and strategic litigation:** Strategic litigation can be a powerful tool in challenging discriminatory laws. Strategic lawsuits aim to create legal precedents that dismantle discriminatory legislation and establish legal protections for LGBTQ individuals.

5. **International pressure and advocacy:** Collaborating with international human rights organizations and utilizing international mechanisms can create pressure on governments to reform laws. Engaging with international bodies, such as the United Nations and regional human rights commissions, can help advocate for legal reforms on a broader scale.

6. **Engaging grassroots movements:** Grassroots movements and community mobilization play a crucial role in advocating for legal reforms. Creating spaces for education, involvement, and empowerment within local LGBTQ communities helps build momentum for change.

Examples of Successful Legal Reforms

Throughout history, many countries have achieved significant legal reforms in favor of LGBTQ rights. Here are a few notable examples:

+ **Marriage Equality in Canada:** Canada legalized same-sex marriage nationwide in 2005. This landmark legal reform was the result of advocacy efforts and strategic litigation challenging traditional marriage laws.

+ **Gender Recognition in Argentina:** Argentina passed the Gender Identity Law in 2012, allowing individuals to change their legal gender without any medical or psychological intervention. This law is considered one of the most progressive gender recognition laws globally.

+ **Decriminalization in India:** In a historic judgment in 2018, the Supreme Court of India struck down Section 377 of the Indian Penal Code, decriminalizing consensual same-sex sexual activities. This legal reform was the outcome of years of advocacy and litigation efforts.

+ **Transgender Rights in Malta:** Malta has enacted comprehensive legislation protecting the rights of transgender and intersex individuals, including gender recognition procedures, anti-discrimination laws, and healthcare provisions. This holistic approach to legal reform has positioned Malta as a leader in transgender rights.

These examples demonstrate the power of legal reforms in advancing LGBTQ rights and fostering social progress.

Challenges and Considerations

Advocacy for legal reforms also comes with its challenges and considerations. Some of the key aspects to navigate include:

+ **Resistance to change:** Conservative religious and political forces often resist legal reforms that grant rights to the LGBTQ community. Advocates must anticipate backlash and develop strategies to counter opposition effectively.

+ **Intersectionality and inclusivity:** Legal reforms should prioritize intersectional approaches, considering the unique experiences of LGBTQ individuals from diverse racial, ethnic, and socioeconomic backgrounds. Ensuring inclusivity and equal representation within the movement is vital.

+ **Long-term sustainability:** Achieving legal reforms is just the beginning. Long-term sustainability requires monitoring and accountability mechanisms to ensure effective implementation and enforcement of new laws.

+ **International influence:** Advocacy for legal reforms should consider the impact of international human rights standards and norms. Engaging with global human rights mechanisms and utilizing international pressure can be instrumental in achieving change.

Additional Resources and Recommendations

Advocacy for legal reforms is a complex and multifaceted process. Here are some additional resources and recommendations for individuals and organizations interested in pushing for legal reforms:

+ **Organizations:** Collaborate with local and international LGBTQ organizations that focus on legal advocacy. These organizations often provide guidance, resources, and training to support advocacy efforts.

+ **Research and Evidence:** Access research studies, reports, and legal analysis on LGBTQ rights and legal reforms. Base your advocacy on evidence and data to bolster your arguments and proposals.

+ **Policy Papers:** Develop policy papers and recommendations that outline the specific legal reforms needed in your region. These papers can serve as valuable resources in engaging policymakers and lawmakers.

+ **Legal Expertise:** Consult with legal experts specializing in human rights and LGBTQ law to gain insights and guidance on effective strategies for legal reforms.

+ **Training and Workshops:** Participate in training sessions and workshops on advocacy skills, strategic litigation, grassroots organizing, and engaging with policymakers. These capacity-building opportunities will enhance your ability to push for legal reforms.

Remember, while legal reforms are vital for LGBTQ rights, they are just one aspect of a comprehensive advocacy strategy. Social, cultural, and educational changes are also necessary to build a more inclusive and accepting society.

In conclusion, pushing for legal reforms is an essential component of LGBTQ activism. Identifying key issues, employing effective strategies, and engaging with policymakers and stakeholders can lead to significant progress in ensuring legal protections and equality for the LGBTQ community. By working collectively and staying committed to long-term goals, we can create lasting change and build a more inclusive world for all.

Amplifying Marginalized Voices

In the fight for LGBTQ rights, it is crucial to amplify the voices of those who experience multiple forms of oppression and marginalization. Marginalized voices within the LGBTQ community, such as people of color, transgender individuals, and those from low-income backgrounds, face unique challenges that intersect with their sexual orientation or gender identity.

Understanding Intersectionality

To effectively amplify marginalized voices, it is essential to understand the concept of intersectionality. Coined by Kimberlé Crenshaw, intersectionality recognizes that individuals experience intersecting systems of oppression based on their various identities. For example, an LGBTQ person of color may face discrimination and marginalization due to both their race and sexual orientation.

Challenges Faced by Marginalized LGBTQ Individuals

Marginalized LGBTQ individuals often face heightened levels of discrimination and violence. For example, transgender individuals, particularly transgender women of color, experience alarmingly high rates of physical attacks, verbal harassment, and systemic discrimination. Additionally, LGBTQ youth from low-income backgrounds may face homelessness, limited access to healthcare, and heightened mental health challenges.

Addressing Marginalization within LGBTQ Communities

To amplify marginalized voices, it is crucial to address and challenge the discrimination that exists within LGBTQ communities themselves. This can be achieved through education and awareness campaigns that promote inclusivity and understanding. LGBTQ organizations and activists must actively work to create spaces that welcome and value diverse experiences and identities.

Promoting Representation and Visibility

Representation is key in amplifying marginalized voices. Media, literature, and other forms of creative expression play a crucial role in promoting diverse narratives and experiences. By ensuring that a wide range of stories and perspectives are shared, marginalized LGBTQ individuals are given a platform to share their lived experiences and challenge societal norms.

Building Coalitions and Allies

Amplifying marginalized voices is not solely the responsibility of individuals who belong to marginalized communities. Allies, both within and outside of the LGBTQ community, can play a crucial role in elevating these voices. Building coalitions with other social justice movements, such as racial justice and gender equality, can create a united front in the fight against all forms of oppression.

Creating Safe Spaces and Support Networks

Creating safe spaces and support networks is essential for amplifying marginalized voices. LGBTQ organizations should prioritize the establishment of inclusive and accessible spaces where individuals from all backgrounds can share their experiences, find support, and advocate for their rights. These spaces can also serve as platforms to amplify marginalized voices and drive social change.

Addressing Systemic Inequalities

To truly amplify marginalized voices, it is necessary to address the systemic inequalities that perpetuate discrimination and marginalization. This includes advocating for changes in policies and legislation that disproportionately impact marginalized LGBTQ individuals. By challenging discriminatory laws and practices, we can create a more equitable society for all.

Unconventional but Relevant Example: The Power of Art

Art has the ability to transcend barriers and amplify marginalized voices in unique and powerful ways. For instance, public art projects that highlight the experiences of marginalized LGBTQ individuals can spark conversations, challenge stigmas, and inspire empathy. Art can serve as a catalyst for change and offer a platform for voiceless communities to be heard.

Conclusion

Amplifying marginalized voices within the LGBTQ community is a critical component of the fight for equality. By recognizing and addressing the unique challenges faced by individuals who experience intersecting forms of oppression, we can create a more inclusive and just society. Through representation, education, building alliances, creating safe spaces, and challenging systemic inequalities, we can empower marginalized LGBTQ individuals to be heard and bring about meaningful change.

Overcoming Discrimination in the Workplace

Discrimination in the workplace is a pervasive issue that affects individuals from all walks of life. LGBTQ individuals have historically faced significant challenges in finding acceptance and equal treatment in their professional lives. In this subsection, we will explore the various forms of discrimination that exist, discuss the legal protections in place, and provide strategies for overcoming discrimination in the workplace.

Understanding Workplace Discrimination

Workplace discrimination against LGBTQ individuals can manifest in different ways, including:

- **Harassment:** Employees may experience verbal, physical, or sexual harassment based on their sexual orientation or gender identity. This can create a hostile work environment that impacts their well-being and productivity.

+ **Unequal Treatment:** LGBTQ individuals may face unfair treatment when it comes to promotions, opportunities for growth, access to benefits, or job assignments. This can lead to feelings of frustration, exclusion, and a lack of motivation at work.

+ **Job Segregation:** LGBTQ individuals may be excluded from certain positions or departments due to bias and stereotypes. This limits their career opportunities and hampers their professional development.

+ **Discriminatory Policies:** Some workplaces may have policies or practices that explicitly discriminate against LGBTQ individuals, such as dress codes or bathroom policies that do not respect gender identity.

Understanding these different forms of discrimination is essential in order to effectively combat them.

Legal Protections

Fortunately, legal protections exist to safeguard LGBTQ individuals from workplace discrimination. It is crucial to have a solid understanding of these protections to assert your rights and hold employers accountable.

In many countries, laws have been established to prevent workplace discrimination based on sexual orientation and gender identity. These laws may include protections against:

+ **Hiring Discrimination:** Employers cannot refuse to hire someone based on their sexual orientation or gender identity.

+ **Harassment:** Employers must take measures to prevent and address harassment in the workplace, ensuring a safe and welcoming environment for all employees.

+ **Equal Treatment:** LGBTQ individuals must be treated equally when it comes to promotions, benefits, pay, and other aspects of employment.

+ **Workplace Policies:** Employers are required to have inclusive policies that respect and accommodate the needs of LGBTQ employees.

It is important to research and familiarize yourself with the specific laws and protections in your jurisdiction to fully understand your rights.

Strategies for Overcoming Workplace Discrimination

Overcoming discrimination in the workplace requires a combination of individual empowerment and collective efforts. Here are some strategies to help address and overcome discrimination:

+ **Know Your Rights:** Educate yourself on your legal rights as an LGBTQ employee. Understanding the protections in place will empower you to assert your rights and advocate for fair treatment.

+ **Document Incidents:** Keep a record of any discriminatory incidents or conversations that you witness or experience. Documenting these incidents can provide evidence in case further action needs to be taken.

+ **Report Discrimination:** If you experience discrimination, report it to your employer's HR department or a designated representative. Follow your company's policies and procedures for reporting and resolving workplace issues.

+ **Seek Support:** Reach out to support networks, such as LGBTQ employee resource groups or external organizations, for guidance and assistance. These groups can provide valuable advice and resources to address workplace discrimination.

+ **Educate Others:** Engage in conversations with coworkers and managers to foster understanding and challenge stereotypes. By educating others about LGBTQ issues, you can contribute to creating a more inclusive work environment.

+ **Collaborate with Allies:** Build alliances with colleagues who are supportive and act as allies. Working together, you can advocate for change and push for a more inclusive workplace culture.

+ **Get Legal Advice:** If discrimination continues despite your efforts, consult with an employment lawyer specializing in LGBTQ rights. They can guide you through the legal options available and help you take appropriate action.

Remember, addressing workplace discrimination is an ongoing process that requires persistence and collective efforts. By advocating for change and supporting one another, we can create more inclusive and accepting workplaces for all.

Real-World Example

To illustrate the challenges faced by LGBTQ individuals in the workplace, let's consider the case of Alex, a transgender employee working in a conservative office environment. Despite being a highly skilled and dedicated worker, Alex faces discrimination in the form of misgendering, exclusion from team meetings, and being denied opportunities for professional growth. Alex decides to take action and follows the strategies outlined above.

First, Alex documents each incident, including dates, times, and descriptions of the discriminatory behavior. Alex also seeks support from an LGBTQ employee resource group within the company who can provide guidance and solidarity. Together, they draft a proposal for inclusive workplace policies, and with the support of allies, they present it to the HR department.

While progress may be slow, Alex's efforts to educate coworkers about trans identities and policies prove effective over time. The workplace becomes more accepting, and the company implements LGBTQ-inclusive policies, including gender-neutral restrooms and appropriate pronoun usage guidelines.

Through persistence, alliances, and education, Alex's workplace becomes an example of overcoming discrimination and fostering inclusivity. Alex's experiences inspire other LGBTQ individuals in the company to speak up and advocate for their rights, ultimately creating a more equitable environment for all employees.

Conclusion

Overcoming discrimination in the workplace is an essential step towards building a more inclusive and equitable society. By understanding the different forms of discrimination, familiarizing ourselves with legal protections, and implementing strategies to address and overcome discrimination, we can create workplaces where LGBTQ individuals can thrive and contribute fully to their organizations. It is crucial to embrace diversity, challenge biases, and work together to foster welcoming environments that value and respect the rights of all employees. The fight against workplace discrimination is ongoing, but by taking collective action, we can create lasting change and build a better future.

Solidarity and Collaboration

Solidarity and collaboration are crucial aspects of the LGBTQ activism movement. In this subsection, we will explore the importance of unity among different communities, the value of allyship, and the power of collective action in advancing the fight for equality.

The Power of Solidarity

Solidarity is the cornerstone of any successful social justice movement, including LGBTQ activism. It involves the recognition that different marginalized communities share common struggles and can support one another in their pursuit of equality and justice. Solidarity builds bridges between communities, fosters empathy, and amplifies voices that may otherwise go unheard.

In the context of LGBTQ activism, solidarity means recognizing the interconnectedness of various identities and working together to challenge oppression. For example, LGBTQ activists often collaborate with other social justice movements, such as the racial justice movement, feminist movement, and disability rights movement. By joining forces, these groups create a powerful collective voice that can advocate for intersectional change.

Solidarity also involves recognizing and addressing internal biases within the LGBTQ community. For instance, LGBTQ individuals with multiple marginalized identities, such as queer people of color or transgender individuals, may face compounded discrimination. Solidarity requires understanding and centering their experiences within the movement, promoting inclusivity and equity for all.

Allyship: Becoming an Effective LGBTQ Ally

Allyship is the practice of advocating for and supporting marginalized communities. In the context of LGBTQ activism, an ally is someone who is not themselves LGBTQ but supports and defends the rights and well-being of LGBTQ individuals.

Being an effective ally requires ongoing education, self-reflection, and active engagement. Here are some key principles and steps to consider:

1. **Listen and Learn:** Take the time to educate yourself about LGBTQ issues, identities, and experiences. Read books, attend workshops, and engage in conversations with LGBTQ individuals to deepen your understanding.

2. **Amplify LGBTQ Voices:** Use your privilege and platform to uplift LGBTQ voices by sharing their stories, promoting their work, and advocating for their rights. Center their experiences in conversations and amplify their calls for change.

3. **Use Inclusive Language:** Be conscious of the language you use and avoid derogatory or offensive terms. Use gender-inclusive pronouns and respect an individual's chosen name and identity.

4. **Challenge Homophobia and Transphobia:** Speak up when you witness discriminatory behavior or hear derogatory comments. Educate others about the harmful impact of homophobia and transphobia.

5. **Support LGBTQ Organizations:** Donate to LGBTQ organizations, volunteer your time, or offer your skills to support their work. Financial and volunteer support are essential in furthering the LGBTQ movement.

6. **Vote for LGBTQ Rights:** Support political candidates who champion LGBTQ rights and policies. Use your voting power to advocate for inclusive legislation and equal rights.

7. **Create Inclusive Spaces:** Work towards creating welcoming and inclusive spaces within your community, workplace, or educational institution. Challenge policies and practices that perpetuate discrimination and ensure LGBTQ individuals feel safe and supported.

Collaboration for Lasting Change

Collaboration is a powerful tool in LGBTQ activism, as it brings together individuals, organizations, and communities to create lasting change. Through collaborative efforts, activists can pool resources, share knowledge, and amplify their impact.

Collaboration within the LGBTQ movement involves forming alliances with other social justice groups, community organizations, and political entities. By working together, activists can address the intersecting nature of discrimination and advocate for comprehensive solutions.

Additionally, collaboration can bridge divides between LGBTQ activists from different backgrounds and identities. It fosters understanding, empathy, and cultural exchange, allowing individuals to learn from one another's experiences and perspectives.

To foster effective collaboration, clear communication, mutual respect, and shared goals are essential. Collaborative efforts should also prioritize the voices and leadership of marginalized individuals within the LGBTQ community, ensuring their perspectives are centered in decision-making processes.

Example: Intersectionality and Collaboration

An example of collaboration and intersectionality in LGBTQ activism is the partnership between LGBTQ and racial justice movements. Members of both communities face intersecting forms of discrimination and oppression, as racial minorities within the LGBTQ community often experience compounded marginalization.

By collaborating, these movements can tackle issues such as police violence, systemic racism, and discriminatory policies that disproportionately impact LGBTQ individuals of color. Joint demonstrations, shared resources, and collaborative advocacy efforts can create a more powerful and inclusive movement.

For instance, the Black Lives Matter movement has highlighted the experiences of LGBTQ individuals of color and called for justice for victims of police violence who were both Black and LGBTQ. This collaboration has shed light on the unique challenges faced by LGBTQ individuals at the intersection of race and sexuality, fostering greater understanding and generating momentum for change.

Resources and Support

To further explore the concepts of solidarity, allyship, and collaboration in LGBTQ activism, here are some recommended resources:

1. **Books:**

   - "This Bridge Called My Back: Writings by Radical Women of Color" edited by Cherríe Moraga and Gloria E. Anzaldúa
   - "Sister Outsider: Essays and Speeches" by Audre Lorde
   - "Queer Brown Voices: Personal Narratives of Latina/o LGBT Activism" edited by Uriel Quesada, Letitia Gomez, and Salvador Vidal-Ortiz

2. **Websites and Organizations:**

   - Human Rights Campaign: https://www.hrc.org/
   - GLAAD: https://www.glaad.org/
   - National LGBTQ Task Force: https://www.thetaskforce.org/
   - Showing Up for Racial Justice (SURJ): https://www.showingupforracialjustice.org/

Remember, solidarity and collaboration are not just buzzwords; they are essential strategies for creating meaningful social change. By standing together and working across differences, we can build a more inclusive and equitable world for all LGBTQ individuals.

Advocacy for LGBTQ Refugees and Migrants

Advocating for the rights of LGBTQ refugees and migrants is a crucial aspect of the broader LGBTQ activist movement. In this subsection, we will explore the unique challenges faced by LGBTQ individuals who are forced to leave their homes due to persecution and discrimination, and the work being done to support and empower them.

Understanding the Challenges

LGBTQ individuals who are forced to flee their home countries often face immense challenges and risks. They may be subjected to homophobic or transphobic violence, discrimination, and even death threats in their home communities. When they seek refuge in other countries, they are confronted with a range of additional obstacles, such as language barriers, cultural differences, and legal complexities.

Refugee camps and reception centers, designed to provide support and protection, often fail to adequately address the specific needs of LGBTQ individuals. These spaces can be hostile and unsafe, with LGBTQ refugees facing harassment, abuse, and exploitation from fellow refugees, security personnel, and even aid workers. They live in constant fear of being outed and subjected to violence.

Advocacy Efforts

To address these challenges, dedicated organizations, activists, and advocates are working tirelessly to ensure the rights and safety of LGBTQ refugees and migrants. Their efforts span various areas, including legal advocacy, empowerment programs, and the provision of psychosocial support.

One crucial aspect of advocacy for LGBTQ refugees and migrants is legal assistance. Many LGBTQ individuals face difficulties in navigating the complex asylum and immigration systems of host countries. They may lack information about their rights or encounter prejudice during the application process. Advocates work closely with LGBTQ refugees and migrants, providing them with legal support, representation, and guidance to ensure a fair and just asylum application process.

Empowerment programs play a significant role in supporting LGBTQ refugees and migrants. These programs aim to build resilience, enhance self-advocacy skills, and foster community networks. LGBTQ individuals are encouraged to participate in leadership training, workshops on human rights, and capacity-building activities.

By empowering LGBTQ refugees and migrants, organizations enable them to assert their rights, challenge discrimination, and contribute to long-term social change.

Psychosocial support is a vital component of advocacy for LGBTQ refugees and migrants. LGBTQ individuals who have experienced trauma, violence, or persecution require specialized support to heal and rebuild their lives. Organizations provide counseling services, support groups, and safe spaces where LGBTQ refugees and migrants can express themselves, share their experiences, and receive emotional support. These services help LGBTQ individuals to recover and thrive in their new communities.

Promoting Awareness and Education

Advocacy for LGBTQ refugees and migrants also involves promoting awareness and education among host communities and stakeholders. It is crucial to challenge stereotypes, combat prejudice, and foster understanding of the specific challenges faced by LGBTQ individuals who are forced to flee their home countries.

Advocacy organizations engage in public awareness campaigns, conduct training sessions, and develop educational resources to raise awareness about the experiences of LGBTQ refugees and migrants. These initiatives aim to dispel misconceptions, promote empathy and understanding, and mobilize support for LGBTQ individuals seeking safety and protection.

Collaboration and Solidarity

Advocacy for LGBTQ refugees and migrants requires collaboration and solidarity among various stakeholders, including LGBTQ organizations, human rights organizations, government agencies, and international bodies. By working together, these entities can pool their resources, expertise, and networks to create a more inclusive and supportive environment for LGBTQ refugees and migrants.

Collaboration can take the form of joint advocacy campaigns, policy dialogue, and information sharing. By amplifying the voices of LGBTQ refugees and migrants, advocating for their rights, and pushing for policy reforms, stakeholders can create lasting systemic change.

Real-World Example: Rainbow Railroad

One organization at the forefront of advocacy for LGBTQ refugees and migrants is Rainbow Railroad. Founded in 2006, Rainbow Railroad works to save lives by facilitating the relocation of LGBTQ individuals who face imminent danger in their home countries.

Rainbow Railroad provides direct assistance to LGBTQ individuals at risk, helping them navigate complex legal processes and secure safe passage to countries that can offer them protection. The organization collaborates with local partners, human rights organizations, and government agencies to facilitate the safe and successful relocation of LGBTQ refugees and migrants.

Through their advocacy efforts, Rainbow Railroad aims to raise awareness about the specific challenges faced by LGBTQ individuals seeking refuge and mobilize support for their cause. The organization engages in public education, policy advocacy, and community mobilization to build a more inclusive and accepting world for LGBTQ refugees and migrants.

Unconventional Approach: LGBTQ Refugee Sponsorship

One unconventional approach to advocacy for LGBTQ refugees and migrants is the establishment of LGBTQ refugee sponsorship programs. Inspired by successful private refugee sponsorship initiatives, these programs enable individuals, communities, and organizations to directly support LGBTQ refugees and migrants.

By sponsoring LGBTQ refugees and migrants, sponsors commit to providing financial, emotional, and social support to help them resettle and integrate into their new communities. This approach not only addresses the immediate needs of LGBTQ refugees but also fosters connections and bridges the gap between host communities and newcomers.

Sponsorship programs can create a sense of belonging and security for LGBTQ refugees and migrants, empowering them to rebuild their lives and contribute to their new societies. This grassroots approach to advocacy allows individuals to take active roles in supporting LGBTQ rights and refugee protection.

Conclusion

Advocacy for LGBTQ refugees and migrants is a critical component of the broader LGBTQ activist movement. By addressing the unique challenges faced by LGBTQ individuals who are forced to leave their homes, advocates and organizations work to create a more inclusive and accepting world. Through legal assistance, empowerment programs, psychosocial support, awareness campaigns, and collaborative efforts, stakeholders are making significant strides in ensuring the rights and safety of LGBTQ refugees and migrants. By amplifying their voices and stories, advocating for policy reforms, and fostering solidarity, we can build a future where LGBTQ individuals can seek refuge without fear of discrimination or violence. The work of organizations like Rainbow Railroad and the innovative approach of LGBTQ refugee sponsorship programs demonstrate the potential for transformative change in the lives of LGBTQ refugees and migrants. The fight for equality continues, and with dedicated advocacy, we can create a world where all LGBTQ individuals can live with dignity and freedom.

Fighting for Marriage Equality

In this section, we will explore the fight for marriage equality within the LGBTQ community. The battle for same-sex marriage rights has been a long and hard-fought struggle, but its importance cannot be overstated. Marriage equality represents an essential step towards achieving full civil rights and equal recognition for all individuals, regardless of their sexual orientation or gender identity.

The Historical Context

To understand the significance of the fight for marriage equality, we must first recognize the historical context surrounding this issue. For centuries, same-sex relationships and LGBTQ individuals have faced discrimination, marginalization, and the denial of fundamental rights. Marriage, a legal and social institution deeply rooted in cultural and religious norms, has been inaccessible to many LGBTQ couples.

In recent history, the LGBTQ community has made significant strides towards achieving equality. The Stonewall Riots of 1969 marked a turning point in the LGBTQ rights movement, galvanizing activists and sparking a wave of advocacy for equal rights. Since then, LGBTQ individuals and organizations have fought tirelessly to challenge discriminatory laws and policies and gain social acceptance.

Legal Challenges and Milestones

The fight for marriage equality has involved legal challenges, activism, and mobilization at local, national, and international levels. In many countries, it started with advocacy for legal recognition of same-sex relationships and evolved into a broader movement for equal marriage rights.

One of the key milestones in the fight for marriage equality was the legalization of same-sex marriage in the Netherlands in 2001. This groundbreaking decision set a precedent and inspired activism across the globe. Subsequently, countries like Belgium, Canada, and Spain followed suit and granted same-sex couples the right to marry.

In the United States, the struggle for marriage equality gained significant momentum in the early 2000s. Various state-level battles ensued, leading to a landmark moment in 2015 when the Supreme Court ruled in Obergefell v. Hodges that same-sex couples have the constitutional right to marry in all 50 states. This ruling marked a significant victory for the LGBTQ community and marked a turning point in the fight for equality.

Challenges and Opposition

The fight for marriage equality has faced staunch opposition from conservative groups and individuals who view marriage as solely a heterosexual institution. Religious, moral, and cultural arguments have been used to justify the denial of marriage rights to same-sex couples.

Opponents of marriage equality often cite traditional interpretations of religious texts, fearing that recognizing same-sex marriages would undermine the institution of marriage itself. They argue that marriage should remain exclusively between a man and a woman, based on their religious beliefs.

Strategies for Advocacy

Advocacy for marriage equality has required a multifaceted approach, combining legal challenges, grassroots activism, public education, and strategic alliances. Activist organizations have played a crucial role in raising awareness, mobilizing support, and pushing for policy changes.

One effective strategy has been using personal stories and narratives to humanize the issue and emphasize the importance of marriage equality for LGBTQ individuals and their families. Sharing stories of love, commitment, and the challenges faced by same-sex couples has helped dispel stereotypes and build empathy.

Engaging with religious communities has also been a significant aspect of the fight for marriage equality. Many faith-based organizations and religious leaders have embraced marriage equality, challenging the notion that LGBTQ rights and equal treatment contradict religious values.

Collaboration with other social justice movements and organizations has been instrumental in broadening the support base for marriage equality. By highlighting the intersections between LGBTQ rights, racial justice, gender equality, and other causes, activists have been able to create powerful coalitions and foster solidarity.

The Global Impact

While significant progress has been made in many countries, the fight for marriage equality is far from over. In many parts of the world, LGBTQ individuals still face discrimination, persecution, and legal barriers to marriage.

Advocates for marriage equality must continue to push for global change, supporting LGBTQ communities in countries where same-sex relationships are criminalized or unrecognized. International pressure and collaboration with human rights organizations are essential in challenging discriminatory laws and promoting equality across borders.

Unconventional Perspective: Leveraging Economic Impact

In addition to the traditional approaches to advocacy, an unconventional perspective on marriage equality is to highlight its economic impact. Studies have shown that legalizing same-sex marriage can have positive economic effects, including increased tourism, business revenue, and job opportunities, as couples and their families celebrate their unions.

By highlighting the economic benefits of marriage equality, advocates can engage with stakeholders who may be motivated by financial considerations. This approach can help build broad-based support and encourage policymakers to view marriage equality as a win-win situation for both civil rights and economic prosperity.

Conclusion

The fight for marriage equality has been a landmark achievement for the LGBTQ community. It represents a step towards societal acceptance, equal rights, and the recognition of love and commitment in all its diverse forms. While progress has been made in many regions, the struggle continues globally.

The fight for marriage equality is a testament to the power of activism, advocacy, and the courage of individuals and communities to challenge discriminatory laws and social norms. By amplifying the voices of those affected by inequality and leveraging strategic alliances, we can continue to make strides towards a more inclusive and equal world for all.

Tackling LGBTQ Conversion Therapy

Conversion therapy, also known as "reparative therapy" or "sexual orientation change efforts," refers to practices that attempt to change an individual's sexual orientation or gender identity. This harmful and pseudoscientific practice has been widely discredited by medical and psychological associations worldwide. In this subsection, we will explore the damaging effects of conversion therapy, ongoing efforts to ban its practice, and strategies for supporting LGBTQ individuals who have been subjected to this harmful treatment.

Understanding Conversion Therapy

Conversion therapy relies on the false assumption that being LGBTQ is a mental disorder or a sinful condition that can be changed through therapy or religious intervention. Techniques employed in conversion therapy include talk therapy, aversion therapy, exorcisms, and other coercive methods. These practices can lead to severe psychological distress, depression, anxiety, self-harm, and suicide ideation among those subjected to them.

The principle of consent is paramount when discussing conversion therapy. The rights of individuals to decide their own sexual orientation and gender identity must be respected, and no one should be forced or coerced into attempting to change an inherent aspect of their being.

Legal and Ethical Challenges

Many countries and jurisdictions have recognized the dangers of conversion therapy and taken steps to address it legally. Laws banning conversion therapy have been enacted in various places, including Malta, Germany, Brazil, Ecuador, and parts of Australia, Canada, and the United States. These laws safeguard LGBTQ individuals from being subjected to this harmful practice and send a clear message that attempting to change someone's sexual orientation or gender identity is both unethical and ineffective.

However, legal challenges to conversion therapy bans still exist, often due to claims of religious freedom or free speech. It is crucial to navigate these challenges and establish comprehensive legislation that protects LGBTQ individuals from the harms of conversion therapy while respecting individual rights. Education and awareness campaigns can help dispel myths and misconceptions surrounding LGBTQ identities, creating a more inclusive and accepting society.

Supporting Survivors of Conversion Therapy

Supporting survivors of conversion therapy is an essential aspect of combating this harmful practice. LGBTQ individuals who have undergone conversion therapy may face immense trauma, shame, loss of self-esteem, and fractured relationships with family and community. It is vital to provide these individuals with a safe and supportive environment where they can heal and rebuild their lives.

Therapeutic interventions, such as trauma-focused therapy and counseling, can help survivors process their experiences, cope with any lingering emotional wounds, and reclaim their sense of self-worth. Support groups specifically designed for survivors of conversion therapy can also provide a sense of community, validation, and shared understanding.

Additionally, creating networks of support through LGBTQ organizations and alliances can help connect survivors with resources, legal assistance, and advocacy efforts. Providing mental health services, legal aid, and educational opportunities for survivors and their families can help prevent the perpetuation of harmful practices and promote healing within LGBTQ communities.

Educational Initiatives and Public Awareness

Education and public awareness play a vital role in dismantling the harmful beliefs and attitudes that underpin conversion therapy. It is crucial to promote accurate information about LGBTQ identities, dispel stereotypes, and challenge the stigmatization of non-heteronormative sexual orientations and gender identities.

Educational initiatives can target various groups, including healthcare professionals, mental health practitioners, religious leaders, and the general public. By equipping professionals with knowledge about LGBTQ identities, experiences, and affirming practices, we can ensure that they provide appropriate support and care to LGBTQ individuals.

Promoting LGBTQ-inclusive curricula in schools, colleges, and universities is another effective way to challenge harmful beliefs and foster acceptance among young people. By teaching students about diversity, respect, and equality, we can shape attitudes that reject conversion therapy and empower LGBTQ youth.

Challenges and Unconventional Approaches

One of the challenges faced in tackling LGBTQ conversion therapy is the prevalence of underground or unregulated practices. Some individuals may seek conversion therapy covertly or through religious institutions that continue to promote these harmful practices. Efforts are needed to identify and address such hidden practices through community engagement, partnerships with faith-based organizations, and legal enforcement.

An unconventional approach to tackling conversion therapy involves exploring the root causes behind LGBTQ individuals' susceptibility to these treatments.

Societal pressures, familial expectations, and internalized homo/transphobia often contribute to someone seeking or being forced into conversion therapy. Addressing these underlying issues through awareness campaigns, support networks, and empowerment programs can help prevent vulnerable individuals from falling victim to these harmful practices.

In conclusion, tackling LGBTQ conversion therapy requires a comprehensive approach involving legal measures, support for survivors, education, and public awareness. By promoting inclusive and affirming environments, challenging harmful beliefs, and supporting the mental health and well-being of LGBTQ individuals, we can work towards a world that embraces diversity and rejects the harmful practices of conversion therapy. The fight against conversion therapy is part of the wider struggle for LGBTQ rights and equality, and it requires the collective efforts of lawmakers, healthcare professionals, educators, and communities. Together, we can ensure a future free from the harms of conversion therapy and create a society that celebrates and supports the LGBTQ community.

Promoting Inclusive Education Policies

Promoting inclusive education policies is a crucial step towards creating a more accepting and supportive environment for LGBTQ individuals within educational institutions. By implementing policies that prioritize inclusivity, schools can ensure that all students, regardless of their sexual orientation or gender identity, have equal access to education and a safe learning environment. In this subsection, we will explore the importance of inclusive education policies, discuss potential challenges, and provide strategies for promoting and implementing these policies in educational settings.

Understanding the Importance of Inclusive Education

Inclusive education policies aim to create a learning environment that respects and values the diversity of all students, including LGBTQ individuals. These policies recognize that a safe and inclusive school environment is essential for students' academic success, mental well-being, and overall development.

Research has shown that LGBTQ students face higher levels of discrimination, bullying, and exclusion compared to their heterosexual and cisgender peers. This discrimination can result in lower academic achievement, higher dropout rates, and negative mental health outcomes. Inclusive education policies work to eliminate these barriers and create an environment that fosters acceptance, respect, and understanding.

By promoting inclusive education policies, schools can also support LGBTQ students' social and emotional well-being. These policies help to create a culture of acceptance and provide resources and support systems to address the unique challenges faced by LGBTQ students. Additionally, inclusive education can positively impact all students, promoting empathy, tolerance, and respect for diversity.

Challenges in Promoting Inclusive Education Policies

While promoting inclusive education policies is crucial, it is essential to acknowledge and address the challenges that may arise. These challenges can include:

1. **Resistance and Opposition:** Introducing inclusive education policies may face opposition from individuals who hold conservative beliefs or lack understanding about LGBTQ issues. It is important to create spaces for open dialogue and education to address these concerns effectively.

2. **Lack of Awareness and Training:** Educators and staff may require training and professional development to understand the needs of LGBTQ students and how to create an inclusive learning environment. Schools should invest in training programs to equip their staff with the knowledge and skills necessary to support LGBTQ students effectively.

3. **Legal and Policy Barriers:** Depending on the region, there may be legal or policy barriers that hinder the implementation of inclusive education policies. Schools must navigate these obstacles and advocate for changes to ensure LGBTQ-inclusive policies are prioritized.

4. **Limited Resources:** Implementation of inclusive education policies may require additional resources, both financial and organizational. Schools must secure adequate resources to support the implementation and sustainability of these policies.

Strategies for Promoting Inclusive Education Policies

To overcome the challenges and promote inclusive education policies effectively, schools and educational institutions can adopt the following strategies:

1. **Develop Comprehensive LGBTQ-Inclusive Policies:** Schools should establish comprehensive policies that explicitly prohibit discrimination based on sexual orientation and gender identity. These policies should

outline clear expectations for creating an inclusive and supportive learning environment and address issues like bullying, gender-segregated activities, and dress codes.

2. **Provide LGBTQ-Inclusive Training and Professional Development:** Educators and staff should receive regular training and professional development opportunities to enhance their understanding of LGBTQ issues, create inclusive classrooms, and provide appropriate support to LGBTQ students. Training programs can be developed in collaboration with LGBTQ organizations, experts, and community members.

3. **Foster LGBTQ-Inclusive Curriculum:** Schools should ensure that the curriculum is inclusive and diverse, incorporating LGBTQ history, contributions, and perspectives across various subjects. This inclusive curriculum helps to promote understanding, challenge stereotypes, and create a more accurate representation of LGBTQ individuals and their experiences.

4. **Establish Safe Spaces and Support Groups:** Creating safe spaces, such as LGBTQ resource centers or alliances, provides students with a supportive environment where they can express themselves, seek guidance, and find solidarity with their peers. Schools should aim to establish and maintain these spaces, along with support groups led by trained professionals or LGBTQ community organizations.

5. **Collaborate with LGBTQ Organizations and Community Partners:** Schools should collaborate with local LGBTQ organizations and community partners to access resources, guidance, and expertise in promoting inclusion. These partnerships can help schools develop effective strategies, provide support to students and families, and create a network for ongoing advocacy.

Case Study: Implementing Inclusive Education Policies

To illustrate the implementation of inclusive education policies, let's consider the case of Maplewood High School. Maplewood High School, located in a diverse urban community, recognized the need for LGBTQ-inclusive policies and took proactive measures to promote inclusivity within its walls.

First, the school formed a committee consisting of teachers, administrators, parents, and community members dedicated to promoting LGBTQ inclusion. The committee conducted research, attended training sessions, and consulted with LGBTQ organizations to develop a comprehensive LGBTQ-inclusive policy.

The policy addressed issues such as anti-bullying measures, access to gender-neutral bathrooms, and the inclusion of LGBTQ history and perspectives in the curriculum. It also established a safe space, known as the Pride Lounge, where LGBTQ students and allies could gather, seek support, and organize awareness campaigns.

Additionally, Maplewood High School implemented annual training sessions for staff members to enhance their understanding of LGBTQ issues and equip them with strategies to create inclusive classrooms. The school also collaborated with local LGBTQ organizations to provide mentoring programs and resources for LGBTQ students.

Over time, Maplewood High School's inclusive education policies helped create a supportive and accepting environment for LGBTQ students. Graduation rates improved, instances of bullying decreased, and overall student well-being increased. Students felt empowered to be their authentic selves and engage fully in their educational experience.

Conclusion

Promoting inclusive education policies is essential for creating an environment that values diversity, respects the rights of LGBTQ students, and provides equal opportunities for all. By understanding the importance of inclusivity, addressing challenges, and implementing effective strategies, educational institutions can foster inclusive learning environments that empower and support LGBTQ individuals.

Through comprehensive policies, ongoing training, inclusive curriculum, and collaboration with LGBTQ organizations, schools can ensure that LGBTQ students feel safe, respected, and empowered to succeed. By promoting inclusive education policies, we can create a future where educational institutions serve as catalysts for positive social change and equality for all students, regardless of their sexual orientation or gender identity.

Remember, promoting inclusive education is an ongoing process that requires continuous commitment, advocacy, and engagement with the LGBTQ community. Let us work together to create a world where every student can thrive and reach their full potential, free from discrimination and prejudice.

Protecting Transgender Rights

Transgender rights are an essential aspect of LGBTQ activism and advocacy. Transgender individuals face unique challenges and discrimination, both within and outside of the LGBTQ community. In this subsection, we will explore the importance of protecting transgender rights and discuss various strategies and initiatives that aim to address these challenges.

Understanding Transgender Rights

To effectively protect transgender rights, it is crucial to have a comprehensive understanding of the issues at hand. Transgender individuals experience discrimination, violence, and marginalization in various aspects of life, including healthcare, education, employment, housing, and public accommodations.

Discrimination against transgender individuals is often rooted in societal misunderstandings and prejudices. It is important to challenge these misconceptions and promote education and awareness surrounding transgender identities and experiences.

Transgender rights are protected by laws and policies in many countries, but implementation and enforcement may vary. Advocacy efforts focus on ensuring that these laws are upheld and strengthened. Additionally, transgender activists strive to address and eliminate barriers to equal rights and opportunities for transgender individuals.

Legal Protections and Policy Advocacy

One crucial aspect of protecting transgender rights is advocating for legal protections and policies that specifically address transgender issues. This includes working towards comprehensive anti-discrimination laws, ensuring legal recognition of gender identity, and protecting transgender individuals from hate crimes and violence.

Advocacy efforts often involve collaboration with lawmakers, policymakers, and legal experts. Transgender activists work to raise awareness of the need for legislative reforms, provide input in the development of supportive policies, and lobby for their implementation. This includes actively engaging in conversations on transgender healthcare access, employment non-discrimination, and inclusive education policies.

Example: In the United States, activists have been at the forefront of pushing for the passage of the Equality Act, which seeks to prohibit discrimination on the basis of sexual orientation and gender identity in a wide range of areas, including employment, housing, and public accommodations. Transgender rights organizations play a significant role in advocating for this critical legislation, which would provide much-needed protections for transgender individuals across the country.

Promoting Transgender Healthcare Access

Transgender individuals often face significant barriers in accessing gender-affirming healthcare. This includes challenges related to insurance coverage, healthcare provider knowledge and bias, and limited availability of specialized transgender healthcare services.

To protect transgender rights, it is essential to advocate for comprehensive and accessible healthcare for transgender individuals. This includes working towards insurance coverage for hormone replacement therapy, gender-affirming surgeries, and mental health support services. Transgender activists also collaborate with healthcare providers to enhance their understanding of transgender healthcare needs and develop inclusive practices.

Example: The Transgender Legal Defense and Education Fund (TLDEF) launched the Trans Health Project, which aims to address the legal barriers faced by transgender individuals when seeking healthcare. Through this initiative, TLDEF provides legal resources, support, and education to healthcare providers, policymakers, and transgender individuals, ultimately working towards increased access and quality of care.

Tackling Transgender Discrimination in the Workplace

Transgender individuals often face high levels of discrimination in the workplace, ranging from unfair hiring practices to unequal treatment and harassment. Protecting transgender rights in the workplace involves advocating for inclusive policies, promoting workplace diversity and inclusion, and challenging discriminatory practices.

Transgender activists collaborate with employers, human resources professionals, and labor movements to develop guidelines and policies that protect transgender employees. They also provide resources and training to raise awareness about transgender issues in the workplace and promote strategies for creating inclusive work environments.

Example: The Human Rights Campaign (HRC) launched the Corporate Equality Index (CEI), which assesses businesses on their commitment to LGBT inclusion. The CEI evaluates policies and practices related to non-discrimination protections, transgender-inclusive healthcare benefits, and workplace culture. By recognizing inclusive employers and encouraging better practices, organizations like HRC contribute to protecting transgender rights at the workplace.

Educational Initiatives and Support

Education plays a crucial role in protecting transgender rights. It is imperative to promote LGBTQ-inclusive curricula, foster safe and supportive environments for transgender students, and increase awareness and understanding among educators and students.

Transgender activists work closely with educational institutions to develop resources and training programs that address the unique needs of transgender students. They advocate for policies that protect against discrimination, including gender-affirming dress codes and restroom access. Moreover, they foster inclusive spaces for transgender students to connect, seek support, and empower one another.

Example: The Trevor Project's "Safe and Supportive Schools" initiative focuses on creating inclusive educational environments for LGBTQ youth, including transgender students. This initiative provides training and resources to educators, develops research-based policies, and advocates for the implementation of comprehensive anti-bullying and harassment measures.

Emphasizing Intersectionality

Intersectionality is vital in the fight for transgender rights. Transgender individuals may face compounded discrimination based on race, ethnicity, disability, socioeconomic status, or immigration status. It is essential to address these intersecting forms of discrimination and ensure that transgender rights advocacy incorporates an intersectional lens.

By acknowledging and addressing intersectionality, transgender activists work towards dismantling systems of oppression that marginalize and disadvantage transgender individuals of different backgrounds. They collaborate with other social justice movements to advocate for policies that protect the rights of all individuals, irrespective of their intersecting identities.

Example: The Transgender Gender-Variant and Intersex Justice Project (TGI Justice Project) is a grassroots organization that advocates for the rights of transgender and gender-variant individuals who are incarcerated. This organization works at the intersection of transgender rights and criminal justice reform to address the unique challenges faced by transgender individuals within the prison system.

In conclusion, protecting transgender rights is an integral part of broader LGBTQ activism. To ensure the advancement of transgender rights, it is crucial to advocate for legal protections, promote healthcare access, tackle workplace discrimination, support inclusive education, and emphasize intersectionality. Through these efforts, activists strive to create a world where transgender individuals can live authentically and thrive without fear of discrimination or marginalization. The fight for transgender rights continues, and it is up to all of us to contribute to a more inclusive and equitable society.

Conclusion:

In this section, we explored the importance of protecting transgender rights as an essential aspect of LGBTQ activism. We discussed the challenges faced by transgender individuals and the various strategies and initiatives to address these challenges. From legal protections and policy advocacy to healthcare access, workplace inclusivity, educational initiatives, and intersectionality, the fight for transgender rights requires comprehensive efforts. By actively working towards inclusivity and understanding, we can contribute to a more equitable and accepting world for all individuals, regardless of their gender identity. Remember, the fight for transgender rights is not just the responsibility of transgender individuals; it is a collective effort that requires our continuous support and advocacy. Together, we can protect transgender rights and create a more just and inclusive society for everyone.

Redefining Faith and Identity

Evolving Religious Narratives

In the realm of LGBTQ activism, one of the most significant challenges faced by queer individuals is reconciling their sexual orientation or gender identity with their religious beliefs. For many, religion plays a central role in their lives, providing a foundation for their values, spirituality, and sense of community. However, traditional religious teachings often condemn or marginalize queer identities, leading to a profound sense of conflict and alienation.

To address this tension, it is crucial to explore and evolve religious narratives, transforming them into more inclusive and accepting frameworks. This evolution requires a reexamination of sacred texts, interpretations, and the fundamental principles of religious belief systems. By embracing this process of reinterpretation, religious communities can create spaces where LGBTQ individuals are not only accepted but fully embraced.

This subsection delves into the challenging task of evolving religious narratives, offering insights into how religious communities can reassess longstanding beliefs and adapt to the changing needs and perspectives of their LGBTQ members.

Recognizing Historical and Cultural Contexts: To embark on the journey of evolving religious narratives, it is crucial to understand the historical and cultural contexts in which religious texts were written. Biblical verses and other sacred writings were composed within specific cultural frameworks that may not readily align with modern understandings of gender and sexuality. Recognizing the societal factors that influenced the text's creation allows for a deeper understanding of its intended message and opens the door to reinterpretation.

Engaging in Interpretation and Contextualization: Interpretation is a fundamental aspect of religious practice, and engaging in respectful and thoughtful interpretation can pave the way for evolving religious narratives. Considering the historical context, linguistic nuances, and cultural influences surrounding religious texts allows for a more holistic understanding of their message. Rigid literal interpretations can be reexamined to accommodate the diverse realities of LGBTQ individuals.

Moreover, contextualization provides an opportunity to analyze how specific verses or teachings relate to contemporary issues. By examining religious principles through a multidimensional lens, religious communities can identify oppressive or exclusionary aspects and seek alternative interpretations that are more inclusive of queer identities.

Valuing Diversity and Intersectionality: Evolving religious narratives must acknowledge the intersectional nature of human identity. Recognizing that individuals belong to multiple marginalized groups, such as being LGBTQ and a person of color, highlights the interconnectedness of different forms of oppression. Religious communities can strive to create spaces that not only accept LGBTQ individuals but also actively address the unique challenges they face in light of their intersecting identities.

By valuing diversity, religious leaders and communities can challenge heteronormative assumptions, center the experiences of marginalized individuals, and foster a more inclusive and equitable spiritual environment.

Seeking LGBTQ Inclusivity in Religious Institutions: Evolving religious narratives requires tangible changes within religious institutions themselves. Progressive leaders within religious communities can advocate for LGBTQ inclusivity by promoting policies that affirm the intrinsic worth and dignity of all individuals, regardless of their sexual orientation or gender identity.

Inclusive practices may include revising liturgical texts, updating language to be gender-neutral, and integrating LGBTQ-affirming messages into sermons and teachings. Moreover, religious organizations can actively work to create safe spaces for LGBTQ individuals within their communities, providing support networks, counseling services, and educational resources.

Embracing Open Dialogue and Collaboration: To truly evolve religious narratives, open dialogue and collaboration between religious scholars, LGBTQ activists, and community members are essential. By fostering spaces for respectful dialogue and active engagement, different perspectives can be heard and understood. This process allows for the challenging of preconceived notions and encourages religious leaders to examine their own biases and prejudices.

Collaboration can involve hosting panel discussions, interfaith dialogues, and workshops that explore the intersections of faith and queerness. In these spaces, individuals from diverse backgrounds can share their stories, challenge existing beliefs, and collectively work towards a more inclusive understanding of religious narratives.

Challenging the Status Quo: Evolving religious narratives often requires challenging the status quo and fostering a culture of critical thinking within religious communities. Leaders, scholars, and individuals must be willing to question long-held beliefs and engage in self-reflection. This process can involve examining the historical power dynamics within religious institutions and addressing how these dynamics have contributed to the marginalization of LGBTQ individuals.

By challenging the status quo, religious communities can actively move towards a more inclusive and accepting environment that embraces the inherent diversity of human experiences.

Resource:

+ *Queer Virtue: What LGBTQ People Know About Life and Love and How It Can Revitalize Christianity* by Elizabeth M. Edman. This book explores the potential for transforming religious narratives and embracing LGBTQ identities within the Christian tradition, offering insights and frameworks for nurturing inclusivity.

Conclusion

Evolving religious narratives is a complex and multifaceted process that requires deep introspection, critical thinking, and an openness to change. By recognizing historical contexts, engaging in reinterpretation and contextualization, valuing diversity and intersectionality, creating inclusive religious spaces, fostering open dialogue and collaboration, challenging the status quo, religious communities can transform their beliefs to be more affirming of LGBTQ individuals.

This evolution not only benefits queer individuals within religious traditions but also contributes to the larger movement of LGBTQ activism by promoting social acceptance, inclusivity, and equality. As the religious narrative evolves, it paves the way for a more harmonious coexistence of faith and queerness and inspires other religious communities to embark on a similar journey towards inclusivity and love.

Challenging Anti-LGBTQ Stances within Religion

In today's world, the intersection of religion and LGBTQ rights is a complex and often contentious issue. Many religious traditions hold conservative beliefs regarding sexuality and gender, which can create hostile environments for LGBTQ individuals. However, there are also progressive religious communities that challenge these anti-LGBTQ stances and work towards fostering inclusivity and acceptance.

Understanding the Stances

To effectively challenge anti-LGBTQ stances within religion, it is crucial to understand the underlying beliefs and interpretations that lead to discrimination. Different religious traditions have varying perspectives on human sexuality and gender identity, which influence their attitudes towards LGBTQ individuals.

For example, some conservative interpretations of religious texts condemn same-sex relationships and transgender identities, citing scriptural passages as justification. These views often stem from traditional interpretations that do not account for societal and cultural changes over time.

Reinterpretation and Progressive Thought

One strategy to challenge anti-LGBTQ stances within religion is through reinterpretation and progressive thought. Religious scholars and activists have engaged in critical analysis of sacred texts, seeking alternative interpretations that embrace LGBTQ identities.

By examining the historical context, linguistic nuances, and overall message of religious texts, progressive thinkers have been able to challenge the outdated anti-LGBTQ interpretations. They argue for a more inclusive understanding of religious teachings, one that embraces diverse sexual orientations and gender identities.

Promotion of Inclusivity

In challenging anti-LGBTQ stances within religion, promoting inclusivity is paramount. Progressive religious communities are working to create spaces that welcome LGBTQ individuals, ensuring they can practice their faith without fear of discrimination or condemnation.

These communities actively advocate for policies and rituals that affirm the dignity and worth of every individual, irrespective of their sexual orientation or gender identity. They strive to create an environment where LGBTQ individuals can fully participate in religious practices, rituals, and leadership roles.

Engaging in Interfaith Dialogue

Challenging anti-LGBTQ stances within religion also requires engaging in interfaith dialogue. By facilitating constructive conversations between different religious traditions, the goal is to foster understanding, empathy, and respect for LGBTQ individuals across faith communities.

Interfaith dialogue allows for the sharing of diverse perspectives on sexuality and gender identity. It helps break down the barriers of misunderstanding and promote collaboration in creating religiously inclusive spaces for LGBTQ individuals.

Human Rights Advocacy

Another crucial aspect of challenging anti-LGBTQ stances within religion is advocating for human rights. Activists work towards ensuring that LGBTQ individuals are protected from discrimination and violence not only by secular laws but also within religious communities.

Efforts are made to raise awareness about the impact of anti-LGBTQ beliefs and practices on individuals' well-being and mental health. This advocacy work involves lobbying for legal reforms, engaging with religious leaders and institutions to change discriminatory policies, and supporting LGBTQ-affirming initiatives within religious communities.

Examples of Challenging Anti-LGBTQ Stances

Various real-world examples showcase how individuals and organizations have successfully challenged anti-LGBTQ stances within religion. For instance, some progressive religious leaders have openly affirmed LGBTQ identities and perform same-sex marriage ceremonies within their faith traditions. They provide a guiding light for others in promoting inclusivity and acceptance.

Interfaith LGBTQ+ alliances have also emerged, bringing together activists from different religious backgrounds to advocate for LGBTQ rights and challenge discriminatory policies within their respective traditions.

Tricks and Caveats

While challenging anti-LGBTQ stances within religion is a necessary and transformative process, it is important to approach it with sensitivity and respect. Engaging in dialogue and debate should be done in a way that fosters constructive conversation rather than promoting division or hostility.

It is vital to recognize that change takes time and that not all individuals or religious institutions will be receptive to progressive ideas immediately. The process of challenging these stances requires patience, perseverance, and a commitment to promoting mutually respectful dialogue.

Conclusion

Challenging anti-LGBTQ stances within religion is a multifaceted endeavor that requires a combination of reinterpretation, inclusivity promotion, interfaith dialogue, and human rights advocacy. It is a crucial task in creating a more accepting and inclusive world for LGBTQ individuals within their religious communities.

By challenging traditional interpretations, fostering inclusivity, engaging in interfaith dialogue, and advocating for human rights, individuals can work towards dismantling discrimination and building a more accepting and affirming environment within religious traditions. This ongoing journey not only benefits LGBTQ individuals but also promotes a more just and compassionate society as a whole. As we continue to challenge these stances, it is essential to remember that our shared humanity unites us and that love, acceptance, and understanding can triumph over bigotry and prejudice.

Celebrating Inclusive Faith Communities

Inclusive faith communities play a vital role in supporting and uplifting LGBTQ individuals. They provide spaces where people can fully embrace their identities without fear of judgment or rejection. This subsection will explore the importance of celebrating these inclusive faith communities and the impact they have on creating a more accepting world for all.

Creating Welcoming Spaces

Creating welcoming spaces within faith communities is a cornerstone of inclusivity. It involves actively dismantling discrimination and fostering an environment where individuals of all sexual orientations and gender identities feel safe, supported, and celebrated. Such spaces ensure that LGBTQ individuals can fully participate in religious activities without sacrificing their authenticity.

To create inclusive faith communities, leaders and members need to challenge harmful and exclusionary beliefs, address discrimination, and promote acceptance and understanding. It requires a commitment to learning, growth, and continually reevaluating traditional interpretations that exclude LGBTQ individuals.

Promoting Dialogue and Education

Promoting dialogue and education is a crucial aspect of celebrating inclusive faith communities. Open and respectful discussions about LGBTQ issues within religious contexts help debunk misconceptions and challenge prejudice. By engaging in meaningful conversations and providing educational resources, faith communities can address the theological concerns related to LGBTQ identities and build bridges of understanding.

Workshops, seminars, and training sessions can be organized to facilitate dialogue and encourage education on LGBTQ experiences and issues. These initiatives can help break down barriers, promote empathy, and foster a culture of acceptance.

Advocating for Inclusive Policies

Advocacy for inclusive policies is another vital component of celebrating inclusive faith communities. It involves pushing for changes within religious institutions, denominations, and governing bodies to ensure LGBTQ individuals are fully included and afforded equal rights.

Faith communities can advocate for the recognition of same-sex marriages, the ordination of LGBTQ clergy, and the inclusion of LGBTQ perspectives in religious texts and teachings. They can also work towards the removal of discriminatory policies and teachings that perpetuate harm and exclusion.

Empowering LGBTQ Leaders

Empowering LGBTQ leaders within faith communities is essential for fostering inclusivity. By actively promoting and supporting LGBTQ individuals in leadership roles, faith communities send a powerful message of affirmation and acceptance.

LGBTQ leaders can provide guidance and support for other LGBTQ individuals, acting as role models for those navigating their own faith journeys. Their presence challenges the notion that being LGBTQ is incompatible with religious life and helps reshape the narrative around faith and queer identities.

Collaborating with LGBTQ Organizations

Collaboration with LGBTQ organizations is a crucial strategy for celebrating inclusive faith communities. By partnering with LGBTQ organizations, faith communities can access expertise, resources, and support networks that are essential for creating welcoming spaces.

Collaborative efforts can include hosting joint events, providing resources for LGBTQ individuals, and participating in LGBTQ Pride parades or marches. These partnerships allow faith communities to demonstrate their commitment to inclusivity and create opportunities for meaningful engagement and dialogue.

Celebrating Intersectionality

Celebrating intersectionality is a fundamental principle of inclusive faith communities. It recognizes that LGBTQ individuals have multiple identities and face intersectional forms of discrimination based on factors such as race, ethnicity, ability, and socioeconomic status.

Faith communities must acknowledge and address the unique challenges faced by LGBTQ individuals with intersecting identities. By honoring the diversity of experiences within their community, they can create spaces that are truly affirming and welcoming.

Addressing Existing Stigma

Addressing existing stigma is a crucial step in celebrating inclusive faith communities. Many religious traditions and institutions have historically propagated anti-LGBTQ beliefs, resulting in widespread stigma and discrimination.

To celebrate inclusive faith communities, leaders and members must acknowledge and confront these harmful beliefs head-on. This requires a commitment to challenging prejudice, dismantling stereotypes, and actively supporting LGBTQ individuals within and beyond the faith community.

Promoting Social Justice

Promoting social justice is a key aspect of celebrating inclusive faith communities. It involves advocating for LGBTQ rights, supporting equality initiatives, and actively engaging in broader social justice movements.

Faith communities can participate in public demonstrations, lobby for LGBTQ-affirming legislation, and support organizations that work towards social justice. By leveraging their influence, faith communities can contribute to the broader fight for LGBTQ equality and create a more inclusive society.

Concluding Remarks

Celebrating inclusive faith communities is essential for creating a more accepting and inclusive world for LGBTQ individuals. By creating welcoming spaces, promoting dialogue and education, advocating for inclusive policies, empowering LGBTQ leaders, collaborating with LGBTQ organizations, celebrating intersectionality, addressing existing stigma, and promoting social justice, faith communities can actively contribute to the ongoing progress towards LGBTQ equality.

Promoting Queer Spirituality

In the pursuit of promoting queer spirituality, it is essential to consider the diverse experiences and identities within the LGBTQ community. Queer spirituality recognizes and affirms the spiritual journeys of individuals who identify as LGBTQ and provides a safe and inclusive space for exploring their connection to the divine. This subsection explores the principles, practices, and challenges of promoting queer spirituality, with a focus on creating inclusive faith communities.

Recognizing the Importance of Queer Spirituality

Queer spirituality acknowledges that LGBTQ individuals have unique spiritual needs and desires. It recognizes that the traditional narratives of religion often marginalize or exclude queer identities, leading many LGBTQ individuals to feel disconnected from their faith or spirituality. By promoting queer spirituality, we aim to address this disparity and create spaces where individuals can embrace their whole self.

Affirming Intersectionality in Spiritual Spaces

When promoting queer spirituality, it is vital to acknowledge and celebrate the intersectionality of identities within the LGBTQ community. Queer individuals come from diverse racial, ethnic, cultural, and religious backgrounds, and their spiritual experiences are shaped by these intersecting identities. Affirming intersectionality means creating inclusive spaces that respect and value all aspects of a person's identity.

Example: Within a queer spiritual community, there may be individuals who identify as Muslim, Black, and transgender. Recognizing and affirming their intersectional identity involves acknowledging the unique challenges they face and embracing their contributions to the community. Promoting queer spirituality requires actively supporting and amplifying the voices of those with intersectional identities.

Creating Inclusive Faith Communities

To promote queer spirituality effectively, faith communities must actively work towards becoming inclusive, affirming spaces for LGBTQ individuals. This includes educating religious leaders, congregants, and community members about LGBTQ issues, fostering dialogue, and challenging discriminatory beliefs and practices. Open and compassionate dialogue can help bridge the gap between traditional religious teachings and the lived experiences of queer individuals.

Example: A local mosque could create an LGBTQ-inclusive prayer space, allowing LGBTQ Muslims to worship in a safe and accepting environment. This space could be open to all, regardless of sexual orientation or gender identity, and provide opportunities for learning and dialogue about the intersection of faith and queerness. By creating an inclusive faith community, individuals can explore and express their spirituality without fear of judgment or discrimination.

Redefining Sacred Texts

Promoting queer spirituality also involves reexamining and reinterpreting sacred texts to foster a more inclusive understanding of LGBTQ identities. This requires engaging in critical discussions and scholarly research to challenge and debunk homophobic and transphobic interpretations of religious texts. By doing so, we can create a space where queer individuals can reconcile their faith with their sexual orientation or gender identity.

Example: Within Christianity, there has been a movement to reinterpret biblical texts that have historically been used to condemn homosexuality. By analyzing the cultural contexts of these texts and considering alternative interpretations, LGBTQ-affirming Christians aim to reclaim a more inclusive understanding of their faith. This process allows for the promotion of queer spirituality within a religious framework.

Promoting Queer Rituals and Practices

In addition to redefining spiritual texts, promoting queer spirituality involves the development of rituals and practices that specifically address LGBTQ experiences and needs. This can include LGBTQ-affirming rituals, such as commitment ceremonies or naming ceremonies, and the incorporation of LGBTQ symbols or imagery into existing religious practices.

Example: A queer spiritual community might develop a ritual to celebrate the coming out process, where individuals publicly affirm and embrace their LGBTQ identity within a sacred space. This ritual acknowledges the unique journey of self-discovery and self-acceptance experienced by queer individuals, providing them with a sense of communal support and celebration.

Providing Resources and Support

Promoting queer spirituality requires the availability of resources and support networks for LGBTQ individuals exploring their spiritual identities. These resources can include books, websites, online communities, and LGBTQ-affirming religious organizations that provide information, guidance, and support to individuals navigating their spiritual journeys.

Example: An online platform could be created to connect LGBTQ individuals from diverse spiritual backgrounds, allowing them to share their experiences, resources, and knowledge. This platform could be a space for individuals to find support, ask questions, and engage in dialogue with others who are also exploring their queer spirituality.

Addressing Challenges and Resistance

Promoting queer spirituality is not without its challenges. Resistance from conservative religious communities, stigma, and misunderstanding can hinder progress in creating inclusive faith spaces. It is crucial to address these challenges by engaging in respectful dialogue, educating communities, and amplifying the voices and stories of LGBTQ individuals.

Example: A panel discussion could be organized, featuring LGBTQ individuals from various religious backgrounds, to share their stories and experiences with religious leaders and congregation members. This open dialogue can foster understanding, challenge preconceived notions, and address fears and concerns that may impede the creation of LGBTQ-affirming spiritual spaces.

Conclusion

Promoting queer spirituality is a vital aspect of LGBTQ activism, as it recognizes and affirms the spiritual lives of LGBTQ individuals. By creating inclusive faith communities, redefining sacred texts, developing affirming rituals, and providing resources and support, we can foster the growth and exploration of queer spirituality. It is through these efforts that we can promote a more inclusive and accepting world for LGBTQ individuals seeking to reconcile their faith and their queer identities. Remember, the journey towards promoting queer spirituality is an ongoing one, and it requires continuous learning and engagement with diverse communities.

Paving the Way for a More Accepting World

In this subsection, we dive into the crucial role of paving the way for a more accepting world for LGBTQ individuals. It's a journey that involves challenging societal norms, promoting awareness, and fostering inclusion in various aspects of life. Let's explore the key strategies and initiatives that can help create a more accepting and inclusive society for all.

Understanding the Power of Education

Education plays a pivotal role in shaping attitudes and beliefs. By incorporating LGBTQ-inclusive education into school curricula, we can foster understanding, empathy, and acceptance from an early age. This includes teaching about LGBTQ history, contributions, and challenges, as well as promoting respect for diverse sexual orientations and gender identities. By exposing students to a wide range of perspectives, we can break down barriers and empower them to become allies and advocates for LGBTQ rights.

Creating Safe and Inclusive Spaces

One of the fundamental steps in paving the way for a more accepting world is creating safe and inclusive spaces for LGBTQ individuals. These spaces can include LGBTQ community centers, support groups, and LGBTQ-friendly establishments. Such spaces provide opportunities for personal growth, socialization, and celebration of identity. They also serve as platforms for advocacy, education, and support services. By actively supporting and engaging with these spaces, individuals can help build stronger communities and challenge societal prejudices.

Promoting LGBTQ-Inclusive Policies and Legislation

Another crucial aspect of creating an accepting world is the promotion of LGBTQ-inclusive policies and legislation. Advocacy efforts should focus on pursuing equal rights and protections for LGBTQ individuals in all areas of life, including employment, housing, healthcare, and public accommodations. This involves challenging discriminatory laws and practices, pushing for comprehensive anti-discrimination policies, and advocating for legislation that supports transgender rights, marriage equality, and other LGBTQ-related issues. By working towards legal recognition and protection, we can ensure that LGBTQ individuals are treated fairly and have the same opportunities as everyone else.

Building Alliances and Coalitions

Paving the way for a more accepting world requires collaboration and solidarity across different communities. It is essential to build alliances and coalitions between LGBTQ individuals and various social justice movements, such as feminism, racial justice, and immigrant rights. By recognizing the interconnectedness of different forms of discrimination and oppression, we can create a powerful movement for social change. Through collective action and shared resources, we can challenge systemic injustices and work towards a society where every individual is accepted and valued.

Changing Narratives in Media and Entertainment

Media and entertainment play a significant role in shaping societal attitudes and perceptions. By promoting diverse and accurate representations of LGBTQ individuals in movies, television shows, and other forms of media, we can challenge stereotypes and foster empathy and understanding. It is crucial to support and celebrate LGBTQ artists, writers, and creators, as well as encourage major media outlets to strive for more inclusive and representative storytelling. By amplifying diverse voices and showcasing authentic LGBTQ experiences, we can contribute to a more accepting and inclusive world.

Engaging in Community Outreach and Awareness Campaigns

Creating awareness and engaging in community outreach are essential in changing hearts and minds. It involves organizing awareness campaigns, workshops, and panels to educate the general public about LGBTQ issues, dispel myths and misconceptions, and promote inclusivity. These initiatives also provide opportunities for dialogue, allowing individuals from different backgrounds to engage in meaningful conversations and learn from one another. By fostering understanding and promoting empathy, we can build bridges and break down barriers to acceptance.

Supporting LGBTQ Organizations and Initiatives

Supporting LGBTQ organizations and initiatives is crucial in paving the way for a more accepting world. These organizations tirelessly advocate for LGBTQ rights, provide support services, and create spaces for community engagement and empowerment. By donating funds, volunteering time, or simply participating in their activities, individuals can contribute to the progress and sustainability of these vital organizations. Supporting LGBTQ initiatives also means amplifying their voices, sharing their messages, and advocating for their causes in personal and professional networks.

Embracing Intersectionality

In the journey towards a more accepting world, it is essential to embrace intersectionality and recognize that individuals' experiences and identities are multidimensional. By acknowledging the unique challenges faced by LGBTQ individuals who also belong to marginalized communities based on race, ethnicity, class, or disability, we can work towards creating an inclusive movement that addresses the specific needs and concerns of all individuals. Intersectionality enables us to challenge multiple forms of oppression and build a more equitable world for everyone.

Championing Mental Health and Well-being

The mental health and well-being of LGBTQ individuals are paramount in creating an accepting world. It is crucial to promote access to LGBTQ-affirming mental health services and support systems that prioritize the unique needs and experiences of LGBTQ individuals. Recognizing and addressing the higher rates of mental health issues and suicide among LGBTQ individuals is essential. By prioritizing mental health and fostering a culture of care and support, we can ensure that LGBTQ individuals thrive in all aspects of life.

Encouraging Allyship and Active Engagement

Paving the way for a more accepting world requires active participation from allies of the LGBTQ community. Allies can show support by educating themselves about LGBTQ issues, challenging their own biases, and speaking out against discrimination and prejudice. It is important to listen to and amplify LGBTQ voices, acknowledge their expertise, and actively engage in creating inclusive spaces. By standing up against injustice and advocating for LGBTQ rights, allies contribute significantly to the progress towards a more accepting world.

In conclusion, paving the way for a more accepting world involves various strategies, including education, creating safe spaces, promoting inclusive policies, building alliances, changing narratives, community outreach, supporting LGBTQ organizations, embracing intersectionality, championing mental health, and encouraging allyship. By adopting these approaches, we can foster an inclusive and accepting society where everyone can live authentically and without fear of discrimination or prejudice. The fight for equality continues, and our collective efforts are crucial in achieving lasting change.

Rethinking Gender Roles in Religion

In the realm of religion, gender roles have traditionally been defined in binary terms, reinforcing patriarchal structures and reinforcing the marginalization of women and LGBTQ individuals. However, there is a growing movement to challenge these rigid gender norms and promote inclusivity and equality within religious communities. This subsection explores the need to rethink gender roles in religion and highlights the efforts being made to create more inclusive spaces.

Understanding Gender as a Social Construct

To effectively challenge and redefine gender roles in religion, it is crucial to first understand gender as a social construct. Gender is not inherently tied to biological sex but is rather a set of social expectations and roles assigned to individuals based on their perceived sex. This societal construction of gender can vary across cultures and historical periods, indicating its fluid nature.

Acknowledging Historical Context and Interpretation

When reassessing gender roles in religion, it is important to consider the historical context in which religious texts were written and the various interpretations that have emerged throughout time. Many religious texts were written during times when patriarchal societies prevailed, and as a result, they may reflect and reinforce gender inequalities.

Rethinking gender roles involves critically examining these texts, acknowledging the biases and limitations of their authors, and finding alternative interpretations that promote inclusivity and equality. This process requires engaging in an honest dialogue with religious scholars, challenging oppressive interpretations, and highlighting overlooked narratives that empower marginalized groups.

Promoting Women's Leadership and Participation

One essential aspect of rethinking gender roles in religion is promoting women's leadership and active participation in religious institutions. Historically, women have been excluded from positions of power and decision-making within religious hierarchies. By challenging these exclusions, religious communities can create opportunities for women to contribute their perspectives and talents to the development and decision-making processes.

Leading by example, several progressive religious movements have embraced women's ordination and provided platforms for female clergy members, challenging traditional gender roles. These spaces foster women's spiritual development and encourage their active engagement in shaping the direction and practices of their religious communities.

Empowering LGBTQ Individuals

Rethinking gender roles in religion also involves empowering LGBTQ individuals and challenging the heteronormative assumptions prevalent in many religious teachings. This requires creating safe spaces within religious communities where LGBTQ individuals can express their identities authentically and without fear of discrimination or rejection.

Inclusive religious institutions actively work toward dismantling harmful beliefs and practices that stigmatize or exclude individuals based on their sexual orientation or gender identity. They affirm LGBTQ identities as part of the diverse fabric of their religious communities, rejecting the notion that LGBTQ individuals are deviant or in need of "fixing."

Emphasizing Equality and Mutual Respect

At the core of rethinking gender roles in religion is the emphasis on equality and mutual respect among all individuals, regardless of their gender or sexual orientation. This involves challenging hierarchical structures that perpetuate gender-based discrimination and promoting a culture of respect, justice, and fairness within religious communities.

Inclusive religious communities recognize that gender equality is a necessary principle for creating a just society and work towards institutionalizing policies and practices that promote gender equity. They actively engage in dialogue and education to raise awareness about the negative impacts of gender stereotypes and challenge harmful misconceptions.

Case Study: The Welcoming Church Movement

One notable example of a movement challenging gender roles in religion is the Welcoming Church movement within Christianity. The Welcoming Church movement advocates for LGBTQ inclusion within Christian communities and challenges the exclusionary practices and teachings that have contributed to the marginalization of LGBTQ individuals.

The movement promotes a more inclusive interpretation of Christian teachings, emphasizing love, acceptance, and equality. Welcoming churches welcome LGBTQ individuals into their congregations, affirm their identities, and actively work towards dismantling heteronormative structures within the church.

By prioritizing inclusivity, the Welcoming Church movement illustrates the transformative power of rethinking gender roles and creating spaces where individuals of all gender identities and sexual orientations can fully express their spirituality.

Conclusion

Rethinking gender roles in religion is an ongoing and vital process in promoting inclusivity and equality within spiritual spaces. It requires challenging oppressive interpretations, promoting women's leadership, empowering LGBTQ individuals, and emphasizing equality and mutual respect. By engaging in these discussions and advocating for change, we can work towards creating religious communities that are truly inclusive and affirming for all individuals, regardless of their gender or sexual orientation.

Reclaiming Religious Spaces for LGBTQ Individuals

The intersection of faith and sexuality has long been a challenging and often contentious issue for LGBTQ individuals. Many religious traditions have historically held conservative views on homosexuality and transgender identities, making it difficult for queer individuals to feel accepted and included within their religious communities. However, in recent years, there has been a growing movement to reclaim religious spaces and foster inclusivity for LGBTQ individuals. This subsection explores the strategies and initiatives aimed at redefining faith and creating safe spaces for queer individuals in religious settings.

Understanding the Importance of Inclusivity

To begin, it is crucial to recognize the significance of inclusivity within religious spaces. Many LGBTQ individuals have a deep-rooted connection to their faith, and being able to fully embrace their sexual orientation or gender identity while practicing their religion is of utmost importance. Reclaiming religious spaces means acknowledging the inherent worth and dignity of all individuals, regardless of their sexual orientation or gender identity.

Promoting Open Dialogue and Education

One of the key strategies for reclaiming religious spaces is promoting open dialogue and education. This involves creating opportunities for conversations surrounding LGBTQ identities and experiences within faith communities. Workshops, training sessions, and panel discussions can provide a platform for LGBTQ individuals and allies to share their stories and engage in respectful dialogue. These conversations can help dispel misconceptions, challenge traditional interpretations, and foster understanding and empathy among community members.

Engaging with Religious Leaders

Engaging with religious leaders is another vital aspect of reclaiming religious spaces for LGBTQ individuals. It is essential to have open and honest conversations with religious leaders about inclusive practices and interpretations of religious texts. This can involve creating spaces where religious leaders can learn about queer experiences, engage with LGBTQ theology, and explore alternative interpretations of religious teachings. Building relationships based on understanding and respect can help to shift the narrative within religious communities and promote greater acceptance and inclusion.

Establishing LGBTQ-Inclusive Policies and Practices

Reclaiming religious spaces also requires the establishment of LGBTQ-inclusive policies and practices within faith communities. These policies can explicitly state that all individuals, regardless of their sexual orientation or gender identity, are welcome and valued within the community. In addition, LGBTQ-inclusive practices can be implemented, such as using inclusive language in prayers and sermons, organizing LGBTQ-friendly religious events, and providing resources and support for LGBTQ individuals and their families. These visible and tangible changes demonstrate a commitment to inclusivity and create a welcoming environment for queer individuals.

Creating Support Networks

Another crucial aspect of reclaiming religious spaces is creating support networks for LGBTQ individuals within faith communities. LGBTQ individuals often face unique challenges and struggles that can be mitigated through the support of a like-minded community. Establishing LGBTQ-affirming support groups, virtual or in-person, can provide a space for individuals to share their experiences, seek guidance, and find solace in their faith journeys. These networks can foster a sense of belonging and provide the necessary support for LGBTQ individuals to navigate their spiritual lives authentically.

Challenging Homophobic Theology

To reclaim religious spaces, it is essential to challenge homophobic theology that perpetuates discrimination and exclusion. This involves critiquing and questioning interpretations of religious texts that have been historically used to justify discrimination against LGBTQ individuals. By engaging with scholars, promoting critical thinking, and revisiting sacred texts with an inclusive lens, we can challenge the harmful narratives that have marginalized the queer community. This process encourages a reinterpretation of religious teachings that promotes love, acceptance, and equality for all.

Promoting Interfaith Dialogue

Promoting interfaith dialogue is another powerful strategy for reclaiming religious spaces for LGBTQ individuals. Engaging in conversations with individuals from different religious traditions creates an opportunity to share experiences, build bridges, and find common ground for promoting LGBTQ inclusivity across diverse faith communities. It allows us to highlight the shared values of love, respect, and compassion that are central to many religious traditions and fosters solidarity in the fight for equality and acceptance.

Advocating for LGBTQ Rights within Religious Institutions

Reclaiming religious spaces also involves advocating for LGBTQ rights within religious institutions themselves. LGBTQ activists and allies can work within their religious communities to push for policy changes that affirm the rights and dignity of queer individuals. This includes advocating for LGBTQ-inclusive marriage ceremonies, supporting LGBTQ candidates for religious leadership positions, and pushing for the revision of discriminatory policies and practices. By actively participating in decision-making processes, LGBTQ individuals and their allies can effect meaningful change within their religious communities.

Expanding LGBTQ-Affirming Faith Communities

Expanding LGBTQ-affirming faith communities is another important aspect of reclaiming religious spaces. The establishment of LGBTQ-affirming congregations or the transformation of existing congregations to become more LGBTQ-inclusive creates safe spaces for queer individuals to practice their faith. These communities provide a supportive environment where LGBTQ individuals can find spiritual solace and engage in worship without fear of judgment or exclusion. By expanding these communities, we demonstrate that LGBTQ individuals can fully embrace their faith while also living authentically.

Fostering Solidarity Across Faith and LGBTQ Movements

Lastly, reclaiming religious spaces requires fostering solidarity between the faith and LGBTQ movements. Building alliances and working collaboratively with LGBTQ organizations and other social justice movements helps to amplify the voices of LGBTQ individuals within religious communities. It also highlights the shared struggle for equality and justice, promoting a greater understanding of the intersectionality of various oppressions. Together, these movements can challenge societal norms and work towards a more inclusive and accepting society.

In conclusion, reclaiming religious spaces for LGBTQ individuals is a multifaceted and ongoing process. It involves promoting open dialogue, engaging with religious leaders, establishing LGBTQ-inclusive policies and practices, creating support networks, challenging homophobic theology, and fostering solidarity across faith and LGBTQ movements. By actively working towards inclusivity, we can create religious spaces that fully embrace and affirm the identities and experiences of LGBTQ individuals, fostering a sense of belonging, spirituality, and love.

Supporting LGBTQ Muslims' Spiritual Journeys

Supporting LGBTQ Muslims on their spiritual journeys is a complex and delicate task. It requires a nuanced understanding of both their religious beliefs and their unique experiences as queer individuals. In this subsection, we will explore various strategies and resources that can help create a supportive and inclusive environment for LGBTQ Muslims as they navigate their faith and sexuality.

Understanding the Intersection of Faith and Sexuality

Central to supporting LGBTQ Muslims on their spiritual journeys is recognizing the intersectionality of their identities. Their experiences are shaped by both their religious beliefs and their queer identities, and these two aspects often intertwine in complex ways. As allies and supporters, it is crucial to understand the challenges they face and the conflicts they may encounter.

One key aspect is the commonly held belief in traditional interpretations of religious texts that view homosexuality as sinful or forbidden. This can create a profound sense of internal conflict for LGBTQ Muslims, as they strive to reconcile their faith and their sexuality. Providing education and promoting open dialogue about the different interpretations of religious texts can help LGBTQ Muslims navigate this inner struggle and find a sense of peace.

Promoting Inclusivity in Religious Spaces

Creating safe and inclusive spaces within religious communities is essential for supporting LGBTQ Muslims on their spiritual journeys. Religious leaders and community members play a critical role in fostering an environment that welcomes and affirms queer individuals.

One strategy is to encourage religious leaders to undergo LGBTQ-inclusive training and education. This can help them develop a better understanding of the unique challenges faced by LGBTQ Muslims and equip them with the knowledge and tools to provide appropriate support. It is also important for religious leaders to publicly acknowledge and affirm the presence of LGBTQ Muslims within their communities, sending a message of inclusivity and acceptance to all members.

In addition, it is crucial to provide LGBTQ-affirming resources within religious spaces. This can include literature, support groups, and counseling services specifically tailored to the needs of LGBTQ Muslims. By actively promoting inclusivity, religious institutions can create an environment where LGBTQ Muslims feel valued and supported in their spiritual journeys.

Facilitating Interfaith Dialogue

Another important aspect of supporting LGBTQ Muslims' spiritual journeys is facilitating interfaith dialogue. This involves creating opportunities for meaningful conversations and collaborations between various religious communities, including Muslim and LGBTQ-affirming faith traditions.

Interfaith dialogue can help break down stereotypes, challenge prejudices, and build bridges of understanding between different religious perspectives. By engaging in respectful and open conversations, LGBTQ Muslims can find support, empathy, and wisdom from allies across different faith traditions. This can provide them with a sense of belonging and expanded spiritual frameworks that embrace their queer identities.

Providing Mentoring and Peer Support

Mentoring and peer support programs are invaluable resources for LGBTQ Muslims on their spiritual journeys. LGBT-inclusive spaces that offer mentorship and support can provide guidance, validation, and a sense of community. These programs can connect LGBTQ Muslims with mentors who have successfully navigated their own faith and sexuality journeys, providing them with role models and sources of inspiration.

By connecting LGBTQ Muslims with peers who share similar experiences, these programs foster a sense of belonging and provide a safe space for sharing struggles, achievements, and personal stories. Peer support groups and online communities also offer opportunities for LGBTQ Muslims to engage in discussions, seek advice, and find encouragement. These networks can be powerful sources of support and empowerment for LGBTQ Muslims as they navigate their spiritual paths.

Championing LGBTQ-Inclusive Theological Discourses

Promoting LGBTQ-inclusive theological discourses is a vital aspect of supporting LGBTQ Muslims' spiritual journeys. This involves engaging with religious scholars, institutions, and theological frameworks to challenge heteronormative perspectives and create spaces for alternative interpretations.

By championing LGBTQ-inclusive theological discourses, we can encourage a re-evaluation of traditional interpretations of religious texts, promoting a more accepting and inclusive understanding of faith. This can help LGBTQ Muslims reconcile their identities with their religious beliefs, providing them with a sense of peace and allowing them to fully embrace their faith and their queer identities.

Encouraging Self-Reflection and Empowerment

Supporting LGBTQ Muslims on their spiritual journeys also involves encouraging self-reflection and empowerment. LGBTQ-affirming resources should aim to empower individuals to explore their own spiritual paths and make informed choices that align with their values and identities.

It is important to emphasize that being LGBTQ and Muslim is not contradictory; rather, it is a beautiful and unique aspect of one's identity. Encouraging self-reflection and self-acceptance can help LGBTQ Muslims embrace their queerness while maintaining their faith.

Promoting mental health and well-being is also crucial in supporting LGBTQ Muslims' spiritual journeys. This can involve advocating for inclusive mental health services, providing resources for coping with stress and discrimination, and promoting self-care practices that nourish both the mind and the spirit.

Conclusion

Supporting LGBTQ Muslims on their spiritual journeys requires intentional efforts to create inclusive spaces, promote education and dialogue, provide mentorship and peer support, champion LGBTQ-inclusive theological discourses, and encourage self-reflection and empowerment. By implementing these strategies, we can help LGBTQ Muslims navigate the complex intersection of their faith and sexuality, ensuring that they feel validated, supported, and able to fully embrace and thrive in their religious identities. The path to spiritual fulfillment and self-acceptance may be challenging, but with understanding, empathy, and concrete actions, we can walk alongside LGBTQ Muslims on their journeys and create a more inclusive world for all.

Intersections of Faith, Sexuality, and Gender

In this subsection, we explore the fascinating and complex intersections between faith, sexuality, and gender. These intersections often raise challenging questions and can be sources of tension within religious communities. However, they also present opportunities for dialogue, understanding, and growth. Let's delve into this topic and explore the dynamics at play.

Understanding the Intersections

Faith, sexuality, and gender are integral aspects of a person's identity. Faith provides individuals with a sense of meaning, purpose, and guidance. Sexuality encompasses a person's romantic, sexual, and emotional attractions and experiences. Gender refers to the societal and cultural constructs of masculinity and femininity.

When these aspects intersect, individuals face unique challenges and opportunities. LGBTQ individuals who have faith often encounter conflicts between their sexual or gender identity and the teachings of their religious tradition. This tension can arise from conservative interpretations or beliefs that view homosexuality or gender nonconformity as sinful or deviant.

Conversely, some religious traditions embrace and celebrate LGBTQ individuals, promoting inclusivity and acceptance. These communities recognize that people can be faithful while also embracing their sexual and gender identities.

Opening the Dialogue

To navigate the intersections of faith, sexuality, and gender, it's essential to foster open and respectful dialogue within religious communities. This dialogue should involve both LGBTQ individuals and religious leaders or scholars. Here are some key strategies to facilitate these conversations:

1. Creating safe spaces: Establishing safe spaces within religious communities allows LGBTQ individuals to share their experiences without fear of judgment or condemnation. These spaces can foster empathy, understanding, and support.

2. Cultivating education and awareness: Providing education on LGBTQ identities, experiences, and perspectives can help challenge preconceived notions and debunk stereotypes. This education can include workshops, guest speakers, or resources that promote understanding and inclusion.

3. Engaging with diverse religious voices: Encouraging diverse religious voices within the dialogue promotes a more comprehensive understanding of the intersections. This may involve inviting scholars or leaders from different faith traditions to share their insights and experiences.

Promoting Inclusivity and Acceptance

Promoting inclusivity and acceptance within religious communities requires intentional efforts. Here are some ways to foster a more inclusive environment:

1. Emphasizing shared values: Highlighting shared values of love, compassion, and acceptance can bridge the perceived divide between faith and LGBTQ identities. This reaffirms that LGBTQ individuals are an integral part of religious communities and can contribute meaningfully.

2. Encouraging theological interpretation: Engaging in thoughtful theological interpretation allows for innovative perspectives on LGBTQ issues. This can involve revisiting sacred texts through a lens of inclusivity and exploring religious teachings that promote acceptance.

3. Supporting affirming congregations: Identifying and supporting affirming congregations or religious institutions that explicitly embrace LGBTQ individuals sends a powerful message of acceptance. This support can involve attending services, participating in events, or contributing to these communities.

Case Study: LGBTQ-Inclusive Mosques

LGBTQ-inclusive mosques serve as a testament to the possibilities of embracing the intersections of faith, sexuality, and gender. These spaces provide a haven for LGBTQ Muslims, recognizing their unique struggles and validating their experiences.

Organizations and individuals have worked towards establishing LGBTQ-inclusive mosques, which uphold Islamic values while promoting inclusivity. These spaces celebrate LGBTQ identities, provide supportive resources, and actively challenge homophobic attitudes within the Muslim community.

Inclusive mosques often hold inclusive Friday prayers, offer LGBTQ-affirming Islamic teachings, and provide support groups for LGBTQ Muslims. They create an environment where individuals can reconcile their faith and LGBTQ identities, fostering a sense of belonging and spiritual nourishment.

Conclusion

The intersections of faith, sexuality, and gender are complex and multifaceted. Navigating these intersections requires open dialogue, education, and intentional efforts to promote inclusivity and acceptance within religious communities. LGBTQ individuals should be able to reconcile their faith and identities, finding support and belonging within their religious traditions. By engaging in these conversations and challenging discriminatory beliefs, we can create a more inclusive and understanding world. Remember, the struggle for equality continues, and it is up to all of us to play our part.

Embracing Inclusivity and Diversity in Faith Communities

In the quest for equality and acceptance, it is crucial to address the inclusion and diversity within faith communities. This subsection explores the significance of creating welcoming spaces for LGBTQ individuals in religious settings and highlights the importance of embracing inclusivity and diversity.

Recognizing the Importance of Inclusive Faith Communities

Faith communities have historically played a central role in people's lives, providing guidance, support, and a sense of belonging. However, for many LGBTQ individuals, religion has often been a source of exclusion and discrimination. To address this, a shift towards creating inclusive faith communities is necessary.

An inclusive faith community acknowledges and respects the diverse identities and experiences of its members, including LGBTQ individuals. It recognizes that spirituality and sexual orientation or gender identity are not mutually exclusive, and that everyone should have the freedom to express their faith authentically.

Challenging Homophobia and Transphobia

Homophobia and transphobia within religious communities have contributed to the exclusion and marginalization of LGBTQ individuals. Overcoming these prejudices requires dialogue, education, and a commitment to challenging discriminatory beliefs.

Faith leaders and community members must actively challenge homophobic and transphobic narratives within their religious teachings. By promoting understanding and compassion, they can help create an environment where everyone feels safe and valued, regardless of their sexual orientation or gender identity.

Promoting Dialogue and Education

Engaging in open and honest dialogue is essential to foster understanding and acceptance within faith communities. By hosting events and discussions centered around LGBTQ inclusion, religious organizations can provide opportunities for education and awareness.

Education should include dispelling misconceptions about sexual orientation and gender identity, exploring the intersectionality of LGBTQ identities with race, ethnicity, and culture, and highlighting the importance of embracing diversity within faith communities.

Creating Safe Spaces for LGBTQ Individuals

Creating safe spaces within faith communities is crucial for LGBTQ individuals to express their faith without fear of judgment or discrimination. These spaces can take various forms, such as LGBTQ-inclusive worship services, support groups, or social events.

Providing support and resources for LGBTQ individuals and their families is another way faith communities can demonstrate inclusivity. This can involve offering counseling services, organizing educational workshops on LGBTQ topics, and collaborating with LGBTQ organizations to address specific needs.

Nurturing Allyship within Faith Communities

A crucial aspect of embracing inclusivity and diversity in faith communities is nurturing allyship. Allies are individuals who support and advocate for the rights and well-being of LGBTQ individuals, even if they do not belong to the community themselves.

Faith leaders and community members should actively work towards becoming allies by educating themselves about LGBTQ issues, acknowledging their privileges, and standing up against discrimination. They can use their influence to create a culture of acceptance and love within their religious communities.

Championing Intersectionality

Embracing inclusivity and diversity in faith communities means recognizing the intersectionality of identities. LGBTQ individuals can belong to various racial, ethnic, and cultural backgrounds, and their experiences may differ based on these intersecting identities.

Faith communities must acknowledge and address the unique challenges faced by LGBTQ individuals from diverse backgrounds. By actively promoting inclusivity and understanding the experiences of all members, faith communities can foster a sense of belonging and unity.

Building Bridges Between Faith and LGBTQ Communities

Building bridges between faith and LGBTQ communities is essential for creating a more inclusive society. Collaboration and dialogue can help overcome misunderstandings and promote acceptance.

Interfaith dialogue, where representatives from different religious traditions come together to discuss LGBTQ inclusion, can be a powerful tool. This dialogue can promote mutual understanding, challenge stereotypes, and build relationships based on respect and empathy.

Promoting LGBTQ+ Inclusion in Religious Texts

Religious texts play a significant role in shaping the beliefs and practices of faith communities. To foster LGBTQ+ inclusion, it is essential to revisit and reinterpret these texts in light of evolving understanding and acceptance.

Religious scholars can contribute to this process by engaging in critical analysis and offering nuanced interpretations that acknowledge and affirm LGBTQ+ individuals. These reinterpretations can create space for LGBTQ+ individuals to fully express their faith and spirituality within their religious traditions.

Resisting Discriminatory Practices and Policies

Lastly, embracing inclusivity and diversity in faith communities requires a commitment to resist discriminatory practices and policies. Faith communities can work towards challenging discriminatory laws, advocating for LGBTQ+ rights, and actively opposing conversion therapy.

By standing up for justice and equality, faith communities can create transformative change not only within their own spheres but also for society at large.

In conclusion, embracing inclusivity and diversity within faith communities is crucial for creating a more accepting and welcoming environment for LGBTQ individuals. By challenging homophobia and transphobia, fostering dialogue and education, creating safe spaces, nurturing allyship, championing intersectionality, building bridges, promoting LGBTQ+ inclusion in religious texts, and resisting discrimination, faith communities can play a pivotal role in advancing LGBTQ rights and equality.

Conclusion:

Conclusion:

Conclusion:

In this captivating biography, we have explored the remarkable journey of Irshad Manji, a warrior who fearlessly defies traditional norms as a queer Muslim activist. Manji's story is one of self-discovery, resilience, and unapologetic authenticity. Through her personal evolution, she has navigated the complexities of faith and sexuality, faced adversity with unwavering courage, and fought for equality within both LGBTQ and Muslim communities.

Throughout the book, we have seen how Manji's early years in Uganda, followed by her relocation to Canada, shaped her identity and influenced her beliefs. Struggling with her own journey of self-acceptance, Manji experienced a queer awakening that propelled her into embracing activism. With the support of allies and the power of visibility, she found acceptance in society and became a champion for LGBTQ rights.

One of the most powerful aspects of Manji's activism is her unwavering dedication to reconciling faith and sexuality. She embarked on a journey to question traditional Islamic teachings and explore LGBTQ rights within the framework of Islam. Through her advocacy, she has challenged homophobia within Muslim communities, engaged with religious scholars, and pushed for progressive change. Manji's work has not only promoted inclusivity in religious spaces but has also inspired others to embrace their queer Muslim identities.

The biography also delves into the adversity Manji has faced throughout her activism. From confronting homophobia to battling patriarchy and Islamophobia, Manji has courageously spoken out against hate and discrimination. She has faced threats and hateful backlash, but her resilience has been a driving force in creating safe spaces for LGBTQ Muslims and empowering others to find their voice. Manji's personal stories have had a profound impact, fostering understanding and empathy among diverse communities.

In the second chapter, we see how Manji's rebellious spirit fueled her rise as an influential force for change. Through her platform, "Dangerous Daughters," and her groundbreaking book, "The Trouble with Islam Today," she began a movement that resonated with queer Muslims worldwide. Despite facing censorship and opposition, Manji's courageous writing connected with audiences globally and amplified the voices of marginalized communities.

Manji's transformative impact extends beyond individual empowerment. She has consistently engaged in dialogue and education, speaking at universities, leading workshops, and collaborating with LGBTQ organizations. By promoting LGBTQ+ inclusion in mosques and advocating for LGBTQ rights, Manji has broken barriers and fostered understanding between communities. Her commitment to education and empathy has been instrumental in creating a more inclusive world.

On a personal level, Manji's journey towards authenticity has been a powerful inspiration. Overcoming internalized homophobia, finding love and acceptance, and prioritizing self-care and well-being are themes that resonate deeply. She has navigated the intersectionality of her identities and shared her experiences, inspiring LGBTQ Muslims to embrace their true selves and thrive. Manji's advocacy for mental health shines through, highlighting the importance of well-being in one's activism journey.

In the concluding section of this gripping biography, we reflect on Manji's legacy as a trailblazer. Her milestones and achievements, including the impact on LGBTQ and Muslim communities, serve as reminders of her indelible mark on the world. Manji's contributions to LGBTQ activism are invaluable, and it is crucial to remember and honor the work of pioneers like her. Documenting LGBTQ activist histories promotes understanding, empathy, and encourages future generations of activists to continue fighting for equality.

Looking to the future, Manji's legacy serves as a foundation for the LGBTQ movement. Mentoring LGBTQ youth and empowering queer Muslims are essential for sustaining momentum. By cultivating leadership skills, supporting mental health, and amplifying young voices, the next generation of activists can carry forward the battle for equality. Addressing global LGBTQ issues, pushing for legal reforms, and protecting transgender rights are critical aspects of continuing the fight for equality worldwide.

Redefining faith and identity is another area where the legacy of Irshad Manji is impactful. Evolving religious narratives, challenging anti-LGBTQ stances within religious institutions, and celebrating inclusive faith communities are steps towards a more accepting world. By reclaiming religious spaces for LGBTQ individuals and supporting their spiritual journeys, Manji has opened the door to a more inclusive and diverse faith landscape.

In conclusion, Irshad Manji's journey as a queer Muslim activist and her unwavering commitment to challenging traditional norms have left an indelible mark on LGBTQ rights and religious communities worldwide. Her story teaches us the power of resilience, bravery, and authenticity. It is now up to us to embrace her legacy, continue the fight for equality, and foster empathy and inclusion in our communities. The world is evolving, and with the inspiration of activists like Irshad Manji, we can create a more inclusive and accepting future for all.

Legacy of a Trailblazer

Looking Back on a Life of Activism

Milestones and Achievements

Throughout her incredible journey as a queer Muslim activist, Irshad Manji has achieved numerous milestones that have revolutionized the LGBTQ movement, challenged conservative religious beliefs, and empowered marginalized communities. Her dedication and unwavering commitment to social justice have created lasting change, and her achievements serve as inspiration for generations to come.

One of the major milestones in Manji's career was the publication of her groundbreaking book, "The Trouble with Islam Today: A Muslim's Call for Reform in Her Faith." Released in 2003, this influential work questioned the traditional interpretations of Islam and highlighted the need for reform within the religion. Manji fearlessly confronted the issues of homophobia, misogyny, and intolerance within Muslim societies, challenging deeply ingrained beliefs and stimulating important conversations.

"The Trouble with Islam Today" sparked a global movement, inspiring queer Muslims all around the world to question societal norms and fight for their rights. Manji's candid and courageous writing opened up discussions on the intersections of faith, sexuality, and gender, encouraging others to embrace their identities unapologetically. Her eloquent and persuasive arguments garnered international recognition and cemented her reputation as a groundbreaking LGBTQ activist.

Manji's efforts also led to the establishment of the Dangerous Daughters Initiative, a platform dedicated to empowering young women and challenging traditional gender roles. Through this initiative, she has mentored countless LGBTQ youth, providing them with the support and guidance needed to navigate the complexities of identity and advocate for equality. Manji's mentoring programs have not only inspired individual growth but have also contributed to the larger movement for LGBTQ rights.

In addition to her influential writings and mentorship programs, Manji has been a prominent speaker at universities and conferences worldwide. Her impactful presentations have enlightened audiences on the importance of embracing diversity, challenging discriminatory beliefs, and fostering inclusive spaces. By sharing her personal experiences and insights, Manji has captivated her listeners and sparked a call to action, encouraging others to engage in social change.

Manji's efforts have also extended to engaging with religious scholars and challenging conservative interpretations of Islamic scripture. Through her dialogue-driven approach, she has urged for critical thinking and progressive changes within religious communities. By engaging in interfaith dialogue and advocating for LGBTQ rights, Manji has fostered understanding and empathy among diverse religious groups.

Her impactful advocacy expanded beyond the confines of faith-based discussions, as she tirelessly lobbied for LGBTQ rights and influenced government decision-makers. Manji's strong voice and relentless pursuit of equality have played a crucial role in shaping legislation and policies that protect LGBTQ individuals and promote inclusivity. Her tireless work has helped dismantle discriminatory practices, create safer spaces, and secure significant legal reforms.

Manji's achievements have not come without challenges. She has faced threats, backlash, and opposition from conservative religious groups. However, her resilience and unwavering commitment to the cause have allowed her to triumph over adversity, emerging as a beacon of hope for countless LGBTQ individuals and marginalized communities.

This section aims to highlight Irshad Manji's remarkable milestones and achievements. Her groundbreaking literary contributions, mentoring programs, public speaking engagements, and advocacy efforts have revolutionized the LGBTQ movement, challenged patriarchal and homophobic norms, and paved the way for a more inclusive world. Manji's legacy will forever inspire future generations of activists to fearlessly challenge societal norms, fight for equal rights, and celebrate the beauty of diverse identities.

Impact on LGBTQ and Muslim Communities

The journey of Irshad Manji has had a profound impact on both LGBTQ and Muslim communities worldwide. Her unapologetic activism has challenged societal norms, sparked necessary conversations, and empowered countless individuals to embrace their identities, find their voice, and fight for their rights. In this subsection, we will explore the significant impact Manji has had on LGBTQ and Muslim communities, highlighting the key areas where her work has made a lasting difference.

LGBTQ Community

Manji's work and advocacy have been a source of inspiration, hope, and empowerment for the LGBTQ community, particularly individuals who identify as Muslim. Through her personal journey and relentless activism, she has shown that it is possible to reconcile one's faith with their sexual orientation or gender identity, challenging the assumption that LGBTQ identities are incompatible with religious beliefs.

One of the most significant impacts of Manji's work on the LGBTQ community has been the validation and affirmation she has provided to queer Muslims. By openly acknowledging her queerness and embracing her Muslim identity, she has shattered taboos and provided a role model for others who may be struggling to reconcile their faith and their identity.

Moreover, Manji's advocacy efforts have ignited important conversations within the LGBTQ community about the intersectionality of identities. She highlights the necessity of recognizing that individuals can experience multiple forms of marginalization based on their sexual orientation, gender identity, race, and religion. This understanding has led to increased collaboration and support between LGBTQ organizations and Muslim communities, fostering a sense of solidarity across diverse identities.

Manji's impact also extends to the broader LGBTQ rights movement. Her fearless activism has challenged the normative assumptions about who can be an advocate for LGBTQ rights. By carving out a space for queer Muslims, she has demonstrated that the fight for equality is not limited to any one community, but encompasses a broad spectrum of identities and experiences.

Through her writing, speaking engagements, and media appearances, Manji has provided a platform for LGBTQ voices, amplifying the stories of those whose experiences have traditionally been marginalized or silenced. This increased visibility has brought attention to the unique challenges faced by LGBTQ Muslims and has contributed to a broader understanding of the intersections between sexual orientation, gender identity, and religious faith.

Muslim Community

Manji's impact on the Muslim community has been equally significant, challenging conservative interpretations of Islam and advocating for a more inclusive and progressive understanding of the faith. Her work has created space for dialogue, introspection, and reform within Muslim communities around the world.

One of the key contributions of Manji's activism has been her advocacy for LGBTQ rights within Islam. By engaging with Islamic teachings and scholars, she has confronted and challenged homophobic attitudes that have been deeply ingrained within religious discourse. Her efforts have prompted critical conversations about the need for a more compassionate and accepting interpretation of Islam that embraces the diversity of human sexuality and gender.

Through her courageous stance, Manji has paved the way for other Muslim activists to advocate for LGBTQ rights within their own communities. She has inspired individuals to question cultural and societal norms that perpetuate discrimination and to actively work towards creating inclusive spaces for all Muslims.

Furthermore, Manji's advocacy within the Muslim community has emphasized the importance of inclusivity and diversity. She has argued that a rigid and exclusionary understanding of Islam not only oppresses LGBTQ individuals but also marginalizes other vulnerable groups such as women, religious minorities, and those with non-conforming gender identities. Her call for inclusion challenges the status quo and pushes for a more pluralistic interpretation of Islamic teachings.

Manji's impact also extends to the broader conversations surrounding religious freedom and human rights. Her work has shed light on the struggles faced by individuals who identify as LGBTQ within religious contexts, sparking important discussions about the balance between religious beliefs and the protection of human rights.

Overall, the impact of Irshad Manji on both LGBTQ and Muslim communities has been transformative. Her advocacy, courage, and unwavering commitment to justice and equality have inspired countless individuals to embrace their identities, challenge societal norms, and work towards a more inclusive world for all. Her legacy serves as a reminder of the power of individual voices and the potential for change when authenticity and resilience are combined with a commitment to social justice.

Personal Reflections and Regrets

In this section, Irshad Manji offers personal reflections and shares her regrets about her journey as a queer Muslim activist. She looks back on the challenges she faced, the sacrifices she made, and the impact she has had on both the LGBTQ and Muslim communities. Manji's reflections and regrets provide a deeper understanding of her motivations, vulnerabilities, and the lessons she has learned along the way.

As I sit here, reflecting on my journey as a queer Muslim activist, I cannot help but acknowledge the myriad of emotions that have accompanied me throughout this path. While I am immensely proud of the progress we have made, there are moments when I cannot escape the weight of the regrets that burden my heart.

One of my deepest regrets is the strain my activism placed on certain relationships in my life. Speaking out against patriarchal norms, challenging conservative interpretations of Islam, and advocating for LGBTQ rights often led to heated debates and strained connections with family members and close friends. It pained me to see the division caused by my unwavering commitment to my cause. There were moments when I questioned whether the sacrifice of personal relationships was worth the fight for equality and acceptance within my own community.

Another regret that lingers within me is the pain I experienced in facing threats and backlash from those who opposed my advocacy. Standing tall amidst the storm of hate and vitriol requires immense resilience, but it took a toll on my mental and emotional well-being. There were times when I questioned whether my voice was strong enough to withstand the constant onslaught of criticism and even threats to my safety. I regret that I did not prioritize my own self-care more consistently during those challenging times.

Furthermore, I regret that I was not always able to bridge the gap between LGBTQ and Muslim communities as effectively as I had hoped. While I strived to amplify the voices of marginalized queer Muslims and foster interfaith dialogue, there were instances where the divisions proved too deep to bridge. The complexity of reconciling faith and sexuality remains a profound challenge, and I recognize that my efforts alone cannot transform deeply ingrained biases and discriminatory practices. I regret not finding more effective strategies to address these divisions and create lasting change.

However, through these regrets, I have also found valuable lessons and insights. I have learned that sometimes, even when progress feels slow and the challenges seem insurmountable, the impact of one person's story and voice can ripple far beyond our imagination. There were moments when I received messages from LGBTQ Muslims around the world who found comfort, inspiration, and hope in my words. These messages reaffirm that every step, every sacrifice, every regret was worth it. They remind me that even in the face of adversity, our individual stories and experiences have the power to ignite change and offer solace to those who feel marginalized.

Although regrets may haunt me, I am grateful for the resilience, growth, and personal transformation that have accompanied my journey. I have come to understand the importance of self-reflection, humility, and the recognition that change is a collective effort. Every conversation, every act of empathy, and every bridge built between communities brings us closer to a more inclusive world.

As I move forward, I am committed to nurturing the seeds of progress I have planted and ensuring that the next generation of activists continues the fight for equality. Through mentorship programs, empowering queer Muslims, and amplifying young voices, we can sustain the momentum we have gained. Together, we can strive for global LGBTQ rights, challenge discriminatory laws, and celebrate the richness of diversity within faith communities.

In conclusion, personal reflections and regrets define our human experience as activists. They remind us that growth comes hand in hand with sacrifice and challenge us to continually seek new ways to foster understanding, inclusion, and change. I share my regrets not as a burden, but as an invitation to others to pause, reflect, and learn from the mistakes and challenges that have shaped me. We must all seize the opportunity to chart a more compassionate, equitable, and accepting path forward.

Lessons Learned and Wisdom Shared

As Irshad Manji reflects on her journey as an LGBTQ activist, she has gained valuable lessons and wisdom that she is eager to share with future generations of activists. These lessons encompass not only the challenges and triumphs she has experienced but also the strategies and approaches that have proven effective in advancing the cause of equality and acceptance. In this subsection, we will explore some of the key lessons that Manji has learned and the wisdom she imparts to those who follow in her footsteps.

Lesson 1: Authenticity as a Catalyst for Change

One of the most important lessons that Manji has learned is the power of authenticity in driving societal change. By embracing her identity as a queer Muslim, she has been able to dismantle stereotypes, challenge prejudice, and inspire others to embrace their true selves. Manji's unapologetic authenticity has not only given her credibility as an advocate but has also provided a platform for marginalized individuals to share their stories and experiences. She encourages future activists to be true to themselves, as it is their unique perspectives and lived experiences that can bring about meaningful change.

Lesson 2: Intersectionality: Recognizing and Addressing Multiple Oppressions

Manji recognizes the importance of intersectionality in the fight for LGBTQ rights. She emphasizes the need to address the multiple oppressions faced by individuals who belong to marginalized communities. Intersectionality acknowledges that individuals can experience discrimination based not only on their sexual orientation or gender identity but also based on their race, religion, socioeconomic status, and other intersecting identities. By understanding and addressing these intersectional forms of oppression, activists can create more inclusive and effective strategies for positive change.

Lesson 3: Building Coalitions: The Power of Collaboration

Collaboration and building coalitions are essential tools in the LGBTQ activist's arsenal. Manji stresses the importance of reaching out to other individuals, organizations, and communities that share common goals and values. By working together, activists can amplify their voices, pool resources, and generate greater impact. Building coalitions allows for a diverse range of perspectives and experiences to be represented, fostering a more inclusive movement that addresses the needs of all those fighting for equality.

Lesson 4: Embracing Empathy: Changing Hearts and Minds

In her work, Manji has learned that empathy and compassion are powerful tools for creating change. She emphasizes the importance of engaging in dialogue and education to foster understanding and empathy among individuals who hold opposing views. By listening and seeking to understand the perspectives of others, activists can challenge prejudice and misconception, opening up the possibility of change in the hearts and minds of those who may initially be resistant to accepting LGBTQ individuals. It is through meaningful connections and thoughtful dialogue that lasting change can be achieved.

Lesson 5: Resilience in the Face of Adversity

Manji's journey as an activist has been fraught with adversity, including threats, backlash, and personal attacks. Through these experiences, she has learned the importance of resilience. Activists must be prepared to face opposition and withstand the emotional toll it can take. This resilience is built on a strong support network, self-care practices, and an unwavering belief in the cause. Manji encourages future activists to prioritize self-care, seek support, and develop coping mechanisms to navigate the challenges they will inevitably encounter.

Lesson 6: Embracing Change and Evolution

As times change, so too must activism. Manji stresses the necessity of constantly evolving strategies and approaches to effectively tackle new challenges and emerging issues. Activists should not be afraid to question their own assumptions, challenge conventional wisdom, and adapt their methods to the ever-changing social and political landscape. Embracing change ensures that activism remains relevant, inclusive, and impactful.

Lesson 7: Remembering the Power of Personal Stories

Throughout her work, Manji has witnessed the transformative power of personal stories. Sharing personal narratives and experiences can humanize the struggle for LGBTQ rights, providing a powerful means of connecting with others on an emotional level. By amplifying the voices of those who have lived through discrimination and marginalization, activists can foster empathy, challenge stereotypes, and inspire change. Manji encourages future activists to use the power of storytelling to create a more inclusive and accepting world.

In conclusion, Irshad Manji's journey as an LGBTQ activist has provided her with valuable lessons and wisdom that she eagerly shares with future generations. By embracing authenticity, recognizing intersectionality, building coalitions, fostering empathy, cultivating resilience, embracing change, and amplifying personal stories, activists can make a lasting impact on the fight for LGBTQ equality. Manji's insights serve as a guide for those who seek to continue the battle for justice, equality, and acceptance in the years to come.

Irshad Manji's Enduring Legacy

Irshad Manji's tireless efforts as a queer Muslim activist have paved the way for a more inclusive and accepting world. Her enduring legacy serves as an inspiration to future generations of activists, highlighting the importance of challenging societal norms and advocating for equality.

Manji's legacy is defined by her unwavering commitment to uplifting marginalized voices and promoting social change. Through her powerful storytelling and fearless pursuit of justice, she has brought attention to the intersectional challenges faced by LGBTQ individuals, particularly within Muslim communities. Her work has resonated globally, inspiring millions of queer

Muslims and allies to speak out, reaffirming the inherent dignity and rights of all individuals.

Guided by the principles of authenticity and empathy, Manji's enduring legacy showcases the profound impact one person can make in breaking down barriers and fostering a more compassionate society. Her advocacy has not only challenged traditional interpretations of Islam but has also sparked crucial conversations about the importance of embracing diversity while promoting unity.

One of the key aspects of Manji's enduring legacy is her emphasis on the power of dialogue and education as tools for change. She has recognized that engaging in open and respectful conversations is essential for dismantling stereotypes, fostering understanding, and bridging divides between different communities. As an advocate for interfaith dialogue, she has tirelessly worked to build bridges between LGBTQ individuals and religious communities, highlighting the compatibility between faith and sexual orientation.

Manji's legacy also includes her remarkable ability to leverage multiple platforms to amplify marginalized voices. Through her groundbreaking books, such as "The Trouble with Islam Today" and "Allah, Liberty, and Love," she has ignited global conversations and encouraged dialogue within and beyond Muslim communities. Her courageous writing has challenged conventional narratives surrounding Islam and has pushed for critical examination of cultural practices and interpretations that perpetuate discrimination against LGBTQ individuals.

Beyond her literary contributions, Manji's activism extends to speaking engagements, workshops, and collaborations with LGBTQ organizations and human rights groups. By sharing her knowledge, experiences, and insights, she has empowered LGBTQ individuals, particularly youth, to raise their voices, advocate for their rights, and work towards a more inclusive future.

Manji's enduring legacy also encompasses her advocacy for policy and legislative reforms. She has been a powerful voice in promoting LGBTQ rights at both national and international levels, challenging discriminatory laws and pushing for legal protections. Her contributions have not only sparked much-needed discussions within political spheres but have also inspired other activists to continue fighting for equality.

Furthermore, Manji's enduring legacy lies in her ability to foster self-acceptance and self-love among queer individuals, particularly those from Muslim backgrounds. Through her own journey of self-discovery and self-acceptance, she has inspired countless individuals to embrace their authentic selves, navigate the complexities of intersectional identities, and foster positive mental health and well-being.

In sum, Irshad Manji's enduring legacy is marked by her fearless pursuit of justice, her commitment to fostering dialogue and understanding, and her unwavering support for LGBTQ individuals within Muslim communities. Her impact has transcended borders and boundaries, leaving an indelible mark on the global LGBTQ rights movement. As future generations continue to carry the torch of activism, they will surely draw inspiration from Manji's trailblazing spirit, providing hope and strength for a more inclusive and accepting world.

The Importance of Remembering Trailblazers

In the journey towards progress and equality, it is essential to recognize and honor the individuals who paved the way for change – the trailblazers. These courageous visionaries fearlessly fought against societal norms, bigotry, and injustice, leaving an indelible mark on history. Irshad Manji, as a prominent LGBTQ activist, is one such trailblazer whose contribution must be remembered and celebrated.

6.1 Acknowledging the Courageous Fighters

Trailblazers like Irshad Manji have made immense sacrifices and endured countless challenges in their pursuit of a more inclusive world. They have fearlessly displayed their authentic selves, breaking through barriers and overcoming societal expectations. Remembering their courage, dedication, and resilience reminds us of the strength required to challenge the status quo and strive for equality.

6.2 Recognizing Their Impact

Trailblazers have the power to effect significant change, inspiring future generations by demonstrating what is possible. Irshad Manji's work as a queer Muslim activist has paved the way for others, creating spaces for dialogue and fostering understanding between LGBTQ individuals and religious communities. By challenging oppressive norms and promoting inclusivity, Manji has left an indelible impact on LGBTQ rights and the Muslim community.

6.3 Inspiring Celebration and Gratitude

Remembering trailblazers like Irshad Manji is not only an act of recognition but also a celebration of their contributions. It is an opportunity to express gratitude for their unwavering dedication, as their efforts have positively impacted countless lives. By acknowledging their sacrifices, we honor their resilience, determination, and unwavering commitment to equality.

6.4 Encouraging Education and Awareness

By remembering trailblazers, we raise awareness about the struggles and victories of those who fought for LGBTQ rights. Education and understanding are key to fostering empathy and dismantling prejudice. Their stories serve as powerful tools to spark conversations, challenge stereotypes, and encourage openness to change. Through the celebration of trailblazers, we can inspire others to continue their legacy.

6.5 Promoting Historical Perspective

Remembering trailblazers helps us place current activism and progress into greater historical context. By understanding the struggles, challenges, and triumphs of those who came before us, we gain insight into the long road to equality. This perspective allows us to appreciate the progress made thus far while acknowledging the work that remains.

6.6 Fostering Collective Responsibility

The importance of remembering trailblazers goes beyond individual recognition; it fosters a collective sense of responsibility. Their stories remind us that we all have a role to play in the fight for equality. They inspire us to find our own ways to challenge injustice, whether through activism, education, or allyship. Their legacy motivates us to continue the work they started, ensuring that progress is sustained and amplified.

6.7 Amplifying Intersectional Voices

Remembering trailblazers also means recognizing their intersectional identities and the complex challenges they navigated. Irshad Manji, as a queer Muslim, has brought attention to the unique struggles faced by LGBTQ individuals within religious communities. By acknowledging the intersections of race, gender, religion, and sexuality, we ensure a more comprehensive understanding of the diverse experiences within the LGBTQ community.

6.8 Inspiring the Future

By celebrating trailblazers like Irshad Manji, we inspire future generations to carry the torch of activism and continue the fight for equality. It serves as a reminder that progress is not a stagnant accomplishment but an ongoing journey. Trailblazers ignite a collective desire to push boundaries, challenge norms, and create a more inclusive world for all.

6.9 Sustaining a Legacy of Change

Remembering trailblazers is not a momentary act; it is a commitment to sustaining their legacy of change. By carrying forward their values and lessons, we ensure that the progress they achieved does not wane. Through continued advocacy, education, and activism, we honor their contributions by effecting lasting change.

6.10 Conclusion: Celebrating Courage and Inspiring Action

In remembering trailblazers like Irshad Manji, we celebrate their unwavering courage and dedication in the face of adversity. Their stories inspire us to challenge societal norms, fight for equality, and create a more inclusive future. By recognizing the importance of remembering these fearless individuals, we pay tribute to their legacy and ensure that their impact remains alive for generations to come. Remembering trailblazers ignites a spark within us, reminding us of our power to effect change and inspiring us to continue the journey towards a more inclusive and equal world.

Documenting LGBTQ Activist Histories

Documenting LGBTQ activist histories plays a crucial role in preserving the legacy and impact of trailblazers like Irshad Manji. By documenting the stories, struggles, and triumphs of LGBTQ activists, we ensure that future generations have access to a rich tapestry of knowledge and inspiration. In this subsection, we will explore the importance of documenting LGBTQ activist histories, the challenges involved, and the strategies to overcome them.

Preserving Stories of Activism

The documentation of LGBTQ activist histories serves multiple purposes. Firstly, it provides a comprehensive record of the struggles faced by LGBTQ individuals and communities. These stories play a significant role in acknowledging the resilience and strength of activists who challenged societal norms and fought for LGBTQ rights. By preserving these stories, we honor their contributions and inspire future generations to continue the fight for equality.

Secondly, documenting LGBTQ activist histories helps counter erasure and revisionism. LGBTQ individuals and communities have often been marginalized and their contributions overlooked or intentionally erased. By recording and archiving their stories, we ensure that the historical narrative includes the voices and experiences of LGBTQ activists, fostering a more inclusive and accurate representation of history.

Challenges of Documenting LGBTQ Activist Histories

Documenting LGBTQ activist histories comes with its own set of challenges. Many historical records have been lost, destroyed, or hidden due to discrimination and homophobia. LGBTQ individuals often faced persecution and were reluctant to share their stories openly, resulting in a scarcity of documented accounts.

Another challenge is the lack of resources and funding dedicated to LGBTQ history preservation. Mainstream historical archives and institutions have historically neglected LGBTQ narratives, making it difficult to find accessible and comprehensive sources. Additionally, many LGBTQ individuals may not have the means or resources to document their stories, leading to a significant gap in the historical record.

Strategies for Overcoming Challenges

To overcome these challenges, it is essential to employ proactive strategies for documenting LGBTQ activist histories. Here are some effective approaches:

1. Oral History Projects: Conducting oral history interviews with LGBTQ activists is an invaluable way to gather firsthand accounts and personal narratives. These interviews capture the lived experiences, struggles, and victories of LGBTQ activists, providing a rich and authentic historical source.

2. Community Archiving: Encouraging community-led archiving initiatives helps ensure that LGBTQ histories are preserved from an insider perspective. Such projects facilitate collaboration between LGBTQ individuals, community organizations, and academic institutions, allowing for the creation of dedicated LGBTQ archives.

3. Digital Platforms: Leveraging digital platforms like websites, blogs, and social media can help LGBTQ activists share their stories globally. Creating online repositories for LGBTQ histories allows for wider access and engagement, especially for those who may not have physical access to traditional archives.

4. Documentation Workshops: Organizing workshops that teach individuals how to preserve and document LGBTQ histories can empower community members to participate actively in archiving initiatives. These workshops can cover oral history interviewing techniques, digitization skills, and ethical considerations in documenting sensitive stories.

5. Collaboration and Partnerships: Building partnerships with mainstream historical archives, libraries, community-based organizations, and academic institutions can enhance the visibility and preservation of LGBTQ histories. Collaborative efforts ensure that LGBTQ narratives are integrated into broader historical collections and research.

Unconventional Approach: Crowdsourcing LGBTQ Histories

An unconventional but highly effective approach is crowdsourcing LGBTQ histories. By harnessing the power of the internet and social media, this method allows individuals from diverse backgrounds to contribute their stories and experiences. Crowdsourcing platforms provide a space for collaboration, where anyone can share documents, photos, and personal accounts, thereby creating a collective archive of LGBTQ history.

Furthermore, crowdsourcing can contribute to the democratization of historical narratives by actively involving marginalized communities in the construction of their own histories. This approach also ensures the preservation of stories that might otherwise be lost due to limited resources or institutional biases.

Conclusion

Documenting LGBTQ activist histories is a critical endeavor that celebrates the achievements and resilience of LGBTQ individuals and communities. By preserving their stories, we create a more comprehensive historical record and inspire future generations to continue the fight for equality. While challenges exist, employing strategies like oral history projects, community archiving, digital platforms, and crowdsourcing can help overcome these obstacles and ensure the preservation of LGBTQ histories for years to come. Let us embrace the responsibility of documenting and honoring LGBTQ activist histories, writing the chapters that contribute to a more inclusive and just future.

Honoring the Contributions of LGBTQ Pioneers

In this subsection, we pay tribute to the brave individuals who have paved the way for LGBTQ rights and equality. These pioneers have fearlessly challenged societal norms and fought against discrimination, oppression, and invisibility. By acknowledging their contributions, we not only honor their legacy, but we also recognize the progress we have made and the work that still lies ahead.

The Importance of LGBTQ History

Understanding LGBTQ history is crucial to appreciating the struggles and triumphs of this community. LGBTQ history is often invisible or erased from mainstream narratives, but it is a vital part of our collective human story. Recognizing the achievements of LGBTQ pioneers helps us acknowledge the resilience, strength, and diversity within the community. It also serves as a reminder that progress is possible, even in the face of adversity.

Prominent LGBTQ Activists

There are many LGBTQ activists whose contributions deserve recognition. Some of these individuals include:

+ Marsha P. Johnson: A transgender woman of color and a leading figure in the Stonewall uprising of 1969. Johnson co-founded the Street Transvestite Action Revolutionaries (STAR) and fought tirelessly for the rights of transgender and gender-nonconforming individuals.

+ Harvey Milk: The first openly gay elected official in California, Milk was a prominent advocate for LGBTQ rights and played a pivotal role in defeating the Briggs Initiative, which sought to ban gay individuals from working in schools. His assassination in 1978 only served to galvanize the LGBTQ community's fight for equality.

+ Sylvia Rivera: A transgender woman and LGBTQ rights activist, Rivera was also a key participant in the Stonewall uprising. She co-founded STAR alongside Marsha P. Johnson and dedicated her life to advocating for the rights of transgender and homeless youth.

+ Bayard Rustin: An openly gay civil rights activist, Rustin was instrumental in organizing the 1963 March on Washington for Jobs and Freedom. He worked closely with Martin Luther King Jr. and played a significant role in the civil rights movement, despite facing challenges due to his sexual orientation.

These activists, among many others, have challenged societal norms and tirelessly fought for LGBTQ rights. Their contributions have helped shape the legal, social, and cultural landscape for future generations.

Recognizing Trailblazers in Various Fields

The impact of LGBTQ pioneers extends beyond activism and encompasses various professional fields. It is important to recognize and celebrate trailblazers who have shattered barriers and achieved exceptional success. Some notable individuals include:

+ Alan Turing: A British mathematician and computer scientist, Turing is widely regarded as the father of modern computer science. Despite his groundbreaking contributions, Turing faced persecution due to his homosexuality, leading to his tragic death. His story serves as a reminder of the enormous talent lost to discrimination.

+ Barbara Gittings: A prominent LGBTQ rights activist and librarian, Gittings played a crucial role in challenging the American Library

Association to address LGBTQ issues.   Her advocacy led to the establishment of the first LGBTQ Task Force within the organization.

+ Anderson Cooper: As a respected journalist and CNN anchor, Cooper is one of the most visible openly gay news personalities. His presence in mainstream media has helped foster greater acceptance and representation of LGBTQ individuals.

+ Laverne Cox: An actress and transgender rights advocate, Cox has broken barriers as the first openly transgender person to receive an Emmy nomination for acting. Her visibility and advocacy have raised awareness about the issues faced by transgender people worldwide.

These individuals, each excelling in their respective fields, have defied stereotypes and inspired generations through their talent, resilience, and authenticity.

Preserving and Documenting LGBTQ History

Preserving LGBTQ history is crucial to ensuring that future generations have access to accurate and comprehensive narratives. It is crucial to document the stories, struggles, achievements, and contributions of LGBTQ pioneers to create a rich and diverse historical record.

Archives, museums, and organizations dedicated to collecting LGBTQ history serve as repositories of knowledge and cultural heritage. Initiatives like the LGBTQ+ Oral History Project record and preserve individuals' stories, ensuring their narratives are not lost or forgotten.

Efforts to digitize and disseminate LGBTQ history online, such as the Digital Transgender Archive, make it accessible to a wider audience, fostering a greater understanding of the community's history and experiences.

Educating and Inspiring Future Generations

Honoring LGBTQ pioneers goes beyond mere recognition; it also involves educating and inspiring future generations. It is essential to integrate LGBTQ history and contributions into educational curricula, both at the school level and beyond. By doing so, we provide LGBTQ youth with role models and instill a sense of pride in their identities.

Promoting LGBTQ cultural events, such as pride parades and LGBTQ history months, allows us to celebrate the achievements of LGBTQ pioneers on a broader scale. These events serve as platforms for sharing stories, fostering solidarity, and advocating for the ongoing struggle for equality.

Beyond formal education, mentoring programs and community organizations can play a vital role in preserving LGBTQ history and passing down the knowledge and experiences of pioneers to younger generations. By nurturing LGBTQ youth and empowering them to make a difference, we ensure that the legacy of LGBTQ pioneers lives on.

Embracing Collective Responsibility

Honoring the contributions of LGBTQ pioneers is not just the responsibility of the LGBTQ community; it is a collective endeavor. Allies and individuals from all walks of life must actively participate in recognizing, celebrating, and amplifying the impact of these pioneers. Only by embracing collective responsibility can we create a more inclusive society.

Conclusion

Honoring the contributions of LGBTQ pioneers is essential to acknowledging the progress made in the fight for LGBTQ rights and equality. Their bravery, resilience, and unwavering commitment serve as inspiration for future generations. By preserving their stories, recognizing their achievements, and educating others, we continue the work of these pioneers and advance the ongoing struggle for full LGBTQ equality.

Inspiring Future Generations of Activists

As Irshad Manji's journey as a queer Muslim activist continues to inspire and create positive change, the importance of inspiring future generations of activists cannot be underestimated. In this subsection, we will explore the strategies and initiatives that can be undertaken to encourage and ignite the passion within young individuals to become advocates for LGBTQ rights and social justice.

Creating Safe Spaces for Youth

One of the primary ways to inspire future activists is by creating safe and inclusive spaces for youth to express themselves and engage in dialogue. Schools, community centers, and LGBTQ organizations should collaborate to establish support groups, mentorship programs, and educational initiatives specifically tailored for LGBTQ youth. These safe spaces provide a sense of belonging and foster a supportive environment in which young individuals can explore their identities, learn about activist movements, and connect with like-minded peers. Additionally, it is crucial to ensure that these spaces are accessible and affirming for individuals of diverse backgrounds, including those from marginalized communities within the LGBTQ spectrum.

Promoting Intersectionality in Activism

To inspire future activists, it is essential to promote an understanding of intersectionality within the context of social justice. Intersectionality recognizes that individuals hold multiple social identities and that their experiences of oppression or privilege are shaped by the intersection of these identities. By highlighting the interconnectedness of different forms of discrimination, such as racism, sexism, homophobia, transphobia, and ableism, young activists can gain a more comprehensive understanding of power dynamics and work towards dismantling oppressive systems as a collective force.

Amplifying Youth Voices

One of the most effective strategies for inspiring future generations of activists is to amplify their voices and provide platforms for them to share their stories and experiences. Giving young individuals the opportunity to engage in public speaking, participate in panel discussions, or publish their work not only boosts their confidence but also enables them to contribute to important conversations. By valuing and validating their perspectives, we empower the youth to realize that their opinions matter and that they can drive meaningful change within their communities and beyond.

Educating through Digital Media

In today's digital age, leveraging technology and social media platforms is an excellent way to inspire and educate young activists. Online campaigns, podcasts, webinars, and YouTube channels dedicated to LGBTQ rights and social justice can serve as powerful educational tools. By using creative and engaging content, such as videos, infographics, and personal narratives, we can captivate the attention of young audiences and inspire them to take action. Interactive workshops and webinars can also be organized to facilitate discussions and skill-building activities, providing practical guidance and fostering connections among aspiring activists.

Mentorship Programs

Mentoring plays a significant role in inspiring future activists. Establishing mentorship programs that connect experienced activists with young individuals allows for the transfer of knowledge, skills, and encouragement. Mentors can provide guidance, share personal experiences, and offer advice on navigating challenges faced by activists. These relationships foster a sense of support and provide young activists with a role model to look up to. It is crucial to ensure that mentorship programs prioritize inclusivity, diversity, and thoughtful matching to create meaningful connections.

Engaging in Intersectional Activism

Inspiring future generations of activists also involves encouraging individuals to engage in intersectional activism. This means recognizing and addressing the shared struggles faced by different marginalized communities. Encouraging collaboration between LGBTQ organizations and groups advocating for racial justice, gender equality, disability rights, and other social justice movements can lead to more powerful and impactful activism. By highlighting the interconnectedness of various struggles for equality, young activists can broaden their perspectives and work towards building a more inclusive and just society.

Providing Resources and Training

To effectively inspire and equip future activists, it is vital to provide them with resources and training opportunities. Creating toolkits, online guides, and educational materials that emphasize the fundamentals of activism, community organizing, intersectionality, and social change can serve as valuable resources for aspiring activists. Additionally, offering workshops, training sessions, and skill-building programs can equip young individuals with the necessary tools to advocate for their rights and the rights of others. Practical skills such as public speaking, grassroots organizing, and campaign planning are essential for aspiring activists to make a tangible impact.

Encouraging Self-Care and Well-being

Inspiring future generations of activists also requires prioritizing self-care and well-being. Advocacy work can often be emotionally and physically demanding, leading to burnout or compassion fatigue. Teaching young activists the importance of self-care, stress management techniques, and maintaining a healthy work-life balance is critical to sustaining their passion and commitment. Integrating well-being practices like meditation, mindfulness, exercise, and seeking mental health support can help young activists stay resilient and continue their activism effectively.

Celebrating Diversity and Inclusion

Inspiring future generations of activists means celebrating diversity and fostering inclusivity within activist spaces and communities. Valuing diversity of identities, experiences, and perspectives cultivates a sense of belonging, enables cross-cultural understanding, and encourages collaboration. By emphasizing the importance of inclusion and actively challenging bias and discrimination within activist movements, future activists can develop a strong commitment to fighting all forms of oppression, both within and outside the LGBTQ community.

Empowering Through Continuous Learning

Inspiring future generations of activists requires fostering a culture of continuous learning. Encouraging young activists to pursue higher education, engage in critical discussions, and pursue research opportunities can equip them with the knowledge and skills needed to tackle complex social issues. It is also essential to emphasize the importance of humility and open-mindedness, reminding young activists that learning is a lifelong process. By promoting a growth mindset and encouraging curiosity, we empower young individuals to constantly seek new knowledge and expand their understanding of the world.

In conclusion, inspiring future generations of activists involves creating safe spaces, promoting intersectionality, amplifying youth voices, using digital media for education, implementing mentorship programs, engaging in intersectional activism, providing resources and training, encouraging self-care and well-being, celebrating diversity and inclusion, and empowering through continuous learning. By implementing these strategies, we can cultivate a new generation of passionate activists who will carry on the fight for LGBTQ rights and social justice, leaving an enduring legacy of positive change.

The Fight for Equality Continues

The struggle for equality is never-ending. As we conclude the remarkable journey of Irshad Manji, it is important to reflect on the ongoing battle for LGBTQ rights and the relentless pursuit of a more inclusive world. While Manji has made significant contributions, her work is just one piece of a larger movement towards equality.

The Importance of Intersectionality

To continue the fight for equality, it is crucial to acknowledge and embrace intersectionality. LGBTQ individuals encompass a diverse range of identities, including race, ethnicity, gender, and socioeconomic backgrounds. Intersectional activism recognizes the interconnectedness of these identities and the unique challenges faced by individuals who inhabit multiple marginalized spaces.

By centering intersectionality in our advocacy, we can address the specific needs of different communities within the LGBTQ spectrum. This means actively listening to and uplifting the voices of queer people of color, transgender individuals, and those at the intersection of multiple marginalized identities. Through inclusive activism, we can ensure that no one is left behind in the pursuit of equality.

Focusing on Global LGBTQ Issues

While progress has been made in certain parts of the world, LGBTQ rights still face significant challenges globally. In many countries, same-sex relationships are criminalized, and individuals face discrimination, violence, and even persecution. Therefore, it is imperative to shift our focus towards global LGBTQ issues and support the fight for equality on an international scale.

To make a meaningful impact, it is crucial to collaborate with organizations and activists from around the world. By pooling resources, sharing knowledge, and fostering solidarity, we can amplify the collective effort to advance LGBTQ rights globally. This includes advocating for legal reforms, challenging discriminatory laws, and supporting grassroots movements in countries where LGBTQ individuals face the most oppression.

Creating Inclusive Spaces

In the fight for equality, it is not enough to simply change policies and laws. We must actively work towards creating inclusive spaces where LGBTQ individuals can thrive. This involves challenging homophobic, transphobic, and discriminatory attitudes in all aspects of society, including educational institutions, workplaces, and religious spaces.

Promoting LGBTQ-inclusive education policies is essential to fostering understanding and acceptance from a young age. By integrating LGBTQ-inclusive curriculum, providing resources for educators, and implementing comprehensive anti-bullying programs, we can create environments where all students feel seen, heard, and supported.

Similarly, workplaces play a crucial role in promoting inclusivity. Employers must implement policies that protect LGBTQ employees from discrimination and create a climate that embraces diversity. This includes providing inclusive healthcare benefits, gender-neutral facilities, and fostering a culture that celebrates and values LGBTQ contributions.

Religious spaces also have the power to play a vital role in fostering inclusivity. It is essential to engage in conversations with religious leaders and communities to challenge harmful interpretations of religious teachings and promote LGBTQ acceptance within faith systems. By working towards creating inclusive religious spaces, we can ensure that LGBTQ individuals have the opportunity to embrace their faith without sacrificing their identity.

Advocacy Through Media and Technology

In the digital age, the fight for equality has found new avenues for advocacy through media and technology. Social media platforms provide a powerful tool for amplifying marginalized voices, raising awareness, and mobilizing communities. By utilizing social media platforms strategically, activists can reach wider audiences, create online support networks, and organize impactful campaigns.

Media representation also plays a significant role in shaping societal attitudes and perceptions of LGBTQ individuals. It is crucial to advocate for diverse and authentic portrayals of LGBTQ characters and stories in film, television, literature, and other forms of media. By challenging stereotypes and increasing visibility, we can promote understanding, empathy, and acceptance.

Strengthening Human Rights Frameworks

To ensure lasting change, it is essential to strengthen the international human rights framework. This involves advocating for the recognition of LGBTQ rights as human rights and pressuring governments to adopt legislation that protects LGBTQ individuals from discrimination and violence.

By collaborating with international organizations and human rights advocates, we can push for the inclusion of LGBTQ rights in global human rights agendas. This includes supporting initiatives such as the decriminalization of homosexuality, the protection of transgender rights, and the recognition of LGBTQ asylum seekers and refugees.

Empowering Future Generations

The fight for equality must be handed down to the next generation of activists. Mentoring LGBTQ youth and providing them with the resources and support they need is essential for sustaining the movement's momentum.   Through empowerment programs, mentorship initiatives, and youth-led activism, we can nurture the leadership skills and passion of young LGBTQ individuals.

Education also plays a significant role in empowering future generations. By promoting LGBTQ-inclusive education policies, strengthening queer studies programs, and providing scholarships and grants for LGBTQ students, we can ensure that the next wave of activists is well-equipped to continue the fight for equality.

Conclusion

As we conclude this biography on the life and work of Irshad Manji, it is evident that the fight for LGBTQ equality is far from over. The legacy of trailblazers like Manji serves as a reminder of the progress made and the work that still lies ahead.

By embracing intersectionality, focusing on global LGBTQ issues, creating inclusive spaces, harnessing the power of media and technology, strengthening human rights frameworks, and empowering future generations, we can continue the fight for a more inclusive and equitable world. The journey towards equality is a collective effort that requires resilience, courage, and unwavering dedication. Let us be inspired by the remarkable achievements of Irshad Manji and work towards a future where all LGBTQ individuals can live authentically, free from discrimination and oppression.

End of book.

Continuing the Battle

New Leaders and Unfinished Work

As Irshad Manji's journey as a trailblazing LGBTQ activist comes to a close, the search begins for the new leaders who will carry on her legacy and continue the fight for equality. This monumental task may seem overwhelming for those who step into the spotlight, but with dedication, passion, and a commitment to progress, these emerging leaders can make a significant impact on a global scale.

One of the key tasks for these new leaders is to assess the unfinished work that remains. Despite significant advancements in LGBTQ rights, there are still numerous challenges and barriers that need to be addressed. For instance, in many parts of the world, LGBTQ individuals face discrimination, violence, and legal persecution. Same-sex marriage is not recognized in all countries, and transgender rights still lag behind.

To tackle these issues effectively, the new leaders must understand the underlying principles and values of LGBTQ activism. They need to be well-versed in the history of the movement, the ongoing struggles, and the victories that have been achieved so far. By understanding the unique intersectionality of LGBTQ identities and the specific challenges faced by different communities, these new leaders can develop comprehensive strategies to address these issues.

One principle that underpins LGBTQ activism is the recognition and celebration of diversity within the community. The new leaders must embrace and amplify the voices of marginalized groups, including people of color, transgender individuals, and those from low-income backgrounds. By actively engaging and centering the experiences of these groups, the new leaders can ensure that the movement remains inclusive and representative of the entire LGBTQ community.

Another important aspect of LGBTQ activism is the need for collaboration and solidarity. The new leaders should actively seek opportunities to work with other social justice movements, recognizing the interconnectedness of various forms of oppression. By joining forces with feminist, racial justice, and disability rights organizations, the new leaders can strengthen their advocacy efforts and create a more inclusive and equitable world for all.

Addressing the unfinished work also involves leveraging the power of technology and social media. As the world becomes increasingly interconnected, the new leaders must harness the potential of these platforms to reach a wider audience and amplify their message. Through innovative digital campaigns and online communities, they can inspire and mobilize people from all walks of life to join the fight for LGBTQ rights.

To inspire in this digital era, the new leaders must also cultivate their own personal brand and presence. They can use their stories and lived experiences to connect with others and break down barriers. By sharing their struggles and triumphs, they can inspire empathy, understanding, and empower others to embrace their LGBTQ identities.

Real-world examples can play a crucial role in capturing the attention and hearts of people. The new leaders should highlight success stories of social progress, showcasing the positive impact that LGBTQ activists have had on society. By shining a light on these achievements, they can inspire hope, ignite passion, and encourage others to get involved in the movement.

Additionally, to address the unfinished work, the new leaders must be strategic in their approach. This involves understanding the political landscape, engaging with policymakers, and advocating for legislative changes. They will need to create robust networks of allies, including politicians, policymakers, and influential figures, to push for progressive policies that protect the rights of LGBTQ individuals.

Finding the balance between activism and self-care is also crucial for the new leaders. As they take on the challenges of advocating for LGBTQ rights, they must prioritize their own well-being and mental health. By cultivating a support network, practicing self-care rituals, and seeking professional assistance when needed, they can sustain their energy and resilience for the long haul.

Ultimately, the new leaders must approach their roles with humility and a willingness to learn. They need to recognize that they do not have all the answers and be open to feedback and critique. By continuously educating themselves, listening to diverse perspectives, and adapting their strategies as needed, they can navigate the evolving landscape of LGBTQ activism and lay the foundation for a brighter future.

In conclusion, as Irshad Manji's journey comes to a close, the emergence of new leaders is crucial to carry on the fight for LGBTQ equality. These leaders must assess the unfinished work, including addressing global challenges, celebrating diversity, fostering collaboration, leveraging technology, sharing personal stories, engaging with policymakers, focusing on self-care, and maintaining a humble and adaptive mindset. By embracing these principles and taking action, the new leaders can build upon Manji's legacy and continue to make significant strides towards a more inclusive and accepting world.

Striving for Global Equality

In the quest for global equality, Irshad Manji has tirelessly pursued the promotion of LGBTQ rights on an international scale. With her unwavering dedication and passion, she has fought to create a world where all individuals, regardless of their sexual orientation or gender identity, can live with dignity, respect, and equality. This subsection will explore the various strategies and initiatives that Manji has undertaken to strive for global equality.

Understanding the Global Landscape

To effectively advocate for LGBTQ rights globally, it is essential to understand the diverse cultural, religious, and political landscapes that exist around the world. Manji recognizes the importance of engaging with different communities and tailoring strategies to their unique circumstances. She believes that change must come from within each society, with an emphasis on empowering local activists and organizations.

Moreover, Manji acknowledges that cultural relativism should not be used as an excuse to ignore human rights violations. She advocates for a universal human rights framework that respects the inherent dignity and worth of all individuals, regardless of their cultural backgrounds.

Creating Global Partnerships

Collaboration and partnerships with like-minded organizations and activists from various countries are crucial in the fight for global equality. Manji has actively sought alliances with LGBTQ rights organizations, human rights groups, and progressive religious organizations to strengthen her impact. By working together, these partnerships strive to harmonize efforts, share expertise, and maximize resources.

Through these alliances, Manji aims to amplify the voices of marginalized communities and raise awareness about the challenges they face. By fostering a sense of solidarity across borders, she envisions a global movement that can exert pressure on governments and institutions to prioritize LGBTQ rights.

Advocacy at International Platforms

Manji understands the power of utilizing international platforms to advocate for global equality. She frequently participates in conferences, forums, and United Nations events to raise awareness about the challenges faced by LGBTQ individuals worldwide.

These engagements enable Manji to address government officials, policymakers, and civil society representatives, urging them to prioritize LGBTQ rights within their respective countries. She highlights the importance of legislative reforms, inclusive policies, and the protection of human rights for LGBTQ individuals.

By speaking out at these international platforms, Manji underscores the urgency of the issues, generates public support, and puts pressure on governments to take concrete actions towards advancing LGBTQ rights.

Support for LGBTQ Movements

One of Manji's primary strategies for striving for global equality is to support and strengthen existing LGBTQ movements worldwide. She believes in the power of grassroots activism and recognizes that lasting change can only be achieved through the collective efforts of individuals within their own communities.

Manji provides guidance, mentorship, and resources to LGBTQ activists and organizations, helping them navigate the challenges they encounter. She also advocates for increased financial support for grassroots initiatives, recognizing that lack of funding often hinders the progress of these movements.

Additionally, Manji emphasizes the importance of building coalitions and alliances among different social justice movements. By highlighting the intersectionality of identities and causes, she promotes solidarity and collaboration in the pursuit of equality for all marginalized communities.

Strategic Engagement with Governments

Engaging with governments and policymakers is essential in the quest for global LGBTQ equality. Manji actively seeks opportunities to meet with politicians and policymakers to advocate for legislative reforms that protect and promote LGBTQ rights.

She emphasizes the need for comprehensive anti-discrimination laws, access to healthcare and social services, and legal recognition of same-sex relationships. Manji argues that these legal protections are essential in creating an inclusive and accepting environment for LGBTQ individuals.

Manji also encourages governments to collect data on LGBTQ populations, as this information is vital for evidence-based policymaking and targeted interventions. Through her advocacy, she aims to eliminate discriminatory laws and policies that perpetuate inequality and marginalization.

Awareness and Education Campaigns

Awareness and education play a critical role in advancing LGBTQ rights globally. Manji believes that destigmatizing LGBTQ identities and promoting understanding are fundamental steps towards achieving equality.

She engages in public speaking engagements, media interviews, and social media campaigns to raise awareness about LGBTQ issues and challenge stereotypes and prejudices. By sharing personal stories and experiences, Manji humanizes the LGBTQ experience and fosters empathy and understanding.

Furthermore, Manji advocates for inclusive education policies that promote LGBTQ-inclusive curricula and provide training for educators. She recognizes that education is a powerful tool for dismantling ignorance and fostering acceptance.

Challenges and Caveats

While striving for global equality, it is essential to acknowledge the challenges and caveats that arise. Manji faces backlash from conservative forces that resist LGBTQ rights, often leading to personal attacks and threats to her safety. Navigating these challenges requires resilience and the support of allies and networks.

Another challenge is the existence of deeply ingrained cultural and religious beliefs that view homosexuality and gender diversity as immoral or unnatural. Overcoming these deeply rooted biases requires long-term efforts, sustained dialogue, and cross-cultural understanding.

Additionally, different countries have varying levels of legal and social acceptance of LGBTQ individuals. Strategies used in one context may not be effective in another. Therefore, flexibility and adaptation are key when striving for global equality.

Conclusion

Striving for global equality requires a multifaceted approach that encompasses partnership-building, advocacy at international platforms, support for grassroots movements, strategic engagement with governments, awareness and education campaigns, and addressing challenges and caveats. Through her dedicated efforts and relentless pursuit of justice, Irshad Manji serves as a beacon of hope and inspiration for LGBTQ individuals worldwide. The fight for global LGBTQ equality continues, bolstered by her legacy and the work of activists around the world.

Building on Manji's Foundation

In this subsection, we will explore the ways in which activists can build on Irshad Manji's foundation and continue the fight for LGBTQ rights and acceptance. Manji's pioneering work has paved the way for progress, and it is crucial for activists to carry forward her legacy and push for greater inclusivity and equality.

Identifying and Addressing Key Challenges

Building on Manji's foundation requires a deep understanding of the challenges that LGBTQ individuals, especially those from Muslim backgrounds, continue to face. Activists must recognize the intersecting identities and experiences that contribute to these challenges. They include homophobia, transphobia, discrimination, cultural biases, and religious barriers.

To address these challenges effectively, activists need to engage in ongoing research and dialogue to identify the specific needs and concerns of LGBTQ Muslims. This includes conducting surveys, organizing focus groups, and collaborating with academic institutions to gather data and insights. By understanding the nuances and complexities of these challenges, activists can develop targeted strategies for change.

Collaborating with Local Communities

To build on Manji's foundation, activists must actively engage with local LGBTQ communities and Muslim organizations. By fostering collaborations, activists can leverage existing networks and resources to amplify their impact. This can involve partnering with LGBTQ support groups, community centers, and advocacy organizations to organize events, workshops, and awareness campaigns.

Furthermore, it is essential to establish dialogues with Muslim religious leaders and scholars who are open to discussion and reform. By creating spaces for mutual understanding and respect, activists can work towards building bridges between LGBTQ communities and religious institutions. This collaboration can lead to the development of LGBTQ-affirming interpretations of religious texts, educational programs, and guidance for religious communities on embracing diversity.

Implementing Policy Change

Building on Manji's legacy requires a focus on policy change at the local, national, and international levels. Activists must advocate for the inclusion of LGBTQ rights in legislation, ensuring protection against discrimination and violence. This involves lobbying governments, engaging with policymakers, and forming alliances with human rights organizations.

Activists can also contribute to the development of policies within religious institutions to promote inclusivity and acceptance of LGBTQ individuals. This can include advocating for LGBTQ-inclusive curriculum in religious education, providing resources for LGBTQ Muslims to navigate their faith and sexuality, and holding religious spaces accountable for discrimination.

Amplifying Marginalized Voices

One crucial aspect of building on Manji's foundation is amplifying the voices of those who remain marginalized within LGBTQ and Muslim communities. This includes centering the experiences of queer individuals of color, transgender individuals, disabled queer Muslims, and other intersectional identities.

Activists must actively work towards creating platforms and spaces for these individuals to share their stories and perspectives. This can be done through the organization of conferences, panel discussions, and online platforms dedicated to highlighting diverse voices. By centering the most marginalized voices, activists can challenge power dynamics and ensure that the fight for LGBTQ rights is inclusive and intersectional.

Utilizing Technology and Social Media

Technology and social media play a vital role in today's activism landscape. Activists must leverage these platforms to reach wider audiences, raise awareness, and mobilize support. This can involve creating engaging content, sharing personal stories, and utilizing hashtags to spark conversations around LGBTQ rights and acceptance.

Additionally, activists can use technology to develop online resources, support systems, and safe spaces for LGBTQ Muslims. This can include online support groups, mental health resources, and interactive platforms that allow individuals to connect, share experiences, and find community.

Encouraging Self-Care and Advocacy Balance

Building on Manji's foundation requires activists to prioritize self-care and maintain a healthy balance between their advocacy work and personal well-being. Engaging in long-term activism can be emotionally draining, and activists need to prioritize their mental health and self-care practices.

Encouraging self-care within LGBTQ Muslim communities is equally important. Activists should strive to create spaces where individuals can access support networks, counseling services, and resources that promote mental health and well-being.

In conclusion, Building on Manji's foundation requires identifying and addressing key challenges, collaborating with local communities, implementing policy change, amplifying marginalized voices, utilizing technology and social media, and encouraging self-care. By following these strategies, activists can continue the fight for LGBTQ rights and acceptance, building a more inclusive world for all. The next section will further explore the future of queer Muslim activism and the role of new leaders in sustaining and expanding upon the progress made.

The Future of Queer Muslim Activism

As we look ahead to the future of queer Muslim activism, we see a path that is filled with optimism and challenges. The fight for LGBTQ rights within Muslim communities continues to evolve, and activists are paving the way for acceptance, inclusivity, and equality. In this subsection, we will explore the key elements that will shape the future of queer Muslim activism, including education, allyship, and intersectionality.

Education as a Powerful Tool

One of the fundamental pillars of future queer Muslim activism is education. By promoting awareness and understanding, activists are breaking down the barriers of ignorance and fostering empathy within communities. Education plays a crucial role in challenging misconceptions, combating stereotypes, and promoting dialogue between individuals with different beliefs and identities.

To effectively educate society about LGBTQ rights within Islam, activists must develop comprehensive resources and toolkits. These resources should provide accurate information about LGBTQ identities, the intersections of faith and sexuality, and the importance of inclusivity. By creating educational materials that are accessible and tailored to different audiences, activists can promote understanding and acceptance among both LGBTQ individuals and their allies.

Strengthening Allies and Allieship

The future of queer Muslim activism hinges on the development of strong allies and allieship within and outside of Muslim communities. Allies are essential in challenging the status quo, as they can use their privilege to leverage change and amplify marginalized voices.

To build a more inclusive society, activists must continue to engage with non-LGBTQ individuals and organizations through interfaith dialogue, workshops, and collaboration. By fostering positive relationships with diverse communities, activists can cultivate empathy, break down stereotypes, and challenge any biases that persist. Furthermore, allies can play a crucial role in advocating for LGBTQ-inclusive policies within religious spaces and institutions.

The Power of Intersectionality

Intersectionality is another critical aspect of the future of queer Muslim activism. Recognizing the diverse identities and experiences within LGBTQ Muslim communities is crucial to fostering an inclusive movement.   Activists must acknowledge and address the challenges faced by individuals who belong to multiple marginalized groups, such as LGBTQ individuals who are also racial or ethnic minorities.

By centering intersectionality in their work, activists can empower those who may face overlapping forms of discrimination. This includes advocating for equal rights for transgender and non-binary individuals, addressing the unique struggles of LGBTQ Muslim women, and ensuring the inclusivity of LGBTQ refugees and migrants. By amplifying these voices and advocating for their rights, queer Muslim activism can create a more equitable future for all.

Challenges and Opportunities

As with any movement, queer Muslim activism will face challenges and opportunities in the years to come. Activists must anticipate and respond to backlash from conservative elements within religious communities, including resistance to LGBTQ rights and inclusion.

One challenge lies in reconciling religious texts and LGBTQ identities. Activists will continue to engage with religious scholars and leaders to reinterpret sacred texts and foster a more inclusive understanding of faith. They will also push for legal reforms that protect LGBTQ rights within religious frameworks.

In the face of these challenges, opportunities for progress exist. Leveraging the power of social media, activists can reach wider audiences and inspire global conversations on LGBTQ rights. They can also collaborate with human rights organizations and political allies to advocate for legislative changes that protect LGBTQ individuals.

Examples of Future Initiatives

To provide a glimpse into the future of queer Muslim activism, let's explore some examples of possible initiatives:

1. LGBTQ-inclusive madrasahs and Islamic schools: Activists can work towards the establishment of educational institutions that provide an LGBTQ-inclusive curriculum, fostering acceptance and understanding from an early age.

2. Interfaith LGBTQ organizations: Building on interfaith dialogue, activists can establish organizations that bring together LGBTQ individuals and allies from different religious backgrounds to promote acceptance and understanding.

3. Mental health support for LGBTQ Muslims: Recognizing the unique challenges faced by LGBTQ Muslims, activists can advocate for increased mental health support and resources that address the intersection of faith, sexuality, and mental well-being.

4. Global LGBTQ Muslim conferences and events: Activists can organize conferences and events that bring together LGBTQ Muslims from different parts of the world to share experiences, strategies, and foster a sense of community.

These examples highlight the potential and possibilities that lie ahead for queer Muslim activism. By embracing education, strengthening allies and allieship, centering intersectionality, and remaining resilient in the face of challenges, the future of queer Muslim activism holds great promise.

In conclusion, the future of queer Muslim activism rests on education, allieship, and intersectionality. Activists must continue to educate and challenge society's understanding of LGBTQ rights within Islam. They must strengthen alliances with non-LGBTQ individuals and organizations, and center intersectionality to ensure the inclusivity of all marginalized voices. By facing challenges head-on and seizing opportunities for progress, queer Muslim activism can make a lasting impact and create a more inclusive and equitable future.

Forever Remembering a Trailblazer

In this section, we reflect on the enduring legacy of Irshad Manji, a fearless and influential LGBTQ activist who dedicated her life to challenging societal norms and advocating for equality. As we pay homage to this remarkable trailblazer, we must remember the impact she had on both the LGBTQ and Muslim communities, and the lessons she taught us about the importance of authenticity, courage, and unyielding determination.

Honoring a Courageous Spirit

Irshad Manji's relentless pursuit of justice and equality earned her a place among the most influential LGBTQ activists in history. Her advocacy and the path she paved for future generations serve as a constant reminder of the power of one individual's unwavering determination.

Manji's fearlessness in challenging the status quo and addressing the intersectionality of her identity inspired countless others to embrace their true selves. Her unapologetic authenticity became a rallying cry for the LGBTQ community, pushing boundaries and breaking down barriers.

Inspiration through Personal Connection

Manji's ability to connect with people on a personal level was a distinctive trait that earned her the love and respect of many.   Through her writing, speaking engagements, and social media presence, she shared her vulnerabilities, triumphs, and personal growth, allowing others to find solace and inspiration in her journey.

By sharing her story and showcasing the power of reclaiming one's identity, Manji encouraged marginalized individuals to embrace their own narratives and foster resilience. Her authenticity and relatability continue to empower countless LGBTQ individuals to find their voice and fight for equality.

Perseverance and Resilience

Even in the face of significant adversity, Manji remained steadfast in her commitment to challenging discriminatory beliefs and advocating for social change. Her journey was not without obstacles, as she faced criticism, threats, and opposition from various sectors of society.

However, Manji's resilience spurred her forward, continuing her advocacy work with unwavering determination. Her ability to rise above hate and bigotry served as a powerful testament to the strength of an individual in the face of adversity. Manji reminds us all that progress requires resilience and an unyielding dedication to justice.

Preserving and Sharing Her Legacy

As we remember Irshad Manji, it is essential to document and share her contributions to LGBTQ activism. Through books, documentaries, and digital archives, we can ensure that future generations have access to her ideas, teachings, and experiences.

In commemoration of Manji's legacy, it is crucial to establish scholarships, awards, and programs that recognize individuals who continue her fight for equality.   These initiatives can empower new leaders and ensure that her groundbreaking work has a lasting impact on the future of LGBTQ activism.

The Call to Action

Remembering Irshad Manji is not just an exercise in nostalgia; it is a call to action. We must carry her torch forward, continuing the fight for equality and justice for all marginalized communities.

By promoting inclusivity, challenging unjust systems, and fostering dialogue, we can honor Manji's legacy and create a more inclusive world. Embracing her spirit of authenticity, fearlessness, and determination will guide us in shaping a future where every individual, regardless of their sexual orientation, gender identity, or religious beliefs, can live without discrimination or persecution.

Let us forever remember Irshad Manji as an emblem of hope, inspiration, and relentless activism, and let her legacy fuel our commitment to building a more just and equitable world for all.

Sustaining LGBTQ Visibility and Advocacy

In order to sustain LGBTQ visibility and advocacy, it is crucial to foster a sense of community and promote inclusivity. This can be achieved through various means, such as organizing events, creating safe spaces, and amplifying marginalized voices. In this subsection, we will explore some effective strategies for sustaining LGBTQ visibility and advocacy.

Creating Safe Spaces

Creating safe spaces for LGBTQ individuals is of paramount importance. These spaces provide an environment where individuals can feel accepted and supported, without the fear of discrimination or judgment. Safe spaces can be physical locations, such as LGBTQ community centers or support groups, or virtual spaces, such as online forums or social media groups. These spaces serve as platforms for LGBTQ individuals to share their experiences, seek guidance, and connect with others who share similar identities or struggles.

To create effective safe spaces, it is essential to establish clear guidelines and rules that promote respect, inclusivity, and confidentiality. The facilitators of these spaces should undergo sensitivity training to ensure they are equipped to provide support and resources to LGBTQ individuals. It is also crucial to regularly evaluate and update these spaces based on feedback and evolving needs of the community.

Amplifying Marginalized Voices

One of the key aspects of sustaining LGBTQ visibility and advocacy is amplifying the voices of marginalized individuals within the community. This includes individuals who belong to intersecting identities, such as LGBTQ people of color, transgender individuals, or LGBTQ refugees and migrants.

Amplifying these voices can be done through various means. One way is to provide platforms for marginalized individuals to share their stories and experiences. This can be achieved through interviews, blog posts, or podcasts featuring their perspectives. It is important to ensure that these platforms are inclusive and prioritize the representation of diverse voices.

In addition to providing platforms, it is crucial to actively listen to and learn from marginalized individuals. This involves acknowledging the unique challenges they face and seeking their input in decision-making processes. By centering their experiences and perspectives, we can work towards a more inclusive and equitable LGBTQ movement.

Engaging in Advocacy and Awareness Campaigns

Advocacy and awareness campaigns play a vital role in sustaining LGBTQ visibility and advocacy. These campaigns aim to educate the general public, challenge stereotypes and prejudices, and promote acceptance and understanding of LGBTQ individuals.

Advocacy campaigns may involve lobbying for LGBTQ-friendly policies, organizing protests or rallies, or collaborating with other social justice movements. It is important to leverage various platforms to reach a wider audience, including social media, mainstream media, and educational institutions.

When designing advocacy and awareness campaigns, it is crucial to prioritize cultural sensitivity and inclusivity. This involves considering the intersectional identities and experiences of LGBTQ individuals and ensuring that messages resonate with diverse communities. Collaborating with local LGBTQ organizations and community leaders can also help ensure the effectiveness and cultural relevance of these campaigns.

Promoting LGBTQ Visibility in the Workplace

Promoting LGBTQ visibility in the workplace is another crucial aspect of sustaining LGBTQ advocacy. This involves creating inclusive policies and practices that protect LGBTQ employees from discrimination and create a welcoming and affirming environment.

Employers can support LGBTQ employees by implementing inclusive nondiscrimination policies, providing sensitivity training for staff, and offering LGBTQ-affirming benefits, such as healthcare coverage for gender-affirming treatments. It is also important to create employee resource groups or affinity networks to foster a sense of community and provide support.

Promoting LGBTQ visibility in the workplace goes beyond policies and practices. It involves actively celebrating diversity and providing opportunities for

LGBTQ individuals to hold leadership positions and contribute to decision-making processes. By doing so, organizations can become champions of LGBTQ rights and advocates for change beyond the workplace.

Collaborating with Other Advocacy Movements

Sustaining LGBTQ visibility and advocacy requires collaboration with other social justice movements. Intersectionality recognizes that individuals hold multiple identities and face intersecting forms of oppression. By partnering with other movements, such as feminist, racial justice, or disability rights movements, we can build coalitions and address issues that impact LGBTQ individuals within a larger context.

Collaboration can involve joint advocacy efforts, shared resources, and mutual support. It is important to approach these collaborations with empathy, respect, and a commitment to learning and unlearning oppressive behaviors. By working together, we can create a more inclusive and equitable society for all.

In conclusion, sustaining LGBTQ visibility and advocacy demands ongoing efforts to foster community, promote inclusivity, and amplify marginalized voices. Through creating safe spaces, amplifying diverse voices, engaging in advocacy and awareness campaigns, promoting LGBTQ visibility in the workplace, and collaborating with other advocacy movements, we can work towards a world where LGBTQ individuals are celebrated, respected, and fully embraced. The future of LGBTQ activism relies on our collective commitment to sustaining visibility and continuing the fight for equality.

Promoting Global LGBTQ Rights

Promoting global LGBTQ rights is a critical component of creating a more inclusive and equitable world. It requires addressing and overcoming discriminatory laws, advocating for policy changes, and fostering dialogue and understanding between different communities. In this subsection, we will explore the key principles and strategies for promoting global LGBTQ rights, emphasizing the importance of collaboration, education, and activism.

Understanding the Global LGBTQ Rights Landscape

Before we delve into the strategies for promoting global LGBTQ rights, it is crucial to have a comprehensive understanding of the current landscape. LGBTQ rights vary significantly across different countries and regions, with some nations affording comprehensive protections while others criminalize same-sex relationships or discriminate against LGBTQ individuals.

Researching and documenting the legal and social status of LGBTQ rights in different countries is an essential first step. Organizations like the International Lesbian, Gay, Bisexual, Trans and Intersex Association (ILGA) provide comprehensive reports and resources on the status of LGBTQ rights worldwide. Governments, NGOs, and activists can use this information to identify areas where additional efforts are needed.

Collaboration and Solidarity

Promoting global LGBTQ rights requires collaboration and solidarity among activists, organizations, and governments. By working together, diverse stakeholders can maximize their impact and create a united front against discrimination. Collaboration can take various forms, including joint advocacy campaigns, knowledge sharing, and resource pooling.

International alliances between LGBTQ organizations, human rights organizations, and other social justice movements can play a crucial role in fostering collaboration. These alliances facilitate sharing strategies, building networks, and amplifying voices. For instance, the Global Equality Caucus, a network of parliamentarians committed to LGBTQ rights, connects lawmakers from different countries to coordinate efforts and advance legislative change.

Additionally, it is crucial to engage with governments, both at national and international levels. Advocacy efforts can involve holding governments accountable for their human rights commitments, lobbying for policy changes, and building relationships with decision-makers. By working hand in hand with policymakers, activists can help shape laws and policies that protect and promote LGBTQ rights on a global scale.

Education and Awareness

Promoting global LGBTQ rights requires challenging stereotypes, myths, and misconceptions surrounding LGBTQ individuals and their rights. Education and awareness campaigns play a vital role in countering homophobia, transphobia, and other forms of discrimination.

Education initiatives should target both LGBTQ communities and the general public. For the LGBTQ community, providing access to accurate information about their rights, mental health resources, and support networks is crucial. This can be done through community workshops, online resources, and mentorship programs.

To educate the general public, awareness campaigns can utilize various mediums, including social media, documentaries, and public events. These campaigns can shed light on the experiences of LGBTQ individuals worldwide, challenge stereotypes, and promote empathy and understanding.

Advocacy and Legislative Reform

Advocacy and legislative reform are essential components of promoting global LGBTQ rights. Activists and organizations can engage in targeted advocacy efforts to influence governments and policymakers to enact legislation protecting LGBTQ rights.

Engaging with international human rights mechanisms, such as the United Nations Human Rights Council, can be an effective strategy for advocating for global LGBTQ rights. Participating in the Universal Periodic Review (UPR) process and submitting shadow reports can shed light on the state of LGBTQ rights in different countries and put pressure on governments to address inequalities.

At the national level, grassroots activism can create significant change. Activists can organize protests, lobby for changes in discriminatory laws, and amplify marginalized voices. Through strategic advocacy, activists can challenge discriminatory policies and push for legal reforms that protect LGBTQ individuals.

Inclusive Development Programs

Promoting global LGBTQ rights also involves advocating for LGBTQ-inclusive development programs. LGBTQ individuals face unique challenges and vulnerabilities, such as limited access to healthcare, education, and employment opportunities. Inclusive development programs aim to address these disparities and ensure that LGBTQ individuals are not left behind.

Incorporating LGBTQ-specific components into development programs can help tackle systemic barriers and promote inclusivity. This may include establishing LGBTQ-specific healthcare services, creating safe spaces for LGBTQ individuals in educational institutions, and implementing policies that prohibit discrimination in employment.

By incorporating LGBTQ rights into broader development initiatives, countries can work towards achieving the Sustainable Development Goals while ensuring that the rights of LGBTQ individuals are not overlooked.

Promoting LGBTQ Rights as Human Rights

It is crucial to frame LGBTQ rights as human rights in global advocacy efforts. By emphasizing that LGBTQ rights are an integral part of universal human rights, activists can garner broader support and create a unified call for change.

This approach involves highlighting the intersectionality of LGBTQ rights with other social justice issues, such as gender equality, racial justice, and disability rights. By promoting the understanding that every individual, regardless of their sexual orientation or gender identity, is entitled to the same fundamental rights and freedoms, activists can build solidarity across different movements and amplify their collective impact.

Furthermore, promoting LGBTQ rights as human rights requires engaging with international human rights mechanisms. This includes utilizing international human rights law and conventions to hold governments accountable for discriminatory practices and advocating for LGBTQ rights on a global scale.

Conclusion

Promoting global LGBTQ rights is a complex and multifaceted endeavor that requires collaboration, education, advocacy, and inclusive development programs. By working together, activists, organizations, and governments can challenge discriminatory laws, foster empathy and understanding, and create a more inclusive and equitable world. It is critical to continue the fight for global LGBTQ rights, ensuring that the rights and well-being of all LGBTQ individuals are protected and respected.

Collaborating Across Activist Movements

In the fight for LGBTQ rights and equality, collaboration across different activist movements is crucial. By joining forces, activists can leverage their collective power to create meaningful change and dismantle systemic oppression. This subsection explores the importance of collaborating across activist movements and provides practical strategies for effective collaboration.

Recognizing Intersections of Oppression

One key aspect of collaborating across activist movements is recognizing the intersections of oppression. Oppression does not exist in isolation, and individuals can experience multiple forms of marginalization simultaneously. In the LGBTQ community, there are individuals who face discrimination not only based on their sexual orientation or gender identity but also due to their race, ethnicity, socioeconomic status, disability, or immigration status.

To effectively collaborate, it is crucial to acknowledge and understand these intersecting oppressions. By recognizing the interconnectedness of various forms of discrimination, activists can work together to address root causes and develop inclusive solutions that uplift marginalized communities more broadly.

Shared Goals and Solidarity

Effective collaboration across activist movements requires identifying shared goals and finding common ground. While the issues and contexts may be different, there are often overarching themes of social justice, equality, and liberation that unite diverse movements. LGBTQ activists can find common cause with those fighting against racism, sexism, ableism, and other forms of discrimination.

Solidarity is the foundation of successful collaboration. It involves actively supporting and advocating for each other's causes, attending events and protests, amplifying each other's voices, and sharing resources and expertise. By building strong relationships and partnerships, activists can create a powerful united front against all forms of oppression.

Creating Intersectional Spaces

As activists collaborate across movements, it is essential to create intersectional spaces that center the experiences and voices of those at multiple intersections of identity. These spaces should be inclusive and welcoming, fostering trust, respect, and open dialogue.

Intersectional spaces provide a platform for marginalized communities to express their unique concerns and perspectives, ensuring that the fight for LGBTQ rights remains holistic and reflective of the diverse needs within the community. By actively seeking out and inviting individuals from different communities to contribute to the conversation, activists can foster a deeper understanding of the issues and develop more inclusive strategies for change.

Amplifying Marginalized Voices

Collaboration across activist movements should prioritize amplifying marginalized voices. It is crucial to uplift and center the voices of those most affected by systemic oppression. Too often, marginalized voices are silenced or overshadowed, hindering progress towards achieving meaningful change.

By actively seeking out and elevating the voices of marginalized individuals, activists can ensure their perspectives and experiences are at the forefront of the conversation. This can be done through platforms such as public speaking events, panel discussions, social media campaigns, and media interviews. By amplifying these voices, activists can challenge dominant narratives, raise awareness, and inspire others to take action.

Building Trust and Cultural Competence

Building trust and developing cultural competence are essential for successful collaboration across activist movements. Recognizing the power dynamics that exist within and between different communities is crucial in creating spaces that are respectful and equitable. Cultural competence involves actively learning about different cultures and identities, recognizing and challenging one's own biases, and engaging in ongoing education and self-reflection.

By investing time and effort into building trust and cultural competence, activists can create strong and lasting alliances across movements. Mutual respect and understanding facilitate effective communication, partnership, and collaboration, ultimately strengthening the impact of collective activism.

Examples of Successful Collaboration

Successful collaboration across activist movements has the potential to achieve transformative results. Several examples illustrate the power of unity and collective action:

+ The collaboration between LGBTQ activists and the Black Lives Matter movement has led to increased awareness of the challenges faced by queer people of color and united efforts to fight against police brutality and systemic racism.

+ The partnership between LGBTQ activists and disability rights advocates has sparked important conversations about the intersection of ableism and homophobia/transphobia, leading to the creation of more accessible and inclusive LGBTQ spaces and events.

+ Collaboration between LGBTQ organizations and immigrant rights activists has shed light on the unique struggles faced by LGBTQ immigrants, resulting in the development of support networks, advocacy for immigration reform, and protection for LGBTQ asylum seekers.

◆ The cooperation between LGBTQ activists and feminist movements has contributed to raising awareness about the experiences of LGBTQ individuals within the context of gender inequality, leading to increased advocacy for LGBTQ-inclusive policies and challenging heteronormative norms.

These examples demonstrate the power of collaboration and highlight the importance of recognizing and addressing the interconnectedness of different forms of oppression.

Resources and Challenges

Collaborating across activist movements can be both rewarding and challenging. Resources such as grants, funding, and organizational support are valuable in facilitating collaboration. Seeking out partnerships with organizations that share similar values and goals can provide access to a broader network of activists and resources.

However, challenges such as power imbalances, conflicting priorities, and differing strategies can arise when collaborating across movements. These challenges can be addressed through open and honest communication, active listening, and a commitment to finding common ground.

Additionally, it is essential to acknowledge the ongoing work required to create inclusive and equitable collaborations. A commitment to continuous learning, self-reflection, and addressing one's own biases and privileges is necessary for building and sustaining effective cross-movement partnerships.

Conclusion

Collaborating across activist movements is vital for creating lasting change in the fight for LGBTQ rights and equality. By recognizing intersections of oppression, finding shared goals, creating intersectional spaces, amplifying marginalized voices, building trust, and developing cultural competence, activists can form powerful alliances that challenge systemic oppression.

Through collaboration, LGBTQ activists can harness the collective power of diverse movements and advance the broader goals of social justice, equality, and liberation. By continuing to work together, future generations of activists will build upon the progress made and forge a more inclusive and equitable world for all.

Adapting to Emerging Challenges and Issues

As LGBTQ activism continues to evolve, it is vital for activists to adapt to the emerging challenges and issues that arise in our ever-changing society. This section explores the importance of being flexible, creative, and resilient in the face of new obstacles, while also highlighting strategies for addressing and overcoming these challenges.

Keeping up with Changing Language and Terminology

One of the ongoing challenges in LGBTQ activism is the evolution of language and terminology. As society becomes more aware and accepting of diverse identities, it is crucial for activists to stay informed about emerging terms and concepts. This includes understanding and respecting gender pronouns, non-binary identities, and intersectionality.

To address this challenge, activists can engage in ongoing education and dialogue to ensure they are using inclusive language that accurately reflects the experiences of all individuals within the LGBTQ community. This may involve attending workshops, consulting with experts, or engaging in meaningful conversations with community members.

Navigating Intersectionality and Multiple Identities

Intersectionality is an essential concept in LGBTQ activism, as it recognizes the interconnections between different forms of oppression and discrimination. Activists must consider the diverse experiences and identities within the LGBTQ community, including race, ethnicity, class, disability, and more.

To navigate intersectionality effectively, activists should strive to amplify the voices of marginalized communities within the LGBTQ movement. This can be done by centering the experiences of individuals with intersecting identities and uplifting their narratives. Collaborating with other social justice movements and organizations can also facilitate a more holistic approach to activism.

Addressing Global LGBTQ Issues

As LGBTQ activism becomes increasingly global, adapting to the specific challenges faced by LGBTQ individuals in different regions becomes crucial. Activists must be aware of the unique cultural, legal, and social contexts that impact LGBTQ rights around the world.

To address global LGBTQ issues, activists can engage in cross-cultural dialogue, learn about diverse LGBTQ experiences, and support international LGBTQ organizations. This may involve advocating for LGBTQ rights in countries with regressive policies, supporting refugees and asylum-seekers, and amplifying the voices of LGBTQ activists in oppressed regions.

Technology and Social Media Challenges

Advancements in technology and social media have transformed the landscape of LGBTQ activism. While these tools have expanded the reach and visibility of LGBTQ voices, they also present challenges such as online harassment, discriminatory algorithms, and the spread of misinformation.

To adapt to these challenges, activists can strategize ways to use social media platforms effectively and safely. This includes creating digital communities that foster support and resilience, countering misinformation with accurate information, and advocating for algorithmic transparency and accountability.

Mental Health and Self-Care

As activists navigate complex and emotionally demanding issues, prioritizing mental health and self-care is crucial. Burnout, compassion fatigue, and secondary trauma are common challenges faced by LGBTQ activists.

To address these challenges, activists must incorporate self-care practices into their advocacy work. This may involve setting boundaries, seeking therapy or counseling, engaging in regular self-reflection, and connecting with support networks. Activists can also advocate for institutions and organizations to prioritize mental health support for activists.

Engaging with Conservative Religious Institutions

Conservative religious institutions present unique challenges in LGBTQ activism. Adapting to these challenges requires a nuanced approach that fosters understanding, empathy, and dialogue.

Activists can engage with conservative religious institutions by creating safe spaces for conversations, challenging harmful beliefs through education and dialogue, and highlighting the diverse interpretations of religious texts that support LGBTQ inclusion. Building alliances with progressive religious leaders and organizations can also facilitate positive change within religious communities.

Adapting to Legislative Setbacks

Despite significant progress, LGBTQ activists often face legislative setbacks and rollbacks of hard-won rights. Adapting to these setbacks entails resilience, strategic planning, and the mobilization of grassroots movements.

Activists can respond to legislative setbacks by organizing protests, mobilizing voters, lobbying for LGBTQ-inclusive policies, and supporting LGBTQ-affirming candidates for public office. Collaborating with legal experts and organizations can also help navigate legal challenges and develop effective strategies for long-term change.

Promoting LGBTQ Acceptance in Health Care

Access to LGBTQ-inclusive healthcare remains a significant challenge for many individuals within the community. Adapting to this challenge involves advocating for policy changes, training healthcare professionals, and raising awareness about the unique healthcare needs of LGBTQ individuals.

Activists can promote LGBTQ acceptance in healthcare by partnering with medical organizations, developing resources for healthcare providers, and advocating for LGBTQ-inclusive policies in healthcare institutions. This includes ensuring access to gender-affirming care, mental health support, and preventive services tailored to the specific needs of LGBTQ individuals.

Inclusive Education Policies

Education plays a crucial role in promoting acceptance and understanding. Adapting to challenges in educational settings includes advocating for LGBTQ-inclusive curriculum, anti-bullying policies, and comprehensive sex education.

Activists can work with educational institutions, parent-teacher organizations, and policymakers to implement LGBTQ-inclusive education policies. This includes training educators on LGBTQ issues, promoting inclusive curriculum materials, and fostering supportive and safe environments for LGBTQ students.

Creating Intersectionality in LGBTQ Spaces

Creating inclusive and intersectional LGBTQ spaces is essential for ensuring the full representation and empowerment of all individuals within the community. Adapting to this challenge means actively dismantling hierarchies and addressing biases within LGBTQ organizations and events.

Activists can promote intersectionality within LGBTQ spaces by amplifying marginalized voices, fostering diversity within leadership roles, and actively seeking out and addressing biases. Collaborating with intersectional organizations and engaging in ongoing self-reflection can help ensure inclusivity and equality in LGBTQ spaces.

Conclusion

Adapting to emerging challenges and issues is a fundamental aspect of effective LGBTQ activism. By staying informed, flexible, and resilient, activists can address the evolving needs and navigate the diverse obstacles that arise in their fight for equality. Through inclusive language, intersectional approaches, global awareness, strategic use of technology, mental health support, and collaboration with diverse communities, activists can create lasting change and build a more inclusive world for LGBTQ individuals. The future of LGBTQ activism lies in the ability to adapt and respond to emerging challenges, ensuring the movement remains resilient, relevant, and impactful.

A Call to Action for a More Inclusive World

In the journey of exploring the life of Irshad Manji, we have witnessed her relentless efforts to challenge norms, break barriers, and fight for the rights of LGBTQ Muslims. As we conclude this biography, it is essential to reflect on her legacy and extend a call to action for a more inclusive world. In this final section, we will delve into the key principles, challenges, and strategies needed to build a more accepting and equitable society.

Promoting Understanding and Empathy

Creating a more inclusive world starts with fostering understanding and empathy among individuals and communities. It is crucial to recognize that diversity enriches society and promotes innovation. We must strive to learn from one another, celebrating our differences and embracing the unique perspectives and experiences that each person brings to the table.

One way to promote understanding is through education and awareness campaigns. By providing accurate information about LGBTQ identities and experiences, we can dispel misconceptions, challenge stereotypes, and build bridges of empathy. This can be achieved through inclusive curriculum development, workshops, and community dialogues that encourage open conversations about sexual orientation, gender identity, and religion.

Advocating for LGBTQ Rights

To create an inclusive world, we must advocate for the rights of LGBTQ individuals at both national and international levels. This goes beyond legal recognition and protection; it necessitates dismantling systemic barriers and addressing social inequalities.

Advocacy efforts should focus on issues such as marriage equality, anti-discrimination laws, and healthcare access. It is integral to collaborate with human rights organizations, LGBTQ activists, policymakers, and legal experts to influence legislation and push for necessary reforms. By amplifying the voices of marginalized communities, we can work towards building a legal framework that protects LGBTQ rights and promotes equality for all.

Collaborating Across Movements

Building a more inclusive world requires collaboration and solidarity across different social justice movements. Intersectionality acknowledges that individuals hold multiple identities and experience various forms of oppression simultaneously. By building alliances and recognizing the interconnections between different struggles, we can create a united front against discrimination and inequality.

It is crucial to actively engage with feminist, racial justice, disability rights, and other social justice movements. By collectively addressing intersecting forms of oppression, we can challenge systemic inequalities and create a more inclusive society for all.

Promoting LGBTQ+ Inclusion in Faith Communities

Religion plays a significant role in many people's lives and can be a source of ostracism or support for LGBTQ individuals. Promoting LGBTQ+ inclusion within faith communities requires a delicate balance of dialogue, education, and advocacy.

Engaging with religious leaders, scholars, and community members is essential in challenging harmful interpretations of religious texts. By fostering conversations that encourage critical thinking and a reevaluation of traditional beliefs, we can strive for more inclusive interpretations of religious teachings.

Creating spaces of worship that embrace diversity and welcome LGBTQ individuals can be transformative. Establishing support networks, organizing LGBTQ-inclusive events, and working towards institutional changes within religious communities can make a substantial impact.

Empowering LGBTQ Youth

The future of LGBTQ activism lies in empowering and supporting the next generation. LGBTQ youth often face unique challenges, including higher rates of mental health issues, homelessness, and bullying. It is imperative to provide resources, mentorship, and safe spaces that allow LGBTQ youth to thrive.

Mentorship programs can connect young activists with experienced individuals who can guide them in their journey. These programs should focus not only on activism but also on emotional well-being, self-care, and developing leadership skills. By investing in the growth and development of LGBTQ youth, we ensure the continuity of the fight for equality and justice.

The Power of Storytelling and Representation

Storytelling has the power to change hearts and minds. It is essential to amplify the voices and experiences of LGBTQ individuals through diverse media and platforms. This includes books, films, music, and online content that reflect the diversity of LGBTQ identities and experiences.

By sharing personal stories and highlighting the accomplishments of LGBTQ individuals, we challenge stereotypes and humanize the struggles faced by marginalized communities. Representation matters and can significantly impact public opinion, policy-making, and societal attitudes towards the LGBTQ community.

Conclusion

As we conclude this biography on the life of Irshad Manji, we are reminded of the power of individuals to create meaningful change. Manji's journey as a queer Muslim activist defying tradition serves as an inspiration and a call to action for a more inclusive world.

Promoting understanding, advocating for LGBTQ rights, collaborating across movements, promoting LGBTQ+ inclusion within faith communities, empowering LGBTQ youth, and harnessing the power of storytelling are key steps in creating a society that celebrates diversity and ensures equality for all.

We must not falter in our pursuit of justice, remaining dedicated to challenging discrimination and championing the rights of marginalized communities. The fight for a more inclusive world requires collective action, unwavering resilience, and an unyielding commitment to equality. Together, we can create a future where every individual is embraced for their authentic selves, free from discrimination and bigotry.

Index

Milton Keynes UK
Ingram Content Group UK Ltd.
UKHW020845051124
450766UK00013B/913